Love, Honor
and
Negotiate

PRAISE FOR THE BOOK THAT
"SHOULD BE REQUIRED READING FOR EVERY
COUPLE IN AMERICA."*
LOVE, HONOR & NEGOTIATE

"At last, a book that really explains couple
relationships as they are evolving at the turn of the
twenty-first century....Betty Carter is the most articulate
voice on this topic in our generation."
—Monica McGoldrick, M.S.W., Ph.D., director,
Family Institute of New Jersey*

"If you read only one book about marriage,
make it this one!"
—Constance Ahrons, Ph.D.,
author of *The Good Divorce*

"One of the most interesting and intelligent books for
women and men of any age who want to understand and
heal their marriages. Reading it is worth at least six
months of couples therapy."
—Laura M. Markowitz, *Ms.* magazine

"Carter is as lucid, straightforward,
and salty as she is theoretically sound,
sophisticated and earnest."
—Richard Chasin, M.D., associate clinical professor of
psychiatry, Harvard Medical School

"Stop arguing and start reading...."
—Fran Ellers, *The Courier-Journal*
(Louisville, KY)

MAKING YOUR MARRIAGE WORK

Love, Honor
· AND ·
Negotiate

Betty Carter , M.S.W.,
AND Joan K. Peters

POCKET BOOKS

New York   London   Toronto   Sydney   Tokyo   Singapore

The personal stories in this book are all based on actual cases from my practice—or are composites of those cases. However, the names and details have been changed to protect the identities of the individuals portrayed.

POCKET BOOKS, a division of Simon & Schuster Inc.
1230 Avenue of the Americas, New York, NY 10020

Carter, Elizabeth A.
    Love, honor, and negotiate : making your marriage work / Betty
Carter and Joan K. Peters.
        p. cm.
    Includes bibliographical references and index.
    ISBN 978-0-671-89625-6
    1. Marriage. 2. Married people. 3. Family. 4. Negotiation.
5. Sex role. I. Peters, Joan K. II. Title.
HQ734.C3312   1996
306.81—dc20   95-43181
                                                                CIP

First Pocket Books hardcover printing July 1996

10 9 8 7 6 5 4 3 2 1

POCKET and colophon are registered trademarks of
Simon & Schuster Inc.

Text design by Stanley S. Drate/Folio Graphics Co., Inc.

Printed in the U.S.A.

"Love, Honor & Negotiate" is the registered service mark of Dr. Norma Barretta,
who is not associated with this book or with its author. Dr. Barretta conducts
workshops under this title and may be contacted at 1 Encanto Drive, Rolling Hills
Estates, CA 90274, 310-326-5545.

For Sam
B.C.

For Peter
J.P.

Acknowledgments

Our mutual thanks to our editor at Pocket Books, Julie Rubenstein, our access to the Big Picture. With humor, tact, intelligence, and warmth, she kept us on track, reminding us always of the difference between an academic thesis and a readable book. And to Judith Riven for her guidance in shaping and polishing the manuscript and her steady editorial hand. Our research was made immeasurably easier by the wonderfully helpful staff of the U.S. Bureau of the Census, the excellent studies done by the Family-Work Institute.

It took the help and support of a lot of people for me to travel the pathways described in this book. My deepest debt is to my late parents, Edna Bennett and James Golden, who lived the values they taught us and provided me a model of a loving long-term marriage. And to my aunt Helen Bennett, who has enthusiastically supported me and my projects since the day I was born. To my dear husband, Sam, a truly committed man, my life partner and best friend, and to our children, Bennett and Tim, and now our daughter-in-law, Jennifer, for being willing to share their lives with me so openly. And to my sister, Edna, and brother, Jim, and their wonderful three-generation families. And to Chet and Vera Kalm, Pat McCarthy, Jean Burns, and Ike Patch for the gift of lifelong friendship.

Bridging my personal and professional life is Monica McGoldrick, soul mate and collaborator extraordinaire, with whom I have worked, written, and discussed every idea I have had in the past twenty-five years, as well as sharing dreams, problems, joys, and sorrows, great and small.

From my friends and cofounders of the Women's Project in Family Therapy, Peggy Papp, Olga Silverstein, and Marianne Walters, I learned how to respect and admire professional viewpoints different from my own as we have struggled together for almost twenty years toward our common goal of identifying and working with gender issues in families and in family therapy, and having fun while doing it. Many of their ideas are included here.

My thanks also for the friendship and professional support I have received in good measure from Evan Imber-Black and Lascelles Black, from Steve and Harriet Lerner, and from all of my colleagues on the staff of Family Institute of Westchester.

Thanks especially for the suggestions on various chapters given by Natalie Schwartzberg, Pat Colucci, and Amy Bibb. Kristen Golden and Barbara Findlen have given helpful professional feedback and personal support beyond measure. And without the efforts of Lily Dispirito it would all have been harder.

From the late Murray Bowen, theoretician, teacher, and a founder of Family Therapy, I learned the central ideas of family systems theory that have been the basis of all of my professional work. And from the groundbreaking research of the sociologist Arlie Hochschild, I gained a broader lens through which to examine the marital problems I saw daily in my office.

My agent, Beth Vesel, first convinced me to write this book and then lived through it all with me, while at the same time producing her son. I would never have done it without her, and the book benefited too from her perceptive suggestions along the way.

No sentence or two is sufficient to convey my deep appreciation of the talents of my collaborator, Joan K. Peters. Writer, teacher, intellectual, feminist, and hard-and-fast worker, she absorbed the ideas and nuances of my professional work like a sponge, added her own thoughts, questioned, listened, argued, wrote, edited, organized, and honed until we were both satisfied. Quite a feat.
—BETTY CARTER

Special thanks to my agent, Susan Ginsburg, who is always the voice of reason and encouragement in all matters literary. Inexpressible gratitude to Beth Rashbaum, whose inspiration brought me together with Betty Carter and whose generosity and keen intellect were invaluable throughout the writing of this book.

A thousand thank-you's Peter Passell, my first reader, gentlest critic, unflagging editor, interlocutor, supporter, and loving companion. And several hundreds to friends whose suggestions and patient listening made all the difference at one or another crucial point along the way: Amy Berkower, Honor Moore, Robert Hamburger, Diane Gottleib, and Myra Goldberg.

To my daughter, Lily, who at age four not only knows something of what it means to write a book, but also knows that everyone in the writer's family has to "help." And she did, even more than she knows.

And, finally, my great thanks to Betty Carter, whose ideas connected so electrically with my own. Her intelligence, irreverence, humor, and originality made the hard work exciting and, more often than I would have believed, a great pleasure.

—JOAN K. PETERS

Contents

Introduction

WHERE MY JOURNEY BEGAN

Although I have been happily married for more than thirty-five years, my husband, Sam, and I have had to renegotiate our marriage contract several times. Much to my present mortification, I was initially such a traditionalist, I even wrote to Sam on the eve of our 1959 marriage that I believed a woman should be led by the hand through life! The conclusion to this profession of love includes as strong an endorsement of the traditional marriage contract as any I have read:

> And so, I need nothing more on this earth than to have you give me your hand, in love, and have you lead me with you on your course through the great world. . . . In return, I hope that I can give you the love, understanding, and support that will sometimes make your seeking of the course easier, your rewards and successes in the course happier, and your frustrations easier to bear. We women, if we are lucky at all, have it easier in life than men, I know.

I was convinced that if a woman found the right man she was fulfilled by marriage alone—that is, by living *his* life with him. What can I say? I was young, in love, and it was the fifties.

Of course, though I went to college, I hadn't prepared for a career. It was totally understood that women got the best office job they could until they had children, at which point they stayed home to do their *real* jobs. This was the pattern every woman I knew followed, and I did the same. As soon as our first son, Bennett, was born, I quit a job I had loved and worked at for eight years. But after two restless and depressed years of full-time homemaking—and a reading of *The Feminine Mystique*—I wanted

1

to go back to work. No one else I knew was doing it, but I was determined, probably because I had worked and lived happily on my own for a longer time than most young women of my day. First, however, we went to a marriage counselor.

Fortunately for my husband and me, the sixties' ethos of liberation gave the counselor a language to help us renegotiate our marriage contract: "Loosen up," he said, "she just wants to do her own thing." And still it took two years of therapy before I felt justified in working and Sam no longer felt that my dissatisfaction was his fault—that maybe he hadn't made enough money or provided enough emotionally. With my wifely lack of entitlement, I kept trying to get Sam's permission and approval. It wasn't until the late sixties, after our second son, Tim, came along and I decided to study family therapy that I didn't ask for permission anymore. By then, we'd reinvented our marriage. Little did I think that our skirmishes would be so relevant to couples in an entirely new era. But they are.

I have practiced family systems therapy, or couples therapy as it is sometimes called, for twenty-five years now. In 1977, I also cofounded a family therapy institute in Westchester, New York, that trains up to seventy-five family therapists a year. There I teach the theories and techniques I've developed to help the many couples who come to us feeling "stuck" in their anger or hopeless about the emptiness of their marriage.

Yes, I explain to my students, these couples *are* "stuck" because they've been trying to solve their problems exclusively in the world of "feelings." And for so many years, we therapists have been treating them as if feeling good about yourself and loving well are sufficient to make relationships better. But love is not enough, and neither is self-esteem.

So many of the very personal complaints a couple will tell a therapist are actually the products of social and economic pressures—and not of their own shortcomings. What's more, our outdated traditional model of marriage just makes those pressures worse. Meanwhile, most people don't even know they're in a traditional marriage or that its unspoken rules don't work anymore.

Too often nowadays people will leave one marriage and then

try another only to fail in their next attempt. Yet all too often neither their personal failings nor their choice in partners turns lovers into enemies. It is marriage as we know it that is failing them.

In *Love, Honor and Negotiate,* I propose a more hopeful alternative than divorce, and one that is far less painful. It offers a way to change our relationships by coming to understand how the forces of money and power govern our intimate lives. And you'll see specifically how those forces play out in today's society, which has little subsidized child care or paid parental leave (and almost none for men). Most jobs demand long and inflexible work hours, and a man is still expected to be successful financially while a woman is expected to take care of the home and children, whether she works outside or not. These are the social and economic facts of our times.

The alternative I propose offers suggestions for renegotiating your marriage contract in the light of these facts so that your marriage can grow as you both do. What this means, really, is a new model of marriage that will support the lives most couples live today.

SNOWFLAKE MARRIAGES

When I started my work with couples in the seventies, I assumed that since women now worked and considered themselves the equals of men, we'd solved the gender problem I had to struggle with. In therapy, I treated every marriage as if it were as unique as a snowflake. But as I began to notice the repetition of complaints, I couldn't help but realize that I was in a blizzard of sex-role issues that had not gone away.

The more I explored couples' "communications" problems, the more I found that one of the main things couples can't communicate about is the power to make decisions. The more I questioned younger couples, the more I heard about their constant arguments. The more I questioned them about the content of their arguments, the more I heard about who spends what money, who does what housework and child care, and—if both partners work—whose work comes first. Or I heard about the backlash from these conflicts in their sex lives, if they still had any. Older couples complained about the emptiness between them or argued bitterly about every detail of their lives. But the more I questioned them, the more I heard about the women resenting their husbands' high-handedness or indifference to family life. And the men were defensively dismissive of these complaints.

Sex-role issues? Yes. First of all, most couples find themselves in trouble after they have children or when the children are grown. That's most frequently when couples come for therapy. I began to see the reason for this pattern is that *most American couples backslide into traditional sex roles as soon as their children are born.* Women cut back at work, quit, or play superwoman because they are *automatically* the ones in charge of children. Meanwhile, men toil even more to "be good providers," ending up just as much the bewildered breadwinner as my husband, Sam, used to be. Some are just furious because of their spouse's incessant complaints. And the divorce rates skyrocket.

I saw all this, but I was stymied. There was no way to use traditional family therapy theory to respond to the problems of gender. So, working with a few like-minded colleagues—Marianne Walters, Peggy Papp, and Olga Silverstein—we cofounded the Women's Project in Family Therapy in 1977 and developed our own techniques. But it meant thinking in an entirely new way for a family systems therapist. To explain the new thinking, though, I should first describe what family systems therapy is.

FAMILIES AREN'T OPTIONAL

Family systems therapy was developed in the fifties as an improvement on individual therapy. The classic Freudian approach treats the individual in a vacuum, as if a person has an emotional problem within himself or herself. Family systems theorists said that the individual doesn't exist alone emotionally but in dynamic relationship with other family members. This means that emotional problems exist not inside the person who happens to exhibit or experience the problem but among all the family members.

Except in rare circumstances, *the family is the most powerful emo-*

tional system we ever belong to. It shapes and continues to determine the course and outcome of our lives. A three- or four-generation family operates as a finely tuned system with roles and rules for functioning as a unit. For example, if one member behaves "irresponsibly," an "overresponsible" member will step in and pick up the slack; if one person is silent and withdrawn, another is usually the one to talk and engage, and vice versa—the sequences are circular.

Everyone in the family maintains problem behavior such as that of an alcoholic father or depressed mother or runaway son. They don't do this because they want or need to but because their automatic and "common sense" response to the problem is *also* part of the problem. The wife who empties her husband's bottles of scotch, the husband who suggests his wife go on antidepressants, and the parents who send their runaway son to therapy to "get fixed" are all trying to be helpful. But they're only making the problem worse, partly because these "solutions" imply that the person's symptom is *the* problem. Instead of looking for the factors in the family system that are producing the person's anxiety or depression, they try to get rid of the symptom.

A person's symptom is really a cry for help. It suggests that there is something wrong in the family system and that the symptomatic person is in a vulnerable position in that system. But to resist having to change themselves, other family members automatically try to keep everyone in place, especially the so-called problem person, whose changing would require the most extensive family changes.

This resistance to changing the system is very obvious in couples. It's almost always the wife who suggests or insists on therapy. Usually she's anxious or depressed about the family or the marriage and has brought in a long list of complaints. But when the therapist asks how the husband sees the situation, he usually says that his only problem is his unhappy wife, or sometimes he angrily contradicts her item by item. In other words, he automatically resists any changes her complaints might call for.

The symptomatic person is generally one of the least powerful people in the system and therefore least able to change the others or the system. This is a person who will try to adapt to difficult emotional circumstances by rebelling, giving in, or making do. When the limits of compromises are reached, the person's level of anxiety will usually express itself in physical or emotional symptoms, or in intense anger.

Most people don't realize the extent to which the marriage and family we create is a product of the family we were raised in, whether we are trying to re-create that original family or do the opposite. Our family relationships—the gears that run the clock, so to speak—are highly patterned and reciprocal. Rules are spoken and unspoken. They are based on our family history, which produces themes, stories, taboos, myths, secrets, heroes, and rebels. This history is passed on, consciously and unconsciously, to the next generation and to all new marriages.

That's what we mean when we say that family relationships aren't optional. They're also not equal or fair. You might say that our original family is like a hand of cards dealt by fate. And that our life task, emotionally, is dealing with this hand.

For all these reasons, the family therapist will help patients actively work out problems with their parents on the assumption that, as I always put it, if you can work them out with your parents, you can work them out with anyone. And you'd better, I tell them, because your parents will always play a significant, if silent, part in all your relationships, particularly your marriage. The more unresolved the problems of the past, the more they influence the present. So if you've married your mother, you'd better have a good relationship with her!

Even when people flee their "families of origin," as we call it, the impact of the family doesn't end. In fact, it actually increases. Not speaking to family members who have caused us difficulty may temporarily relieve the pain of trying to deal with them. But the poison of the cutoff spreads throughout the family as members expend enormous emotional energy taking sides, justifying some people's action and vilifying others. Every subsequent family event takes place in the shadow of the cutoff, and when the conflict that supposedly caused it is almost forgotten, what remains are families whose members are disconnected from one another and who live with broken hearts or hearts covered with calluses. Worst of all, the legacy suggests to future generations that family members we disagree with should be discarded. This is not a healthy resolution of conflict.

The other side of the coin—what we call enmeshment or fusion—occurs when family members become overinvolved and entangled in their relationships, taking inappropriate responsibility for one another, wanting peace at any price, insisting on ignoring differences through denial and compromise or eliminating differences through endless conflict. There is no "live and let live" in this smothering system. Attempts to get space in such an enmeshed family lead easily to emotional cutoffs that are disguised by dutiful, superficial contact. These are simply other forms of not really dealing with family.

Family therapists normally believe that for a person to have a mature relationship with family members he or she must be authentically oneself—even in ways that may break the family rules—while still having a meaningful personal connection. Of course, as everyone knows who has ever tried to achieve this with parents, spouses, and siblings, it is very difficult to do. Most of us will spend a lifetime trying to do it. Family therapy just helps us move in that direction.

Because I believe so deeply that people can only understand themselves in context, I have always used a therapeutic tool called a "genogram." When a couple comes in for therapy, I routinely draw a family tree for each partner, questioning them about the major problems with and among their siblings, their parents, grandparents, and children.

Answers to the simplest questions will immediately reveal the important patterns that show the partners the familial themes they are repeating in their marriage. A "faithless husband," for example, may be following in the footsteps of his own philandering father or rebelling against a father he thought of as pathetically dominated. A man who accepts punishing work that keeps him from family life may have a father who did the same thing. That's certainly the case with Gary and Sharon, the first couple you'll meet in this book. But whatever the themes, the couple can begin to think of their marriage as part of a larger picture—they can put their marriage in the context of family.

The family context, however, wasn't enough to explain the gender complaints I was constantly hearing. So I had to discover on my own that family systems therapy—like Freudian therapy—wasn't drawing a large enough picture. Marriages, I realized, were not only two people enmeshed in family structures, they were also families enmeshed in cultural structures—structures that often exert unbearable pressures on these families, making spouses blame each other for what are really social problems. So I began to realize that the genogram had to be expanded to make the picture larger, placing every couple's story in the context of family *and* culture.

Each family tries to teach its members the "right way" to live in our time and the "right values" to have about money, marriage, work, parenting, sex, and so on. A family does this without realizing the degree to which these "truths" are dictated by the family's place in our very stratified culture—for example, their race, gender, ethnicity, social class, or sexual orientation—and how those values play out not only *against* the family, but also *within* it. Therapy is an opportunity for couples to examine their emotional and social "programming" and decide which values they actually believe in and want to keep for their own.

Without an understanding of the impact of family and cultural beliefs, couples are left with the crazy idea that they are inventing themselves and their lives, or that they could if only their spouse would change. It is this false notion of independence that leads to marital power struggles and divorce.

This cultural perspective is still a radical expansion of most family therapy. When I lecture on my therapeutic methods, other therapists will often say, "But we have to accept a particular couple's style of life. We can't change that." And I always answer, "Well, why not? If that's what needs changing?" And I've come to believe that nine times out of ten, that is precisely what needs changing.

Improved communication is supposed to solve a couple's problems, but in the majority of cases, it cannot. For example, if a woman who works outside the home still does the lion's share of housework and child care, communication can only name the problem or identify the source of the wife's unhappiness. Unless

the talk leads to a change in how the couple divides up housework and child care, it won't help at all. Too often "communication" can become an argument without end and lead to mutual
blame and psychological name-calling. With a cultural perspective on their problems as well as a psychological one, couples can
start to evaluate their problems in the context of their families
and our culture.

THE GOLDEN RULE

What can couples learn from this cultural perspective? Exactly
what I've learned from working with couples over the years and
from other therapists who have been studying gender problems
in marriage. Simply put: Our society forces couples to backslide
into traditional marriages when they have children, which re-
duces the woman's power in a previously equal marriage. This is
not to say that partners can never maintain their equality in a
traditional breadwinner-homemaker arrangement. They can if
they are not ambivalent about these roles, if they do not penalize
the nonearner, and if they value both contributions to the marriage equally—despite society's indoctrination. Some couples
truly march to a different drummer; in others, the nonearning
partner may have a talent or avocation so valued by society as to
"equalize" power. But for the vast majority of today's couples,
going backward is the worst mistake to make. For no matter how
much love you feel, relationships in our money-driven society
tend to be governed by the Golden Rule: Whoever has the gold,
makes the rules.

The Golden Rule means that the power balance can be disas-
trously upset if the woman cuts back at work or quits to take care
of the children, thereby losing her economic muscle in the marriage. What usually happens with these transitions is that money
and power reshape our relationships without our knowing it. If,
instead, she takes the superwoman route and winds up working
at the office and doing everything at home, she's generally too
exhausted and resentful to enjoy the relationship.

This is where American culture intrudes into the inner sanc-
tum of marriage. On the one hand, it has given us new expecta-

tions of marriage; on the other, it has failed to allow the new marriage to fulfill these expectations. The American economy requires that most husbands and wives both work outside the home but offers little workplace or social support for the two-earner family. And couples *have* changed—but not enough. At our current stage of semi-enlightenment, a man often wants to have a real relationship with his children, but not at the risk of his career. A woman often wants her husband to be more emotionally involved with her and the children yet still wants him to be the *main* breadwinner so that she can feel free to work less if she wants to stay home with the children.

That's why I've come to believe in resolutions that combine the personal, social, *and* political. First, we have to give up the myths that women can't have it all except by doing it all and that men don't have to do it all but can have it all. We seriously have to question the idea that men's careers must never be disturbed and that mothering is different from—and more involving—than fathering. These are the sacred cows of our culture.

As frightening as it may feel at first, women and men must truly share parenting. Both mothers and fathers today need to cut back at work or redesign their career goals, trading some fame and fortune for time to have a fulfilling family life. These same mothers and fathers will also have to press for changes in the workplace.

Renegotiating the marriage contract so that the marriage maintains the partners' equality and allows ample time for family life may seem like an overwhelming task for most couples. But it is my hope that this book—filled with its many success stories of couples at every stage of life who have dramatically improved their relationships—will contribute to the reexamination of marriage that will enhance love and family life.

WHY LOVE, HONOR AND NEGOTIATE

Although a book can never substitute for therapy, I believe that much of the work I do with couples can be done by the couples themselves if they understand the internal and external pressures on their marriages. Of course, couples struggling with severe problems like violence or substance abuse cannot change without professional help. But the majority of couples can learn to do the very things I've helped my clients to do: find personal solutions to these cultural problems and realize the options they actually have for changing their lives, even when it means scaling down and cutting back on certain luxuries. Many of the methods I use in therapy to help couples think in new ways about old problems can be used by all couples to prevent the frustrations that might later bring them to therapy, or to divorce. Many of the questions I ask couples, couples can ask themselves. Their honest responses will give them a glimpse of the unstated social and economic themes of their marriage.

In the first part of *Love, Honor and Negotiate,* I explain in detail how cultural beliefs and social forces not only account for many of our marital decisions *without our knowing it,* but they are also at the root of most marital strife. I show how money and power control our intimate, even our sexual, lives. Here, as elsewhere, each discussion is grounded in a couple's story so that you will see how couples learn to step back and view the larger picture of their intimate lives, and to work out a happier marriage.

The second half of the book will focus on method, laying out the principles of renegotiating the marriage contract at the major marital stress points or whenever a crisis occurs. It also examines the processes of change for men and women, and the ways we can overcome our strong resistance to change. And finally, it explores the particular problems involved in divorce and remarriage.

In the final chapter, I'll take a look outward and forward to how the culture could change in ways that would make our marriages work better. It is my statement of hope about the future of marriage, community, and America. Not that I think of what I'm doing as changing the world. But as couples change their individual marriages, they can—and must—change the world around them to make it better support our families and ourselves.

Backsliding into Traditional Marriage

Marriage, I sometimes remind couples on the brink of divorce who have come for therapy, can ruin a perfectly good relationship

Not that I wish to make light of their unhappiness—or of marriage. Few experiences are more meaningful than sharing a life with someone, knowing another and being known, creating a family together. That bond between two people, which is the essence of marriage, is surely one of life's great joys. What I do mean is that successful relationships are most often undermined by *traditional* marriage, marriage defined by fixed gender roles and women's second-class status.

Whether couples have consciously rejected traditional marriage or not doesn't matter. They have all changed enough with the times to feel hemmed in by the rigidities of the institution. Religious couples routinely have the word *obey* deleted from their wedding ceremonies; others write their own vows to express their personal definition of marriage. Often now both the mother and father of the bride will escort her down the aisle. But even the bride whose father "gives" her to her husband can tell you how her marriage will not be traditional; the groom who awaits her swears he won't be the kind of husband his own father was.

Today's *Modern Bride Magazine* may superficially resemble the 1949 premier issue, but as its editor in chief says of their current readers, "They want traditional weddings, *not* traditional marriages!" Most of their readers, all women, have careers (as opposed to jobs) and earn the same money as their husbands. In the pages of the bride magazines today—there were seven at my local newsstand—are articles that would never have appeared before the sixties, such as advice on prenuptial agreements, shared finances, or on how to make the wedding night special even though you've been living together.

Apparently, the penchant for Victorian wedding gowns and Wedgwood china no longer reflects an allegiance to the old code. Couples may still love to dress up and create a dramatic rite of passage for themselves, but as much as they crave a grand and solemn ceremony, no one buys into the symbolism. A lot of brides will tell me they're wearing a white gown, quickly adding with a smile, "off-white, of course."

Even conservative contemporary marriages start on a profoundly different basis from marriages before the sixties. Couples often meet at college or on the job. Both partners are likely to work at similar levels, and since they both work, they usually share housework, which is minimal anyway. In the evenings they might make dinner together or each go out on their own with friends, including those of the opposite sex—neither of which their parents were apt to do. Just look at the young married couple in the TV sitcom "Mad About You." As one friend from an older generation commented after watching the show for the first time, "It's not about marriage. The husband and wife are more like two friends having a good time." They usually are. And while they might not use feminist language, they almost always consider themselves equal.

In fact, these newly married couples are more equal now than they are ever likely to be again—once they have children. What they don't know is that the institution of marriage has changed, but it hasn't changed enough to make their egalitarian dreams work.

Most unhappy marriages today are unhappy in a very particular end-of-the-twentieth-century way. In therapy the patterns are startlingly clear. As I mentioned in the introduction, couples rarely come for therapy before they have children. Why? The explanation is simple. Until then the relationships work because there *is* more equality. But as soon as the baby arrives, the new parents discover that their world isn't organized to allow them to remain equal. What may surprise them even more is to discover that they won't allow themselves to remain equal; their own psyches pull them back into traditional roles. "I never thought I'd feel this way," new mothers tell me to explain why they quit their jobs to stay home to care for their child. New fathers will tell me how anxious they feel about their future financial responsibilities. Are these just our "real" selves emerging? Our inescapable maleness and femaleness? No, not at all. However, deep in our hearts, underneath our sense of ourselves as equals, is very strong familial and social programming to be mothers and fathers in the old mode.

Because we live with these two conflicting ideas of ourselves, tensions within new parents and between them are inevitable. If they carry on without examining their "programming" and do not renegotiate their marriage contract, they often have very angry child-rearing years—these are, in fact, the years when most divorces take place. If the couple stumbles through such angry child-rearing years without renegotiating, later on—once the children have grown and left—the partners often find they're tired of living in a constant battle. Either that or they discover the "emptiness" between them (read withdrawal brought about by anger and resentment) and decide that there's nothing to keep them together anymore. The result: divorce has become as common as marriage.

WHY DO WE DIVORCE SO MUCH?

Fifty percent of American marriages end in divorce. That figure is the highest in the world, and a very sobering one. But there are other noteworthy figures, too. The divorce rate for second marriages—once thought to be based on better and wiser choices—is up as well, even higher than for first marriages. And couples who have lived together before marrying have a higher divorce rate than couples who have not.

Americans divorce so frequently that for half of our couples, the family life cycle is now most accurately outlined as: marriage—divorce—remarriage. For many of these couples, there will be more than one divorce and remarriage. In all honesty, do any of us know more than a handful of people who've stayed married to the same person through middle age? Probably not.

What could account for so much divorce? Many people point the finger of blame at our culture's lack of family values or at women's "selfishness" or at men's "irresponsibility." The flaw in such thinking is that it's based on the assumption that something is wrong with men and women today. No one ever blames marriage itself. Yet that is exactly what logic and my experience as a family therapist lead me to conclude. Such high divorce rates must mean that something is wrong with marriage, *not* the people who marry. And because women are the ones who most frequently initiate divorce, it stands to reason that something is *more* wrong for women than men. My professional observations bear this out as well.

Women are not getting what they need from marriage today. They usually do before they have children, but when the children are born, they often lose their financial independence. As a result, they lose their ability to negotiate with their husbands on a level playing field. And if they cannot negotiate, they cannot insure that enough of their needs are met. Eventually, when too few of a woman's needs are satisfied, she'll ask herself, What am I getting from this marriage? And that's not the only way marriage ends up failing women.

Women also lose a great deal more by being married than their husbands do. Marriage's two most predictable stress points—when couples have children and when the children leave home—are far more stressful for women than men. They leave women reeling while men's lives are often relatively undisturbed. To help you understand why, let me first explain what we mean by "stress points" in a marriage and why having children, and then having them leave home, can be so threatening to a marriage.

MARRIAGE'S MAJOR STRESS POINTS

Two people usually decide to marry because they are so happy together they want to join their lives and create a permanent home together. What disturbs their bliss is stress of one kind or another. It may be something as simple as trying to agree on furniture they both like or something as complex as one of them losing a job. But the greatest stress in an emotional system, whether it's a couple alone or a family, will always be caused by the loss or addition of one of its members.

Whether a particular loss or addition to the family happens to be happy or sad isn't what determines the extent of the family's upset. What matters is how much emotional shifting around the couple has to do so they can adjust to the new or missing member. For example, a wonderful new daughter-in-law is usually a happy addition to a couple's lives, but it means they will now have to relate to their son in an entirely new way. An elderly parent dying is a loss that creates a different kind of stress for a couple. But unless the grief for a parent is complicated by painful or unresolved problems between them, or unless the dead parent played a major role in the couple's relationship, such predictable additions or losses will not drastically change the day-to-day relationship of spouses. But the birth of a new baby will.

The New Baby

Having children creates such intense stress for a couple because the "new member" requires a major change in their relationship. When a baby is born, parents usually endow it with dreams and expectations, and enormous importance. But what happens to the twosome who were the most important people in the world to each other before the baby? What happens if those dreams and expectations aren't fulfilled? The couple may believe a baby will bring them closer, but what if it doesn't? What if each partner experiences the baby very differently, as often happens. What if one or both partners "lose themselves" in their new parenting roles? Or panic at the new responsibilities? One of them may even suddenly have a strong urge to flee. And if the baby was unplanned or has a disability, the parents may have to deal with more anxiety than they've ever experienced before. Whatever way the new arrival makes its entrance felt, the couple will never be the same. The challenge here is how to be together in a different way.

The Children Leaving Home

Couples whose children grow up and leave home also face the challenge of how to be together differently. During the child-rearing years, these couples have usually been too distracted to be clearly aware of how satisfied they were with each other. Too much of their energy has gone toward the children and worrying about money and careers. And if they weren't too tired to argue about their relationship, they might have been too concerned about the children to risk a confrontation, or worse yet, divorce. They may have bickered or they may swallow their anger, but they have been waiting—consciously or unconsciously—for the time when they can deal with the problems between them without bringing down the roof on the family.

That time comes during or after the launching of the children. Then the husband and wife—alone as a couple—have to figure out how they want to reorganize their relationship for the many years still ahead.

Today, these two stress points are much more difficult for couples than they were even a generation ago. They require much more emotional shifting and practical reorganization. Traditional marriage gave couples a formula for weathering such stress and reorganizing: when the children arrived, women became homemakers and men got serious at work. But that formula isn't effective when women also work. We might even say it's counterproductive. The formula is too often unthinkingly applied, intensifying the stress for women.

When the children left home a generation ago, a woman waited for the grandchildren to arrive and then helped out with them while her husband made retirement plans. But if she didn't go back to school or get a job, she often faced the empty-nest syndrome. Of course, the name itself downplayed the serious depression that sometimes ensued in women whose "job was done" (read "useful life was over"). Today, when the wife works, this part of the transition is clearer for couples. The focus of any discontent is usually squarely on the couple's relationship, where it belongs. It does, nevertheless, vastly increase their stress to realize that the problem is with them, and not with the loss of the children.

Becoming parents and launching the children aren't the only marital stress points. In Chapter 9, "Renegotiating the Marriage Contract," I'll describe many others, mapping out the emotional and behavioral changes required in each. For now, let me just flatly state that the stress points need not result in anger, withdrawal, or divorce if couples can renegotiate their contract to keep their relationship equal. If they do, they can use their crises to grow—independently and as a couple. If they can't figure out how on their own, smart couples go to see a therapist.

"I'M COPARENTING WITH OUR NANNY"

Gary and Sharon came for therapy because, as she explained on the phone, "I can't cope anymore. I work, I run the household, and he acts as if we don't have any children."

In fact, as I soon learned, Gary and Sharon had a three-year-old daughter, Sophie, and a five-month-old son, Max. The household was a large home in Scarsdale, one of New York's most affluent Westchester suburbs. Gary was forty-three; Sharon, forty. They'd been married for eight years.

Their first appointment was for 5:30 P.M. When I came out to the waiting room to greet them I found Sharon alone. "*This* is my problem," she said. "He promised he'd get out of the office on time, but he never does. So what do we do now?"

I suggested we wait ten minutes then begin without him. Just as Sharon sat down in my office, Gary arrived. "Sorry I'm late," he said and, glancing at Sharon, joked to her, "but I *did* make it?" She looked away.

When I invited them both to explain the problem, Gary said, "Go on, Sharon, this was your idea." Then he crossed one knee over the other, as if in patient expectation, but actually he was quite tense. *Wired* is the word that came to mind. Of course, arriving directly from the office, he looked more formal than his wife, starched and somewhat severe in a three-piece navy blue suit and red silk tie. Still, he seemed less exhausted than Sharon, who had obviously come from home and had time to change out of her work clothes.

Although Sharon wore brown suede slacks with a sumptuous sweater, she still seemed unkempt. The sweater was stained at the cuff, her pants were worn at the knees, and wisps of her thick black hair had come loose from her ponytail. And yet, although her eyes were puffy with sleeplessness, they had the same intensity as Gary's did. Both husband and wife created the impression of energy and readiness.

"Okay, let me draw you this picture," Sharon said. "Saturday afternoon. I had specifically asked Gary to take care of the children while my mother and I prepared a birthday dinner for my sister, Lydia. It was just for a couple of hours, but what does he do? Without telling me—"

"I just forgot to mention it," Gary interjected.

". . . he offers Alma, our nanny, who's off weekends, a whole day's pay to work Saturday afternoon, just so he won't have to be alone with the children, God forbid—"

"Where is it written that I have to be *alone* with them?" Gary whispers, and Sharon, ignoring his remarks, continued.

"So he's in the living room with Alma and the children, supposedly *being* with them, you know, like playing with them, since he's been at the office most of the day. And suddenly we hear a crash, then everyone's crying. We run in. There's Gary, his *Fortune* magazine in one hand, the other pointing to the lamp that's broken into pieces at his feet, and he's yelling 'Look what you've done, Sophie.' Meanwhile Sophie is hysterical, and Alma, who has Max and his bottle in one arm, is trying to pick up the lamp and comfort Sophie and explain to me that it was just an accident, she'd been feeding Max, and Sophie was needing some attention. And Gary storms out like a madman, muttering, 'She always needs attention,'—as if that's a crime in a three-year-old. My mother hides in the kitchen she's so embarrassed. And there I am, as always, with Alma, trying to deal with the kids, telling Sophie Daddy's just tired."

"I *was* tired. I'd been up since six-thirty in the morning," Gary said gently. "I *had* to have some quiet time. I told Sophie that. Alma put out crayons and paper for her, but she had to keep turning off my lamp. And when that didn't work, she threw it over. On *purpose*, Sharon."

"She's three, Gary. She's very jealous of her new brother, particularly when Alma is attending to him. You don't even know what's going on with her. All you do is work."

"Gary," I asked, "what's your view?"

"Look," he said, his palms open, as if to show he had no secrets. "I'm a corporate lawyer for a big New York firm. Even my women colleagues don't say, 'I'm going home to take care of my kids now.' Not if they want to make partner. We have a house, a vacation home on Fire Island, a live-in nanny, two cars, and now we pay for her parents' condo in Florida as well. Does she think we can do that if I work forty hours a week? I can't. And I can't walk in the door and deal with a baby who screams the minute no one's koochying him, plus Sophie, who's turned back into a baby, plus Sharon, who's had postpartum depression ever since Max was born."

"I do not," Sharon snapped. "That's ridiculous."

"Well, I think I get the picture," I said. Then, to remind them of why they were together and to learn more about them, I asked if they would tell me how their life was before the children came.

Sharon said that they lived in Manhattan until Sophie was six months old, then decided the city wasn't the place to raise children. A clinical psychologist and graduate school professor, she felt she didn't have enough time for Sophie and so left teaching.

After they moved, she started a private practice in Scarsdale, which they had chosen to be close to her sister, Lydia.

They both seemed to enjoy talking about their early life together: "We'd start the day jogging around the reservoir in Central Park. We both worked late. Then we'd maybe go to the symphony or have dinner and watch Ted Koppel. It was idyllic, really."

Now I caught a glimpse of the pleasure they had in each other, and their tenderness. And as if telling the story in concert, Gary chimed in, "We played tennis on weekends. She'd take me to all these crazy neighborhoods I'd never seen. Or we'd go visit her family in Brooklyn."

"That's right," Sharon said. "You used to like my family, remember? Now you just resent them."

He spoke softly and extended his arm along the back of the couch toward her: "I *do* like your parents. You know that. I even like their visits, though months at a time is a lot for me. What I resent is that you won't even ask your brother to help pay for their condo."

I turned to Sharon for confirmation. She explained that when her parents closed their shoe store, she and Gary and her sister and brother-in-law bought them a condo in Florida. But since her sister's husband left her a year ago, Lydia could barely make ends meet, so they've been paying for the condo and helping Lydia, too. Her little brother, Josh, just "kissed us all goodbye and moved to California. We're lucky if we see him every couple of years. So I take care of the family because that's how Jewish families are. Gary doesn't understand that."

"What about your family, Gary?" I asked, and with pained hesitations, Gary, an only child, told me that he saw his parents, who lived in Chicago, about once a year. His father, a retired banker, was "critical and controlling." His mother was "cold and withdrawn." Gary's eyes misted when he said, "I'd rather not see them any more than I have to."

Hoping for a way to explore the connection between him and Sharon, I said, "I wonder if you adopted Sharon's warm, close family as an antidote to your family's more distant style?"

Gary nodded. "I think that's true. Sharon had what I didn't, a real family." While Gary spoke, looking over at her several times, she fixed her eyes on him. "They were so accepting of me. Except for Josh, who's more like a WASP." For the first time that evening, Sharon and Gary exchanged a smile.

For their next session, I had asked them to think about the changes each would like to see in their home life. Although "lawyerly" to the last vest button, Gary seemed more open than before and began to speak, unprompted. "I really think Sharon ought to cut back or quit her practice until the kids are in school. She has the latitude that I don't, and if life is too hectic, why not work less? I'd also like to reduce our expenses, and it would help if she even knew what they were, but she won't listen to a word I say about money." Sharon stared at the ceiling as he explained why earning jointly over $250,000 a year wasn't enough.

Sharon, herself dressed for success that morning with a black dress and thick silver necklaces, said, "Gary, all you talk about anymore is money. All I want is for us to enjoy our family. Why be together if we don't? Don't you remember how we'd fantasize about kids and a dog?"

"Please, Sharon, no dog," Gary said, his hands held up like two stop signs. "No more dependents." Just as Gary was about to launch into a defense, I moved them back into the deeper thinking about themselves they had begun in the last session.

"Gary," I asked, "you were quite lonely as a child, am I right?" He nodded, and we talked for a while about his being an only child, his gloomy home, and his father's always being at work or at the club. "At dinner, he'd just give me his lists of expectations and disappointments in my behavior." Then I asked if he didn't think he might be reproducing his father's distant and angry parenting?

Gary's cheeks reddened. He didn't answer. "Gary," I asked, "would you be willing to work on breaking this pattern?" Closing his eyes for a moment, he listened as I explained, "Things won't change for you and your kids unless you do some work on your relationship with your parents."

"They're hopeless," he replied. "They depress me and I really don't see what they have to do with how I raise my kids."

"Everyone assumes their parents are hopeless. But I think that if you come to terms with who they are and could stop running away, it would change everything for you with your kids." I could tell from the way he tightened his lips that he heard me but was still guarded. I knew I couldn't press him anymore right then. Instead, I said, "Sharon, what about you. If you could magically arrange your life just the way you wanted it, what would you do?"

"Well, I certainly wouldn't stop working," Sharon said. "I did that when we first moved and wasn't happy. I might work three half-days a week instead of four and one evening instead of two, but I worked so hard to build this practice when we moved here. If I turn people away now, I'm just throwing out the last year's gains. And besides, if I work less, he'll work more. Before Sophie, I was earning more than Gary was. He never worked on the weekends then. If I had a magic wand, *he'd* work less."

Gary looked at me. "I keep trying to explain to her I can't cut back. She knew I was a lawyer when she married me. She knows these are the tough years. Everyone left and right is waiting to jump into my place if I slack off for a minute. The children are fine. I really don't see what the problem is."

"Do you believe this?" Sharon said. "He really thinks that children raise themselves. He's never seen Sophie's nursery school. He's never been to the pediatrician with them. He has no idea what Max is eating now. The children don't even want to go to him. They think Alma and I are their parents."

When I asked Gary exactly how many hours a week he worked and when he saw the children, he admitted that he averaged sixty to seventy hours and got home after the children were asleep. "I see them on weekends and in the mornings."

Before Sharon could tell me that he worked most Saturdays and just waved at them in the mornings, I asked if he could get home early enough a couple of days a week to spend an hour with them before bed?

"I could try," he said, but I told him I was thinking of something the children could depend on. By the end of the session, he agreed to get home one evening by 7:00 P.M.

Over the next several sessions, we discussed how difficult it was for Gary to engage Sophie, who did prefer Alma or Mommy. But with our support, he began the ritual of taking Sophie for an ice cream so they could be by themselves. It was still "forced," Sharon said, but she felt they were making progress on "daddy night."

As their therapy progressed, Gary was still primarily concerned about money, so I asked Sharon if she could commit to going over the budget with Gary. Although she protested, she did agree, then I wondered out loud why it was so hard for her to ask her brother to help pay for her parents' condo? "Does he have the money?" I inquired.

"Oh, yes. He's very successful in computers. But he doesn't want anything to do with family. And I don't want the hurt of having him say it for the umpteenth time. It would kill my parents if they thought I asked him. And *I* might kill *him*."

"It sounds to me as if you're protecting the whole family, Sharon. More like a mother than the daughter, am I right?"

"Well, I'm the oldest," she said, nodding, and we talked about her "overresponsible" position in the family constellation, constantly bailing out her younger sister and taking over for Josh so he could just "cut loose." "My mother was always ill or depressed or both," Sharon said, "and my father was always at the shoe store, so I had to take care of everything."

"Yes, I see. But that was then and this is now. You don't still have to take care of everything, do you?"

After weeks of talking about how Sharon could be responsible to her family, not *for* them, she decided she would try to renew her relationship with her brother and eventually deal with the issue between them instead of just angrily writing him off. When she called just to say hello and ask Josh what he'd been up to, he told her that he was now living with a woman he was "very serious about." Not only did this make him much more open to his family than usual, apparently he'd even been thinking about bringing his girlfriend to meet all of them. By the time Josh and Sharon were exchanging regular friendly phone calls, Sharon took the risk of telling him how much it would help if Josh could take over Lydia's part of their parents' mortgage payments. The money was no problem, he told Sharon. It was a relief to him to do something concrete and "limited" for his parents.

Sharon was so excited by her success with Josh, she agreed to tell Lydia that she and Gary needed to cut back financially and wouldn't be able to help her anymore. Lydia stalked off saying, "I won't be any trouble to you," and at first wouldn't return Sharon's calls. But I helped Sharon to stick to her position and not get angry at Lydia. Eventually, Lydia did come around and decided that it was time for her to sell her big house and get an apartment instead.

For Sharon, these small changes were miracles. "I feel so much lighter," she kept saying, and Gary was clearly impressed by how much Sharon was changing as she asserted her own needs with her family instead of trying to take care of them all the time. That's when I approached the subject of his family again, explaining that it was no accident that Sharon was happier, less "on the attack" with him. "Your relationship with your own family is like a blueprint for how to have intimate relations. If the blueprint is faulty, so are the relations," I said. I told him that if he didn't change his relationship with his parents, he would probably have the same problems of distance and anger with his children when they were older.

"I know I don't want them to feel the way I did," he said, and that's when I was able to persuade Gary to write his mother a letter to tell her how much he wished she knew his children and that they could all be closer.

Gary's mother called him, almost immediately, and responded warmly. Over time, their talks grew more personal, and when Gary had to make a business trip to Chicago, he suggested he visit. Alone with her, he confessed that he always felt she regretted having a child and was disappointed in him. "Oh no—no—no," she gasped. "I was just so unhappy." She told him that his father was much sterner and more reserved than she'd understood. She had married him because he was above reproach. Her own father, an alcoholic, had once spent two years in jail for forging a check, leaving his family to public assistance.

"I never knew any of that," Gary said. "Apparently, my father married her anyway, and she had to be eternally grateful. No one mentioned my mother's father, and we hardly ever saw her family. Now I realize it was because she was so ashamed of them."

Gary had been thunderstruck by his mother's revelation. "I can remember her telling me how important it was to 'work and earn' and be 'respectable' like my father. It's as if I was delegated to make up for her malingering father." This was the first time that Gary was moved emotionally to view his workaholism as a possible problem instead of a successful man's career track.

Gary's father was much more difficult to "get through to." But with coaching, Gary kept talking to him about his own life and work and how much he missed having time for his kids. His father, who understood that Gary was also talking about his own childhood, usually said something like "Gary, I really don't enjoy these conversations of yours" or "Your responsibility is to provide for your family." But once, instead, his father replied, "I never was very good at emotions. I guess you and your mother suffered because of that."

"It wasn't much," Gary said. "But I glimpsed a person in there somewhere." The truth was his father had mellowed. Gary persisted in his efforts to relate to his father, asking him about his own childhood in the twenties and thirties and what his parents were like. Eventually, his father talked more easily with Gary, and when Gary went with him to his club to meet his friends, he saw his father glow with pride.

The changes Gary made with his family resonated in his marriage immediately. He was more open and talkative with Sharon, more at ease with the children, and he also agreed to two "daddy nights" a week. "I bring them both onto our bed and let Sophie hit me with pillows while I bounce Max. It's rather relaxing. Then I read the mail while Sharon puts them to sleep and we have our own quiet dinner. If my in-laws aren't there."

"Or mine," Sharon said. She was referring to his parents' visit, the second they had made since the wedding.

Over the next sessions, we talked about Sharon's reasons for marrying a reserved and emotionally distant WASP. It was clear that she had aspired to Gary's "classy WASPness," as she called it. And also, she wanted to control their home and make her own extended family central.

"So, in a way, Sharon, it was convenient that Gary had 'no family.' He really became a part of your family." She nodded. "I wonder if you're feeling threatened now. After all, if Gary becomes the full partner you've said you wanted, then you have to make room for his family."

"Ayyyy, save me," Sharon said, shaking her head, her ponytail wagging.

Gary laughed at her, and the two of them, obviously comfortable with each other now, seemed quite happy. When I mentioned that, Sharon said, "Yes, we're almost human again."

"Good," I responded. "Then what shall we work on now?"

"Gary's working less," Sharon said.

"Any less and I'd be taking Alma's job," Gary said.

"No, really, I wish you didn't have to fly out the door at dawn to commute to the city, and you still stay late a lot."

"What would you have me do, Sharon? Make pottery?"

Sharon rolled her eyes and said, "Do you have to stay at your firm? Aren't there different ways to practice law?"

"Sure. I could work for a small corporation, I suppose."

"Is that so horrible?" Sharon asked, her eyes wide with surprise that she was actually "interfering" in Gary's career.

"Yes," Gary said. "This is what I like to do."

"But do you like paying the price? You hardly see us."

Gary was silent. I wondered out loud if he was thinking about his father.

"Well, maybe," he said, brushing the idea aside. He turned back to Sharon. "Look, if I were even to consider a 'smaller' job, we'd have to sell Fire Island. We couldn't afford it."

Sharon sat back. Her breathing became heavier.

"What does that mean to you?" I asked. I knew that her parents lived in the Fire Island house for two months every summer, with Sharon's and Lydia's families visiting on weekends and all of them together for August.

"That would be hard. It's like the family compound. It's a dream for my parents."

While Gary's challenge was to connect to his family, Sharon's was to extricate herself from her chief caretaker role in hers. And she had made so much progress that, although she struggled with this radical suggestion for a couple of months—as Gary did—she found the courage to give up "the family compound" when Gary agreed to "research" alternative jobs, particularly in the Westchester area. Since Sharon had been doing the monthly budget with Gary for some time now, she knew they couldn't maintain two homes if Gary reduced his income. But for once she didn't try to solve the problem for her family. She just told her parents that they would have to sell Fire Island and all find another summer arrangement. It was her father who came up with the plan that the parents would spend a few weeks with Lydia, a few with Sharon, and a few with his brother who still lived in Brooklyn.

They did sell their vacation home, which vastly reduced their monthly nut. Now Gary was faced with the real possibility of working and earning less, but he resisted it for many months and protested with all his "old" anxious questions:

- Am I supposed to think that changing diapers is as rewarding as writing briefs?
- Why should I rush home so she can tell me what to do every minute?
- If she wants me to worry less about money, why doesn't she take over the finances?

On her part Sharon expressed just as many fears. Although she wanted him to change, she had all her "old" anxious questions about the changes she would have to make in their relationship:

- Do I need him home arguing with every household decision?
- Why doesn't he know how to take care of the children?
- Why should I do the finances? I'm terrible with numbers.

Yet, all their work over the last year and a half had paid off. In the following months, they made a plan. They decided that Gary would seriously inquire into other kinds of law practices, which he hadn't yet done. Sharon promised to stop criticizing his style of caring for the children. They also agreed to set aside one week-end evening for themselves, come hell or high water.

Soon their child-rearing battles stopped entirely. Gary had come up with some interesting work possibilities, and while he wasn't pursuing any, he did talk with Sharon about them. On the weekends, he worked at home but no longer went into the office, and now there were several "daddy nights" a week. For her part, Sharon decided to cut back to sixteen hours a week over the next six months and work only one evening instead of two. Alma worked Saturday mornings so Gary and Sharon could "play," but she was off every evening after six instead, when *they* took care of the children. Most revolutionary of all, Gary took care of them alone on the evening that Sharon worked.

It was obvious how much more Gary and Sharon were enjoying themselves. "We've even been playing tennis again. I almost like our life," Gary said. Liking it, he'd begun to resent his commute and his associates' disapproval of his new schedule.

Now the time was ripe for a major change. During his "research" period, he'd spoken to an acquaintance whose partner in his small Westchester law firm was retiring. When the man called Gary to ask if he might be interested in the partnership, Gary went to talk it over. "It's not as exciting as New York but it's a surprisingly attractive place. The commute's ten minutes! I'd be able to take Sophie to school so Sharon doesn't have to rush out, and I could relax when I got home. Sharon and I would have a lot more time together. My income will drop at first, but it will go up again later on."

Gary did take the partnership in Westchester. Although their combined income was reduced by almost a fourth—to $170,000 annually—so were their expenses. During the rest of that second year, they came to see me monthly "to keep us on track," as Sharon put it. "I feel like we're free," Gary said. "It's true," Sharon agreed. "Gary's office never calls, and now both our families visit and play grandparents for the kids, like normal relatives. Now that I don't feel the burden of mine, we're all so much more comfortable."

I don't see Gary and Sharon anymore, but I get a holiday card every year with a family picture. In the last one a slobbery Labrador wearing a party hat was sitting between Sophie and Max.

There's much more to Gary and Sharon's therapy, some of which we'll see in subsequent chapters. But I hope what I've included here illustrates the challenge of contemporary marriage. At the first marital stress point—having children—the equal relationship between husband and wife will backslide into a traditional one. The women are then doubly stressed because they either have to give up their work and with it their power in the marriage or, like Sharon, they have to juggle so much they're about to snap. By that point they're so angry they're often ready to leave a relationship that was perfectly satisfying before the children came along. But if the partners can separate their own wishes and current needs from their programming, they can renegotiate their marriage contract to restore their equality. In doing so, they will also make their lives together more emotionally satisfying for themselves and their children.

The Mothering Problem

Much of the reason why Sharon wanted to cut back at work was because she wanted to be home more with her children. Gary, who wished he could be home more, didn't feel the urge so strongly that he would consider cutting back *his* work at all. He did give up weekends in the office, but he still worked full-time. How is it that Gary, who saw his children after work and on weekends, was satisfied with his fathering while that arrangement didn't satisfy Sharon's idea of mothering? Answering this question takes us right to the heart of the contemporary marriage problem: our almost absolute belief that mothering is different from and more deeply involving than fathering.

Most people today no longer believe that a woman has to be a mother to be fulfilled or that motherhood alone is fulfilling for all women. Forty percent of American women between the ages of eighteen and forty-four do not have children. We readily accept that women who are mothers can also run bulldozers or perform heart surgery, and that they well might be as professionally ambitious as men. But although we've disavowed many nineteenth-century notions about women, we can't quite bring ourselves to truly challenge the classic idea that, as Freud put it, biology is destiny. Women, we think, will always be the primary and often exclusive nurturers of children. Of course, as several feminist thinkers have pointed out, like begets like. As long as mothers do the mothering, our culture will reproduce girls who nurture and boys who don't and thus perpetuate the traditional family structure. But let's look for a moment at the pressures we are under to be mothers and fathers in the traditional way.

"Mother and child" is one of the most powerful icons in Western culture, romanticized, sanctified, and scrutinized. Growing up with this overwhelming image, men and women may well respond in opposite ways. A man may feel like an outsider to the charmed circle of mothers and children. He will hardly feel guilty for not being "good with children" and may even be embarrassed if he is.

A woman, on the other hand, may think she isn't "normal" if she's not a good nurturer or if she isn't the primary parent the culture expects her to be. And whether or not she's had any experience with children, she will usually trust her "instincts" about caring for them above her husband's because she believes so strongly that women just *are* mothers. By the same token, she may become terribly anxious if her decisions about the child don't prevail. That's why it's often more comfortable for a woman to adopt a conventional mother role and cast her husband into the role of "helper," even if it means doing most of the child care. And all the while, she may also want—and in a practical sense—she may *need* to share the parenting. But her "mothering" image creates the greater of these two opposing desires. It's no wonder. She's probably never seen shared parenting that worked, if she's seen it at all.

Like most of us, Sharon and Gary were parented primarily by their mothers. In their parents' generation, fathers were only expected to "make appearances." That's why no one's buttons were ever pushed when men were practically absent from the home. Children were a mother's province, not a father's. I remember my mother's story that when I was born, my father, on some great occasion, held me not in his arms but on the flats of his hands, like a cake or a crystal bowl he was afraid to drop and was uncomfortable having to guard. Her amusement as she told this clearly conveyed her belief that men were just naturally awkward around children.

Times have certainly changed. Most men can hold, feed, and diaper their babies. Yet children are still a mother's province. Just look in any playground on any weekday and see who's watching the children. Look at who's wheeling children in shopping carts through the supermarket aisles or taking them to school. Mostly moms. And most moms will tell you they *want* to be there. "Children need their mothers," everyone says, especially in the first three years. So how can we avoid falling into the traditional roles? The answer is that we can rethink our definition of mothering.

THE PSYCHOLOGICAL TRAPS

Mothering *is* more intensely involving than fathering when a child is in very early infancy. It certainly was for me. Since I was thirty-two when I had my first child—ten years late for my generation—motherhood was all the more special for me. Here was the extraordinary experience I was so afraid I might miss. In fact, I was so carried away by the romance of motherhood that whenever we took the baby to visit my parents in Brooklyn, I insisted we take along his portable outdoor screened crib and a portable aluminum folding rocking chair I could use to feed him. I was so swallowed up by the anxiety of new motherhood, I remember calling my pediatrician to ask how much orange juice I should let my six-month-old drink. "Oh, not more than a quart at one time," he said, and only later, after I hung up, did I realize he was teasing me.

Although my husband was overjoyed too throughout my pregnancy and Bennett's early years, I was keenly aware that this was something that had happened outside his body and inside mine. By the time the baby arrived, I had a far more detailed vision of parenthood than Sam did. Although it changed later on, his relationship to Bennett came after the baby's birth, after work, and after he learned my rules for taking care of him. Of course, I liked this special maternal power, but I now see the price I paid in the early years for having it.

The mother's bond with an infant is surely special. In the early months of a newborn's life, she is the primary parent. She has a bodily intimacy that cannot be disregarded, nor should it be. But we draw far too many conclusions from this biological reality. For example, we do, truly, believe mothers know their children better and are naturally protective of them. However, much of a mother's experience of intimacy and protectiveness comes as a result of being the one who's taking care of the child. In other words, some of the "mother-child" bond is in the doing.

A recent study done by a Yale psychiatrist followed seventeen families in which the fathers were primary caregivers for their children. Some of the men were unemployed but others simply had more flexible jobs than their wives, even those earning up to $125,000 a year. The point is that nearly all those fathers expressed the same feelings new mothers are known to have, among them, a fear of leaving the baby alone with anyone else, including the baby's mother!

As hard as it is to believe, many of the feelings a new mother has are part of the job, not part of her female nature. In fact, the results of five new studies on the subject are that "men become mothers when they do not have wives to do it for them." That is, men have the capacity for "mothering," but it is rarely activated. Furthermore, if it is activated when the child is an infant, "men continue to feel competent to be involved in their children's lives."

Let's assume, however, that the mother is the one to have this first bond with the child, as is usually the case. Why does she have to remain the child's primary parent? As early as possible, fathers, siblings, grandparents, and close friends can be allowed full access to the "mother's child." It is often very difficult for a new mother to relinquish the exclusive care of her infant. But as any mother who has several older children knows, the babies are very happy when their siblings, grandparents, or dads care for them. The babies are rarely the ones to object.

In her excellent book, *Kidding Ourselves*, Rhona Mahony argues that women will never achieve equality with men as long as they insist on, or fall into, primary parenting. To change this ingrained pattern, Mahony says, women have to actively help their husbands catch up with the mother's prenatal head start by encouraging the new dads to spend lots of solo time with their infants from the earliest days. Otherwise, Mahony warns, mother's "head start" leads inevitably to her "gatekeeping" on all matters involving the baby. This naturally "tips" the system back to familiar mommy-daddy roles.

The whole notion of mothers having exclusive care of their children is a rather recent American phenomenon. On the farm or the ranch or in crowded urban tenements, whichever females were around often did most of the child care while mother did the work around the place: laundry, farming, making clothes, making meals, etc.

The more responsibility and access other adults have in relation to the baby, the more *they* will bond and become known and loved caregivers. If the mother shares the nurturing, she'll be surprised at how quickly others learn what the baby does and doesn't like.

Everyone benefits from shared parenting. Babies learn to trust and engage a few different people. They aren't as dependent on one person for getting what they need. And mothers aren't compelled to provide everything for a child.

We must remember too that shared parenting is as much a necessity as it is a benefit. Modern life can't be lived unless the mother shares the romance and the power of the experience. The reality today is that most mothers have to work. Most children do spend part of their time with a baby-sitter, day-care counselor, or family member. What happens, then, if mothers don't really give up their idea of being the primary parent? They'll be anguished when their maternity leave is up, and so will their baby, who won't have grown used to other parent figures. They'll be fighting for control of the parenting at the same time that they have to give it up in order to free themselves for work.

When should a woman go back to work? This is a personal choice and will vary from family to family. The usual three-month leave feels too short to some women while others are eager to "get back." Most working women choose between six weeks and six months. Often, though, a woman needs more time than she otherwise might because she, alone, is tending the child, reorganizing the household, finding the necessary services, creating a new social parenting network, etc. These same women might have an easier time of integrating their new mothering role into their work and social lives if they didn't feel the baby depended solely on them and if their place of work allowed them to phase back slowly or begin again part-time. Even women who breastfeed find ways of alternating breast and bottle feedings so that they can go back to work.

The woman who chooses to make mothering her primary work may quell her mothering anxieties, but she will face new ones as she gradually loses her power in her marriage, and she most likely will. Because a new mother's maternal power is so thrilling, she may not be aware that the power balance is shifting in her marriage. But her status as a mother is ultimately related only to her child. She may be the one to decide when the child goes to bed and the one to decide that she and her husband stay home with a feverish child instead of going to a party. If her husband is now earning all the money, however, he'll be the one making the important family decisions. For example, they won't take out comprehensive health insurance if he feels it's unnecessary or they'll move if it's best for his job, no matter how it affects his wife's work future.

Even if a new mother isn't aware that she's given up power, she will eventually get some inkling. In therapy, Sharon and I explored her ideas about motherhood and work. Originally, despite her professional status, she'd been eager to quit work when Sophie was born. She explained, "I just loved being able to spend the whole day with her without worrying about time." But her delight at staying home wasn't just her desire to nest. Motherhood also provided an opportunity for Sharon to cut back on, then leave, her demanding jobs. Being an overachiever, Sharon had worked and studied throughout her college and graduate

school years, and her clinical training. She had never given herself very much time off and never felt she'd really worked unless
she'd put in a ten-hour day, at least. But unlike Gary, she hadn't
been trained to "work and earn," so she felt free to leave the
driving world of work behind when her first child came along.

"Well, then, what made you return to work?" I asked.

"Hmm, when Sophie was about nine months old and we'd
settled into Scarsdale, an old graduate school friend of mine
came to visit from Boston. Gary was away, and we had time to
spend by ourselves. She arrived in the evening, after Sophie was
sleeping, so I took out some pictures to show her and then felt
the tears. I think, actually, I had become depressed staying home,
and there was my friend so excited about her work. She was in
New York to lecture and to promote her first book. The next
morning she'd be taking the train into Manhattan. Also, something had happened between Gary and me the night before. We
were having an argument about whether we could afford to
spend Christmas in the Caribbean the way we always had. It
meant plane tickets and the hotel for us and my parents, and I
knew it would cost a lot but we'd always gone before and I really
wanted to get away. But Gary said, 'I'm not going to discuss this
anymore. We can't afford it,' and he left the room. He never
talked to me that way before, like he was the boss of the house
now."

Sharon hadn't consciously connected her earning power with
the power to make decisions, yet it was no accident that soon
after that argument and their missing Christmas in the Caribbean, she decided to build her new practice. "I miss work," she
told Gary to justify her going back into practice. Her conscious
need was acceptable to both of them; her unconscious need—to
rebalance the power in her marriage—might not have been.

Sharon's return to work took care of her conscious and unconscious agenda. She did enjoy building a new clinical practice,
and they did go to the Caribbean the next year. Also, she was
much happier building a practice. But Sharon paid a price, too.

"How did you feel working again?" I asked her.

"Guilty," she said. "I hated to leave Sophie, and then, also,
Gary liked my being home, taking care of everything."

SHE CRIES WHENEVER I LEAVE

Sharon's guilt is typical. Guilt is the inevitable result of our definition of mothering. I certainly remember feeling guilty leaving my children to return to work. And if during some rare period when everyone in our family was happy and my guilt abated, there was no shortage of people who inspired some more. This Greek chorus of "guilt inducers" may be our own disapproving parents, the nursery school teacher who can't imagine why a mother has no time to volunteer at the school fund-raiser, or the culture at large, which characterizes the children of working mothers with words like *neglected,* as if no one was caring for the children in their mother's absence.

Guilt is also created by two misconceptions about full-time mothers—that they are deliriously happy and that they spend much more time with their children than mothers who work outside the home. Recently, two sociologists determined that married working mothers spend just as much time as stay-at-home mothers in *direct* child care, such as bathing children, reading to them, helping with homework, and playing.

Working mothers generally don't realize that mothers who stay at home may feel just as guilty because they're *not* happy all the time and they're not playing with their children all the time. I can remember during my tenure as a homemaker feeling guilty when I wanted to read a book rather than play with Bennett, or when I just felt lonely and isolated on the long winter shut-in days if Bennett had a cold. I remember how irritable I could be when one of the children didn't want to eat a lunch I'd fixed or I had to read the same book for the hundredth time. However, many of these parenting tasks became a pleasure when I didn't have to perform them relentlessly, and when I got to do some of what I needed as well.

We should also be careful not to confuse the detrimental effects of insufficient parenting with the effects of a mother's working. A mother's working need not be harmful to a child—even a very small child—if the child has loving and consistent care in her absence. That is, if the mother and father are both involved parents. But if she has to take up the slack for the father's lack of involvement *and* she's away at work a great deal, then, yes, the child might be neglected. But then it's fathering that's missing, not mothering. If both parents work and neither has enough family time, of course, a child will suffer. That's a parental problem, however, a problem of family priorities—and not the inevitable result of a mother's choice to continue working. Children, especially in the first three years of life, do need to establish secure attachments, but those attachments need not be with mother alone or even father and mother alone.

Some mothers do truly enjoy caring for their children full-time, and they certainly should have society's concrete supports in the form of health benefits and job security. Nonetheless, when a mother would rather be working outside the home but thinks she *should* stay home she'll often make her unhappiness felt. Studies have shown that children are happier with mothers who work than they are with mothers who stay home when they'd prefer to be working. And recent studies on work, family, and stress have shown that women with more than one identity or role to make them feel good about themselves are mentally healthier and enjoy more marital stability.

Nevertheless, there is so much pressure for women to be primary and stay-at-home parents that I wasn't shocked to read recently that more and more women in "Generation X" (people in their twenties) are planning to stay home when they have children; they're leaving "power" jobs to be "power moms." Homemaker/breadwinner is the fastest growing marital structure among the young marrieds! Not the majority structure, but the fastest growing one. When these women are interviewed, they'll often say that their choice is a reaction to their own harried feminist mothers who worked double time at home and at work. But isn't it interesting that instead of seeking an alternative to their mother's "doing it all," they've reverted to their grandmother's idea of mothering.

What these young women haven't come to terms with is how different they are from their grandmothers. A woman who has been educated, trained, and done well in the work world may be far more unhappy with homemaking than her grandmother who, in a sense, trained exclusively for that job. And these young couples face other problems as well. In some cases the woman was earning so much more than the man that she couldn't opt out of working. Sometimes it turns out that her husband doesn't want the pressure of being the sole breadwinner and didn't realize that's what having children would amount to, particularly when he and his wife had been moving up the career ladder together. Or perhaps because she's been such a high earner, he'd been able to pursue work he loved rather than profitable work and now resents having to give it up.

If there weren't a mothering problem, these couples wouldn't be trying to shoehorn themselves into traditional roles. They wouldn't consider turning their relationships upside down when they become parents. Rather, they might try to figure out how to find a parenting arrangement that fits their actual lives, regardless of gender. That's what I always try to help them do. But, then, of course, their parenting arrangement has to fit the real world as well.

THE SOCIAL TRAPS

To some extent, a mother ends up being the only one to stay home with a new baby—and therefore becomes the primary one to bond with the baby. This sequence usually occurs because only she gets any paid maternity leave or feels free to take it. Then she ends up quitting her job or cutting back while the father continues to work long hours because few companies offer paid paternity leave. Without it, only very wealthy people can take significant time off to be with their new children. In effect, even though we finally have a family-leave bill, the American workplace doesn't support mothers or fathers who want to be involved in their children's lives.

Our government is so traditionally protective of business that we have thus far been unable to require that businesses automatically give men and women paid parental leave the way they do, for example, in Sweden. We have recently seen our society's resistance to making businesses contribute to health insurance coverage for employees. And flextime is considered a privilege, not a right. Without any guaranteed flextime, paid family emergency leave, and no guaranteed health care, many mothers quit work—if it's financially possible—when children arrive in order to handle the child care problem. I hear women all the time saying, "By the time I paid the sitter, the clothes and dry-cleaning bills for myself, the transportation, the take-out food, I was only making about five thousand dollars a year! For what? For someone else to be my little boy's mother?" Everyone understands her reasoning. But let's step back a moment to consider the logic of the common argument: how is it that the cost of child care immediately becomes the mother's problem? Not the father's?

HONEY, WHERE DO WE KEEP MICHAEL'S SOCKS?

Fathers still play a major role in perpetuating the mother problem. They are certainly more involved in their homes than their own fathers were. I know many who are gourmet cooks; most are proud to carry their babies around in their Snuglies, with diaper bags slung over their shoulders. And a handful with more flexible jobs than their wives sometimes do the lion's share of child care. But for the most part, fathers are still just "helping." According to a *Modern Bride* survey, their readers have husbands who expect their wives to work as well as be in charge of the children. The latest statistics tell us that men are on average doing about a third of the domestic work. This is a vast improvement, but it's still significantly less than the two-thirds their wives are doing. Yet most of their wives believe they should be grateful that their husbands help as much as they do. After all, all women know husbands who refuse to help at all.

Remember, too, that even those fathers who are involved enough to play with kids, help with homework, bathe, and put them to sleep leave the planning and scheduling to the women. This means that mother rather than father knows the ins and outs of the children's play dates, medical and dental affairs, haircutting, and school business. In other words, she is the children's manager.

In one of our sessions, Sharon described a typical morning before leaving for work. First she called the local firehouse to arrange for Sophie's after-school visit (that took three calls), then the nanny who would be taking them, and next the mother of another child who was going with them. She then had to call the pediatrician to discuss whether Max needed a refill on his antibiotic prescription. It was a Monday, before Gary left for the airport on a business trip. She said, "He got angry at me when I waved him away instead of talking with him. I heard him muttering about how I was in another one of those moods. I wasn't in any mood. I had a thousand things to do before leaving for work. He only had to eat breakfast and pack his bag."

Few fathers really understand what goes into child care. And few are prepared to reduce their own work hours to do it, yet that's what it takes. Men who do are penalized—passed over for promotions and socially dismissed. A journalist I know believed that if he took the three-month parental leave he was entitled to it would be the end of his career—even though a woman covering a similar beat took her leave with impunity. A lot of men feel they have to put in overtime as well or it won't seem as if they are part of the team anymore.

If the pressure that average men feel doesn't make the case strongly enough, the sensational Houston Oilers' controversy of the fall of 1993 certainly does. When David Williams, the starting offensive right tackle, missed a game to be with his wife for the birth of their child, the team docked Williams $125,000 pay, threatened him with suspension, and announced that he had let the team down. So much for the Family and Medical Leave Act, which had been passed earlier in the year.

Men are also afraid of the intimacy and difficulty of caring for small children. In a *New York Times* Op Ed piece explaining why men don't *want* to take family leave, magazine editor Colin Harrison made both male prerogative and fear of intimacy quite clear:

> After having dutifully puffed and panted through natural childbirth classes and then sweated out the actual delivery, suddenly being cooped up with a squalling, mysterious infant and a tired, distracted wife isn't necessarily the transcendent joy it's advertised to be. . . . The prospect of immersion in

this environment is, for some men, a panicky proposition. The office, even with its pressures, suddenly seems sweetly attractive, affording a regular pattern, a *known* role. Returning to work, we should admit, can be a guilty but genuine relief (italics mine).

Harrison's response illustrates how entitled men feel to stop being new men whenever they wish, and that almost always means when it turns out to be difficult instead of fun. He also gives voice to how claustrophobic some men feel when intimacy is required of them.

Yet it's men who lose when they opt out of fathering or take a safe backseat to their wives. And perhaps those who do participate fully are the best ones to explain what the others are missing. Benjamin Cheever, son of John Cheever (that most reserved fifties novelist whose placid description of suburban life hid his homosexuality, alcoholism, and troubled marriage), clearly rejected the oppressive masculine role that very likely ruined his father's life. In one article, Benjamin, who is also a writer, talks first about the price he pays for being a stay-at-home dad while his wife works outside the home: "I can tell you what I don't like about staying at home. What I don't like is the ignominy. . . . [My wife] writes for *The New York Times*. She has a byline. I've been called Mr. Byline. This I do not like." But is it worth it? Benjamin Cheever thinks it absolutely is:

I've been a man with a rocket ship. I've had an office, an office I went to no matter what. Sometimes I miss that. But there are compensations. Mr. Byline may not get the good table at the Russian Tea Room, and he may get snubbed at some cocktail parties. But when he comes home from the 7-Eleven, the parrot will start right up. "Daddy, Daddy!" he squawks.

Then John will run into my arms. "Daddy, Daddy!" he cries. When this happens, I'm glad I don't have antlers.

Andrew has fallen down. He's hurt his knee. "Kiss it," he says.

My reason for living, I think, nuzzling a mass of baby curls. My shot at immortality. My ace in the hole.

If only his father had been allowed to enjoy that connectedness. If only there were no social "ignominy" attached.

As much as we can learn from such rare examples, most men won't follow their lead. Most, unfortunately, will never even see men who don't largely conform to their usual roles. And most women won't either. Given our powerful social and psychological programming, is it any wonder that after the first child is born, the burden of child care falls heavily on the woman? This is the moment where the power balance between husbands and wives changes, throwing relationships out of kilter.

WHEN DID WE TURN INTO "OZZIE AND HARRIET"?

The mothering problem is hard enough with one child. The birth of the second child generally tips the marital scales. A couple may have muddled through with one child by virtue of the wife's cutting back at work, reducing travel, or giving up sleep. But unless she is as important professionally as Murphy Brown, she will have paid a price in promotions and raises—and possibly in the confidence of her employers, who may well consign her to the mommy track. In my local Westchester "women's" newspaper, one former corporate superwoman writes that "when I became visibly pregnant with my second child, it became a whole new ball game. I somehow *felt* that I was no longer 'one of the troops' along with my unencumbered (mostly male) colleagues but one of the fourteen other pregnant women executives aptly dubbed 'the mothers.' " She got the message that with two children she could no longer be the executive she had been.

With a first child, there is fun and novelty in a woman's public presentation of herself as a mother. If the mother does work and the workplace is informal enough, she might even take the child with her occasionally, and somehow, with only one, there's still enough time to lead a married life that bears some resemblance to what it was before. With two children, however, housework and child care increase disproportionately. The couple must fit themselves into the children's lives, not vice versa. Their schedules and needs are too complicated to circumnavigate.

In my own life, our second child changed our lives in a way we never expected. When our first, Bennett, was a baby, we took him everywhere—even to parties. Before he was born, Sam and I used to love to go to fancy restaurants for Sunday brunch. After he was born, we just took him along and put his infant seat in the middle of the table. Of course we thought everyone in the restaurant would think he was as wonderful as we did, and whatever they actually thought, they always came to admire him. So we kept up our precious Sunday tradition. Well, that ended abruptly when Tim was born. One child in a fancy restaurant is sometimes possible; two are not. When we absolutely had to eat out with the kids, we'd look for the nearest fast-food joint and inspect it first to make sure it was "child friendly." I couldn't "stash" two children at a neighbor's to run to a meeting. I couldn't take two children along to a seminar. With two, my long career as a child care manager began.

When the logistics become too much and the pressures too great, couples like Sharon and Gary may groan that "they can't go on this way," and sit down to discuss their options. It is soon obvious to both that they are more financially dependent on the husband's career and salary, which has been progressing while hers has not. Or if, miraculously, her career has progressed, the couple generally still banks on the husband's, since the wife's is perceived as supplemental. One "solution," then, if they can afford it, is for the wife just to stay home with the children. And that's what Gary wanted, even though they couldn't afford it and maintain their lifestyle.

Because *she* is the one feeling so harried and preoccupied with the children, a woman will often opt to stay home, find a less demanding job, or cut back as Sharon did. We all know women who downscaled professionally after the birth of a second child. A dozen examples pop into mind: the computer programmer who switched to teaching computer skills at a community college; the corporate executive who became a consultant; the physician in private practice who took a less demanding hospital job. The trouble is that none of these women and their husbands actually worked out a plan about child care and her outside work. But it happened all the same, based on their programming. And because they didn't renegotiate their marriage contracts, the old model of marriage dictated their roles.

By this point, the structure of their marital relationship, which the wife has tried so hard to keep equal, commonly collapses back to a quasi-traditional marriage. One of its clearest vestiges is the couple's tacit agreement that the responsibilty for the children is the woman's. Even the feminist with a career will frequently rediscover her option to stay home and be supported by a man when her second child is born. Often, my women clients don't even know how they came to be home full-time with no plan for returning to paid work. "It just happened," one of them said to me, "and now I can't figure out my life."

This particular woman had had a lucrative career as a residential real estate agent. When her husband complained about being left with the child on weekends and evenings, her busiest work time, she began to work less, telling herself that it was really because the market was drying up. Instead of figuring out a plan, changing careers, or readjusting the real-estate job to, say, commercial property, she drifted into full-time homemaking. Her stockbroker husband had reached a similar professional dead end when the market collapsed in the late eighties. But he adapted by switching to commercial insurance sales. One of the reasons women don't press on professionally is because doing so has a much higher personal cost than it does for men.

WHAT'S A WORKING WOMAN TO DO?

Mothers who opt for the "solution" of full-time work usually find themselves on the superwoman path, whirling from work to a second shift at home. These women commonly do emergency laundry in the middle of the night, buy Halloween costumes on their lunch hours, and spend Saturday taking children to the orthodontist, the barber, the violin lesson, the shoe store. A colleague of mine always cooked and froze meals for the family to cover the days she would be away at conferences. I myself vividly remember the years I built my practice, feeling as if I'd lived a life and a half before even getting to work in the morning. After work, I'd race from the train to the bus, then stagger home at 7:00 P.M. Tears would sometimes jump into my eyes when I put the key into the lock, for in that brief moment before my boys, my baby-sitter, and my poodle would all fling themselves at my skirts, I so keenly felt my bewilderment at there being no other way.

As I learned, superwomen don't set out to do it all but quickly end up doing it all. One sociologist discovered that when home and child-care hours are factored in, women in the workforce actually work fifteen hours longer each week than men. That's an additional three months of labor a year! It shouldn't be surprising, then, that many working mothers are so resentful and exhausted they begin contemplating divorce. If they cannot bear the thought of divorce, they sometimes become symptomatic in some way—for example, they'll become depressed, chronically ill, or even alcoholic. In other words, their misery will express itself in some indirect way if they cannot confront their husbands directly. Another view of a symptomatic wife is that she's turning her anger inward—which she may feel safer doing—instead of allowing herself to feel her anger at her husband.

Poor and working-class women who have no choice but the superwoman role may have expected to do both their outside jobs and all the housework and child care, but they are no less exhausted or resentful—however unacknowledged their resentment may be. Even women who feel they agreed to the traditional arrangement find that they just cannot keep their part of the bargain. As one woman client said to me, "I've given and given, and gotten nothing in return. Who could expect anything from a man who worked ten hours a day? I never made demands, even though I work all day, too. And being a secretary is no picnic. But I always knew how important his work was to him, especially since he worked his way up from mail-room clerk, so I didn't even ask him to buy a container of milk. Now I have no more energy to work on holding us together. If he can't do something different, we're history."

Another woman said in a joint session with her husband, "*I* go to the kid's school when there's some special event or a problem, *I* take them to the dentist, *I* keep food in the house and dinner on the table—*I, I, I, I, I*. Where are you?" She turned to her husband, then back to me and dropped her head in her hands, "I might as well be divorced."

This is how the mothering problem turns out to be the crux of the contemporary marriage problem. Like Sharon, many women who come for couples therapy are mothers who accepted the traditional mothering role without realizing it. They just never realized that the role itself ends up being either very nearly impossible when they also have to work outside or very frustrating when they've prepared to work outside and then have to stay home. Without ever questioning their own or their mothers' conception of the mothering role, they find themselves bitter and unhappy about how much more they give to the family than do their husbands. And yet, driven by guilt about being good mothers, they will remain the primary parent at all costs, even if it means depression, exhaustion, or finally divorce. Divorce, after all, is an American tradition; shared parenting is not.

3

Why Isn't Marriage Fifty-fifty?

The institution of marriage has changed so much and in such a short time that it has left us dazed. Perhaps the most fundamental change is its purpose. In my parents' generation and the generations before them, marriage was for raising children—which occupied most adults for their entire active lives. A woman had an average of five or more children. And usually, in those prepenicillin times, some of them died. No matter how many children a woman ended up with, she was probably pregnant, nursing, or tending to little ones until menopause. When her children were grown, she often continued her mothering role by helping her children—who usually lived nearby—with their families.

Before the sixties—a mere thirty years ago—you married to have a family; there was no other way to have one, or often no other way to have sex either. If the marriage was loveless, it didn't dissolve. It existed for the children. For the family. Today, husbands and wives expect personal fulfillment from marriage, and not just the job of parenting.

In some of the Irish Catholic families I knew growing up, the husbands and wives were no longer speaking to each other—the children carried messages back and forth! And yet those husbands and wives wouldn't have dreamed of divorce. Their marriages existed for the family. It was never meant for personal satisfaction, so their love or lack of it was almost irrelevant. Now the terms of marriage are incontrovertibly changed. Why? In a word: science.

More than any other factors, birth control and longer lives have changed the purpose of marriage. Child rearing is no longer the center of marriage; the couple is. Most couples have only one or two children. Raising them doesn't occupy a couple's whole married life, especially now that we live longer and are youthful longer. Child rearing might end up occupying only *half* the parents' adult life before old age, which means a couple could spend some twenty years alone together! That is too long to endure if they haven't found significance in their relationship.

Because the *primary* purpose of marriage today includes the couple's happiness as well as the raising of children, unhappy partners don't automatically stay together even if there are small children at home. Partners today expect companionship. If it's not there, why bother? Especially when there isn't much social stigma attached to divorce.

Such short child-rearing years along with the support of the women's movement have also prompted women to define their lives by something other than motherhood. They may opt not to have children. They invest in their own work lives, not their husbands'. Before the sixties it was common for women to look upon their husbands as an investment. Often a woman would earn the money to send him to school. Organizations of student wives at progressive universities would "award" women "Ph.T" degrees—"Putting Hubby Through"—when their husbands earned doctorates or law degrees. But such "investments" are very rare nowadays. A woman might well become a full-time wife, but she probably didn't start out her marriage thinking she would be.

Scientific advances and women's entry into the workforce have certainly changed the nature of marriage, relocating its center from the children to the couple. Yet in themselves these changes need not necessarily have made marriage or family life more difficult. The problem, really, is that the rest of society hasn't changed along with women. Also, we've had so little time to adapt to this new idea of marriage we shouldn't be amazed that we're not more successful at it. Especially when the tasks at the marital stress points have changed so profoundly that couples can't learn from their parents how to navigate transitions.

The stresses of the childbearing years for today's couples are so different from what they were for yesterday's that parental advice often seems hopelessly irrelevant. How many women I've heard saying, "My mother doesn't have a clue about my life" or "I can't talk to my parents about our problems, they'd never understand." And that was true for me as well. My husband, Sam, and I went to a therapist at our first marital crisis, not to either of our parents. When I grew up it was unheard of for a married woman to go back to work after she had a child, so my parents could hardly guide me through that difficult period in my life.

Every other stage of family life has changed just as much as the childbearing years. Just think, for example, about how thirty years ago, middle-class parents rarely had to face the problems of raising children while they both worked and had no relatives close by to help. They didn't have to steer teenagers through the shoals of drugs and sex. And, now, just when you think you've launched the kids, the not-so-empty nest syndrome appears because children often can't afford to move out and then the divorced ones return. A friend of mine said, "When my last child left, I removed the door and had them put in a revolving one." Older couples may not be able to retire because of the economy or because their children still need their help.

So here they are, today's newlyweds, plunging into marriage without a blueprint or advisers. The bride defines herself by her work, her interests, her family and friends, and so does the groom. The schools they attend and the places they work are invariably "equal opportunity." And so are they, consciously at least. Fine, everything's even-steven. And yet society today is less, not more, supportive of this equal marriage than when the idea was still shocking.

Back in the sixties when Sam and I renegotiated our marriage contract for the first time, the women's movement had just popularized this new concept of marriage. Not that I had any affiliation with the women's movement at that time. You didn't need one to be affected by their ideas. After all, it was in 1966 that the National Organization of Women—a very visible and "respectable" part of the women's movement—stated their goal that men and women should share equally in raising children and supporting them financially. So, luckily, Sam and I were able to renegotiate our contract based on a more or less socially accepted attitude, at least among younger people. The right attitudes are necessary, of course, but not, as it turns out, sufficient. What may have helped us and others like us as much was an economy growing rapidly enough so that couples could experiment with jobs, create their own businesses, or work fewer hours if they wanted. Relatively few Americans had to worry about being impoverished in middle age if they took some financial risks. So workplace rules never really had to bend to accommodate these new equal marriages. We were simply a nation optimistic enough about our economic future to give equal marriages the room they needed to work. We no longer are.

THE ECONOMIC SQUEEZE

Some of the middle-aged couples I see in therapy now did have equal marriages back in the sixties but haven't been able to keep them equal. Time and again I learn that back in the sixties these couples identified with the counterculture. They rejected mainstream values and went into "human scale" businesses or lived off the land or their crafts—and on very little money. They supported themselves on fellowships and grants, opened health-food stores and co-ops, taught school, worked for poverty programs. The success of their equal marriage depended on their anti-materialist values and a booming economy that could support its fringe. On a teacher's salary of $10,000, a person could support a family, own a car, and rent a house.

Middle-aged couples today don't understand the social context of their marriages. They either blame themselves or else one partner blames the other for "selling out." What actually happened is that as the economy tightened in the late seventies, these counterculture couples had to worry about making a better living. By the time blue jeans started costing what they'd once paid for rent, they ran smack up against the rigidity of the social system. Money for fellowships and poverty programs dried up. As couples were forced into more conventional jobs or longer work hours, they were no longer able to maintain their equality. Men—more than women—went to law school, medical school, or expanded their small businesses into large, profitable ones, à la Ben and Jerry's ice cream company. Inevitably, one of the partners—usually the woman—took up the domestic slack when the man became a professional. So the once-equal partners never realized how much they relied on a prosperous society to make their equality work. Everyone thought they just "grew up."

Yuppies also got caught in the economic squeeze. They rejected the "adolescent" behavior of the counterculture in favor of material success. And although yuppies usually believe in gender equality, it turns out to be very hard to have an equal marriage when both partners have long work hours, high pressure, and stiff competition. Neither partner has enough time left over from work to care for children. So when children come along, the wife turns into superwoman, but like the woman who wrote the article for my Westchester newspaper, she won't really be "one of the guys" in the office anymore. Meanwhile the men will focus even more on work in order to meet the financial needs of their new—much more expensive—family life. They generally want to be good parents, too, but it turns out to be very difficult to be the new loving, caring, feeling man most aspire to be when you're working long hours in businesses that require split-second decisions, hype, and more than a bit of the killer instinct.

All told, the scientific and economic changes over the last thirty years have affected marriage profoundly. They've changed a traditional ideal into an egalitarian one. And yet, we end up thinking that the new ideal of marriage doesn't work when actually we haven't—and the society hasn't let us—fully commit ourselves to it. The mothering problem and men's "careerism" keep the new marriage from being new. So like Sisyphus of the Greek myth, doomed eternally to pushing a boulder up a mountainside only to have it roll down again, we keep trying to make this "new" marriage work, then try again when it doesn't. What we don't do—and neither does the society—is change enough.

Change makes everyone nervous. It's a double-edged sword, as frightening as it is tantalizing, as irrationally threatening as it is logical. Because we're afraid to change—and because society— the largest system to which we belong—doesn't want us to—we end up stuck in a no man's land between the old marriage and our new lives. We're all straddling the present ideal of equal partnership and the bygone world of at-home moms and breadwinning dads. And nearly all of us are teetering as a result.

CAN WE PLEASE BE NEW MEN AND WOMEN WITHOUT REALLY CHANGING?

From my personal life and my experience treating troubled couples, I am convinced that although we have created a "new" marriage script for today's men and women, we haven't really changed the substance of the play. Our real domestic dramas are still controlled by the patriarchal vision that produced traditional marriage. The awful irony is that today, the force of traditional marriage has become even *more* powerful precisely because everyone believes traditional marriage no longer exists. Couples either assume the influence of traditional marriage has died out or won't affect them, since they don't believe in it. Believing they're equal, partners reject the traditional division of labor, but the new, supposedly equal, marriage script leaves them playing the same old roles.

I think this script is nowhere spelled out as plainly as it is by Hollywood, our cultural barometer. *Mr. Mom,* a hugely popular comedy written by John (*Home Alone*) Hughes in 1983, captures the contemporary marriage problem perfectly. It might well have been called *How to Be New Men and Women Without Really Changing.* Watch and see how the couple in the movie "solves" the problem of equality in the same way Gary and Sharon did—before I encouraged them to explore their assumptions and re-negotiate their marriage contract.

The movie opens on a sort-of-happy marriage with three children just before dad gets fired. Since he faces few prospects, the wife suggests she should look for work too. After all, she graduated college and has two years experience in advertising. Well, what can an egalitarian man do but agree?—and then become "Mr. Mom" when she lands a great job in advertising.

Within a few weeks, they both suffer the occupational hazards of fixed gender roles, but in reverse: he turns into a soap-opera watching slob, and she's so preoccupied with work that she barely notices her family. When she chides him, he becomes a "new man," finally learning to take pride in caring for his home and children. When he chides her for not even noticing that he's potty trained the baby, she recognizes the personal cost of being on the fast track and quits.

The "solution" is presented when—miraculously—both their ex-bosses arrive to offer them "anything to come back." The husband secures *his old job* and encourages his wife to accept her offer because "she loves her work" (not because they should both support the family). So she does, "three days a week, two at home." He, presumably, will return to his grueling schedule and become as preoccupied as ever. Nonetheless, the reconstituted couple sits down to watch her first commercial produced for television. Its message is about tuna . . . and marriage: "Schooner tuna will drop their prices by fifty cents until these trying economic times are over, then return to its normal price."

Here's the point, and the movie's subtext: marriage may be fifty-fifty for a while, but as soon as the economy is better and wives don't *have* to work, everyone will return to the "normal" division of labor, softened a bit by what they've learned about expanding (not changing) the old sex roles. It's Rosie the Riveter all over again. What began as an adventure in a new kind of marriage ended, as it usually does in real life, with a contemporary variation on the theme from *Taming of the Shrew*.

And like most Hollywood movies, *Mr. Mom* presents personal life without any political or social context. This couple appears "free" to choose whatever arrangement they want because their bosses have given them carte blanche if they'll just come back to work. There is no suggestion that the reason the husband will return to his grueling schedule is that his boss expects him to and won't agree to his working fewer hours. And the wife has the three-day option because only women get that. Lucky women, of course. Isn't it interesting that these two now phenomenal career successes couldn't both work half-time? The inflexibility of the workplace is a given, an untouchable, even in a comedy. Hollywood allows everything to go topsy-turvy but not the workplace. In this country it's more sacred than marriage.

THE OLD GENDER MYTHS JUST WON'T GO AWAY

What keeps couples from taking that next step out of their traditional marriage and into a new one? Why haven't we just set our feet squarely in the world of today? Although the greatest obstacles may be the rigid workplace and lack of social supports, they aren't the only ones. I believe it is also because we haven't entirely given up the old assumptions about women and men. We just can't seem to let them go.

Many women today, if really honest, would admit that like the heroine of *Mr. Mom*, they still assume that men's professional lives are more important than their own. They still look upon a husband's income as if it's the "real" one. A man's success in the world is crucial while a woman's is just a wonderful "extra." Most women also believe that the children are fundamentally theirs. At the same time, women today have a hard time admitting such outmoded ideas because they were raised to believe in their professional dreams and their equality with men. So in order to make the old assumptions feel acceptable, we've packaged them in new wrapping. And the culture—ever ready to uphold the status quo—has applauded our efforts.

One point of view that has become fashionable among scholars and pop social critics alike (despite its sounding alarmingly similar to the one that produced our "separate but equal" racial policy) is that men and women are just different—biologically *and* culturally. They're from different planets, in fact. In the hey-

day of the women's movement, "unisex" was the buzzword. People believed that boys and girls were essentially the same and just
bred to be different. Now everyone wants to believe that gender
differences have been bred into the bone.

Not too long ago, *Time* magazine ran a cover story that read:
"Why Are Men and Women Different? It isn't just upbringing.
New studies show they are born that way." When you read the
article, however, it turns out that the so-called evidence was scant,
ambiguous, and even ridiculous. For example, one previously
skeptical professor of psychology decided there must be inborn
gender differences because he saw his fifteen-month-old daughter flirt with men! Even the article itself concluded that "in the
final analysis, it may be impossible to say where nature ends and
nurture begins because the two are so intimately linked." So why
did the *Time* cover misrepresent the findings? To appeal to the
popular demand for proof that men and women are vastly different.

And what do we get from believing that men are from Mars
and women are from Venus? It may help couples to understand
their differences, but it does not necessarily help them to change
the way they interact. In fact, this polarization suggests that men
and women just *are* different, and that's that. We are relieved
of the responsibility of changing, and that, of course, keeps all
members of the system in place. We don't have to change, and
neither does society. Like the gears of a clock, we all still fit, even
if some of us are suffering rather too much just to keep everything ticking. But that's not the part of this idea that we tell ourselves about.

In much of the current discourse on gender that I hear, the
sexes are thought of as essentially different, but not necessarily
unequal. In fact, the subtext among women is often that women
are somehow better than men, who are emotionally stunted dun-
derheads and incapable parents. Not because they were raised
that way or because they won't try, but because they just are. The
current quip among women is, "You think men are missing the
gene for hearing the baby cry?"

In the nineteenth century, women did all the emotional and
household work because men were superior beings who needed

peace of mind to pursue their noble goals. Now women do every-thing because men are inferior beings who just can't.

Practically every day we can see or read about a savvy man who will readily acknowledge, parrot, explain, parry, and often satirize this view. In a recent review of several new books on mas-culinity, the male reviewer humorously sums up the position.

> Men are defective: brutal, competitive, exploitative, insensi-tive, disconnected from meaningful social relationshps, out of touch with their feelings and oblivious to things they do not want to hear. It is impossible to get them to do house-work, even when they are unemployed. Why not simply re-place the unit? They just lie around and make noise. Feeding them is an act of charity. Or so the indictment goes.

Women today take comfort in feeling superior, but cold comfort it turns out to be. Actually, the ready acceptance of men's "de-fects" has landed us back at ground zero in domestic relations by helping to resurrect the gender myths that work to keep tradi-tional marriage in place.

We are more comfortable believing that men and women are different because it explains why we can't have the equality we want. That's not the stated premise of such arguments, of course, but it is the unconscious agenda behind them. Everyone talks as if we're much more sophisticated now about gender differences than we were during the early years of feminism. But it seems to me that what most of the "new" thinkers are doing is just putting a modern spin on the old myths of "the eternal feminine" and "the dominant masculine" principle.

Again and again in the couples I see, women assume that men are too fragile or too "out of it" to face life's emotional stresses as well as women. Again and again, I see wives still trying to live their husbands' emotional lives for them. They will be the ones to talk to their in-laws, buy them birthday gifts, make nursing home visits to his aunts, get close to his sister, and get angry at his boss when he's turned down for some special recognition.

Women regularly excuse men emotionally. Although Sharon very much wanted Gary in the delivery room with her when she gave birth she hadn't insisted on it because he "couldn't take seeing me in that much pain." Like many women, Sharon let Gary off the hook emotionally. "And if it had eased your pain?" I asked her. But Sharon protected Gary by saying, "I would have been less comfortable seeing how uncomfortable he was." And then I said, as I always do, "If you can experience the pain, why couldn't he tolerate it enough to give you support? Why don't you expect that of him?"

Typically, when it comes to the mysteries of life and child rearing, women can do and men (supposedly) can't. Women either believe men can't deal with closeness or that they are such softies that they must be vigilantly protected from family crises or from outside threats to their self-esteem. In particular, women help men maintain the myth of masculine autonomy by never acknowledging (or expecting them to acknowledge) their degree of emotional dependence. How many women whisper to their friends about their husbands, who might well be captains of industry, "He's really such a baby." Yet how few women will insist that their husbands take emotional responsibility for themselves.

This assumption about men's inability to deal with closeness means that a woman doesn't expect her husband to be as connected to the children as she is. Even in marriages of presumed equals, the woman generally does not expect the man to be as involved in home and children, whether or not she is as involved (and successful) as he is in work. She will do not only her own work but all or most of the family work if it is necessary to advance his career. She accepts—consciously or not—the value our culture puts on a man's career achievements. Rather than question whether it's really so important that he get a promotion or another account she will often accept—like Sharon—his work-related reasons for absence from family life because he's "doing this for me and the children" or "he warned me he's always been a workaholic," or "men are just like that."

Often women believe that their husbands would like to do more at home, but, as they explain to me and to their women friends, "He just doesn't have any time." And many therapists well might have encouraged Sharon to accept Gary's punishing work schedule. Period. After all, if a man doesn't know the names of his children's teachers or where their pajamas are kept, no one thinks that odd. And usually the fact that a man doesn't have any time for his family is expressed as if it were an absolute so that no one can ask, as I always do, "Well, why can't he make the time, like you do?"

It may sound as if women are getting nothing from all this indulgence. But that's not entirely true. From what I've observed, the benefits are these: in exchange for his wife's acceptance of these myths, the husband will support her and the children financially to the extent he is able. That means if he is able to earn enough to support her, she can stop working or cut back if she wants to. He will also defer to her rules and ideas about domestic life and child rearing, believing at heart that she really does know better about such things. And this is how those myths actually serve to exclude him from the emotional life of the family even as they protect him from its burdens. What this all boils down to is: he'll earn the bread and bow to her "mother power" just as his own father did with his mother.

And why is it that men and women don't realize that these attitudes are nothing more than old wine in new bottles? Because of the one new myth that keeps the others from full consciousness: We are now equal in our marriages and in our lives.

WHERE DOES THE MYTH OF EQUALITY LEAVE US?

Women—and men too—believe in gender equality in principle but not in fact. The problem is that women want to believe in their rights and equality, but like myself when I was a new mother, they don't quite—or at least not enough to challenge their husbands. Yet the idea is so vital to women's identity today that they will believe they have an equal relationship in the face of blatantly conflicting evidence.

A couple came to see me recently because of a problem with their fifteen-year-old daughter. The mother complained bitterly that the daughter was a slob and didn't pitch in because her husband babies and protects her. The husband said that he felt strongly that their daughter should enjoy life.

I asked them to tell me how they split the housework between them. "Oh, we're fifty-fifty," said the wife. "Stan does all the cooking. He's a terrific cook." Then she tried to turn the issue back to her daughter. But I pursued my train of thought, asking her who shops, who cleans up after dinner, who takes things to the dry cleaner, who does the extra laundry between visits from the cleaning lady, etc. It turned out that the wife did all the household organizing and cleaning, except for cooking dinner. And, actually, she did part of dinner, too, setting out and chopping all the ingredients her husband would use for his dish that night.

My questions alone made it clear to both of them that I didn't think they had a fifty-fifty deal. What they hadn't yet grasped was that they expected next to nothing in housework from their son, while their daughter was supposed to take the place of the help the wife wasn't getting from her husband. Although the husband made a token gesture of cooking dinner, he did nothing else in the house. It didn't seem to matter that, as an opthamologist, he was able to make his own schedule while his wife, the director of a mental health clinic, had a long and inflexible day at work.

This wife was overworked and irritated. But rather than confronting her husband, she took it out on her daughter. When I questioned her as to why she wouldn't ask her husband to do more, she said, "He hates housework. When he has to do it, he makes me pay. But he does all the cooking, so it works out pretty evenly."

As much as we might gasp at the wife's self-delusion that their marriage was equal, many women and men today are similarly deluded. That is, they pay lip service to the dream of equality, but they put their money on the old myths.

Either women delude themselves into believing their relationships are equal or else they complain to other women instead of confronting the men. Incredulous, they'll ask each other, "What is it about these men? I mean, I have a job, too." Or, "He wasn't like that when we got married." Women shake their heads, roll their eyes, and say, "Men just don't get it." They screw up the corners of their lips and mutter, "I don't even ask him anymore." Sound familiar?

In the end, women are left viewing the work/family problem

as an unsolvable one, but that is because they—and everyone—continue to assume it is entirely *their* problem. It always takes men by surprise when I redefine the work/*child-care* problem in therapy to include them. Not that marriages then miraculously transform. Hardly. Whether a husband is sympathetic to his wife's demands or resentful, educated or not, his responses to my questions about why he doesn't do his share of household work are always pretty much the same. To summarize:

1. I agree it's unfair the way boys and girls are raised, but I wasn't raised to do women's work.
2. Remember the time I cleaned up for the party without being asked?
3. When I do try, she supervises me and complains.
4. I take total responsibility for the cat and the dishes.
5. If this is what it takes to avoid divorce, I'll try to change.
6. I have a killing work schedule, but I'd do more if I had time.

All couples resist change to some extent or another. Resistance is in our nature. But once the issues are on the table the real work of challenging those old assumptions and changing the conditions of our lives can begin.

The reasons, then, why our marriages are not fifty-fifty is that our society and our workplaces won't let them be. Furthermore, we still devoutly believe in the old gender myths. Rather than challenge them—and therefore the culture at large—a woman will convince herself that she *wants* to do most of the housework and child care or that she's happy to cut back at work or that her husband really does do his share. And the couple will cope, almost. But add any additional stress to the marriage, such as another child, a sick parent or child, the husband's losing his job, or a professional opportunity for the wife, and the inequities crack the veneer of stability. The clock stops ticking.

Most women who arrive at this impasse believe their husbands failed them. It rarely occurs to them that today's marriage has set both of them up to fail. Some women understand their complaints but can't challenge either the old myths or society to make their marriages different, at least not on their own. Although the social forces that have stopped change short are rarely obvious to couples, the result often is. As one observant young wife once said in therapy, "I'm both husband and wife. But he's still only the husband," which aptly describes the problem with contemporary marriage. Our society has "allowed" women to do two jobs, if they can manage them both, but has pressured men to keep doing only one.

Discovering the Golden Rule
Whoever Has the Gold Makes the Rules

For a marriage to thrive, both partners must be mature, autonomous individuals. That may sound reasonable enough, but people don't always recognize that in a society such as ours maturity and autonomy usually require financial independence. Without the money to support yourself, you are rarely free to do as you think best.

If a parent or spouse supports you, *they* will have the final say as to what you can and can't do. You might convince them to "let" you visit your aunt in Idaho or buy your nephew the computer he wants so much, but you do so at *their* pleasure. Most young people can't wait to be independent financially. They are extremely sensitive to the golden rule and know full well that as long as their parents pay, their parents "rule." Everyone seems to agree that depending on parents for money has a tendency to infantilize young adults.

In a marriage, however, the power of money is far less apparent than it is in a parent-child relationship. Money is supposedly beside the point. Romantic love is thought to be "above" money, as if money should never muddy the pure waters of love. So if a wife supports her husband during his internship, we say she's doing it for love. If a husband supports a wife who's raising the children, he's doing it because he loves his family. In marriage, what's mine is yours. Right? No—wrong.

What's mine is yours. Think about the idea honestly. It has to be one of the last great myths of romantic love. At most divorce hearings partners are more than ready to assert that what's mine never really was yours to begin with. Although they may have spoken differently when they married, their unspoken agreement always was "I will share my money with you *as long as you make me happy.*" Prenuptial agreements have helped to put the lie to the mine-is-yours myth, but we still don't quite accept that every marriage has a bottom line, which, unfortunately, is more likely to be about control than about sharing.

Yet couples don't have to wait for a divorce hearing to figure out which money really belongs to which partner. Our everyday lives make it perfectly clear to those who wish to see. As I mentioned earlier, when one partner is financially dependent on the other, he or (usually) she rarely has the *power* to negotiate the visit to Idaho or the computer purchase or who has what household responsibilities and who'll take care of the children when. And, as we will see, trivial as these subjects seem, they enhance or diminish each partner's individuality.

Because we live in the consumer, money-worshipping society that we do, money exerts its massive force on all marriages. And while most partners can neutralize that force by balancing the power between them or changing their lifestyle, few do. Like it or not, earnings almost always establish the power balance in relationships. Let's take a hard look at homemaking, for example.

Many men and women agree homemaking is more important than half the jobs people do outside the home. Nonetheless it doesn't carry real power either in a relationship or outside it. Ironically, it carries less power now, when homemaking is a relatively invisible job, than it did in the nineteenth century, when homemakers actually made—or supervised the making of—every household essential from candles to clothing. As a society we no longer value the homemaker's work. Society may raise a glass to homemakers on Mother's Day, but otherwise they are not recognized, paid, or insured. They don't get workman's compensation if they are injured on the job, and as all homemakers know quite well, there are no sick days. However much the partners themselves believe in their equality, the larger society, including its legal system, does not. At the time of divorce, the couple's income is considered the husband's alone (if he earns it). Her work as a homemaker is not toted up. The law does not view them as matching contributions to a partnership. In most states, if a couple has accumulated assets, women usually get at most a third.

And what do these realities mean to the couple? Generally this: a homemaker may spend her partner's money as long as he approves, but she will rarely feel entitled to spend it when he doesn't. Usually, the dependent partner or the low earner feels compelled to defer to the other's choices while the high earner feels entitled to veto decisions. What you have then is a situation in which one partner "asks" and the other "allows."

Such subtle power differences between lovers can't help but have emotional ramifications. When one partner is economically dependent, distrust and resentment will fester. The powerful partner may not believe he (it's usually a he) is freely loved, since he's well aware of how much his partner needs his support. It's the same principle that makes the wealthy fear others value them only for their money and not for themselves. As for the dependent partner, who is well aware of how little power she has, she will find emotional (or sexual) ways to "even the score." Or she may simply lose so much sense of self trying to please her partner that she can no longer be a real companion. The truth is that because our society values earnings over homemaking, neither partner can really believe in *her* equality if *he* supports her financially.

Sound extreme? I guarantee it's not. It's just that we're so unaccustomed to thinking about the role of money and power in our love relationships, we aren't aware of how these issues affect us. Money isn't a petty issue at all. Whether and how we earn money, how much we have, and what it means to us is an integral part of who we are. So if couples don't acknowledge the role of money in their lives, they are overlooking an important piece of information about themselves both as individuals and as partners. In addition, if there is a problem of unequal power in a marriage, it can't be solved without first acknowledging the role money plays in the couple's life—and unfortunately, couples and therapists rarely do so. At one time I myself didn't either.

IT'S NOT NICE TO TALK ABOUT MONEY

By 1981, when I had long since found myself caught in a blizzard of sex-role issues that wouldn't go away, I was just beginning to realize that the classical therapeutic techniques weren't digging us out. This glimmer of frustration turned into painful awareness when Dottie and Ben came to see me.

Dottie and Ben were one of those couples who come into therapy when their children are grown and the woman senses something is terribly wrong in the marriage. They'd been together for thirty years, and now that the youngest of their four children had graduated from high school—now "it would just be the two of us," Dottie explained—she wanted "more say" in the relationship.

Dottie had never earned a living. She married young and at a time when women weren't expected to work outside the home. Until recently, she hadn't questioned that choice and had felt more fortunate than most because Ben had done so much better than their working-class backgrounds had led them to expect. But Ben, who owned a successful window-installation company, made all the money and all the family decisions. Actually, the problem that brought them to me was the consequence of one of those unilateral decisions. Some years earlier Ben had bought a condo "hideaway" in rural Pennsylvania without consulting Dottie. She refused to set foot in it. For years that hadn't been a problem because Ben had been happy to go there by himself on the weekends. But now that the children were gone, he wanted to make it *their* retirement home.

I was struck by the contrast between husband and wife. Although they were the picture of the older suburban couple, each wearing roomy khaki slacks and tennis shirts, they were nonetheless quite different from each other. Ben was a vigorous, fast-talking, outgoing man who waved his arms around when he talked. He was candid about wanting "the old-fashioned marriage where the man brings home the money and the wife serves him dinner . . . sex, whatever," he added somewhat self-mockingly, since the opening discussion made it clear that he'd given up on sex or even affection from Dottie. Dottie was quiet and withdrawn, her face half-hidden by her large eyeglasses, her head tucked down into her shoulders, her voice small. But she proved unexpectedly firm, like a cornered boxer in a crouch toward the end of a losing round, defended and determined.

Dottie never smiled during our sessions. She had a long list of complaints about Ben and was almost unstoppable once she began it: he dropped his clothes everywhere, not bothering to put his freshly washed laundry away; he didn't even take his dishes into the kitchen; he took her for granted and treated her like a household servant. Ben, on his part, had no complaints at all, except that Dottie wouldn't live in the condo. As for her complaints, he either made light of them or he parried, as in "I do so think about you. On Saturday night when you were sick, I left the bathroom door open for you." Or he dismissed them entirely, blaming Dottie's friend Vivian for "putting ideas in her head." Or he "joked" about them: "If this is menopause, I like it even less than I thought I would."

I couldn't take Dottie and Ben back to their original feelings for each other the way I usually do with a younger couple because there was so much water under the bridge. And also, Dottie, in her open-and-shut way, insisted "then was then and now is now." Besides, I felt that Dottie had hit on the central issue: she had no power to say how the relationship should be. Since she just had the power to refuse, that was what she did. She refused practically everything he wanted—from sex to retirement in the country.

I'd begun to grasp the idea that I needed to address the unequal power of couples like this, but I didn't know how. I realized vaguely that money was part of the picture but had not yet questioned the training that had taught me to regard money as a smoke screen, never to be literally discussed. Besides, I was afraid the topic would make Ben drop out. He'd already said that if he had to change "too much," he didn't think he'd stay in the marriage. So, like a "good" therapist, I moved the whole discussion to the emotional arena and called it "Ben's unilateral decision and Dottie's anger about that"—as if these were separate and equal factors bearing no relation to the money issue.

The time-honored method I'd been taught for changing the emotional climate was to engage a wife's sympathy for her husband. In the second session, Ben had given a poignant description of himself as an outsider looking in at life, exactly the way he'd felt as a young man in the navy visiting foreign ports. In business, he said, he met people and moved on to new ones. "That's all I know: tell the same jokes, don't get involved. That's how it is at my hideaway, only more so—talk to whoever is around, don't know anyone in particular." He said this in the spirit of confession, his usual jollity tempered by regret. He very much wished Dottie's company there.

Throughout his confession I kept looking over at Dottie, who stared at him warily. Had he ever told Dottie how lonely he was? I asked, hoping to move her. In the last session, Dottie had been moved to tears telling me about how Ben's own sister also wished for more intimacy with Ben but could never get through to him. Now, however, Dottie wasn't buying his sad song—or mine.

"I don't like superficial relationships," she snapped. "I don't want to live on the outside. I don't know anyone in the country. *I* don't want to live there. We have a perfectly nice house already where I know plenty of people. If he's so lonely, why did he buy a hideaway in the first place?"

On and on the sessions went while I continued to talk as if Dottie should be pleased that Ben was finally opening up and inviting her into his other, private life. Until, after six sessions, they quit. Or rather, Dottie quit.

I knew I'd failed them. By then, I felt I was failing many of the couples I saw despite the fact that they stopped battling and became friends again. I knew that even if they'd learned something about their covert emotional agendas and the behavior they'd brought from their own families, their relief would only be temporary. I wasn't helping them to change the inequality that was the major cause of their conflicts. It would be years before I realized that the key was money—money and how it is connected to gender and power in our society.

THE PROBLEM IS MONEY

Fortunately, my colleague Monica McGoldrick and I were beginning to realize that whenever we discussed a case (including the case of Dottie and Ben), we would immediately ask each other, "How much money does he make? Does she make any?" If not, we'd both sigh, "Oh, that's a problem."

We had an inkling it was *the* problem, but we still deferred to the established idea that you don't talk about money with couples in therapy. And as a therapist you don't think about the impact money makes on a couple's relationship. Such a notion was never even articulated. And yet, little by little, we started to articulate the idea to each other. We even began to discuss money, earnings, and power with patients. When I say "little by little," I mean that it took years and a great deal of experimenting before we really understood what we were doing. That was true even though our results were so striking that we began to teach the technique to the therapists in training. Eventually, it became a part of our professional exchange with the field at large.

In 1988, I wrote an essay called "The Person Who Has the Gold Makes the Rules" in which I argued that while a couple's presenting problem may be "we can't communicate," the underlying problem in traditional marriages is that the couple's money is not *theirs,* but *his.*

To illustrate the point, I used a case that was so typical I could be sure every therapist saw such a couple weekly: the husband accused his wife of being a "spendthrift" while she, in turn, felt he was "stingy." Instead of helping them to "communicate," I asked them directly about who earned what money and what power that gave each of them. Within a session, the couple quickly uncovered the essential terms of their relationship (and every other like it): the wife burst out that she felt as if they were "master and chattel," and the husband responded coolly,

"I wouldn't go that far, but I certainly do think as far as responsibility for money goes, we *are* parent and child."

By the end of their therapy, this couple rejected the parent-child model of marriage they had fallen into. Although it wasn't easy, the wife reestablished her catering business as a serious financial venture and the husband took an active parenting role.

That was still pretty straight talk for 1988. In fact, talking about finances in relationshps had become so routine for Monica and me and my three colleagues in the Women's Project in Family Therapy, we failed to notice that most of the profession still considered the subject taboo. So much so that later in the year when I presented a talk on the importance of money in couple's therapy at a workshop at an annual family therapy meeting, there were gasps of surprise in the audience. On the standard workshop evaluations, some people expressed outrage at "Carter's crazy ideas about money" and at how "disturbing" my talk had been. And this from an audience that had come to hear the new theories about gender issues.

Of course, we were all surprised by their surprise. But we were also made suddenly aware of how radical the subject was: of all the things said at that workshop about couples therapy, asking about money was the most controversial!

My colleagues' reaction actually helped me to realize that I'd struck oil. That's when I went back and watched the tapes of Dottie and Ben's sessions, confirming my suspicion that I had never once mentioned money. As I watched, I finally saw the problem with such clarity that I now use those tapes to teach my students how vital it is to raise the issue of money and power directly.

Ben, charming though he was, had been stonewalling Dottie and me. He purported not to understand why Dottie objected to his buying the condo, since "it's such a nice place." Then, he didn't see why negotiation was necessary, since he "never made unreasonable requests of Dottie."

At the end of the second session, I had asked Ben to think about whether he wanted to try negotiation instead of his usual unilateral decision making. I asked Dottie to consider what role her anger played in their relationship—as if it didn't matter which one of them changed as long as the conflict stopped.

To Dottie's credit, it hadn't worked. Dottie felt entitled to her anger as long as Ben "ruled." And as for Ben, even when I tried to get him to "delegate" some power to Dottie, he refused. He wouldn't consider letting Dottie look for another house that suited them both. He refused, even though, as I later realized, my request for him to "delegate" responsibility to Dottie validated his right to do so. It acknowledged the power he could choose to share—or not. Could the outcome have been worse if I had just asked them straight out about money and power? I doubt it.

I never raised the dread subject because it was outside the accepted territory of therapy and because couples themselves didn't discuss it. Much as they might have argued about *spending* money, they never talked about how it structured their relationships. I never asked who earned what, what each thought about whose money it was, what role it played in a wife's decision to remain in the marriage, or in the freedom a husband felt to spend or veto spending. Today, well over a decade since I saw Dottie and Ben, most mental health professionals still don't discuss money with their patients, except to dismiss it. It's much easier and more acceptable to both therapists and couples to talk about sex.

IT'S ONLY MONEY

Inequities in money and power create problems in all marriages, not just *traditional* ones. And whether the couple cares about money or not, the issue is always lurking in the background of their relationship.

Sam and I hardly ever argued about money although, Lord knows, we should have. But here we were, the passionate musician and the "do-gooder" therapist, and that left nobody in the counting house.

My brother tried his best to help us: once he bailed us out of trouble with the IRS, and later he gave me advice on how to invest. But I just wasn't able to follow through because it involved "nuisances" like filling out forms and going in person to discount stockbrokers. Isn't it interesting that my brother and I came out of the same family—he who is so adept at money management and I always remembering my mother saying, "It's *only* money." As an artist, Sam had "renounced" money. So we both felt it was "tacky" to be concerned about such a mundane thing. Nevertheless I realize now that we were constantly engaged in a silent struggle trying to get the other to take charge of the money so that the one who didn't have to bother could concentrate on "higher things."

I see now that in our relationship, although we never discussed it, greater power still went to the one earning the most— not because the high earner insisted, heaven forbid! But because the lower earner hesitated to make unilateral financial decisions. I can still remember myself as a frugal young mother standing for ages in front of a lipstick counter trying to convince myself that it was all right to buy another lipstick. And even now, I notice that Sam, who's retired and not earning as much as I am, will check with me before buying a fancy present for someone, although I'd never think to check with him. Only during the middle years when our earnings were close to equal do I remember feeling free of unspoken tension about money.

Individually, I would say that Sam has suffered most about money because he could never fully reject society's financial measure of a man's success and insistence that "providing for the family" is a husband's major responsibility. Most men do worry about the money and feel responsible for it regardless of who earns what.

As for me, raised to expect to work at a low-paying job and then "retire" forever into family life, I have *over*achieved. And it feels good, no matter how I still pretend or try not to care about money.

"WHOEVER CONTROLS THE PURSE STRINGS CONTROLS THE RELATIONSHIP"

Often, financial control seems entirely irrelevant in relationships, particularly where the men are "reasonable" and sincerely want to think of their wives as equals. But if the husband is still the primary earner and decision maker, the power of his money is usually at the heart of their problems.

In one such case, a severely depressed wife who was managing her husband's small advertising agency and raising their two boys was becoming "increasingly hostile" in therapy. Their therapist had called me in to consult when, after many futile sessions, the wife, Laura, had "run away" from home. With the family's permission, I watched through the one-way mirror and saw the therapist listening almost exclusively to the husband, who was, admittedly, at his wit's end trying to hold his home and family together. Matt was a kind, caring man, genuinely concerned about his wife's depression, which he believed had nothing to do with him or their marriage.

As Matt related how earnestly he'd tried to reason with Laura and how bewildered he was by her continuing misery and "acting out," the female therapist, unaware of her automatic deferral to a "reasonable" man, ignored Laura's attempts to speak and instead colluded with the husband to "cure" the wife. So while Matt made a hundred suggestions about what Laura should do to help herself and described his own plight, Laura kept up a mumbling Greek chorus of contemptuous remarks, each made from an increasingly hunched posture: "Well, if *he* says so . . ."; "Yeah, a holy terror . . ."

When, at my suggestion, the therapist challenged the husband's patronizing and started to listen to what the wife was mumbling—this brooding sullen woman came alive. "I'd be fine," she screamed at her husband, "if I were holding a paintbrush in my hand more of the time instead of a dishrag or a typewriter." By the end of the session, she was sitting up in her chair and speaking clearly in complete sentences, obviously hopeful now that the therapist didn't seem allied with her husband against her.

Soon after that session, the therapist called to let me know that the couple's therapy was going very well. Laura had quit the unpaid "job" in her husband's office to return to painting, which (the therapist had just learned) she had given up to "raise a family." Laura had done this even though her canvases had started to earn her money and recognition. And although Matt fought the change at first, pressuring her with his fears that "no one would manage his office as well as she" and that "they'd be really stretched financially," he did concede. The therapist helped Laura not to give in to Matt's pressure, and once he hired someone else who was competent, his fears disappeared. Money had never been discussed in their therapy before.

Therapists' expectations of men very much color how they interpret a couple's problems. This is particularly true when the man in question is as concerned and well-meaning as the husband in the previous case. As a colleague of mine noted, "Acceptable masculinity is still domination, but domination that appears reasonable and not striven for." And one reason money is such an uncomfortable subject is because it challenges that deeply rooted—and respected—domination.

Even now, when I discuss my technique of suggesting to certain couples that they go to a legal mediator to divide the family assets equitably, putting the wife's part in the wife's name and the husband's part in the husband's name, then return to marital therapy on a very different footing, a stunned silence comes over professional audiences. But as a friend of mine described, the silence is "soon broken by claps, not applause, but claps of surprise and delight—but only from the women. Looks of deep dread seep from the shaded eyes of the men."

Resistant as we all are to thinking about marriage and money, we do so more and more. As I was leafing through *Bridal Guide* recently to see what was new in today's view of marriage, I was struck by their running column on "Love and Money." The one in the issue I picked up was entitled, "The Power of Money: Whoever Controls the Purse Strings in a Marriage Also Controls the Relationship." Ironically, family therapy hasn't yet caught up with *Bridal Guide.* Why?

HOW THERAPY CAN (BUT OFTEN DOESN'T) HELP

Most family therapists, myself included, have been trained to focus on *how* a couple argues and ignore the content of the argument. This means we treat an argument about money as simple administrative detail or translate it into emotional currency, as if it were a symbol of a partner's feeling that he or she is not getting enough love. No therapist was ever supposed to ask how much each partner earns, who manages the money, or what impact the disparate earnings have on the couple's decision making.

Most therapists work within the framework of the couple's financial lifestyle. They try to help the couples themselves understand that the material details of life—from earning money to cooking dinner—are trivial, emotional background music. When the man earns most or all of the income and the woman does most of the child care, everyone still thinks it's "normal"—a reality to which therapists will help couples adjust. But there is nothing inevitable about this arrangement; it is just the familiar patriarchal one, which many people never question.

Simply put, if we do not have money to support ourselves, we usually do not have a clear enough "I" to form an abiding relationship. When older couples, like Dottie and Ben, have had a lifetime of "Father Knows Best" or worse, "All in the Family," they may have to completely renegotiate their marriage contract to make a fresh start for themselves. When I worked with them, the best I was hoping for was helping Dottie to adjust to a new life stage with her domineering husband and loosening Ben up a bit so he would delegate more power to Dottie. Now, I would work with them very differently. I would help them to understand the nature of the contract they agreed to and why Ben needed to listen to Dottie's wish to change that. Not only because a more equal relationship is simply fairer, but also because without equality, the self becomes so threatened that the relationship will automatically destabilize.

NO MONEY/NO SELF

Money is inextricably a part of relationships, and not only in the obvious and aboveboard family accounting. Money talks, as it were, at the level of the bank account and also deep below the surface of a marriage, where the essential tension between the needs of the couple and the needs of the individuals is in constant play. For a marriage begins with two separate people whose individuality must remain intact if the couple is to thrive.

A person's individuality is supremely important. It is the sum of those beliefs, thoughts, and feelings that are nonnegotiable. Individuality, in other words, is *self:* who you are.

The problem with talking about partners' individuality within a marriage is that the culture still defines individuality—or self— differently, and I think erroneously, for men and women. For men, self is autonomy, which is self-direction and self-sufficiency. For women, self is emotional connection: caring about others, supporting them, being liked.

If we really believed in the equal importance of autonomy and connection (which we do not), wouldn't we believe all people needed both? As a therapist, I can assure you, all do. Most women who lack autonomy eventually feel they have not lived a full life—and they have not. If they have lived their husband's life, letting his dreams, his work, his goals, and his decisions about their life predominate, then at the end of the day they always wonder what might have been if they had followed their own dreams and used their own talents outside of the family.

When women (or men) temporarily stay home with small children but have planned for a return to work, they remain economically viable and therefore autonomous. But when home-making is a permanent career choice and someone else always provides the necessities of survival, it makes it that much harder—if not impossible—for the couple to continue to grow emotionally.

It was no accident that Dottie wanted to change things once the children were launched. Her late midlife crisis, if we want to call it that, consisted of her taking stock of her life and deciding she hadn't lived the way she wanted to. She regretted not having "done something" with her life, as her friend Vivian had. Although Ben said that Dottie would have been fine if she hadn't been listening to her friend Vivian, it was because Vivian's ideas resonated for her that Dottie was moved by them. Vivian, who had been widowed ten years earlier, had recently brokered her active PTA, school board, and community involvement into a political appointment. Although Dottie wasn't interested in politics, she agreed with Vivian that a woman can have her own life, her own opinions, and her independence. She admired Vivian's "expertise" in the wider world and wished she had some as well.

Ben now wanted Dottie to come away with him to the condo on weekends. He hadn't insisted she do that before because she had to supervise the children's weekend activities. "Now," Dottie said, "Ben expects me to drop everything and do whatever he wants, but I have my own interests. While the children were home, I never noticed how bossy Ben was because he accepted whatever I said about the children. I didn't realize I had no other authority with him."

Like many women, Dottie didn't realize she'd given up her autonomy until the busy child-rearing years were over. As for men, we all know some who discover, usually too late, what their families and friends mean to them. Or like Ben, finally realize at age fifty-five that they've been lonely and unconnected all their lives.

So what could a therapist do with a couple like Ben and Dottie? Dottie obviously wasn't able suddenly, at age fifty-two, to earn a living. Ben clearly wasn't going to turn into a "new man" or even a benevolent despot. Yet making their relationship successful would have meant that Dottie had to have enough money to enable her to act on her needs, to do what she wanted, about which she was very clear. She loved her husband enough to negotiate, but not enough to give in entirely to his demands. *His* money, then, would have to have been redefined as *their* money. Ben would have had to put enough assets in her name and perhaps divide the money still coming in from his business. He may not have been willing to do this. Had I been playing my role more effectively though, I would have pointed out to him that if they were to divorce, he would be forced by a court to do *some* financial sharing. Why not do it before? I would also have pointed out to him how much less lonely he'd be if he had a real companion rather than a resentful dependent.

Traditional definitions of male and female self are neither accurate nor emotionally viable; mature individuality requires *both* connectedness and autonomy. And not only for the well-being of the individual, but for the happiness of the couple. If maturity were defined as autonomy *with* connectedness for both men and women—and boys and girls were raised accordingly—the imbalances in relationships would more often than not right themselves.

As complicated as this theory of mature individuality in relationships may sound, it is really quite simple. In 1917, without the benefit of any fancy theories, a writer named Floyd Dell expressed it this way:

> When you have got a woman in a box, and you pay rent on the box, her relationship to you insensibly changes character. It loses the fine excitement of democracy. It ceases to be companionship, for companionship is only possible in a democracy. It is no longer a sharing of life together—it is a breaking of life apart. Half a life—cooking, clothes and children; half a life—business, politics and baseball. It doesn't make much difference which is the poorer half. Any half, when it comes to life, is very near to none at all.

Although we might disagree with Dell that it makes no difference which is the poorer half, his point is well taken. The traditional roles are "a breaking of life apart," an impoverishment of self.

The surest way to avoid such impoverishment of self in marriage is for partners to have relatively equal and adequate incomes, which generally means that they have equal power and can take care of their family. But in the real world, partners rarely have equal incomes and may also have much more or less than their family needs. Then, the influence of money in marriage and its connections to power have to be assessed. Usually, they take one of the several following forms, some subtle, some blatant.

1. The husband earns most of the money and controls all significant financial decisions. In most instances when the wife earns nothing, has no significant marketable skills, and has never worked, she loses her autonomy. She will eventually feel trapped

in her marriage and will most likely take her anger out not only on her husband but also on herself.

2. The wife stays home temporarily with young children but has the skills to support herself and her children if necessary. This couple can maintain equal power because she is "financially viable." *If she's vigilant* about maintaining her equality, she need not suffer the loss of autonomy or of power in her marriage. Since she retains choices and options, she's not trapped and therefore can continue to negotiate from a position of strength.

3. The wife is "financially viable" but still earns significantly less than her husband. If she has great difficulty in getting her husband to negotiate decisions with her, she may experience her lack of power and options within the marriage. If so, she will be resentful and might even consider divorce, or she will consider earning more to increase her power in the marriage.

4. The wife earns significantly more than the husband. One or both partners' anxiety over the husband's "failure" to fulfill his "role" and be the main provider of his family may drive a wedge between them. If the wife doesn't share power (and she usually does), the husband's resentment may grow even more quickly than a woman's does in the same "low earner" position.

5. Affluent marriages. "Financial viability" is often redefined as a "need" for more and more money to support an extravagant lifestyle. The partners may complain about the emotional costs of consumerism ("Now that we can afford the country club, we have no time to use it"), but they are rarely motivated to make changes that would affect the bottom line. Even if both are equally high earners, the stress of earning so much money may undermine their relationship.

6. Poor couples. They lack the money and power necessary to take care of themselves and their children. The stress of their struggles—i.e., unemployment or partners working different shifts or two and even three jobs, leaving no time for each other—may pull the partners and the family apart.

Therapists (especially male therapists) often support what they call "equitable" as opposed to "equal" arrangements. "Equitable" means "fair," and I have nothing against it. Equitable relationships can work: e.g., he makes more of the money and she does more of the child care. But it can only work *if* the couple can override society's conditioning with their personal belief that earning money and homemaking are *equally valuable* contributions of equal partners who share important decision making and have equal access to the money. In truly equitable relationships of this kind, the higher earner will often put some of the assets and savings in the other's name, thereby "equalizing" the real power each has.

Power can be wielded through assets other than money if partners agree. Let's say a husband's earnings pay for a house and a wife is in charge of renovating and reselling it. These partners can certainly weigh their contributions fairly and split the revenue accordingly. After all, time is money; she's put her time into raising the value of the house. When a wife has the personal connections in a network important for her husband's business, she definitely has a power equal to money. But this kind of power will only "count" if both partners agree that it does.

There are other special circumstances in which partners do successfully override social conditioning and value some intangible contribution equally with money. If one partner is an artist, let's say, and the other, revering such a talent, is willing to support the family and still believe in his partner's equality. Sometimes fame, great social or political skill, or even having a very strong, cohesive family can endow a partner with power equal to money in the eyes of his or her spouse. And, of course, if one partner has a trust fund, he or she can choose not to earn money without losing power. All these equitable arrangements are fine for the lucky few who can make them. Unfortunately, these "comparable" contributions to a marriage rarely count as power in a society where only money talks. And this is why not earning too often means giving up power . . . and self.

Thus, to be whole people and therefore able to be true companions to each other, partners have to examine the nature of their unspoken financial contract and acknowledge the power of money in their relationship. If we really strive to be connected and autonomous—and to help our partners do the same—we'll avoid the kind of permanent financial dependence that so often destroys mutual respect and turns love into obligation. The subject of money won't muddy the "pure" waters of love. Rather, it will reflect the patterns of light and dark in those waters. That is, it will reflect our *real* relationships. Ironically, the more the power of money is recognized—and balanced—in marriage, the freer love can be.

5

The Search for Intimacy in Marriage

To explain how the power of money affects a couple on the deepest levels, I have to discuss the nature of intimacy so it isn't confused, as it often is, with togetherness. For while equalizing money and power can threaten togetherness, it enhances intimacy. Let me explain.

Not too long ago a woman phoned me to make an appointment for herself because of her depression. I asked her to bring her husband along who, it turned out, was "happy to do anything to help her." They were then in their midthirties and living in New York City, though my Westchester office was near the garden shop where Dawn worked. Harry, a successful television writer, earned a lot of money, but erratically—one year, $400,000, the next year, nothing, the next, $80,000. Dawn loved her work, though she earned less than $40,000 a year doing it, a fraction of Harry's earnings even when averaged out. She'd often thought she'd like to be a landscape architect but never quite mobilized to pursue it, she said, "Because there is no future for landscape architecture in the city and Harry absolutely refuses to move to the suburbs or get a weekend house in the country." She also explained that they'd always been so busy traveling to Los Angeles for Harry's meetings, going on wine-tasting trips where they'd buy wine for Harry's collection, or "just taking off for Bali or Thailand."

Harry, with a giggle, said, "But we were having too much fun, so we had to stop. Dawn's got a thing about hedonism." Although Harry was smiling at her, Dawn, whose voice lowered several decibels, said that she enjoyed the trips, but always taking time off put her job at risk. Then Harry responded, "She knows she can get another job any day. It's not as if they pay her enough to deserve such loyalty."

Dawn, almost inaudible now, whispered that Harry never seemed to understand how much her job meant to her or how much she'd love a house in the country. And Harry, who spoke directly to me, said that they'd agreed they didn't want children, so "what would we need a house for? It would just pin us down. It's just her depression talking. Anyway, she only thought of it when her old friend bought a country house, but they have three kids and her husband's idea of a great Sunday is mowing the lawn."

Without going into any more detail about their lives or their therapy (which bore out my impression that first session), I want to point out how Harry and Dawn's discussion illustrates what I mean by togetherness—as opposed to intimacy. Dawn was right. Harry truly couldn't understand that Dawn wouldn't want to do exactly what he wanted to do. She always had, or so he thought. And they only started to argue when Dawn began to say "no" to him.

The problem was that Harry saw his wife as an extension of himself, not as a separate person. That's why he chuckled at her refusal to continue traveling and explained why she shouldn't care about her "puny" job. From his point of view, her desire for a country house wasn't really about her but about her old friend, whom she emulated. Or her depression, as if it were a demon who gave her strange ideas. Dawn, as he perceived her, wouldn't have such opinions. And I can assure you Harry and Dawn are hardly unique in this regard. Many women are like Dawn, who assumed Harry would read her real feelings and respond in a caring manner. Instead of her stating her desires and negotiating for the life she wanted, Dawn was living Harry's life and complaining about it. She was also constantly hurt that he "couldn't understand" her.

When couples are merged this way, partners begin to act as if one person is an extension of the other or *reflects* on the other. How many of us have witnessed couples in which one partner is embarrassed by the other's opinions. One might even tell the other not to talk about politics or religion or whatever topic upsets them. "Steven, you know I can't stand it when you start in on the corruption of the church." "Claire, you don't know anything about business, so why don't you just keep quiet."

Such censorship is enforced because it's as if the outspoken partner shouldn't have his or her own—and different—opinions. Or shouldn't be responsible for them, whether they are right or wrong or silly or irrelevant. How hard it is for people to sit quietly by when their spouses "mouth off" about something or are, in their opinion, ridiculous, angry, or argumentative. Usually, a wife will say, "Allen, please, you're embarrassing your uncle," as if Allen is her responsibility. Yet if Allen were a friend, not a spouse, she wouldn't feel his opinions reflected on her and therefore wouldn't feel as compelled to shut him up. More likely, she would just disagree with Allen's points. She might even admire his passion. And husbands do the same. Most partners learn to stay away from certain subjects so they are not confronted with their "irreconcilable differences" and can maintain the illusion of their togetherness.

The belief in the togetherness of married partners is so basic in our culture that it usually takes a great deal of discussion before couples accept that two should *not* be "as one." And why shouldn't they? Because too much togetherness destroys intimacy! I'll be discussing intimacy—including sexual intimacy—in greater depth in Chapter eight, but I would like to begin the discussion here by making clear the distinction between togetherness and intimacy.

Togetherness is when partners cling to each other in an emotional dependency, scared to disagree for fear their differences will break them up. Wives who give up friends their husbands don't like or husbands who quit playing or watching sports because their wives don't enjoy sports are protecting their togetherness, not their intimacy. They're acting as if they are a two-headed unit who should think and feel the same about everything. They're frightened their differences will cause conflict.

Intimacy, on the other hand, is when two partners, secure in themselves, are able to take care of their own moods and wishes. They enjoy being close and sharing their lives, but they also accept each other's differences and separate pursuits, thoughts, and feelings. Each acts as a separate individual, autonomous but emotionally connected to the other. If Harry were secure in himself, he wouldn't have been frightened by Dawn's work or her wish for a country house. Although it may have been "easier" to have a wife who was free to go on his trips and wanted to live full-time in the city, as he wished, it was actually much harder emotionally. With Dawn resentful and depressed, she really wasn't "there" at all; furthermore, both of them participated in the deception that Dawn wanted Harry's life. So while they had an abundance of "togetherness," they had little intimacy.

Equalizing money and power in their relationship would have threatened their togetherness because Dawn wouldn't have so automatically lived Harry's life. For example, if half the money were hers, she might well have felt entitled to say, "I'd rather buy a small country house with *our* money and travel less." Then Harry and Dawn would have had to resolve their conflicting desires. Doing so, however, would have given them far more insight into their partnership and greater opportunity for mutual respect. If Dawn had become a landscape architect, Harry might have had less of her company, but when they were together, they could have had a closer and more satisfying relationship, one laced with the excitement each might bring from sharing their own meaningful worlds.

Equal marriage, with its goal of lifelong commitment and emotional fulfillment, is both the most difficult and the most likely framework for intimacy between two people: most difficult because disagreement seems like "biting the hand that feeds you" (emotionally); most likely because commitment is necessary if trust is to grow between people. Without trust, there can be no intimacy.

INDIVIDUALITY VERSUS TOGETHERNESS

Even if we all had mature individuality, maintaining that individuality would still create a tension in all couples. Murray Bowen, one of family therapy's first theorists, believed that every couple's relationship consists of an effort to balance the partners' needs for individuality and the pull toward togetherness. These are two opposing life forces: the first is the drive to be in charge of your life, and the second is the impulse to merge with another.

If people have insufficient individuality (what's often described as low self-esteem or immaturity), they feel like prisoners of the relationships they so desperately need. In response, they often give up their fragile sense of self to convince themselves that everything the other wants, they want, too. What they really need is to be with the other person in order to feel good about themselves. As Bowen puts it,

> Despite the limited development of his individuality, a poorly differentiated person can "fill his tank" with togetherness and take to the highway of life. His "mileage" will be low, however, because of the almost constant need to turn to the relationship for reassurance and a sense of purpose.

Most of us have known at least a moment in our lives when we've felt so empty and frightened that we produced what a friend of mine used to call "the vampire effect," sucking the strength to live from other people, asking too much of our friends and partners. We may have felt such need for approval that instead of thinking through to our own views, we searched for strong people and adopted their views instead. Even a successful and seemingly confident man can be so desperately needy with his wife he may have to tell her everything that happens at work, making her take his part in any disputes; he may wake her in the middle of the night to soothe his anxiety attacks and insist that she be constantly available to help him. Mature individuality has nothing to do with intelligence, education, or "success." Indeed, many people at every level of society live their whole lives as emotional dependents.

Very needy people aren't necessarily clingy. Although women will often respond to their desperation for others by clinging, desperately needy men are more likely to detach themselves. We're all familiar with people who are cold, remote, distant. Although they might be charming or exciting they are not "accessible," we say. But this kind of emotional distance should never be confused with autonomy. In a relationship, fixed emotional distance is often an indication that someone can't hold on to himself and also be with another person, and therefore must pull back, cut off, or even avoid relationships altogether. In other words, the Marlboro Man is scared to death. He may be a rugged individual, but he doesn't have sufficient individuality to connect intimately with someone else.

When people have enough individuality, they can experience both self-fulfillment and intimacy with others because they don't lose their bearings in relationships. They aren't threatened by conflict or by the natural fluctuations of distance and closeness in all relationships. They don't have to take care of the other person; they don't confuse what they want with what the other person wants.

Harry wanted Dawn to want whatever he wanted. He felt she should be thrilled to travel with him and live in New York City. Like Dawn, he had lost his bearings in the relationship and was unable to see where he ended and she began. If Dawn had become more resentful of her loss of individuality, she may well have done what women often do. She may have gone "underground." What I mean is that she might have kept her real self private and not tried to share it with her partner. Then he, too, would have gradually withdrawn, assuming that his fate was to be emotionally alone.

Chet and Christie, a couple in their late fifties, had done exactly this. She asked him to come for therapy because he never talked to her, expressed no interest in her career, and was so consumed by golf, which she loathed, that—to her horror—he now wanted to retire to a golf resort.

Essentially, Chet and Christie had shut each other out. For years, he went on golf vacations while she went to Europe with a dear friend. Chet, an accountant earning $250,000 a year, had become a conservative Democrat as he aged, while Christie, an editor of a women's magazine, had become more and more liberal. Chet said he wouldn't talk to her about her work because she used the subject to launch attacks against conservatives and against men. They never discussed politics except to make contemptuous remarks about the other's beliefs. As for his complaints, he summarized them in the only comment he volunteered: "Let me tell you, this isn't the girl I married. The girl I married was thin, loving, and lighthearted."

In such long-term marriages, after years of togetherness without intimacy, couples like Chet and Christie may begin to treat each other like fixtures. That's when familiarity can breed contempt and boredom—when it becomes a substitute for intimacy. These going-through-the-motions kinds of partners usually aren't even aware of the distance that's built up between them. Ironically, their assumed need for togetherness drove them apart. They couldn't be themselves and also be together. They didn't bring their different experiences, thoughts, and feelings to the marriage to enliven it. In the hurly-burly of child rearing, they lost touch with each other, not having enough private time to muse together and share their visions of life the way they once did. They took for granted that they knew each other when, in fact, they no longer did.

For the most part, Chet and Christie had grown insensitive to each other because of the years of emotional distance. His complaint about her weight is quite common in long-married couples where one partner is, in effect, blaming the other for their lack of sexual connection. Just as often, the wife will say the husband has become "a slob." But these complaints can often be interpeted as an attempt to reach out and tell the other, finally, who you are and what you want. Coming to therapy, Christie was trying to be separate from Chet, instead of just settling for their separate lives. And she was giving him a chance to respond to her as an individual and exchange their distance for intimacy.

There's nothing inherently impossible about Chet and Christie becoming intimate. Intimates can have different politics and different passions, which should enrich each other and the relationship. However, most going-through-the-motions couples can work things out only if the men are willing both to open themselves up and to share power and if the women are willing to *insist* on being heard. Also, both the partners have to risk facing the differences that emerge when people level with each other. They have to invest in each other instead of burying themselves in work, sports, or saving their real selves for their friends—or therapists. In the end, the outcome depends on the combination of their emotional programming and the power arrangements they set up in their marriage.

The main impediment to older couples finding each other again and building trust is that sometimes they are so bitterly embattled they seem to hate each other. Chet and Christie had argued so angrily since he had announced "their" retirement plan that they had eaten away at any remaining goodwill. Really, they were so afraid to have an adult exchange of differences when retirement decisions forced them into it that he just stonewalled while she raged. Ultimately, they did decide to divorce, as do many such estranged couples once their children are launched. Ironically, the force of togetherness drove them apart.

THERE'S SUCH A THING AS BEING TOO CLOSE

Although togetherness is often called "closeness," it is actually entanglement. When partners use togetherness to solve their individual problems, their need for togetherness will overwhelm their individuality. Such entangled "togetherness" (also called "fusion") is a formula for marital disaster. Yet, actually, we all tend toward togetherness to some degree as we become more emotionally dependent on our spouses. Here, however, are three common examples of relationships in which togetherness has completely won out over individuality:

- *The parent-child marriage.* One partner always needs the other's approval or permission.
- *The stormy marriage.* Couples who argue constantly and even break up, then make up passionately.
- *The "perfect" marriage.* One partner or both partners set out to live a conflict-free life of peace and can't tolerate any arguments or even disagreements.

Familiar? You may even see these dynamics at work in your own relationship. All marriages fall into them from time to time, especially under stress. But some relationships operate in one of these patterns *most* of the time, and increasingly such partners find that they are losing their individuality, and therefore their intimacy. Often couples aren't aware of what's making married life so hard for them when they are "so close," or, as they might think of it, "so passionately in love." But that's exactly the problem. Let's take a look at our three examples.

The parent-child marriage. When one partner feels unable to act without the other's permission and invariably defers to the other's wishes and ideas, afraid to risk disapproval, the marriage slowly but surely takes on the characteristics of a parent-child relationship. Only one of the partners acts in the adult role of someone who is in charge of his or her life. The "adult" may be the husband, who controls the money and decisions, or it may be the "she-who-must-be-obeyed" wife, who has the final say about every family activity. Whichever one plays the role, he or she speaks for both of them.

Things are not what they seem, however. The "adult" derives much of his or her "adulthood" from the dependency of the other, not from having greater maturity. Both are equally immature and needy, but the one who defers is the most vulnerable to symptoms.

A very common example is the wife who decrees that they must all go to dinner at her parents' home every Sunday "because *we* want our children to have a strong sense of family. Family is very important in *our* lives. And anyway, they'll think there's something wrong if my husband doesn't come with us."

I always go on red alert when I hear one spouse saying "we"

all the time, as though the couple had one set of thoughts and feelings. I always say to them that every marital "we" ought to consist of two "I's." And I usually have to point out to the dissenting partner that even though he or she disagreed with every statement the other made, no one corrected the use of "we."

In this couple, the husband protested having to go to his in-laws house every Sunday, but still he went. When I asked why, he explained, "Because she'll pitch a fit." To which I responded as I always do.

"So what? You can't survive if she doesn't agree?"

Then his wife, incredulous, asked, "Are you saying that he can just come or not come as it suits him?"

"Well, of course," I answered. I probably say this with so much gusto because I'm remembering back to the time when I thought I had to get my husband's approval to get a job or pursue a career or even buy a lipstick.

You can see that a couple with one adult and one "dependent" would find it hard to be intimate, since intimacy would require the "adult" to show vulnerability and the "dependent" to handle his or her own decisions. So they settle for togetherness instead.

The stormy marriage. These couples are "madly in love" but can't find a balance between angry distance or a stifling "closeness," so they go back and forth between the two. For years, the tumultuous relationship between Liz Taylor and Richard Burton captivated the public with their continual bitter breakups and their fabulous reunions—complete with extravagant gifts and honeymoon trips. It was as if no couple had ever been so "in love." But their pattern isn't so extraordinary.

These partners will argue constantly over small things. For example, one of them might be on the phone and won't hang up when the other comes in from work. Their irritation with each other will escalate immediately into "you don't care about me" and "I can't trust you" and "you won't let me have a life." Usually, both the partners grew up with unstable parents who themselves weren't dependable, at least not emotionally. Often there's a depressive parent or an alcoholic, and the contract is that the spouse is going to "rescue" them from that tumultuous past and make up for it by being ever-dependable, ever-available, ever-loving. Which, of course, no one can be, so the inevitable disappointment leads them to re-create the past they're trying to escape.

They invariably have a colossal argument and break up. But when they separate, they don't just go on and build a new life. They feel angry, devastated, guilty. They never stop thinking about their "missing" half who "filled the emptiness" and so fall again into each other's arms. There is a "predestined" romantic aura about their relationship that we often associate with "first love" or "young love"—but then most young couples graduate to a more mature, perhaps less dramatic, form of partnership.

Of course, getting older doesn't necessarily make people more mature. Like adolescents, the older stormy couple may believe that this person is their "other half" and they would never find anyone who "fits" them as well. But they can't manage the anxiety and anger that their entanglement produces, nor can they control their impulsive reactions to each other. They react rather than respond, which might mean screaming, "Not again! Every goddamn Sunday I have to put up with your father's war stories?" Then slamming the door, sullenly putting on a white shirt instead of simply saying that you don't care to go to your in-laws this week.

Since neither of the partners in a stormy marriage is able to stand for long on his or her own two feet without clutching the partner for support, they cannot risk the acceptance of differences that is the bedrock of intimacy. "If we are too different," the feeling goes, "you might leave me—and then I couldn't survive."

Even divorce doesn't necessarily separate a stormy couple who continue to relate to each other negatively with life-and-death intensity. These partners often launch bitter court battles and require loyalty from their children and friends. It's as if they're always wearing "binoculars," their eyes trained on their former partner. And whatever the other does, they *react* to, usually as if they've been slapped. Other relationships pale by comparison, even a new marriage. The hatred is a strong bond that prevents them from moving on. I know one such divorced couple where the mother went to the daughter's wedding and the father to the reception. I know another couple who had separate bar mitzvah parties for their son.

The "perfect" marriage. The partners in a "perfect" marriage don't come initially for marital therapy. They come about one of the children, or the in-laws, or for an "individual" problem like depression. In the first session, they assure me, "We never argue." And I always say, "That's an ominous sign. Why not?"

Eventually I will hear either that their parents never argued and they don't know how. Or their parents never stopped arguing and they promised themselves they'd have a different kind of marriage. They don't know how to manage conflict either, having seen it go on and on and on between their parents—with no resolution. So this husband will go every Sunday to his in-laws' house—even though he'd prefer not to, without a murmur of opposition—even to himself.

Couples determined to live "in perfect harmony" can't handle any difference at all because difference always raises the possibility of conflict. Conflict, in turn, means the end of the relationship as they need it to be. Potentially divisive topics are avoided. Secrets and taboo subjects abound. Bored resignation. Resentful togetherness. Lonely isolation and, perhaps, quiet desperation. "Anger destroys me," one of my clients said, "and she knows that, so she keeps upsetting things to herself. What's wrong with that?"

What's wrong is that it rules out intimacy, the arena where you can tell someone what upsets you without their reacting to their own emotion instead of listening to what you're saying about yourself. That's how people can know each other. Without differences, there can be no intimacy.

INTIMACY: BEING TOGETHER SEPARATELY

Unfortunately, stifling togetherness is too often our ideal of romantic love. It pervades the culture and the counsel of "marriage experts," who should know better. Marriage, by extension, is imagined to be a life of such "closeness" that a person will have all his or her needs met, will never have to be lonely again or face disagreement. This is the unconditional love of a parent for an infant, which we all crave but shouldn't expect in adulthood. And yet we do.

The image of "the love of one's life" is the overly romantic one we get from most novels and films. And what relief we usually feel when, at the end, the two "true lovers" finally find each other again. But truly intimate love comes to partners who can live with give and take, and who know that despite their love, both could have been happy with others as well. In other words, their lover is their best friend instead of their salvation.

It surprises me how often I find myself saying to couples in therapy: "You need to stop thinking of yourselves as 'husband and wife' and start thinking of yourselves as friends. If he were your friend, what would you say about this problem? If she were your friend, how would you respond? For example, if your friend said, 'I want to be alone this weekend to concentrate totally on my report,' you might be disappointed, but you'd understand. So why take it personally when it's your spouse? If you can't stand your friend's best friend, you might say, 'I know how close you and Lee are, but we just don't hit it off. Do you mind if we see each other without him?' What if it were your spouse's best friend? Well, isn't it all right if your spouse has a truly separate relationship with his or her best friend? If your spouse adores sports and you loathe them, why go along to the game? If it were a friend, you'd probably just say, 'Football's not my thing, but let's you and I go to the movies on Thursday.' "

If partners could just give each other the courtesies and space they give their friends, they wouldn't be so tense or resentful. Of course, we don't feel as emotionally dependent on friends as we do on spouses. We don't usually expect friends to fill mutual infantile needs. Instead, what we expect of friends is cooperation and friendship and affectionate caring. Should we ever expect more than that from another person? Popular movies and books suggest we should.

The closest we've come in Hollywood to portrayals of what I would call love are the great comic romances of the thirties and forties, like the ones starring Katharine Hepburn and Spencer Tracy, or Fred Astaire and Ginger Rogers, where both partners have strong—mature—individuality. Of course we never see these couples after they have children, when *her* autonomy might be threatened. When, for example, if the wife no longer works, she might no longer be able to go off on dance tours with her husband, or take a stand against him in court, on the newspaper, or at the office where they tussled and played, affirmed their equality and enjoyed their friendship.

What's so appealing about those old Hollywood romantic comedies is, in a sense, how realistically unromantic they are. Instead of swooning with love, the partners genuinely like and respect each other; they're intimate—loving and close, but they're clearly capable of operating on their own, too. In truly intimate relationships, partners want to get close enough to feel the rich pleasures of togetherness, but also to remain separate enough to keep their own individuality intact. And the machinery of that regulation is in the negotiation of "trivial" details, such as housework, child care, and how daily life is lived.

What would intimacy mean in our own day-to-day married lives? It means making yourself vulnerable by telling the other your own self-doubts, fears, uncertainties, or private dreams. It requires that the other listens and acknowledges the importance of what's being said. That's it. Let's look at a couple of examples:

WIFE: Today, when Bobby kept crying and crying and I couldn't comfort him, I got so angry I hated him. It made me feel like a bad mother.

HUSBAND: How awful. I can imagine how upsetting that would be for you, especially when your own mother was so patient.

If the husband had tried to "solve the problem," as men are taught to do, and had given suggestions for handling the baby's crying, they would not only have missed an intimate moment, but also probably would have had an argument because the wife would have felt "unheard." For the same reason, an argument would certainly have followed if he had tried to reassure her that she was really a good mother or had negated her feelings by telling her she shouldn't get so angry over nothing. It's the wife's own job to reassure herself and to solve the problem of reacting to the crying.

Another intimate exchange might sound like this:

HUSBAND: I'm really worried about my standing at work since this new boss came on.

WIFE: Oh, I'm so sorry about this. I know how problems at work upset you. What's this new boss like?

Many wives, however, because of the wife's gender programming as emotional caretaker and regulator of her husband's moods, might be inclined to respond by defending their husband. "Are you kidding? There is nobody in that department who works harder than you do—nobody. And the boss will soon find that out. Come on, now, have some dinner. I made something you love." The husband may not call her to task for not responding helpfully, but he will feel unheard and alone with his worry.

Intimacy is deeply rewarding, but hard. It takes respect for the other's individuality and the ability to control impulsive reactions, really listen, and really say what's on your mind. Understanding relationships, then, in terms of each partner's need for individuality versus the pull toward togetherness heightens the meaning of day-to-day arguments. You can see that arguing with your husband or wife about work or housework, buying houses or even a new toaster, can make you feel as if you are fighting for your life.

To understand how important it is for both partners to be autonomous individuals—and that means being financially viable—let's look again at the common complaint I examined in my article on the Golden Rule: the husband is a "tightwad" and the wife a "spendthrift." The classical therapeutic technique is to cajole the husband into giving his wife an "allowance" that she can spend however she sees fit. But here's the catch. Although this adjustment may stop arguments about money temporarily, it won't right the imbalance of power in the relationship—namely, the wife's limited access to their resources. Therefore, it won't penetrate the heart of the problem, the reality that she may have lost more of her autonomy than she can bear and still be able to hold on to her individuality.

If it is the wife who earns more money than her husband, as almost one quarter of working wives now do, you would think that she, too, might become openly or even "reasonably" dominant the way husbands usually do. Instead, I usually find that the wife downplays the difference and denies her power in the relationship, as Gina does in our next case example.

MY WORK'S IMPORTANT TO ME, TOO

Like many of today's professionals, Gina and Dale waited until they were established in their careers before they married. Now, both forty, they were newly married and also expecting their first child. Because of their age, they explained, they didn't want to wait to have a child. As a result they were faced with many developmental tasks at once: setting up a marriage, facing midlife career questions, and having a child. But they weren't aware of any problem between them. In fact, the only reason they were in therapy was because Gina's gynecologist referred her to me when she told him about her recurring headaches and insomnia.

They really did seem quite happy with each other, though in a low-key, reserved way. Both of them were rather serious people. Dale, prematurely bald, with horn-rimmed glasses, beard and mustache, looked bookish. I thought, because he was mild-mannered and matter-of-fact, he might be a science professor. Actually, he was a computer programmer with an independent consulting business that he ran from their home.

Gina was an executive in her father's company, which manufactured landing gear for small aircraft. As matter-of-fact and plainspoken as Dale, she appeared to be a no-nonsense sort of woman, straightforward and unadorned both in her manner and style. Her hair was cropped short; she wore simple collarless dresses for the most part, no makeup and no jewelry except for gold button earrings. Though she looked tired and drawn—her dark eyes ringed with sleeplessness—Gina was as attractive as Dale, her face as guileless, her black hair and pale skin as striking as his auburn coloring.

They'd met when Dale created the computer program for Gina's father's business. Gina was the one in charge of such things, so they'd worked together for several weeks. Gina said she was impressed by how Dale had negotiated his contract "firmly but in a nice way." And then by how patient and clear he was in explaining the program. Dale said he admired her business sense, her knowledge of aircraft, and her understanding of how to deal with people. "Everyone in the company liked her, and I did too, though she was obviously tough. But she was fun under her somewhat *stern* exterior," he said a bit teasingly. They spoke so courteously and good-naturedly to each other, I was taken aback when one of my first questions—how much each of them earned—startled them.

Dale unhesitatingly told me he earned about $55,000 a year. But Gina, nervously—and in an offhand way—mumbled that she made $75,000. With this, Dale's jaw literally dropped. "Wait a minute," he said. "I thought you made sixty-five thousand. When did you get a raise?"

She shrugged. "Oh, yeah, just the other day my father gave everyone a raise."

"Dale, is this the first you heard about it?" I asked.

"Well, yes," he said, his eyebrows raised above the frames of his glasses.

"So, Gina, how come you didn't tell Dale? Seems like it would have been the evening news."

Gina still hadn't cracked a smile. "I thought I'd mentioned it," she said. "Anyway, it just happened. I didn't think it was important."

"But it's clearly important to Dale. Look, Gina, you've been earning more than Dale all along, and now you're earning a lot more. What do you think the impact of your different earnings has been?"

Gina thought a second, then said, "None."

Dale crossed one leg over the other. "It's true. We've been able to talk things over and come to agreements on most everything."

"Who does the housework?" I asked, and Dale said he did most of the housework—laundry, straightening, calling the plumber. He didn't mind. It gave him a break from the computer. Gina added that she always stopped at the market and made dinner when she got home. They both said things are pretty equal, and I agreed, it seemed as if they were. "But what's going to happen now, with the baby? How are you going to slip that little addition into your lives?"

They both looked utterly perplexed. "Have you talked about that?" No, they hadn't. "Well, Gina, what did you think you'd do?"

"Uhmm, take a couple of months off, maybe cut down on traveling, then go back to work four days a week. You see, there's a lot going on at work that is really satisfying to me. My work's very important to me. And now with my dad about to retire—"

Dale, who looked as if he'd seen a ghost, was suddenly sitting forward in his seat. "Wait a minute, my work's important to me, too. I get a lot of satisfaction from being able to work at home and do the work I do—"

At this point, I stopped them. "You know why this is happening, don't you? The added pressure of having a child has made your lives much more complex. Now, you've got to figure out whose job comes first, who does what for the child. And, Gina, I think you're minimizing the importance of how much money you make. Things can't work—automatically—in the same equal way unless you work it out so they do."

Gina, ever businesslike, said, "Right. So how do we work it out?"

"That's what you'll have to determine between yourselves."

Until then, Gina and Dale were equals. They each respected the other's work; they each earned their keep. But they both sensed that their lives were about to change in a way that would threaten their identities. Being newlyweds, however, they weren't comfortable yet with facing their differences and confronting the fact that each would sometimes be out purely for himself or herself—a reality that usually doesn't hit until the "honeymoon is over"—a year or two into the marriage. For that reason, they didn't just talk things over the way they had been able to do. They didn't even dare think them. As a result, Gina, who was feeling the reality of the child in her body, became symptomatic.

She, who had never been sick a day in her life, as she put it, was suddenly unable to sleep and was plagued by blinding headaches.

In addition, Gina was under some special pressure. Being firstborn, she was very much the recipient of her parents' expectations. Her father, about to retire, wanted Gina to take over the business. She didn't know what he thought she'd do about the baby, since he behaved as if her pregnancy weren't happening. At the same time, her mother made it clear that she thought Gina should stay home with her child and give up her role in the business. Gina's parents weren't talking to each other about their different attitudes, which was typical of the family style.

Gina's parents were second-generation Italian immigrants. Her mother believed in women's roles, but that included never questioning her husband, who was the undisputed head of the family. The family never aired their differences, which is how Gina learned to avoid talking about problems. But with *this* problem, the family style was leading *her* to be symptomatic. Since she had never fully become an adult in her dealings with her parents, her mother and father's conflict over her proper role was being played out through her and was obscuring her own wishes.

In the next session, when I asked Gina how she would handle her life as a mother if she didn't have to take the wishes of her mother, father, or Dale into consideration, she repeated that she'd work four days a week.

"But then I'd be upset," Dale said. "I want to do my fair share, but if you work four days a week, that leaves me with eighty percent. That's more than my fair share!"

When Dale looked to me for support, I said, "This is kind of reminiscent of what women have been complaining about for years. People take it for granted that they'll do most of the home and child care, and then don't value what they do."

"Exactly," he said, "if I were doing most of the child care, I'd probably feel like I was a househusband."

"And feel bad about it?"

"Well, yes," he said. "The world isn't going to judge me by how good a father I am. They're going to judge me by my work."

Then I asked him what his thoughts about fathering were.

"I definitely want to be involved, but the part that really scares me is the first two years. When a child is so helpless."

"What was your father like?" I wanted to know.

"Not involved," Dale said. He was the youngest of three brothers. He didn't remember his father even playing with them. "It wasn't until we were much older that he took an interest in us."

"And what do you think your father gained and lost?"

"He gained feeling that he was doing what he was supposed to do. He was very proud of his work, managing the experimental laboratories for a drug company. But he definitely lost out on the bonding part. I don't want to have that happen."

"I see from your genogram that your two brothers have children, so that makes four men in the family who must have some feelings about fatherhood. Do you ever talk about it with any of them?"

"Never."

We all laughed. It was obvious to them both that neither of their families talked things over, and further, that Dale was learning to be a father from his own very traditional father. Although he wanted to be "a significant part" of his child's life, he had no experience with children. He and his brothers did housework with their mother, but his brothers never baby-sat for him, though they were five and eight years older than Dale. They were never encouraged to take care of their little brother. Their mother did that. "So you want to bond with your child but also have the same career satisfaction that your father had?"

"Yes," Dale said. I sent them home to work out a plan so they could each have their work and parent too. Not that the lack of a practical plan was their real problem. But risking an honest discussion about their different wishes would be an important step for their marriage. Their real problem was figuring out what their own wishes and beliefs were in the midst of conflicting expectations their families and society held for them.

What they came up with was that they would each work three consecutive days a week and hire a part-time nanny to cover the overlapping day and to help the parent who was "on."

"Good," I said. "You each got some of what you needed and

gave up something, too. Now comes the hard part. What are you going to tell your folks, Gina? And Dale, how are you going to learn to be a different kind of father?"

Dale agreed to begin talking to his father and brothers about fathering in order to open new lines of family communication and better define fathering for himself. The prospect of doing child care made Dale feel in danger of losing his autonomy, the part of his self he had been taught to value most. But motivated by his desire for a close relationship with the child he awaited, he learned in therapy to connect better to others. Although this process took a lot of time and work with his family, Gina's problem was even more difficult. Therefore I'll give more details about that work in order to give you an idea of what's involved when we really confront issues of individuality.

Gina was caught between a rock and a hard place: her father's wish for her help in preserving his business and her own ambition, on the one side; on the other, her mother's (and the culture's) insistence that a mother's place is home with her child and Gina's own desire to be a "good mother." In getting herself out of the middle of her parents' silent struggle on this issue, for the first time, she had to think through to her own position and then take a personal stand with her parents. By doing so she paved the way for assuming a more mature adult role with them instead of the powerless child role she'd always taken before.

Gina's inability to disagree with her parents had a long complicated history. This is true for everyone who has trouble being themselves with their parents (which means *everyone*). Gina's younger brother had a drug-abuse problem and lived a dissolute life, neither of which was acknowledged by the family. With her brother being the rebellious child, Gina became "the good one," a role so rewarded by her parents, she found herself unable to disagree with them at all lest they be disappointed in their "perfect daughter." So Gina went underground with her real self, telling her parents only what they wanted to hear. When they each wanted to hear different or opposite things, the frustration would turn to anger at her mother.

Although Gina said she was "much closer" to her father, who didn't discuss family disagreements with her, her answers to my questions revealed that she wasn't, in fact, closer to her father, she just felt more warmly toward him. In reality, Gina and her father seldom discussed anything except business, and she acknowledged that she had little idea of what made him "tick." On the other hand, she knew her mother very well, since they talked about their feelings and the family. Gina, however, was also angry at her mother for the pressure she felt from her always to agree or else be accused of taking her father's side. Unable to express her own feelings, Gina would flush, lower her eyes, and be silent. I believed that description because I saw her do the same thing whenever she disagreed with Dale.

One thing was clear. Gina had to learn to disagree with her mother and then deal with her mother's anger over her "taking her father's side" by returning to work. She had to understand that although her mother might feel that Gina was betraying her and rejecting her whole way of life, Gina knew that wasn't true, and she had to do what she believed was best for herself and her own new family. She also had to break the silence about the coming baby and its consequences in her life—and all the family issues—that continued between herself and her father.

"You go along with his unexpressive style so he won't be uncomfortable with you," I said to Gina, "and you end up hardly knowing each other. Can you really understand Dale—and let him know you—if you can't have a real talk with your own father? How would you feel if you found yourself complaining to your daughter one day because you couldn't openly disagree with Dale?"

It took quite a few such questions and quite a few months for Gina to begin talking to her parents in a new way. Every time we discussed the "worst things her parents could say" and also who her parents were—their childhoods, their Italian backgrounds, etc.—it helped reduce her anxiety about changing her relationship with them. In fact, her earliest talks with them were simply about their memories of their own families growing up. These talks excited Gina because they allowed her to understand her parents better; they also prepared her for telling them about the parenting arrangement she and Dale agreed on. Before each talk with them, she'd have a sleepless night. After, she was exhilarated: "When my mother said—'So you're giving up your family life to please your father,' I didn't get angry at all. I simply said, 'No, Mom, it has nothing to do with dad—it's what I want,' I just felt ten feet tall." At one talk with her father she said, "I'm going to raise my own child, Dad, and I'm going to work as well. I can do my job in three days instead of five." Slowly the voice of Gina, the adult woman, emerged as she calmly told her mother and father what she did and did not plan to do, what she thought and felt. After that, expressing her thoughts and feelings to Dale came easier all the time.

Gina and Dale's renegotiation was relatively easy to accomplish. For one thing, they were relatively mature to begin with. For another, they caught it early before they'd built up resentments and destructive patterns of interacting. Also, they had enough money to allow the luxury of choices. Gina was more willing to relinquish the power her higher earnings gave her than a man in her position might be, and she couldn't ignore the parenting role as a man might have. Most important, Gina and Dale both were willing to do the emotional work with their parents that would make such changes possible and lasting.

Generally, when women earn more, both husband and wife believe that the husband's autonomy—his "masculine" self—is threatened by her higher earnings and/or status. They may both worry that society will recognize him more for his connection to her than for his own achievements. Sometimes a successful woman will worry that while her husband may actually be self-sufficient, he may no longer *feel* self-sufficient. Because women value men's autonomy, couples like Gina and Dale in which women are the higher earners will be *more* motivated to confront the problem of a power imbalance than couples in which the men earn more money. And, as in all couples, if the power imbalance is confronted soon enough, it can prevent a split during the early childrearing years.

In this case, the work increased Gina's autonomy and Dale's abilities to connect emotionally. Strengthening their individuality in this way increased the likelihood that they could establish for themselves a level of intimacy that they had not seen growing up. They had also clarified their own beliefs and were thus less likely to react impulsively to past or future pressures to return to old familiar roles. They were now set on a different, more equal path.

In our last session together, Gina was very pregnant but also rested, excited about the birth, and tremendously interested in pursuing her new adult identity. I asked them how their relationship had changed. Dale said he felt much closer to Gina, as if they really knew each other. "We argue a bit more, I'll say that, but I'm getting used to it." And Gina added pensively, "I'm amazed that it's okay to just say what we're thinking about. We never did in my family. And I used to think that just having differences would break up a marriage. That it meant people didn't really love each other. Now I think it means we do."

Not all women define themselves by their work, as Gina did. However, those who define themselves primarily as homemakers have a harder time changing than Gina or Sharon. If, like Dottie, they do try to change, their marriages often prove far less flexible than dual-earner marriages.

If marriage and family are the main focus of life, they must understand the consequences, just as Dale did instinctively. They put their autonomy at great risk, and therefore they put their marriage at risk as well. Without two autonomous individuals, there can be no intimacy. A husband and wife must both be self-sufficient individuals or one partner will be more dependent on the marriage for a sense of purpose and self-esteem than the other partner, and that's when intimacy fades. As revolutionary as this idea may seem, suffragist Susan B. Anthony expressed it in 1875:

> Marriage, to women as to men, must be a luxury; an incident of life, not all of it. And the only possible way to accomplish this great change is to accord to women equal power in the making, shaping and controlling of the circumstances of life.

In other words, when people stop controlling the circumstances of their lives, they will lose the individuality they cultivated before marriage. Use it or lose it, as the saying goes.

6

Matrimonial Duets
Power Games and Power Plays

I worked with a couple once where the husband was the president of a well-known sportswear company. Laurence had had absolute power for so long, he was oblivious to his abuse of it. When, during one of their sessions, his wife expressed her grief that their toddler was more attached to the nanny than to her because she worked such long hours, her husband said, "Well, just fire the nanny and get a new one. That's what I always do when anyone gets too attached to someone besides me at work."

His shocking suggestion jolted his wife into a new assessment of the situation, and of her marriage. Miko, who was herself a coat designer for a popular outerwear company, said she wouldn't dream of firing someone who did such good work. "It would be unfair to her and unfair to the baby." With my help Miko realized that even though she felt bad, it wasn't the nanny's fault, and soon she decided to take one afternoon off a week to spend with her daughter alone. She also instituted a "five o'clock rule." This meant that the office went on notice that she left every day at five and could be reached—for emergencies—at home.

That was the easy part. During the next session, Miko only wanted to talk about one thing: "How could you make such a suggestion? It chilled my blood," she said to Laurence. "That's really how you think about people, isn't it?"

What Miko realized is the fundamental difference in the way she and her husband used power. Laurence exploited his power over others. He hired and fired on whim, made the "help" walk on tiptoes, and, as Miko was slowly understanding, vetoed all her decisions that differed from his. "I didn't make demands before the baby. There was no need. Now, I do." Miko had quite a bit of worldly power in her own right, but not nearly as much as Laurence. The power she used, however, wasn't the *power over* but the *power to*. In this case, she had the power to reorganize her own relationship to the baby so she didn't need to use her power over the nanny and child to feel better.

Miko certainly enjoyed the spoils of Laurence's power and her own: the lavish lifestyle, the people who always wanted to wine and dine them, but she had never before realized what it was based on, and it created something of an ethical dilemma for her.

"POWER IS THE GREAT APHRODISIAC"

When Kissinger made that remark in 1971, everyone knew he was talking about *power over:* the ability to dominate, and that he was referring only to men! Our culture reinforces the idea that men will and should have "power over," even progressive "new men" who handle power in subtler ways. Powerful women, on the other hand—and I mean women with the "power to"—are not considered alluring. Actually, they've usually been demonized, called "feminazis" on talk radio, portrayed as scary, heartless, and in the Hollywood version, even homicidal.

Domination, however, isn't really attractive for very long in anyone. In fact, I think of it as a perversion of real power, which is access to options and control over your own life. As I tell my clients, the difference between "power over" and "power to" is sort of like the difference between bad and good cholesterol: only the good kind of power is an asset.

Classical couples therapy, based as it is on the ideas of reciprocity and complementarity, mutes the difference in power between the sexes. The assumption in this kind of therapy is that both partners contribute in some way to a marital problem. True, but I had to learn to ask, is the contribution *equal*? Is the ability to resolve the problem *equal*? Only then did I realize that a wife's nagging about her husband's work schedule isn't only a reciprocal part of the problem. It is the *result* of the work schedule. And even when the man "feels" powerless, he often still has enough concrete power in the form of salary to block his wife's attempts to change their relationship. Her nagging can't make him come home earlier if he doesn't want to. If her nagging gets unbearable for him, he can leave the marriage and continue to work as much as he wants. On the other hand, if his long work hours become unbearable to her, stopping nagging won't bring him home, and if she leaves the marriage, her standard of living will probably plummet. So who has the real power here?

Times *are* changing, thank goodness, and younger women, at least, are beginning to appreciate the difference between bad and good power, feelings and facts. They're more comfortable acknowledging their desire for the power to be in charge of their lives than their mothers were. In a recent *Esquire* poll of what women want, the editors concluded that "this generation would rather be a workaholic wife like Hillary Clinton than a princess like Di. . . . They'd rather have a Pulitzer Prize than Miss America's crown. And if they admire Madonna, it's Madonna the CEO more than Madonna the sex symbol."

Yet as much as these young women want power, within their relationships, men will often have more. And men who have most of the power in a relationship must solve the problem of unequal power by sharing the power. Women must give up their culturally instilled desire to relinquish power and be taken care of by a man. Otherwise, distrust and resentment will gradually erode the love and companionship partners once enjoyed.

LOVE AND THE ART OF NEGOTIATION

When Sam and I were having our round-robin fights about whether I should go back to work after our first son was born, negotiation was the furthest thought from our minds. We fought the way lovers do—taking it personally, calling it a lack of love and caring, being rejected and "hurt," and bringing in expert witnesses (Betty Friedan vs. Freud). In addition, I contributed copious tears and sobbing.

This was a power struggle. I was challenging Sam's—and certainly society's—definition of the "correct" marital structure: husband at work, wife home with the children. On the surface, Sam had all the power. He earned our income, and his was the socially sanctioned position. I had a few wild cards, however. I had worked in Europe and New York for ten years before Bennett's birth at what passed for a "career" in office management in those days, and so could legitimately claim "special difficulties" in adjusting to staying home. Most importantly, my old boss was a good friend and would let me return to work at whatever part-time hours suited me.

But before we could begin to negotiate, we had to stop fighting and start listening to each other. Finally, our therapist and friends helped us to calm down enough to have quiet, nonaccusatory discussions. I discovered that Sam's definition of "good husband" was completely threatened by my idea of returning to work. He thought it meant I didn't trust him to provide for us. Sam learned that working had become a fulfilling way of life for me and that I wasn't rejecting him and the family; I just wanted something for myself. He also found out that I did realize that my earnings would just about cover child care and commuting costs, but I wanted to do it anyway—for the experience itself—to hold on to a part of myself that I valued: the person who did interesting things out in the world.

In effect, I was asking Sam to share the marital power with me because it would make me happier to live that way; because it was so important to me. I wouldn't yet be earning as much as he, but I would earn enough to go out to work if I wanted. I don't like to think what might have happened if he had refused. But finally, reassured that it was not a move directed against him, he agreed—"so long as it's not full-time." I happily assured him that it would only be two and a half days a week—"if you can get home a little earlier on those days, for the baby."

At the end of these discussions, which we never realized were full-scale "negotiations," we concluded our dispute with each of us having gotten something important to us, and neither of us having given in entirely. And we now understood for the first time the reasons for the other's position.

The most important outcome of that first renegotiation of our couple-contract, of course, was the unspoken agreement to share power and responsibility: Sam gave up some of his power as "head of the household," and I started down the road toward sharing the responsibility for household finances. More than anything else in our history together, I think this agreement set the stage for the development of our marriage into the strong lasting bond that it became.

Sometimes, instead of appearing as conflict, a couple's differences or problem areas become taboo topics. A rule of thumb is: *the taboo subjects in a relationship are the areas of real disagreement.* But the partners may feel that broaching such subjects could disrupt or even break up their marriage. Gina, for example, a powerful executive, was afraid to bring up the thorny subject of child care with Dale. She had made some assumptions about their parenting arrangement silently because voicing them was too frightening to her. But to maintain the togetherness of her relationship, she developed headaches and insomnia instead of raising the subject with Dale. That's why their power imbalance was about to turn into a power struggle—albeit in reversed gender roles—without their ever knowing what went wrong.

When Dale heard Gina's plan for child care, he disagreed strongly, but had they not been in therapy, he might have backed away from her assertiveness about it. Then resentment and distrust would have created tremendous tension between a previously happy couple. However, when Gina and Dale honestly acknowledged their power imbalance and decided their equality was important to them, the power struggle ceased; they were able to air their disagreement and then negotiate a fair arrangement.

WHEN MATRIMONIAL DUETS BECOME TRIOS

Gina and Dale are the kind of couple therapists identify as "pseudo-mutual" because they never argue. They are the kind of couple that fits into the "perfect marriage" pattern I described in the last chapter. Either they learned to avoid arguing in their original families, as was the case with them, or a couple's "togetherness" is of such importance they can't risk acknowledging *any* differences. Newly remarried couples are often like this when both partners are scarred by divorce wars. So are immature partners who cannot bear the tension between individuality and togetherness.

However, you don't have to be pseudo-mutual or newly remarried to avoid conflict. In all twosomes, disagreement creates anxiety because it threatens that wonderful sense of togetherness. But because disagreement and difference are inevitable, if they aren't acknowledged, they will express themselves somehow, perhaps in a spouse's symptom, like Gina's headaches, or in conflict over trivial or "safe" subjects, like style or politics. Most frequently, however, couples "triangulate" in the face of difference, turning their duet into a trio *by involving a third party*. Maybe they'll exaggerate their superficial disagreement about whether their teenage daughter Kimberly can stay out past eleven o'clock in order to mask their *real* disagreements. By locking themselves into an ongoing problem with another person (Kimberly), they deflect the attention from themselves. In relation to Kimberly, after all, they can argue without putting their own relationship on the line, or their parental concern can draw them closer just when they might have been feeling dangerously separate.

Triangulation is so common in relationships that it often goes unnoticed. So adaptable, it can take many different forms: partners may have as their focus a so-called problem child whom they argue over or join together to "help"; a husband may be having an affair; a wife may be having her most intimate emotional relationship with her best friend or her therapist. Whatever the form, the function of a triangle is always the same: triangles reduce the anxiety between partners—a third person either absorbs the anxiety or provides a refuge from it. By distracting partners from their real disagreements, triangles help them to maintain the illusion that they never *fundamentally* disagree. It's easier for partners to "fight" about someone else or seek emotional refuge with another than to confront each other about their actual dissatisfactions or needs within the relationship.

The price tag for handling anxiety about differences by triangulating is that the differences cannot be resolved. The anxiety is just detoured, and the twosome becomes more emotionally distant (as in the case of one partner's having an affair) or they substitute togetherness for intimacy (as in the case of avoiding their own differences by joining to help a "problem child"). Think about how alcohol or drugs reduce a person's anxiety at great cost to their health and functioning. Entrenched triangles do the same thing for the couple's emotional health and functioning.

Eugene and Devita had been married ten years and had two small children, Gene Jr., four, and April, two. Eugene was an engineer, and Devita worked part-time as a drug counselor. She had cut back her work schedule when April was born, and Eugene had agreed to cut out overtime and travel. Instead, he took an unexpected promotion although it meant he worked later and traveled more than before. When Devita complained, he silenced her by reminding her that she had agreed to the promotion and they needed the money. True as that was, Devita began to feel whispers of fear that Eugene didn't want to spend more time with her and the children and found his main happiness in his career.

One day, in a flood of tears, she confided her fears to her older sister. Her sister, Dolores, comforted and reassured her that Eugene really loved her—"Men are just like that." In the next month, Devita confided more and more in Dolores, telling her all her complaints about Eugene: he missed Gene Jr.'s nursery school picnic; he forgot their anniversary; he no longer called her punctually at 6:00 P.M. whenever he was away. Sometimes Dolores joined in Devita's anger at Eugene, sometimes she pooh-poohed it, but Devita always felt better after they talked. It kept her from feeling so angry at Eugene, and she stopped complaining to him. Sometimes she was so preoccupied with her own thoughts that he would ask her if she was okay. "Was anything the matter?" But she would just smile and tell him she was thinking about work.

Devita was no longer afraid that Eugene didn't care about her because, to tell the truth, she found herself less inclined to think about him at all. Marriage was really too hard, she thought. Her sister Dolores was having a hard time with her own husband, Craig. Dolores complained to Devita about him, but unlike Devita, Dolores also took the complaints to Craig and insisted that they do something about them. So Craig and Dolores were struggling with their issues while Eugene and Devita were silently withdrawing from each other.

I met Devita and Eugene several years later when she asked him for a divorce. Dolores and Craig had moved away and were doing well, she told me.

Devita and Eugene eventually worked things out, but the turning point in their therapy didn't come until I asked Devita when she'd given up on Eugene. She burst into tears and told me about how she had brushed those whispers of fear aside and stopped complaining. When I heard about the triangle with her sister, I understood how Devita had contained her anxiety but then failed to resolve the issues with Eugene. When Dolores moved away, some other "solution" was needed.

Triangles come and go daily in the lives of all of us. We whisper to each other instead of complaining to the boss; we laugh about our parents' foibles with a sibling; we roll our eyes with one friend at the antics of another. These and other fleeting triangles are inconsequential. But when a particular triangle recurs rigidly over time and prevents family members from dealing with important emotional issues, the result is serious trouble in the emotional system.

The most common triangles for couples are those with one or more children and with in-laws, especially mothers-in-law. Affairs create a most destructive triangle, as does any intimate relationship that replaces the spouse, such as therapist, best friends, or colleagues. Ultimately, undoing a family triangle requires deconstructing gender roles so that there are three separate appropriate twosomes: father and child need to have a significant relationship that can stand on its own; mother and child need theirs; and partners have to have their own intimate personal relationship.

Each spouse needs to conduct a personal relationship with his or her own mother and father, and not expect their wives to do it for them, as men are taught, or to exclude their spouse, as women sometimes do when relating to their mothers and sisters. Once again, society's rules that put women in charge of children and extended family make these balanced personal twosomes harder to imagine or to accomplish. At the same time, these gender rules burden both men and women with tasks that lead them away from each other.

If married partners cannot face their real disagreements with each other and/or if the power imbalances between them prevent negotiation so they have no way to resolve their differences, relationships do not change and grow. That's when triangles flourish and couples become stuck in whatever power games they play. Unfortunately, these games don't change the power relations that imperiled one partner's autonomy and the other's emotional connectedness to begin with. And then you have a stalemate.

POWER GAMES

After triangulation, the three most common stalemates in a marriage are what I call the power games of tug-of-war, pursuit and distance, and seesaw. And as you'll see, they all create such high anxiety, the "players'" next step will be a triangle after all, and then there goes mother-in-law, the kids, his secretary, her ornery brother, any of whom might get roped in to "restabilize" the couple. In this section, I'm going to present a series of "snapshots" from different couples' lives so that you'll see the same power issues played out in different ways, and in the several different "up-down" roles of the seesaw.

Tug-of-War

Partners involved in a tug-of-war are the only ones who do confront differences directly; however, they're locked into their power battle and can't get out. A battle, remember, is never a reasoned negotiation. They don't really understand the terms of their battle. All they know is either that they both want to be the boss—this I call the "seniority" struggle—or both want to be taken care of, which is the "juniority" struggle. In the first case, partners are often both oldest or only children who may have had too much responsibility in their original families. The second is most likely to occur between partners who are both younger or youngest siblings and have been babied or neglected. Let's look at how they work.

1. THE SENIORITY STRUGGLE: **Andrew and Janet**

> JANET: He turned our daughters against me, telling them I gamble secretly and have affairs. Ridiculous ideas, both of them.
>
> ANDREW: I never said any such thing to the girls, but they're both true anyway. And why did she tell them I was an alcoholic?

They were an elegant pair, both lawyers, though Janet, serving liberal causes the conservative Andrew noisily disapproved of, earned only a tenth of what he did. The girls were away at college, and although Andrew and Janet sought therapy to improve communication, all they did was attack each other. Every argument represented a judgment on one another or an attempt to get the other to be like them. Every step of their therapy reflected their power struggle. Both phoned me between sessions to "correct" what the other had related in the session. During sessions, I had to constantly break up their bickering over such "facts" as whether Andrew was an alcoholic. For them, therapy was just another opportunity to vindicate self and blame the other; in other words, to win. It's hard to believe such a marriage had endured for thirty years, but remember "bitter enemies" are often very close; it's just that intense anger had replaced what was once distance.

Janet and Andrew had never negotiated any difference. Instead, they handled their anxiety with alcohol, gambling, mutual workaholism, triangulating their daughters, having affairs, and trying to control each other. She, as the oldest child of an alcoholic mother, had "survived" by her ability to "control." And he, as the only child of elderly and infirm parents, had done the same. Powerful as they both seemed, they weren't strong enough to face the demands of individuality. Nor were any of the therapists they went to able to help them.

Remarkably, after thirty years, the power game had become a way of life for Janet and Andrew. If either one had suddenly decided to cooperate or change for the better, that one would "lose" the game. Had they come for therapy earlier, they probably could have broken their deadlock. For when two such "over-responsible" take-charge types focus their attention on *themselves*, they are usually able to make a significant amount of change on their *own* unresolved problems, which are, after all, the only problems anyone can really change.

2. The Juniority Struggle: Susan and Gabriel

> GABRIEL: Why can't she understand what I'm going through at work? It's my third job in three years. I need her support.
>
> SUSAN: He used to give me back rubs, put my head in his lap and I'd tell him about the day. He doesn't listen to me anymore.

These two fought constantly, too, but their complaints were very different from Janet and Andrew's. They weren't angry so much as hurt and whiny, like tired children. All their complaints boiled down to "he/she doesn't nurture me."

Susan and Gabriel had had their first child three years before and had been fighting ever since. Clearly, now that they had to nurture a child, they couldn't nurture each other to the enormous extent they had: spending all their time together, buying surprise presents, cooking favorite meals, etc. The stress of having a child was harder for them than it normally is because they both felt so needy. Gabriel's father, who was also the youngest in his family, was a "failure" at work and a sporadic provider; his mother had been too overwhelmed by money problems and the four children who came before Gabriel to give him much special attention. Susan's parents were the opposite—successful and extremely attentive to their three children, especially "baby" Susan. In other words, both Susan and Gabriel struggled over who would be "taken care of" though they did so because of almost opposite childhood experiences.

As in most juniority struggles, Susan and Gabriel "appeared" to be equally powerless. Their fight was covert, marked by tears, sulking, recriminations, helplessness, incompetence, and mutual blame for their problems. However, like many couples in juniority struggles—and unlike partners who both want control—Susan and Gabriel did have some intensely good times with each other and a warm sex life. They both wanted the stalemate to end but didn't know how to break it.

It is often very difficult to break a juniority power struggle because neither partner is used to taking charge of him or herself, and that's what's required. During one of our sessions, I finally said to them, "You seem like two people in the middle of the lake drowning and grabbing each other around the throat. And you know, both of you are capable of swimming to shore by yourselves. All you need from each other are some encouraging words and an occasional supporting shoulder." They got the point, and soon began to ask each other for less and depend more on themselves. Gabriel said he "caught himself" every time he was about to blame Susan for his own problem, "like not having energy for our daughter because I have so many problems at work that I come home upset." They both had a lot of growing up to do, but at least now they weren't making it harder for each other.

Pursuit and Distancing

I recently saw the following videotape of a female therapist's session with a couple in their thirties.

ISABEL: All he does is work. The kids and I hardly see him during the week, and on weekends he wants to run over to his office for a few more hours.

CHRISTIAN: *(Grimaces, folds arms across his chest.)*

THERAPIST: Isabel, perhaps if you weren't always reminding Christian about what his responsibilities are, he might take charge of them himself?

This therapist is typical. According to classical theory, one partner distances in order to preserve the emotional space necessary for the individuals to feel (though not necessarily really be) autonomous while the pursuer gives voice to the couple's togetherness needs. And despite the fact that we all know which gender is taught to play which role most often, therapists still suggest by their intervention that it's the wife's problem. If she would stop pursuing, her husband would stop distancing.

Too many therapists, reflecting their own gender socialization, fail to see this as a gendered pas de deux. Instead, they interpret the power game as a one-sided "intrusion" by the woman into the man's (sacred) space. They see the man's distancing solely as an understandable response to her nagging and tell the woman that if she "backs off" the man will stop running away and move toward her. The sad truth, however, is that maybe he will but *probably* he won't.

As a group, therapists don't question why its almost always the woman "pursuing" the man with her checklist of emotional items to be taken care of: "call your mother, ask Jessie how his overnight was, think about what you'd like to do for our anniversary." Too many therapists protect men from emotional involvement with their families that could "threaten their work," "anger them," or "make them leave therapy." And so the game continues to get played even after the couple leaves the therapist's office. Or perhaps eventually she will "back off" and satisfy her emotional needs (and their children's) without him. And then, down the line, they'll find themselves strangers to each other, like Eugene and Devita. The real work is helping both of the partners to change. The wife might well have to focus more on her own options, and she'll most certainly need help doing that. And the husband almost always needs to take more emotional responsibility in the family, and always needs help learning how.

Seesaw

When couples seesaw, one partner up while the other is down, the partners may feel "glued together." They may feel, and even look to others, as if they're perfectly complementary. Opposites attract, don't they? In fact, these marriages can be extremely enduring because the partners are involved in a power game whose terms they both accept. Depending on their original families, they might think this is the way life is. Also, these roles will often seem "normal" simply because they are so culturally familiar. Think about how many of these couples you recognize from family, acquaintances, film and fiction, and maybe your own life:

1. the Angry Mommy and the Naughty Boy
2. the Princess and the Commoner
3. the Dreamer and the Doer
4. the Steamroller and the Doormat
5. the Doctor and the Patient
6. the Boss and the Secretary

Familiar as the roles are, however, they mask emotional avoidance, marital stagnation, and sexual boredom. The marriage may "endure" (like Janet and Andrew's), but the couple cannot grow, either together or individually. However they appear to others, in private they are lonely and pained.

Most of these roles are gender related. They can also be played by both sexes and in same-sex relationships although in somewhat different form. They don't necessarily reflect directly on the real power relations, which are often the opposite. For example, a woman who has no real power might become "angry mommy" to her husband who earns $300,000 a year. He may *appear* henpecked even though their life choices are his. In all the one-up one-down pairs, the partners are adapting to the unequal power conferred by money and/or success in the outside world.

As you read through the examples, think about how fundamentally similar they are.

1. THE ANGRY MOMMY AND THE NAUGHTY BOY: Toni and Nick

> TONI: Life's just not a bowl of cherries with three kids. All he does is play, like ruining their appetites when I've made a big dinner, joking with them about "the momster." That's what they call me. He's like having another kid.

> NICK: She has a rule for everything and a fit if I don't obey. We used to be great partygoers, a fun couple, but she's become a mad housewife.

Looking at Toni's tense face and Nick's easygoing manner, it would be easy to believe that Nick's the fun-loving nice guy while Toni's a controlling bitch. Now it turned out that Nick was afraid of his wife's anger, as he also was of his mother's. His reserved New England mother, he told me, "Could chill the room with mild annoyance." And when I asked him for an example of Toni's "rules" he said, "Well, just this morning I poured the kids' juice into the grown-up glasses instead of the children's glasses and she made me do it all over." And if you just told her you decided to use these glasses today? "She'd blow the roof down," he said. "Oh, you mean she'd get angry?" I asked, and Nick immediately understood. We talked about how he was "allergic" to anger and had learned to use evasion and "horseplay" to placate both his mother and his wife. But this was his problem, not Toni's.

In therapy he found new nonreactive, direct ways to disagree with his mother and to disagree with his wife, so he no longer needed the children to gang up on her. Little by little, freed from the triangle with the kids, his real conflicts with Toni surfaced. For example, as a commercial artist, Nick was making a good salary, but Toni kept pressuring him to ask his boss for a raise. Nick resented this enormously and finally was able to tell her he was earning as much as the other senior artists at the agency and didn't feel comfortable asking for more.

Toni understood a portion of their game, that Nick was sabotaging her parenting, allying himself with the children against her instead of parenting responsibly. But what Toni didn't see was that to stop the power game she needed to explore her role. As the oldest daughter in a close-knit Hispanic family, she had spent her childhood training for career motherhood. By making herself the expert, there was no room for Nick's parenting except as her assistant. And by having no life outside the family, she was losing her sense of self.

After a lot of work with her mother, Toni began to figure out what she wanted to do when she "grew up." After talking with friends and researching career possibilities in the library, she decided to capitalize on being bilingual. She soon settled on a training course for simultaneous translation, and once she started going to school, she was grateful for Nick's taking over at home. "Whatever juice glasses he uses are fine," she laughed. The two of them, I noticed, were laughing a lot more, and I could finally see the "fun couple" Nick had nostalgically described.

2. THE PRINCESS AND THE COMMONER: Jennifer and David

DAVID: I can't stand her needless show-offy spending. She doesn't know the meaning of a dollar because she's never worked. First her father supported her and now I do. She's a princess and I'm supposed to pay the bills.

JENNIFER: David has always lacked taste. He'll let us run around in rags so he can buy another car and gamble.

It was soon obvious that both Jennifer and David were serious consumers but disapproved of what each other consumed. Jennifer shopped *daily* for home furnishings and clothes for herself and their two little girls. They had a maid, nanny, baby-sitter, and gardener. David, a divorce lawyer "to the stars," had three cars, traveled, and played the stock market, which she deplored.

Indeed, Jennifer came from a privileged background. She'd studied art history at a fine women's college and had been her doting father's "princess." David initially admired her "class."

He'd come from a rough neighborhood and had gone to a city college, but at his prestigious law school, he'd been exposed to "the elite." In the early years their marriage worked. But not for long.

The princess is usually a benevolent version of the angry mommy. But her imperiousness reveals just as much desire for power. Jennifer had the power to buy things, but she never cultivated real autonomy for herself, nor did she have any clout in their marriage. When I probed, I learned that David did almost nothing with his family, preferring to race cars on the weekends, go to car auctions, or take yachting trips with friends (where his children weren't welcome).

Although at first Jennifer seemed like the more inflexible one, she turned out to be much more open to change. For one thing, she was lonely in her marriage and very much pained by David's lack of interest in her and the children. For another, her family "gave her everything," but they had expected her to "do wonderful things with her life," and she very much regretted not having "done anything," as she put it. She completely changed her little-girl deferential relationship with her father and then turned her attention to the marriage. When Jennifer understood the power game she and David played, she was determined to stop it. She began the process by returning to school for a master's so she could do museum work, a world in which she had many "connections" to help her.

David, who actually had the decision-making power in the marriage—and used it—wouldn't give an inch. He practically came out and said that he had worked so hard for the status he had, he wasn't about to give it up. He constantly tried to sabotage Jennifer's efforts to change, laughing at her "schoolgirl number" and continuing to live his separate life. They left therapy after Jennifer changed, so I don't know what happened. My guess is that Jennifer would end up getting a divorce because David wouldn't stop playing the game and actually preferred a "trophy wife" to a real companion. Perhaps she decided to borrow power from her own family's wealth instead of waiting to inherit it later in life.

3. THE DREAMER AND THE DOER: Anita and Gordon

> ANITA: All he does is sit around the house thinking up "black" get-rich-quick schemes, like franchising Sylvia's soul food. That's this week. Meanwhile, I'm bringing home the only check, but he went out and bought the kids a computer when I told him we couldn't afford it.

> GORDON: My kids are going to have the same advantages as any white kid. Besides, we've been having fun with it. I'll be bringing in some money soon.

Gordon's Black Arts Company, promoting African-American furniture, crafts, and art, had failed almost a year before. His brother, who had been his partner, had found another job, but Gordon hadn't. Anita was a caseworker for the city, earning $40,000 a year. It was enough to support the family because they lived in a house owned by her aunt and only "sometimes paid rent." Also, Anita did a great deal of overtime. While Gordon did take care of the children after school, he did no housework, not that Anita wanted him to. She wanted him to get a "realistic" job—any job—so she could stay home more with her kids.

"You used to say blacks needed dreams. You didn't want me to get a nine-to-five job," Gordon said.

"But, Gordon, we have two kids, and I can't keep this up," Anita answered.

Anita had always planned to work but wanted a "break" and was afraid she'd end up being the sole support of her family like her mother had been. Her mother "did nothing but work," leaving her younger sister to raise Anita and her brothers. Knowing how much she missed her mother growing up, she wanted more time with her children.

Many therapists might have accepted Anita's goal without examining the couple's power struggle. As the "doer," Anita held the cards but didn't want to. However, she also didn't have the power to change things around. By the end of therapy, Anita had agreed that Gordon's dreams mattered. As long as Gordon brought home at least $25,000 a year from a steady job, she'd stop criticizing his schemes to "do well by doing good." She also came to understand that *her* dream of the happy stay-at-home wife was a Hollywood delusion and was content to cut out overtime and take the sabbatical that was available to her. In addition, Anita had the hard job of talking directly and honestly with her aunt to clarify the question of "rent." She was thrilled when her aunt thanked her for bringing up the subject and finally gave them the house.

"You know," Anita said, "my aunt really raised us, and I was the oldest so, as she said, 'You earned that house taking care of all the little kids, including mine.'" Now that the lines of communication were open between her aunt and herself, Anita said she felt closer to her mother as well. They'd all been afraid to talk about their relationships for fear the sisters would be jealous or angry about Anita's "loyalty." Once she could talk "as an adult" with her mother and aunt, she found it much easier to let Gordon know what she wanted and thought. Gordon had his emotional work cut out for him, too. As the baby of his family and the "talented" one, he'd been indulged by parents and siblings. Gordon had to learn to accommodate his goals to his family's needs as well as his own. After much trial and error, he ended up running a community after-school arts program for kids and spent mornings trying to set up an art gallery. When they left therapy, they were headed in a direction that looked good for both of them.

4. THE STEAMROLLER AND THE DOORMAT: **Elaine and Donald**

ELAINE: *(Weeping uncontrollably)* I just want to move back to the city, that's all.

DONALD: She just needs to get out and find volunteer programs where she'll meet other women. She could join the health club. It's a gorgeous new one, practically a social center.

Elaine had agreed to move to a Massachusetts town because Donald, a textile designer, had been offered an excellent job with a factory there. But she was miserable in "the sticks," had made no friends, and wasn't able to find any work at all, much less work that was comparable to her previous job directing a successful program for inner-city kids in New York.

While she wept and explained, Donald, a handsome, easygoing young man with an impish smile, just sat back in his chair, one leg crossed over the other knee, and gave his advice at every juncture. Since Elaine was somewhat disheveled and hysterical, a therapist might have bought into Donald's self-help program for his wife, believing that she was failing to adjust to a perfectly reasonable situation. But Elaine had clearly relinquished too much power to maintain her sense of self, about which she was now absolutely clear: she liked the urban life and needed her work. Moving had been a mistake. She'd done it because Donald, who both earned more and was more self-assured, had "steamrollered over her," dismissing her every objection. Her constant refrain was, "I told you I didn't want to go."

"Well," I finally asked, "why did you?" and that began our exploration of their covert power struggle. Elaine had given up power because she thought she had to. "Every woman I know moves where their husbands work," she said. "How can I deny him this opportunity?"

"You both need opportunities," I told her. "It won't help Donald if you sacrifice your life for his career."

Although he had expected me to help her adjust, Donald had to agree. "And it won't help either of us if you keep having tantrums." They decided on a temporary separation to decide what to do. When I encouraged Elaine to think about what she really wanted, she—alone—went back to the city, and back to the job she had left. Their "deal" was that they would make a final decision about their marriage six months later, and meanwhile they'd meet in my office for therapy as well as on weekends for "dates." Like all steamrollers, Donald needed to learn to listen to what his wife said she wanted instead of insisting on his own preferences and giving her *endless* suggestions as to what she should do. Once back in the city, Elaine blossomed again, and they worked hard on their relationship. He finally decided that the career move wasn't worth his marriage and also returned to New York. For her part, Elaine equalized the power between them by taking her job seriously and learning to speak forthrightly about what she wanted. Once she saw she could do that, she no longer felt caught between tantrums and giving in.

5. THE DOCTOR AND THE PATIENT: John and Sarah

> JOHN: My only problem is Sarah's illness, and I don't think it has anything to do with us, since her mother was a serious depressive. At least once a week, she'll have these terrible migraines and won't be able to go to work. I told her she should just quit and take the pressure off.
>
> SARAH: He's probably right, but I don't want to quit.

Sarah was the articles editor at a prestigious magazine but earned far less than what John earned as a successful architect. She had a staff of five at work and no problem asserting herself there, she said. But when I pressed her, her only complaint about their marriage was John's mother, whom they had to visit more than she liked and whose last-minute invitations often preempted whatever plans they'd made. "I do understand it. She's a very imposing woman." In other words, Sarah couldn't criticize or challenge John at all.

However, when therapists see a depressed, symptomatic wife and a concerned, caretaking husband, they will often be sucked into the clients' game. It will then go unnoticed that the man holds the power cards and the woman has given up asserting herself in the relationship, even when she is impressively assertive in her work. But their genogram revealed their inherited power roles. John, an only child, supported his widowed mother financially and emotionally. He had been his mother's emotional support ever since his father died when he was seven. His mother had told him he was "the man of the house now" and began deferring to him even at his young age. So John, of course, easily assumed a "man of the house" role with deferential women.

Sarah found it very hard to confront John both because she was afraid she might be "unreasonable" and because she had never learned to negotiate anything with her own father. Her father, who owned a large commercial baking business, had been a benevolent despot at home and at work. Sarah, his only daughter, was "daddy's girl." As all daddy's girls know, the deal is that he will give them everything in his power to bestow and in return they will never challenge daddy's authority. This meant that Sarah knew just how to please powerful men, which had helped her in her professional life. But at home, where a person's real needs are of crucial importance, such deference doesn't make for success. Sara did make periodic feeble attempts to challenge John, which John would hear through then rebut in a "kindly" way.

Neither Sarah nor John understood that they were re-creating the power imbalance they were most familiar—but not most happy—with. They were, however, eventually able to examine the power games they had grown up in and change those relationships enough so that they could organize their own system on a much more equal basis.

It took Sarah a long time to "come out from behind her migraines." For a long while, she got migraines every time she talked to her parents or visited them. Her mother's depression felt "contagious" to her. But as she began to be more of an adult with her own parents and was able to say no to her father, she was more and more able to assert herself with John, and to insist that he set some boundaries with his mother.

As frightening as it was for John, he finally did make it clear to his mother that he loved her and wanted very much to see her, but he couldn't continue to respond to every invitation because he needed time alone with Sarah to build his own family. His mother reacted by being "so hurt she got sick." Although at one point she said she never wanted to see John again, she did of course see him—and Sarah—on their terms.

6. THE BOSS AND THE SECRETARY: **Elliot and Meg**

ELLIOT: She can't do anything right. I ask her to send a package to 32 West Thirty-fourth and she'll send it to 34 West Thirty-second. Every day I leave her a to-do list, bills to pay and errands, whatever, and she still forgets or gets mixed up, even though I write it down for her.

MEG: I very rarely forget and I get plenty right, especially
        with Elliot's daughters and his ex-wife Marissa. *We* get
        along fine.

Meg realized that she was taking care of Elliot's emotional life for
him, dealing with his children and his ex-wife, as she thought she
should. But she had not taken charge of her own life. Elliot, who
owned an athletic supply company, earned $200,000 a year. Meg
had worked in the same travel agency for a decade and "hadn't
gotten anywhere," according to Elliot, who constantly pressured
her to do more with her life while treating her like his underling.
Meg and Elliot were like a lot of couples caught between two
conflicting norms. On the one hand, they both wanted Meg to
be an independent person, but on the other, they were emotionally stuck in gendered power roles.

In Meg's family, she had mediated between her older brother
and her dictatorial father. She was disdainful of her mother's
"helplessness" and inability to stand up to her father, so she
swore, "I'd never take that from a man." Instead she argued constantly, which prevented her from recognizing that her husband
had the same dictatorial style as did her father. When she realized it, she stopped playing the game. She stopped "assisting"
her husband, stopped bickering with him, and put her mind to
getting a better job for herself. Eventually, she opened a new
travel agency with two other agents who were also dissatisfied
where they were. And Elliot, who was now busy learning how to
conduct his own relationships with his parents, his daughters,
and his ex-wife, was far less critical of Meg.

All of these couples might have stayed in their roles until death
did them part—unhappily and within one rigid triangle or another. But there are also unequal couples you will remember who
live in apparent happiness in "perfect" marriages. Such relationships will "work" if the "underling" doesn't want anything the
"boss" hasn't granted. If he's sufficiently benevolent (if he gives
in enough) to satisfy her, and *if she is never aware of desires he doesn't
approve of,* they will get along just fine. However, that's a lot of
if's. And I am reminded of one woman who told her feminist

daughters that she couldn't see what all the fuss was about since *she* always did exactly as she pleased. But Mother, they said, don't you think there's a reason why it pleased you to teach third grade, then to abandon it when we came along? Many women without autonomy will convince themselves that they like it like that. But their children, who are aware of their parents' limited lives, usually don't choose the same path.

Generally, however, underlings will recognize and resent their powerlessness, and then the power struggle begins, soon freezing into a stylized power game with cartoonishly exaggerated roles. And power games won't change on their own. Beyond the fact that people are frequently reared to take a particular role, men are often more skilled at negotiating on their own behalf and will therefore keep the power. Women were usually raised not to assert directly what they want. Instead they might use any of the usual tactics of the powerless: tears, sulking, nagging, pleading, whining, and hence fall into one of the roles that allows them to express their wish for power sharing but do so in a counterproductive way. Often, too, when a woman thinks she's negotiating, she's really just telling her husband what she likes or doesn't like and hoping he'll act accordingly. Elaine told Donald she didn't like small-town life, but she didn't say, "No, I won't live in a small town." Negotiation is not about venting the emotions, although it takes the emotions into account. It's about decisions: we will live here or there, have a second child or not, take on extra work or not. What I do is to help couples get out of the triangles and gender roles that have imprisoned them. Once they have, they can each step up to the plate and state their wishes clearly, and negotiate as equals.

Thus, power and romance are tightly woven into every marriage. If couples don't balance the power between them, they'll end up in power struggles where the "weaker" tries by whatever means to regain, if not real power, a "feeling" of power. And if the couple is engaged in an overt or covert power struggle, they cannot grow. They'll be locked into a stalemate where they might switch roles but never change their system. And as familiar as these roles are, whether they're angry mommy/naughty boy or the doctor and the patient, they are neither healthy nor emotionally fulfilling for either partner.

This is why the power balance between partners and its inevitable appearance in the "mundane" details of daily life is of such central importance to relationships and to the family. In evaluating any marriage today, it is more germane to ask who controls the money, who does the housework, and who does or arranges the child care than to obsess about who expresses what feelings. Any couple or any therapy that avoids the issue of equal power is simply rearranging the deck chairs on the *Titanic*.

Exceptions That (Dis)prove
the Golden Rule

Monica McGoldrick, my colleague and codiscoverer of the Golden Rule, made me laugh out loud recently when, in a talk on multiculturalism, she said the following:

"Growing up, I didn't even know that I myself had a cultural background. But when I made a trip to Ireland in the seventies, I had an overwhelming sense of having come home. I seemed to see my relatives everywhere, people using humor, teasing or ridicule to keep others in line or to maintain distance in male-female relationships; failing to talk about vital emotional issues staring them in the face; and expressing anger by giving others the silent treatment. Suddenly, patterns I had taken for granted all my life fit into a larger picture. It wasn't that my family was 'crazy'—I was just Irish!"

I laughed because that was exactly my own experience except that—as lower-middle-class Irish instead of upper-class—we *knew* we were Irish and wore green every St. Patrick's day to prove it. What I didn't know growing up was that those patterns of denial were part of the deal. So much of my difficulty then—as I graduated from "problem child" to "rebel" to "black sheep"—was my failure to live by "ethnic rules," especially the one that called for me to "sit down and be quiet" or what would the neighbors think? I couldn't stay silent when I was the kind of person who always noticed the slightest emotional disturbance. In fact, I probably chose to become a family therapist because it was a profession that rewarded me for noticing. And yet, to this day, it's still hard for me to deal with any disagreement or controversial issue in my extended family because it's against the rules to talk about it.

Usually our particular set of rules for living comes from a distinct heritage, whether we know that heritage or not. And I don't just mean race or ethnic background. For within each group, distinctions are ever more subtle: when did your family come over? Under what circumstances? Are you southern or northern? From what tribe? What class? And yet as much as these rules vary in our society, we somehow always imagine that *ours* are written in stone. At the same time, we also manage to believe that some groups' rules are "more true" than others. So if you have marriage partners from two different cultural backgrounds, more than likely a "my rules are the right rules and yours are wrong (bad, tasteless, funny, crazy)" will creep unseen into decision making.

Now it's true that ethnic, racial, and gender stereotyping has a long and malicious history. These days, most people are quite relieved to let go of stereotypes, except in private amongst their own. At almost any Jewish gathering, Jews will tell Jewish jokes; at Irish get-togethers, the Irish jokes make the rounds. And usually those jokes do capture some characteristic ethnic behavior or attitude. A colleague of mine, Carol Anderson, who is of Swedish descent, jokes about her uncle "who loved his wife so much he almost told her about it." The one quip is a comment both on Swedish reserve and on Carol's own different perspective.

Naturally, no one wants to be stereotyped or discriminated against, but in order to understand ourselves, we have to acknowledge the kernels of truth that characterize our heritage.

We first need to "recognize" them, as Monica did, and then find out how they apply to our lives. A good family therapist will always help couples unbraid their behavior from the strands of race, ethnicity, gender, class, and sexual orientation that are woven around it. Only then can they decide what needs changing. And, as you will see, exceptions to the Golden Rule actually demonstrate that if some groups can handle money, power, and emotional nurturing more equitably, then there's hope for everyone.

CHANGING THE RULES

Cultural patterns have such a powerful influence on people, they can change the power of money in their lives. One of the most famous recent studies of American couples documented that *money establishes power between partners of all races, backgrounds, and sexual orientations, except among lesbian couples.* As the researchers observed, women and men value money differently. To men, money is identity and power; to women, it means security and independence. Therefore two women together are less likely to use money to dominate and often "make a conscious effort to keep their relationships free of any form of domination, especially if it derives from something as impersonal as money." And while it is true that with more women earning large incomes, some lesbians do get into the money-is-power trip, this is still very much the exception. The same sociologists also found that *among all couples, partners who feel they have equal control over how money is spent have more tranquil relationships.* Naturally, they concluded that there is much to be learned from how lesbian couples typically handle money. And I agree.

When Nancy and Patricia sought therapy, they had been a committed couple for six years. Their problem was Nancy's growing unhappiness that after this many years together Patricia was not "completely out" and, in public, would rarely acknowledge her or be affectionate.

Patricia, a fifty-year-old lawyer for the city of New York, had spent much of her past "semicloseted." Nancy, thirty-five, had been "out" to her family and friends since she herself recognized she was a lesbian. As a writer, she only earned a fifth of what Patricia did. However, Nancy showed none of the usual hesitancy of the lower earner. She was forthright about her complaints and viewed me as a kind of "arbitrator in their negotiation."

As I talked with them, I saw that they were completely satisfied with their equitable division of chores and expenses. They explained their money arrangement this way: Nancy contributed one-fifth of what Patricia put into their joint account to cover household expenses. Patricia paid for vacations and special celebrations because "she has more money," Nancy said. But each bought her own clothes and gifts. As for household chores, they made a list from which each chose the tasks she was better at or minded least, and then rotated the ones that were left. They were especially grateful that New York City uses a "domestic partners" registration, which permits city employees to extend their health insurance to their partners, married or not.

The only issue between Nancy and Patricia was about how "out" to be in terms of their relationship. A lot of what upset Nancy was that she equated Patricia's being out with commitment and love. To Patricia, it had been a lifelong dilemma. Nancy had been out from jump. In most other ways, they accepted each other's different styles. Patricia, dressed in classic tailored clothes, could have walked out of a Talbot's catalogue, while the long braid down Nancy's back, her jeans and T-shirt, suggested a more bohemian self-image. Yet they were having trouble accepting their deeper differences about disclosing their sexual orientation. We worked on this issue, helping Patricia to examine her willingness to stand by her sexual identity as long as she didn't feel endangered, which, she said, she always did on the streets. I also tried to help Nancy appreciate the different consequences of coming out for different generations. I emphasized the impact of the trouble Patricia had had with her family and colleagues, who accepted—but didn't at all support—her sexual identity.

"She doesn't really understand how it used to be," explained Patricia. "When I first started practicing law, I was one of very few women lawyers. Being lesbian wasn't even talked about in those days in any of my circles." Patricia also acknowledged that such

silence had had a price tag: "I guess I felt a little weird sometimes, a lot weird actually. And ashamed. Thank God, I've lost
the shame now that things have gotten more open, but I guess
the silence is a habit. And I know it hurts Nancy."

It was very important for Nancy to understand that Patricia's
hesitancy to come out to others was not about her commitment
or love for Nancy, but rather a reflection of the different stages
they were at in accepting their lesbianism. After several sessions,
Nancy felt less anxious about Patricia's love for her and Patricia
became less defensive, which freed them up to really hear what
the other was saying. After that, they were both more able to
accept each other's differences.

Of course, Patricia still had to learn how to acknowledge
Nancy in public. She began by introducing her as "my companion" in informal settings and agreed to have people to dinner
who weren't just their closest friends. What really broke the ice
for them, however, was a successful family dinner party. Although
Patricia's elderly mother long ago refused to visit their home,
Patricia's brother and his wife along with Nancy's sister and her
husband did come, and the evening proved to be a turning
point. After that Patricia felt ready to try more combinations and
more family. She was surprised that the two of them could have
almost anyone over and feel just like "regular folks," talking
about their vacation, their work, their life. By this time, Nancy
had stopped pressing Patricia for public demonstrations of affection. "So we don't hold hands outside," she said in their last
session, "I can live with that." She wished it were otherwise, but
she understood Patricia's reasons.

Notice how Patricia—the higher earner—was able to take
Nancy's complaints seriously and use them as a springboard to
examine unresolved problems of her own. She then made
changes that benefited the relationship and herself. That is, she
shared the power and decision making.

While the power of money may not be a problem for many
lesbian couples, they do have all the usual couple difficulties and
other unique problems as well. Homophobia in society makes
same-sex couples experience what I call the "fox-hole buddies"
syndrome, which pushes partners together for survival but makes

it harder for them to accept their differences. Patricia and Nancy had to learn to expand their small social world, to let others in, and to reduce the stress of being stigmatized by sharing with others. Their socialization as women can also create problems when they each bring full emotional intensity to the couple relationship. The fact that both of them focus on the relationship is good up to a point, but when the focus is too intense, it can be "stifling." No issue is ever dropped. Arguments and hurts can replace intimacy. But when power is equal—even when earnings are not—partners have a better chance of negotiating an equal relationship.

A recent study has shown that when lesbian couples become parents together they most often strive for and often achieve a near fifty-fifty sharing of all aspects of family life: decision making, child care, and household tasks. In this respect, the researchers concluded, the lesbian family is a viable and valuable model of an effectively functioning family in contemporary America.

"MONEY MAY BE POWER, BUT RICH MEN HAVE A LOT MORE POWER THAN RICH WOMEN"

Although unequal earners *can* choose to share power, it is more difficult when a man is involved and most difficult when two men are. In the same study on American couples referred to earlier, the researchers found that competitiveness and power are often at issue in gay male couples. This pronounced difference in attitude toward money that lesbian and gay male couples have reflects society's usual gender programming. Because men identify money with power, a very low earner in a gay male relationship will often feel so bad about himself, he will eventually leave or destroy the relationship. The higher earner will "wield" more power than in the average heterosexual relationship. The competition between the two male partners will often drive equal earners to work longer hours, earn more, buy more, or just do more of whatever symbolizes power. The overidentification with money can often turn job loss or health problems into a catastrophe. Richard and Norman, the couple I'm about to describe, were caught in a stalemate. Instead of Steamroller and Doormat or

Boss/Secretary, their power game was one I call the Saint and the Sinner. To some extent, they played the game exactly like any heterosexual couple would, but as you'll see by the end of their story, their overidentification with money made the game all the more difficult to end.

THE SAINT AND THE SINNER: **Richard and Norman**

> NORMAN: Just go over to the other side of the room and leave me alone. I can't stand that look on your face.
>
> RICHARD: Are you sure you'll be all right?

Everyone who knew them rolled their eyes and wondered how Richard put up with Norman. Although Richard, a hard-working internist, was ever soothing and kind to him, Norman just browbeat Richard in public. Norman had been in a wheelchair for three years after a serious car accident. They'd been together for more than a decade and raised Richard's two children together. Norman was still very involved with the boys, who were now teenagers, but he no longer went to watch them play soccer or play in the high school orchestra because he "couldn't stand to watch Richard play the noble father" any more.

"You used to think I was a good father," Richard said, and sweetly reminisced about how they had been such gung-ho parents together. He seemed genuinely—and innocently—perplexed. But things are seldom what they seem between the saint and the sinner. Being deemed a saint is the emotional overfunctioner's "reward" for putting up with the other partner's bad behavior. These are the roles each slips into when the saint is unable to confront or leave the sinner for either emotional or financial reasons. No one sees what the saint does to provoke or maintain the cycle. But as I asked more questions, I found out more about Saint Richard.

In a private session, Norman finally told me that Richard had been having an affair ever since the accident, even though they had committed themselves to a monogomous relationship. As "concerned" as Richard appeared, he'd never gone with Norman to see any of his specialists, or even done the research to see what Norman should do, although as a physician, Richard was in an excellent position to help. I also learned that they had never once discussed how Norman's injury affected their relationship. Because they couldn't level with each other, layers of deception and resentment grew.

Richard dismissed my suggestion that Norman's injury created great difficulty for them and wouldn't discuss any arrangement that made him feel that he was abandoning Norman. Norman denied that he was in a rage at his helplessness (and took it out on Richard), preferring instead to blame Richard for his distress. Norman never shared with Richard, or anyone before therapy, the depths of his anguish about "being crippled" and the fear that he had "trapped" Richard.

As therapy uncovered the layers, the two men raged and fought but finally stopped playing their power game and arrived at a point where Norman seriously offered to leave so Richard could have a life with his lover. Richard seriously considered it, discussing it for weeks with Norman before deciding to give up the affair and stay, "now that they could talk again." Meanwhile, Norman started to create a support system for himself so he wasn't so dependent on Richard, and that included reconnecting with his parents, difficult though that was for him.

Where does the overidentification with money come in? Norman, a teacher who earned far less than Richard, automatically assumed a large part of the household responsibility—even though the children were Richard's. Norman had traditionally catered to Richard, though they told themselves it was because Norman worked fewer hours and had more vacations. But one of the reasons why Richard found it so hard to cope flexibly and honestly with Norman's disability was that he had never "taken care" of Norman. Norman had always been the caretaker. On the other hand, when Norman couldn't work, he felt so bad about himself, he couldn't "ask" Richard to help him by taking him to see his doctors or involving himself in the medical decisions, etc. The truth was that Norman, whose self-worth was based on being an exemplary teacher, a leader of kids, and a decent wage earner, was filled with self-loathing when he couldn't perform. Once Norman was confined to a wheelchair, he and Richard simply reversed the roles in their one-up, one-down relationship, without changing the system of "powerful-powerless." But Richard's acting out (the affair) and Norman's increasing bitterness brought them to therapy, where their power relations and the impact of Norman's disability could be addressed.

Norman was one of those uncommon men skilled in nurturing. Sometimes gay couples find that because neither partner has any experience at caretaking, no one raises important emotional issues or offers the intimate support that will sustain them. Of course, necessity is a great teacher, and when AIDS struck the gay community, formerly competitive men became tender nurses of the sick and dying. They now routinely take personal care of their friends and lovers in ways that heterosexual men usually leave to wives or daughters. Because of AIDS, gay men are far more ready to express their own vulnerability and to share money with more vulnerable, less self-sufficient lovers or friends or members of the gay community. In fact, I would say that the gay community is proof of just how adaptable people are and how men can learn to share power and nurture, rejecting the competitive individualism they are often reared to.

WAITING TO EXHALE: THE AFRICAN-AMERICAN PERSPECTIVE

Another major exception that disproves the Golden Rule is the African-American couple. My friend and colleague Nancy Boyd-Franklin, an expert on the subject, explains that African-American women are somewhat more likely than white women to be better educated and have access to better jobs than their spouses. When that's true, African-American partners have to learn not to be angry with each other for not fitting the traditional pattern. Also, because racism makes people feel (and often *makes* them) powerless, partners frequently "compensate" by trying to control their spouses. The helplessness and understandable anger they bring to the relationship from the outside world may be the real source of conflict. The therapist then needs to help them join together to combat racism, not each other.

According to another African-American therapist, Audrey

Chapman, black boys and girls receive very different gender messages than whites do. The saying "We raise our daughters, but we love our sons" reflects the common parental practice in which, Chapman says, "Black girls are taught self-reliance and independence and black boys are pampered and protected . . . [because] the world is a threatening place for black males." Then, paradoxically, the other part of the message teaches the girls that their strongest adult identity is to be a mother and nurture others, while the boys soon learn that "success" for males of any race means earning money and providing for your families, whatever the obstacles. Chapman notes that the effect of parents pushing their sons and daughters in different directions sometimes gives rise to relationship difficulties, with issues of control, resentment, and frustration vented on each other as they struggle to form new families in a racist society.

Jerry and Denise were married for four years when they came to the Family Institute, and I supervised the therapist in charge of their case. Jerry was thirty-five and working two jobs, one for the Transit Authority at night and the other as a substitute gym teacher. Denise was a personnel administrator who earned $48,000, which was more than Jerry, but not if he took on an exhausting load of teaching assignments. The problem, according to Denise, was that he "subs" too much. Even though Jerry took care of their daughter, Joy, during the days he didn't teach, they had no time together as a couple or a family. All his free time went to his buddies.

Denise saw herself as "a strong, independent black woman," and indeed, she came across that way. She sat forward in her chair, ready to engage. Her bright black eyes seemed to welcome attention, much as the beads on the bottoms of her cornrowed hair attracted it. She stated her complaint forthrightly: "If Jerry keeps up working as much as he does and then going out on top of that, the three of us, *we* don't exist." After giving examples, she sat back in her chair and sighed. "Jerry thinks I'm overreacting, and there may be some truth to that. I did grow up with a father who was never there. But Jerry and I were a real *couple* before Joy. I loved that. We'd go bicycling together on Saturday, go to the movies, go to church then have lunch with my family.

Now we go to church and he leaves to meet a friend." Her smiling face had become solemn.

Jerry was laid back, relaxed-looking in his plaid shirt and jeans. He always took a few seconds before giving a considered response. When the therapist asked how he saw their situation, he answered, "Well, I hear her. I understand what Denise is saying. But at the same time, I have *no* time for myself anymore. If I'm not working, I'm with Joy. Being with Denise means taking care of Joy with her. Being with my friends is the only thing that takes the pressure off for me."

"Let's talk about the pressure. There seems to be a lot of it," the therapist said, then asked if Jerry was working much more than he really had to. "I wonder if you're not 'overreacting' too, given your background?"

Jerry thought a moment, then said, "Well, it's true. You see, I came from a very duty-oriented family. First of all, they're a very religious, small-town family from North Carolina. So whatever free time there was, everyone gave it to the church. You sang in the choir, you helped rebuild the rectory, you cooked for the church picnic. My mother and father just worked. My mother cleaned houses, every day including Saturday. My father still works two jobs. He's a watchman and a carpenter. He'd get home from work then put on his overalls and do repairs and such until it was dark. Sometimes I'd see him collapsed in front of the TV, but my mother never even did that. She was always sewing, canning, cleaning."

"It's true," chimed in Denise. "I never knew people like that. They are *serious.*" The two of them began to laugh, obviously enjoying a long-standing joke.

As Jerry relaxed and began to talk more, answering the therapist's questions, he concluded, "I guess I've been *programmed* to work this hard, at least after we had Joy." And it was true, the role of father as provider had been drummed into him by word and example. His father, grandfather, and all of the other men in his church had set the standard for him. The result was that Denise fell by the wayside. He'd also *never* seen his parents together "in a couple way" and had assumed that once partners become parents, they no longer take bike rides together or time for themselves.

"Then he wonders why I don't want to have sex. But I'm too angry at him, and I don't want sex when I'm angry."

In his considered way, Jerry slowly turned to her and said, "Denise, you were angry at me before you met me. Why don't you tell her a little bit more about *your* father."

Caught, Denise filled out the picture of her father by telling the therapist, "He was always drinking or getting high with his friends—and his girlfriends, one of whom he left my mother for. He broke my mother's heart and he broke my heart. I'm not going to live any such life."

At that point I interrupted their session for a conference with the therapist. I had suggested to her that she ask Denise if she had many women friends or relatives who were able to turn to their husbands for emotional support. Denise thought for a while, then shook her head. The therapist asked, "Well, were *all* of them abandoned by their fathers?" "No, of course not," Denise said. And the therapist asked, "Why, then, are none of them able to lean on their husbands?"

Jerry was smiling. "She doesn't know what you're talking about."

The therapist explained that she had asked because she was aware that racism had made it impossible for many black men to provide for their families. As a result, black women were often raised not to rely on their men or acknowledge their own vulnerabilities—even to themselves. They had to be the backbone of the families they were left to raise.

So you mean I've got Strong Black Woman Syndrome, like my mother," Denise said.

"Yup, S.B.W.S. I usually call it 'overresponsibility,' but in your case it's definitely S.B.W.S." And that became the running joke and a serious theme in their therapy. Instead of just showing anger about Jerry's "disappearing," as she called it, Denise learned to talk about how lonely she was for him, how much she wanted to be with him and to talk over the day. "Sometimes, honestly, I even resent my own child for getting more affection from Jerry now than I do," she said.

When Denise first tried, with the therapist's coaching, to verbalize such feelings, she would often giggle self-consciously like a teenager. But Jerry didn't crack a smile at her struggle. He listened intently, answered immediately, and often reached out a hand to her. Her comment about wanting the kind of affection he gave to Joy made Jerry's eyes glisten. Without a second's hesitation, he said to her, "You've got it, baby."

As for Jerry, the therapist tried to help him reconsider his need to overwork in order to be the main provider. Jerry frequently referred to how smart Denise was, and how successful she'd been in her career. When he spoke about his own future prospects, he was obviously filled with great anxiety. "I'm doing okay *so far*—but you never know what will happen."

Jerry had a lot of emotional work to do with his family before he would be able to stop working so hard. He needed to feel comfortable enough with who he was rather than who he thought he should be before he could spend more time with his family and less working.

The therapist encouraged Jerry to have a quiet talk with his father about life, work, and family during their next visit. But Jerry's father was not receptive to his son's questions about whether both were giving over their life's blood to work. "Would you rather be like Stanley and Joseph?" he asked Jerry, referring to an alcoholic brother and nephew. "Stanley's the only one of us who didn't make something of his life, and now Joe is following him. You've got two choices—work and do right or fall by the wayside. I learned that from my father and I tried to teach it to you."

The therapist then suggested that Jerry run all of this past his mother and see what she thought. Jerry had several conversations with her before he worked up the courage to ask if she thought she and his father had enough time together. "No, we didn't. We still don't. But I count my blessings every time I help out at the church's soup kitchens. I know you're not talking about that. You mean about being a man and a woman. No, we didn't have time for that in our life."

As Jerry heard the deep regret in his mother's voice, he felt an almost irresistible urge to run away from the pain of it. Instead, he took a deep breath and started talking to his mother about his own life, his need to make something of himself and Denise's complaints that they didn't have any couple time. His mother said she thought it could be different for him and Denise. She didn't see why he shouldn't cut back at work if *they* had enough money, but she added that his father wouldn't ever understand.

The talks with his mother did relieve some of Jerry's anxiety. He was more understanding of Denise's wishes and seemed to wish he could do things differently, but while his father disapproved so much, he couldn't seem to. During the end of their first year of therapy, however, Jerry's dad suffered a major heart attack and had bypass surgery. The time Jerry spent with him in the hospital moved him profoundly. "I saw my father turn into an old man before his time." Apparently, the ordeal had weakened his father terribly. In addition, the doctors said he would have to change his life, giving up carpentry, all strenuous activity, and most of the foods he loved. "And still," Jerry said, "there he was sitting on the porch, stoical as ever, telling me, 'I lived the way I was supposed to. The way you're supposed to.' "

The shock of his father's heart attack made Jerry more open to talking about how to be a man different from his father. Though he still struggled with his powerful programming, he finally agreed to cut back his substitute teaching. When he did, he found himself relieved. His father, however, was distant and angry. "There he is," Jerry said, "barely able to walk and he's mad at me for working less. His work almost killed him." The therapist understood Jerry's frustration but coached him not to react with equal anger. Jerry didn't. In fact, in every phone call, he expressed his love for his father and his concern about his health. Eventually, his father became warmer but made it clear he still didn't approve of Jerry's decision. Jerry made no apologies or excuses for his choice and occasionally tried kidding his father about having a "lazy son." His father was not amused but did seem to get used to Jerry's life. His brush with death had also made him more appreciative of Jerry's caring and his visits. Denise, of course, had a lot of work to do with her family as well, but this couple did "find each other again," as Denise put it.

Like Denise and Jerry, many African-American partners can be extremely competitive. Bell Hooks, an African-American professor and writer, points out that among people who have been deprived, "There is a sense that there are never enough goodies to go around, so that we must viciously compete with one another." And this may be as true within a marriage as within a community. However, it's important to remember, except for college graduates, the *majority* of African-American women don't even have the possibility of competing financially with their husbands. On average, they earn less than their male counterparts, and many are unemployed or work at the most menial jobs. But when African-American women are financially successful, they may bend the Golden Rule in yet another way.

Financial counselor Glinda Bridgeforth explains that "many of us believe that we're in a high-stakes competition for a shrinking pool of available black men. We try to buy love, believing that we can't get a man to commit to us any other way." So here, a woman's financial power in a relationship—particularly if she's overly generous with her lover—can reflect her lack of self-esteem and her sense of emotional powerlessness. Many young black educated women feel despair about finding a partner. Sometimes, it's not so much a lack of self-esteem as it is a chronic insecurity in relationships because black men are such "rare, precious commodities," as one client put it. With 25 percent of black men dead or in prison by age twenty-five, many women are reluctant to use their financial power to change a relationship, even an abusive one. Instead they might just turn that power over to their partners, if they marry at all.

While racism can reverse the Golden Rule, it can also reinforce it. John and Bernadine's story in Terry McMillan's best-selling novel *Waiting to Exhale* illuminates that situation. This stereotypical successful couple lived a lavish life on John's $400,000-a-year salary, but Bernadine confides to a friend what motivates his spending: "'One day I'm going to have exactly what they have,' he'd say. 'They' being rich white folks. He'd taken it to the extreme, gone completely overboard. . . .''

To please John by playing *her* role in the American Dream marriage, she kept postponing her own dream of starting a catering business. Instead, she became John's bookkeeper. When she got a job elsewhere after John didn't need her help with his business, "he had a series of fits . . . because now not only did she have her own money but for the first time in years she had interests outside of him and the kids and this stupid house."

John's hunger to "have what they have" was never satisfied. When the novel opens, John has left Bernadine for his new bookkeeper, a twenty-four-year-old white woman. Along with Bernadine, we learn that John has liquidated his assets, put his properties in his mother's name, and sold his half of the company to his partner so that on paper his income dropped to $80,000 a year. What Bernadine got of this didn't even cover the mortgage payments on the house. In other words, *their* money and the business *they* built was *his* all along.

As contemptible as John's behavior is, it's important to understand that African-American men are under extraordinary pressure to maintain a "male identity." Despite their successes, they know they will never reach the top of the power pyramid, which is reserved for white men. In America, skin color is of enormous social consequence. It's no accident that John left Bernadine for a white woman. Or, that in Spike Lee's movie *Jungle Fever* the African-American hero leaves his wife for a white woman. As Nobel prize-winning author Toni Morrison lamented in *The Bluest Eye,* even among African-Americans, the lighter your skin, the higher your status. In other words, African-American marriages are as vulnerable to the power of color as they are to the power of money.

CLASS: THE LAST TABOO

The issue of socioeconomic class difference is one of America's last taboos. We value our egalitarian society and like to believe that we're all equal and we still treat everyone the same, providing everyone with the same opportunity to succeed—rich and poor alike. And yet, recent widely publicized studies reveal that we have the greatest class gulfs of *any* industrialized Western nation. Furthermore, the vast gap between rich and poor is growing fastest in America, where one percent of the households control 40 percent of the nation's wealth—twice as much as in Britain, which we all think of as an extremely class-stratified society.

The denial of class differences operates on the social level of the system the way denial of individual differences operates between couples: it makes it harder to deal with differences. And yet, the factors that distinguish the different social classes— income, education, and occupation—create radically different experiences and ideas about almost every aspect of life. Still, as a society we haven't found a way to talk about or understand class differences. People trying to comment on differences in class levels below theirs risk being called snobs and bigots, even if their comments are not meant to demean, while comments from below on classes above can be perceived as jealousy.

For couples, such mystification of class differences intertwined with gender and ethnic norms creates problems that can't be discussed in a rational way early in a relationship. One couple I am working with, Vincente and Joanne, have marital difficulties based almost entirely on the class difference of their families. Both are in their twenties and had been married for two years when they came to see me because of their constant arguing over whether Joanne should finish college or quit and have a baby. Both their extended families are deeply involved in the dispute, and the couple's mothers are no longer speaking to each other. It is obvious to Vincente's working-class Puerto Rican family that it's time for Joanne to start a family. It's equally obvious to Joanne's middle-class professional parents that she should finish her education and prepare for a career. Like all couples at such an impasse, both Vincente and Joanne have to figure out what *they* want, apart from family pressures, then they'll have to change their relationships with their families so that they can remain close to both sides and still have a marriage based on their own ideas.

In some families, only one sibling will "move up" in class through education or marriage. The strains in the family are inevitable. Many African-American couples are stressed to the breaking point by their attempts to provide needy family members with every possible assistance while they are struggling to move themselves ahead in their own careers. In some other ethnic groups, couples distance from their "lower-class" family, becoming increasingly cut off from them and depriving their children of grandparents, uncles, and aunts who don't fit in to their new surroundings.

Reflecting and also exacerbating our ambivalence about differences in class, culture, and gender, corporate leaders "talk the talk of inclusion" but actually fail to advance women and minorities to the top ranks of business. So concluded a federal commission appointed under President Bush in 1990 to investigate the "glass ceiling."

Until we are ready in families and in the larger society to acknowledge these problems, they will continue to rankle couples who marry naively, believing that differences in background don't matter in America.

What does all this tell us? Whatever their sexual orientation, ethnicity, class, or race, couples must define power themselves instead of accepting society's definitions, or external power structures of money, class, maleness, and whiteness will insinuate themselves into their intimate lives. If couples don't make a conscious effort to reject the money=power equation, earnings will be inseparable from power, forcing them to live under the tyranny of the Golden Rule. The good news is that as we've seen with lesbian couples, couples *can* consciously redefine power in their marriages to maintain their equality. And, as shown with gay male couples, men can redefine maleness to include nurturing, caretaking, and power sharing. The lives of some African-American couples illustrate that partners can identify the forces outside themselves, such as racism, that have made them pull away from or blame each other. And once couples understand the power hierarchies at play in their relationships, they can fight them as a *couple*—on the outside—and reject them within their homes.

8

Erotic Equality:
Sex and Power

I've always thought that in the sex department, men are given a double message about power. After all, if "power is the great aphrodisiac," men stand to lose quite a bit in giving it up. But actually, "power over"—power in the sense that Kissinger meant when he made that remark—is no more an aphrodisiac than black lace lingerie and a curvy figure. They may arouse a lover at first, but if the person isn't fully sexual and fully *there*—i.e., isn't a mature individual—sexy underwear won't hold a couple together emotionally. In other words, domination, like beauty, doesn't translate well in bed or in marriage. On the other hand, equality does. But you'd never know it from the images of sex and romance that we grow up with and carry in our fantasies.

SLAVES OF LOVE

The erotic love story *9½ Weeks*, a popular book that was made into a popular movie in 1985 and an even more popular video after that, shows very explicitly what we, as a culture, call sexual fantasy.

John, the hero, is a currency trader; Elizabeth, an assistant in a SoHo art gallery, is a serious independent woman. Within no time, though, her response to John's sexuality of dominance is "beyond her control," and she becomes his love slave.

John pursues Elizabeth *sexually* but is emotionally detached, never telling her more about himself than his first name. She tries to talk to him about her life, the gallery, whatever, but when he says, "No friends. I don't want to see your friends or mine. Just you and me," Elizabeth accepts his terms because she finds him irresistible. He initiates all of their sex games, which progress from the sensuality of food play and the thrill of making love in outrageous places to Elizabeth's sexual degradation, complete with John's cracking a whip and making her crawl to pick up the money he's strewn on the floor.

The power games escalate and the sexual degradation intensifies until finally Elizabeth finds herself in a tawdry Forty-second Street hotel, blindfolded, having sex with another woman while John "directs" the scene. At that point, Elizabeth leaves John, returning to his apartment only to get her things. The S-M sex was thrilling, but she could no longer pay the price and hold on to her *self*.

The message of *9½ Weeks*—and it is a male message—is that women find sexual ecstasy in total submission. The fact that the author is a woman doesn't matter: the culture provides sexual fantasies for women, its images *teach* women where their pleasures lie. Men, too, are taught their fantasies. John is shown enjoying—not sex—but the thrill of power and possession of a beautiful woman. No one seems to think it strange that sexual ecstasy should involve women's slavery and humiliation by a man who controls and creates the sexual terms. And that's because these ideas have been culturally reinforced since the beginning of time. However, erotic power relations may actually be more familiar than mutually satisfying, more tolerated than embraced, so to speak.

WHY ARE THERE NO SEXY EQUALS?

It's difficult for us to believe that equality is sexy when everything we've learned about sex is based on an age-old idea of men's "natural" need to dominate sexually and women's "innate" desire to submit sexually. We somehow still believe that this behavior is instinctual rather than conditioned. Our foremost sexual image is still Scarlett O'Hara being carried off by Rhett Butler. However much we *wish* to be equal, in our mind's eye—and in a million movies, books, and perfume ads—we see something very like the image of a passionate and powerful man bent over a woman who, weak with rapture, is arched back in his arms, her hair flowing to the floor. If you reverse the genders, the image is instantly ridiculous because it *seems so right* that dominance is male and submission female.

Few of us actually personify either one of these polar opposites. In fact, people usually have to ignore a larger and more subtle array of sexual feelings in order to fit these predefined roles. Even though the roles have expanded since the Victorian era and now include more sexual aggression in women and more passivity in men, the basic male-female power relations are unaffected.

ROLE REVERSAL DOESN'T HELP

In the matter of sex, tradition haunts us. The images of surrender and dominance follow us into the boardroom and lurk in the bedroom. Try as we might, we haven't been able to break loose. We can reverse the polarities, making women dominant and men submissive, but we can't get rid of them.

As I see it, role reversal is the sign of our times, our way of *attempting* to move beyond sexual stereotypes. But we shouldn't confuse the one with having achieved the other. A dominatrix isn't any more loving or connected than John in *9½ Weeks*. And now we have the new "Madonna" image for women, which seems to me to be an attempt to combine "male" dominance with "female" submission. Unfortunately, what you get is a twisted hybrid I like to call "swaggering submission." Madonna may project power, but it is the power to be an object, and that is an emotional contradiction.

Role reversals and hybrids aren't the answer. Taking the dominance out of sex is. But of course that's easier said than done.

The allure of dominance is enormous. Some women only understand the compliment implied by it and not its darker message. I have a client who was flattered when her husband introduced her as his "trophy wife." "Oh," I said, "does that mean he's going to sit you on the mantel and leave you there while he's at work?" Only then did she begin to understand that she was an ornament and an object to her husband, not a companion. Women who have equal sexual relations worry that they're missing out on the "grand passions" of life, by which they mean being "swept away" by someone. They sometimes wonder if it wouldn't be nice to have a man who would take care of and possess them. Some women worry that equality will mean losing their femininity or abolishing gender entirely, which is impossible.

Maleness and femaleness is a fact of life. The differences are there, physically, and no one can take them away. But exaggerating the differences so that they mean opposites is just a way for the insecure to reassure themselves that they are truly masculine or feminine. The problem is that men and women aren't *opposites.* No one has successfully tracked just what our inborn sexual differences are. And, after all, masculinity and femininity have entirely different meanings at different times and in different cultures. Unfortunately, in ours, they continue to mean sexual opposites, which always amounts to dominance and submission. This definition makes for a limited sexual connection at best and, at worst, a destructive one.

SLAVES OF MARRIAGE

In my clinical experience, neither men nor women find the eroticism of power fulfilling. And yet, although marital relationships are rarely as extreme as John and Elizabeth's, they are still often based on dominance and submission. Sasha and Adam, a young couple married five years, came to see me after they had been separated for over two months. Adam had left in a jealous rage after Robert, an old boyfriend of Sasha's, had shown up in their lives and begun pursuing her. A few weeks after Adam left her, Sasha had started to date Robert, but when she and Adam then met by chance, they both realized they wanted to get back to-gether. Their "problem" was that Adam "couldn't get past it."

"I still love her," he said, "I just can't forgive her. I thought if we went to our honeymoon inn in Vermont there would be no ghosts. And we were fine until we got into bed that night. But then when I closed my eyes, all I could see was Sasha in bed with Robert. We ended up crying, both of us, and we left the next morning. That's why we came to see you."

Adam was a boyish-looking man who, in a certain physical sense, seemed less "powerful" than his wife. He was dressed in "soft" clothes, a pastel-colored Lacoste shirt, corduroy slacks. Sasha dressed flashily, wearing lace-up boots, tights, a miniskirt, and a leather jacket. She was brassy and bold. In that first session, to "prove" how furious she was with Robert for "interfering" in her marriage, she said, "I threw a glass of wine in Robert's face at lunch when he propositioned me. Adam's who I want sexually. I'm always the one jumping *him*, sometimes as soon as he walks through the door at night. I've always been like that with Adam."

Her eyes desperate, she turned to him to corroborate. He did, reluctantly, with a nod of his head, but then shot back at her, "So why did you sleep with him as soon as I left? I haven't slept with anyone."

Sasha leaned far over her chair to reach Adam so that she was nearly prostrate. "Robert's nothing to me. I was just so hurt, don't you understand? I couldn't eat, I couldn't go to work, I fell apart." She reached her hand toward him but withdrew it and sat up when he didn't respond. Then, she cried, "How could you have just walked out on me? I hadn't done anything, I swear. Not then, I swear. I only want you." As Sasha sobbed, shaking with misery, Adam looked at her askance—angry and distrustful.

In order to understand for myself what the "real" issues were, I calmed them down and asked them to tell me about their lives together before the incident. I asked them, as I always do, who earns what, what they each do for a living, what their families were like, and I soon discovered a relationship based on domi-nance and submission. Sasha thought of herself as a strong woman. But Adam was the center of her life. Drying her tears, she told me that in college, she had majored in French with no thought of a career. At age twenty-eight, she was doing catalogue modeling to support them while Adam, a fledgling architect, got established. She clearly had no power in the world. She hated modeling and said the man who ran her modeling agency was "a maniac who had fired her once for coming in late. But I don't mind," she said, "it's only until Adam makes his mark. He's an extraordinary architect." Animated again, she began to tell me about Adam's brilliant architectural ideas and how well he had done in school, but I interrupted.

"So, in other words, you've decided to live Adam's life?"

"No, not at all," she said, annoyed. "We're planning to have children soon. And I want to raise them."

Without realizing it, Sasha had begun a traditional marriage. She already did all the housework and cooking. When I asked them what kinds of things they argued about before Robert, Sasha said they hardly argued.

Rubbing her lips nervously, she said, "Oh, sure, we'd have spats about, you know, he'd leave his clothes all over the floor, then I'd get furious, but usually we'd end up on the floor in the pile of clothes making love. I'd probably have thrown him down after hitting him."

In effect, they never argued because Sasha went along with Adam's life. When they had spats (over, what else? her having to clean up after him), they ended them with ever more passionate lovemaking. In other words, she expanded her sexual role but never challenged it. Real role departure would be something else entirely. For example, could they have made love at all if, instead of a moment's petulance, Sasha had said to Adam, "Hey, how come you don't clean up, too?" Not quite. Although they weren't aware of it, their sexual passion, as traditional as their relationship, was based on her being a *selfless* and *primarily* sexual being. For all her boldness, Sasha always remained in her sexually submissive role. Women, after all, were always expected to be tigresses in defense of their children and their men, just never for themselves. So she threw a glass of wine in a man's face. And as sexually agressive as Sasha was, she and her husband both still considered that she *belonged* to him. On the surface, it seemed that all Sasha wanted was "to belong" to Adam again. But that wasn't really true. And that's where Robert came in.

"Tell me about Robert," I asked her, but Adam jumped in with what *he* considered the most significant point:

"He's rich." As he said this, Adam clenched his teeth.

"Who cares? I never cared about that," Sasha said. "I didn't marry *him,* did I?"

"That could have been for a million reasons. Maybe you weren't in the mood to get married at nineteen."

At this point, Sasha put her head in her hands and began to cry again. When she could control herself, she murmured, "This is what he always does to me. I don't love Robert, I don't."

After she dried her face on her scarf she began to talk again and slowly. The story emerged that by chance Sasha and Robert had met again on the street at lunchtime. He hadn't married and was obviously flirting. "I told him I was married and how happy Adam and I were, but I went to lunch with him when he invited me because he was an old friend and I thought we could put the sex part behind us. I like Robert, why shouldn't I?"

"Why shouldn't you? He took you to Chanterelle," Adam said with scorn, mentioning an expensive restaurant and adding, "Mr. Big Business told her he'd been too busy earning money to have a relationship. And then, she saw him again. Another wine-soaked lunch."

Sasha said, "He was there, waiting, when I left the morning shoot. He'd called to find out when I'd be done. He was so sweet. He'd brought this picture of me as the prom queen in my high school and told me how intimidated he'd been by me. I was so smart. I'd been in the honor society. I don't know. He made me feel good, which was nice, particularly after a shoot, where they treat you like a piece of meat."

At this point, I thought about the fact that sexual attraction doesn't just rise from our loins alone. It was no accident that Robert was rich. Remember, the need for power—the good kind—is natural in everyone. If suppressed, it will emerge somehow. Sasha's only expression of power at that time in her life was by her association with a rich man. In other words, the issue of money and power, suppressed in her marriage, came out in her flirtation. Being a good girl, she couldn't crave status for herself.

But she, who was actually powerless in her marriage, got back—as the powerless often unconsciously wish to do—by getting a man more powerful than Adam.

"So I wasn't making you feel loved?" Adam asked. "That's why you slept with him?"

"I didn't sleep with him until you left me. I wouldn't have. I swear . . ."

Adam's accusations and Sasha's pleading were bound to go on and on. Sexual jealousy is such a strong emotion, the hurt lover can't really focus on anything else, especially men, who feel humiliated by the rival. So the same scene would repeat itself until, as we'll see in the upcoming discussion of affairs, the hurt subsides and I can help the couple put the affair behind them. Then, the partners can begin the work of deconstructing the triangle to get at the real problem. But for now, I could only help Sasha and Adam understand why Sasha was so vulnerable to Robert. That's why I encouraged her to talk about how she felt after Adam left her.

"I fell completely apart. I wanted to die, really. I'd never been so depressed in my life . . ."

Eventually, when she could hear me, I said, "Well, I guess once you've made Adam the center of your universe, his walking out on you must have been a catastrophe."

Sobbing, she said that it was, but she also began to understand that since he was *everything* to her, she felt like *nothing* without him. This also allowed Adam to glimpse just how dependent his wife was on him, and why this old boyfriend, who reminded her of a time when the world was her oyster and she felt powerful, could come in and rescue her from an overwhelming loss. Eventually, Adam and Sasha did understand that their real problem was that Sasha had submitted her life to Adam, which had left her frustrated and resentful, in need of the kind of ego boost Robert represented.

Sasha and Adam are an ordinary couple. Because they seldom argued and still had a passionate sex life, they didn't think they had any disagreements. But they did. When a relationship "explodes" the way theirs did, you can be sure that the disagreements were being suppressed. One of their main disagreements was *her* unexplored and unexpressed desire for equality, and *his* unthinking assumption that he and his life would be central to their marriage, that she would want what he wanted. The images of dominance and submission wouldn't have rung any bells with Sasha and Adam. His "softness" and her "outspoken" personality made the relationship almost seem equal. All the same their life together, including their sexual lives, was based on his dominance of her. And that always destroys love.

WHERE DID OUR LOVE GO?

Despite Sasha and Adam, most couples don't express their discontents by having affairs. The recent survey on sex in America surprised everyone with "a subdued picture of few partners and less exotic sexual practices." Three-quarters of American couples are faithful to each other, and almost half have six twice a week, while few singles have that much sex. However, many couples I see feel unsatisfied with their sexual life together. They don't know why, but their sex lives have gone from excitement to routine to duty. And sometimes to little or nothing. Why? Because the eroticism of power doesn't last.

Women today usually resent their powerlessness, whether they know it or not, and retaliate by "having a headache" or in some rare cases, having an affair, as Sasha did. However attractive a man's power may have seemed at first, however fulfilling of women's fantasies and conditioning, the resentment a woman inevitably feels kills the sexual attraction she felt.

This eroticism of power doesn't last because today our changing lives so constantly contradict the ideal of submission and dominance. Women nowadays have a hard time acting like a sexual object in bed while maintaining a high profile in their social and professional worlds. What often happens in this situation is that the man, who can no longer believe in his CEO wife as an object, is the one with the headaches!

Men whose formerly traditional wives have become equal partners in their marriages do sometimes react by losing interest in sex. This is a new symptom therapists are seeing more and more often now. Until this last decade, if a husband had no interest in sex, we assumed he was having an affair. We now ask about recent changes in her income and status. Fearing his loss of interest, the woman, as much as the man, still tries to fit herself into the traditional erotic roles, no matter how assertive she may be in the rest of her life.

Often, also, women, when they become wives, abandon their sexuality entirely. The wifely—submissive—role seems to require that they not be the assertively sexual people they once were. That is, it's okay to be erotically free when you're single, but once you marry—and once you become a mother—you have to be "good."

When women desexualize in marriage, people often assume that it's because women don't really like sex and once they have their men, they simply turn off. Being wives and mothers means that women are supposed to live for others now, and that is what contradicts being sexual. Being sexual means getting pleasure for yourself and giving as a mature, assertive person. Fulfilling sexuality, then, requires that a woman be an equal partner, not the subordinate member of a relationship, which she often becomes in marriage. Or is forced to become when the children arrive. And, as we've seen, the birth of a baby is typically when sex goes out the window and stays out long after the baby is sleeping eleven hours a night.

What then happens is that many couples begin to argue constantly about how often to have sex. Typically, with the couples I see, the man's complaint is that his wife doesn't want to make love as much as he does. She says:

- I'm too exhausted
- I'm angry at him, and if I'm angry I don't want sex
- There's no romance anymore. He just wants to "do it." We don't even talk.
- I'm a morning person and he's a night person, so I'm always tired when he's not and vice versa.
- I don't feel comfortable. One of the kids is always getting up and wandering in. And no, I won't lock the door. They need us now.

- We have no emotional relationship. Why would I want to make love?

And what does he say? Nearly always some version of:

- If we had more sex, maybe we'd have more of an emotional relationship.
- The romance is gone. I can't get all lovey-dovey the way we used to.

Then I tell them, "What you have is a stalemate. And the one good thing about a stalemate is that no one has to change." Only then will they consider some of the problems underlying their "unequal" interest in sex.

These are the backlash problems, in which sex is used as a battleground for issues in their power struggle. With negotiation, discussion, and good faith, all of these actual sexual differences would just be a part of the couple's sex life. What compounds the difficulty of simply negotiating for mutually satisfying sex is that most people never expect to have to talk about sex with their partner. After all, movies show lovers simply hurling themselves into each other's arms and letting blind passion guide them to ecstatic sex. So when this doesn't work, or doesn't last, partners think they are just not sexually compatible or that the other person got "off track" somehow. Most partners are so unsure and embarrassed about sex—despite our seemingly open sexual society—that they prefer to remain silent rather than discuss and negotiate how to have a satisfying sex life together.

Finally, many women fall into the role of good wife, caretaking wife, *and sexually reluctant wife,* the way, probably, they saw their mothers do. They never suspect that losing power may have ruined their sex lives. In fact, ironically, couples often won't examine the power relations between them because they're afraid of destroying the "mystery" of sexual relations, the "magic" of love, even when the magic is gone. But their fears are based on what I believe is a basic misunderstanding of the erotic impulse.

THE NATURE OF THE BEAST

Many of us in the mental health professions now consider that a child's crucial sense of self comes not from being "merged" with the mother but from the child's attachment to her *and* others. Its interactions and communications (smiles, cries, excitement) with others are then *recognized* by others.

Our human need to connect with another human being is so urgent that people will go to extremes of erotic dominance and submission if that is the only way they can experience connection. And yet, ironically, like Elizabeth and John in *9½ Weeks*, such S-M lovers remain strangers. In their story, the underlying wish—to connect—is portrayed in the ending when John, watching Elizabeth pack her things, begins to tell her about himself for the first time: "I have four older brothers," he says, "my mother worked at the checkout counter. They're retired now and I support them. . . ." After Elizabeth leaves, he says into the emptiness, "I love you." His real desire—to know and be known by another—has come out too late.

No matter which sex dominates, the eroticism of power does not last. Unlike mature passionate love, which grows, domination and surrender just escalate, further alienating the partners from themselves and each other. The ever greater attempts to "know" each other by possession and being possessed instead of through self-disclosure and empathy quickly descend into ever more frightening experiences of aloneness. The more alone and empty the lover feels, the more he will try to possess, dominate, or force the togetherness he yearns for. The woman, far from feeling pleasure in pain, surrenders more of her self and submits to more humiliation in hopes of that magical togetherness she imagined she could have. And the same is true of young married partners like Sasha and Adam.

Patterns of dominance and submission are really expressions of the kind of clutching togetherness I described earlier. And this is true whether partners act out their feelings in sex or live out their lives with one person dominating the other. The more immature a person is, the more anxious he is about his aloneness. As a result, that person will continually try to use another to fill the vacuum where a greater sense of self should be. The prescribed male role can make men appear strong and mature, while women's roles can make them seem just the opposite. But appearances deceive. These roles are steps in a dance requiring two partners—one to give up power and the other to look powerful in the eyes of the world. Yet they are equally frightened. Sasha, for example, never developed her autonomy, but Adam, who *seemed* more mature, was not secure enough to expect, accept, or encourage Sasha's autonomy.

Without mature selfhood, people fall easily into and accept the culture's sexual roles instead of being sexual in their own unique way. And those given sexual roles, generally learned from traditional models in society and family, lead to the sexuality of power. As many a mother has been known to say, "Everything I do is for you." Sexualize that attitude and you get "submission." Add the stifled wish for power to it and you get "swaggering submission," whether it's in Madonna's show-biz style or Sasha's more everyday version.

Many prominent feminists have argued that as long as we have a patriarchal system that leaves mothers primarily responsible for raising children, we will reproduce sex roles as we know them. And *sexual* roles as well. As long as mothers are trained to be self-sacrificing—and therefore lacking in autonomy—we will have some degree of male dominance and female surrender. This is quite a different way of understanding behavior from the Freudian notion of "natural" female masochism and male sexual aggression.

THE EROTICISM OF EQUALITY

In the wedding ceremony, when partners vow to "worship" the other with their bodies, they are expressing the desire for joining body and soul. Erotic union is the deepest form of mutual recognition because it is where we encounter another with our fullest selves: heart and mind, body and soul, as all the songs say.

Of course, sexual passion can be purely carnal. We can send our bodies into the arms of another and withhold ourselves entirely, then leave. Maybe never see the person again, though we may remember the sexual tenderness, the pleasure or excitement. Or we may forget those lovers and wonder, years later, talking to someone at a party, was she the one I spent the night with in Boston? That is, sex can mean nothing more than a great workout. But that's not really what we mean when we use the word *lovemaking*. If sex involves love, we mean for it to involve our whole selves.

Bringing so many parts of ourselves together in one moment can make lovemaking sound as impossible as angels dancing on the head of a pin. Because lovemaking isn't as automatic as sex, it feels like "magic" when it happens. Sexual passion based on intimacy—or the desire for intimacy—will grow into that sexual communion only if the partners preserve and then reveal their individual selves. The exultation we feel in love, says psychiatrist Ethel Person, is in our transcending (not capitulating) self in order to "know" another, as the Bible aptly describes sex. It is transforming because if we truly reveal ourselves, we confront our dependency, our tenderness, our limits, our weaknesses, and our strengths as they are recognized by the lover. We discover capacities we didn't know we had. We discover a depth of connection we didn't quite believe possible.

The hallmark of falling in love is discovering our similarity to another. This is true of friendship too. It is the way we connect. "Oh you love old movies, too?" Or, "You're a Pisces too." But in erotic love we confront a person's differences much more, and have to live with them. Yet tolerating differences, which will always be there, requires a strong enough sense of self to overcome the urge to merge, to make the other like you or "submerge" the self into the beloved. In a sense, what makes for sexual ecstasy is not just bodily pleasure but the momentary experience of total connection that *we* are there to witness. Far from blotting out consciousness like alcohol or S-M sex, lovemaking heightens the awareness of the self connected to another.

The paradox of sexual love is that it requires greater individuality in the partners. The stronger their separate selves, the greater their potential for closeness. Each partner's individuality, if it is strong enough to begin with, is then strengthened more by the lover's recognition and acceptance. However—and here's the point everyone overlooks—*clutching* a dependent or a superior in no way provides the transcendent experience of *connecting* with a peer—someone just as alone and just as afraid and just as strong as you are. True lovers, then, must be equals.

One of the most interesting new sex therapists, David Schnarch, argues that individuality is the life blood of what he calls "wall socket sex." What makes Schnarch so different is that while most sex therapists counsel couples to close their eyes and lose themselves in fantasy, he thinks that just shuts people into their aloneness. Schnarch counsels couples to look into each other's eyes during orgasm; that is, to let themselves see and be seen for who they really are.

Intimacy, he says, is for mature people because intimacy requires knowing another and being known. A man's sexual peak may be at age seventeen, but not his "erotic" peak. At seventeen, the last thing a boy wants is to be known, particularly because he doesn't know himself. The more maturity we have, the stronger our individuality, the greater our ability to depend on ourselves, soothe ourselves when our partners reject or disappoint us. And hence the paradox: by becoming more distinct as individuals, lovers get closer. As I always put it, if you want to keep a couple together, push them apart.

"UNTANGLING" LOVERS

In the early seventies, as my career got under way, Sam and I began to confront situations that were new for us and for others of our generation. I was regularly off working with male colleagues, having evening planning sessions, going out for lunch and away for conferences that included social activities as well as work. This was not supposed to happen after marriage! Married couples were supposed to turn the world into Noah's ark and go everywhere two by two.

Our early reactions to this predicament flowed right out of our traditional upbringings and are now the family anecdotes we laugh hardest about:

- Sam once appeared at the house where I was planning a workshop with a male psychologist and demanded that I come home "immediately."

- One time while I was talking to Sam on the phone from a distant city where I was at a conference, he asked, "Who else is there?" and I hung up on him! (How dare he question me?)
- Every time I returned home from a conference, we had a "ritual fight" and stayed mad at each other for hours because "he/she didn't even ask about *my* weekend."

We were so afraid that separate activities were going to destroy our relationship. In characteristically gendered responses, Sam acted the jealous husband, afraid that I'd surely have an affair, and I was like a rebellious teenager, oversensitive to any suggestion that I interpreted as "questioning" me. And, mind you, he acted the jealous husband even though, as an actor and an opera singer, he routinely did summer stock, television shows, and print advertisements in which he hugged and kissed often scantily clad beauties. I had never been jealous. I wasn't supposed to be. After all, it was for his *work*.

After a few stormy months like this, I decided it was time for more family therapy. The southern gentleman and the Irish girl from Brooklyn seemed to have very different ideas about how we would live.

The therapist helped us to stop "reacting" and instead to take an "I position," which meant calmly telling each other what we thought and what we were (or weren't) willing to do. The therapist also told us that we'd put all our eggs in the one basket of marriage, and that now we were acting married, like a two-headed unit instead of two individuals having a relationship. We'd given up some of our individuality and had fallen back into the old roles from our original families. I, for example, had been a rebellious adolescent, and Sam was the "talented one" who got special treatment from his mother.

Under stress, we reacted to each other as we had to our parents, me arguing and resisting the "rules" and Sam expecting things to go his way. This round of family therapy reconnected us to our roots and helped us to become more "separate": we expanded our identities by actively restoring daughter and son, sister and brother, aunt and uncle, niece and nephew to the wife/mother and husband/father roles we had shrunk into. Having taken the standard route to adulthood and coupledom of being dutiful but distant from our families, we'd nearly lost our real connections to them. Being connected again to a larger family network helped to absorb some of our anxiety and gave us the emotional support the therapist predicted it would. But most important in terms of our marriage, reconnecting with our families revealed us to ourselves. What I mean is that by confronting the old familial roles and patterns, we found it was much easier to stop blaming the other for playing them out in our marriage.

During that period, we also worked at expanding our circles of friends and colleagues and explicitly changed the "rules" to include some separate friends, acquaintances, and socializing. Now, our joint activities were truly voluntary. Anything we did separately, we told the other about but didn't need permission or agreement for. At first, Sam still didn't love my going to out-of-town conferences, but I'd simply say, "By the way, I'll be gone from Thursday through Sunday." Whatever he felt, he *accepted* it.

In time, he didn't mind at all because all of this "separateness" brought us closer than ever. What used to be a big fight was now a routine decision, such as my professional activities. Whereas before we'd throw "Oh, that would be too much time away from the family" at each other, we now made our decisions individually and trusted each other to be responsible. That was that. Including when Sam decided to go back to graduate school in addition to working. Before, we didn't stop to think, Is my partner making a responsible decision? We were just having anxious, knee-jerk reactions to each other. Once we stopped trying to control each other, we could see that each was making responsible decisions and neither of us wanted to escape from or hurt each other or our family life. Once the arguments stopped and we learned to trust each other, our anxiety faded. We were even able to joke about Sam's sexual jealousy. Once, as I left for a conference, he said, "Well, either I have to hire a detective or trust you, and it's cheaper to trust you." With our new separateness, the warmth and passion that had marked our early years together flooded back.

COUNTERPOINT, NOT HARMONY

As Sam and I learned during this second renegotiation of our marriage contract, erotic love is a growth experience. You reveal yourself because it makes you less alone. It is desire out of fullness, not emptiness—not jealousy, not the need to possess the other and not fear of losing the other. Even the new generation, free of the old-fashioned constraints Sam and I faced, still has this lesson to learn. Although few husbands today would "demand" that their wives leave a professional meeting, women clients often tell me that they would never make a dinner date with friends unless their spouses were out of town. Most wives wouldn't dream of spending a weekend with an old friend. Some won't even talk on the phone once their husbands get home in the evening for fear of hurting or annoying them. And, really, this is the same clutching togetherness as the old-fashioned marriage rules prescribed—the very thing that couples must let go of.

This "letting go" applies to sex itself. So often in the couples I see, the woman is in a rage because, as she explains it, "I tell him how *I* feel but then he never tells me how he feels." And I say to those women, "You share your emotions with him because it makes you feel better to do it. Maybe it doesn't make him feel better to do the same or maybe he just doesn't feel like sharing at that moment. You can let him know what it means to you to know how he feels, but that's all you can do." Once the men don't feel that professions of love and their most intimate thoughts are being demanded of them, they will generally say how they feel because, well, it does feel good. At least when it's voluntary. It may make you anxious to have a lover who doesn't reveal as much as you do, but if you can live with the anxiety, you can grow. Of course, if you have a lover who almost never reveals himself, you will inevitably reevaluate the relationship.

I now find myself completely in agreement with Schnarch's theories of mature sexual love. Whereas conventional sex therapy tries to reduce anxiety to enhance performance, Schnarch encourages partners to learn to tolerate anxiety in exchange for growth. To learn real self-disclosure, self-validation, and recognition of your lover. And that means partners who have equal individuality. Partners who are different and can disagree. Who aren't asking for basic reassurance that they're "okay."

The assumption that agreement equals love, that couples should do everything together and be alike, that they should "live in harmony," leads to a dull erotic union. If couples are afraid of conflict, they are less likely to self-disclose, innovate, or allow themselves to grow for fear of threatening the relationship. The more self-protective the partners are, the more likely their passionate courtship sex will flatten into repetitive or perfunctory sex. Harmony blends tones into a single sound. Counterpoint, like that in Vivaldi's *Four Seasons* is a far better musical analogy for a successful relationship: two distinct melodies playing simultaneously, creating a new, more exciting sound.

As frightened as men are of giving up power and women are of assuming it, what everyone must understand is that the great benefit of equal power is the potential for real intimacy, the kind only two mature individuals can have. What that means is real involvement in each other's lives, being able to exchange your thoughts and feelings freely and having them listened to (not reacted to impulsively), and being mutually considerate and thoughtful while still willing to argue and disagree. In other words, being friends. Many people believe that lovers can't be friends. They believe that being friends means you can't have good sex. But that's because they're defining friendship too narrowly. Each friendship is different. There are surely things you share with some friends that you don't with your spouse, particularly, perhaps, friends in your profession or friends you grew up with or friends of your own gender who like to do and talk about certain things your spouse doesn't.

What marks the intimate friendship between husband and wife will always be unique and doesn't have to include every potential for intimacy. But it means that they will each know the other deeply, know about the important aspects of their lives, their families, their friends, and their dreams. Intimacy is not a synonym for sex, nor is it one for togetherness or even "talking about relationships," which women, more than men, reared as differently as we are, often like to do. Intimacy is emotional connectedness. Sexual intimacy is the act of equally mature and separate people sharing a moment of emotional, sensual, and physical connection.

NO ONE EVER GIVES UP POWER WILLINGLY (EXCEPT WOMEN)

The real quandary for most couples and family therapists is the husband's resistance to giving up power, which is precisely what usually needs to happen if a relationship is to become equal. And the flip side of this quandry is women's resistance to challenging their husbands' power. If women don't clearly state, "I can't live with this. I need more say, and we have to negotiate until I have it," men will not change, even though both partners will benefit from equality.

Usually I explain the equality principle this way: *a relationship cannot survive if one person always loses the arguments. A husband needs to think about the fact that every time he "wins" or vetos his wife's decisions, he puts a shadow over their marriage, diminishes the intensity of their erotic union, and impairs his and his wife's ability to grow.* Every time women suppress their legitimate desires and give in instead of negotiating, they are betraying themselves and their partners. They think that by avoiding short-term conflict they are insuring a long-term marriage. What they don't understand is that each time they give in on the issues that mean most to them, they lose *self,* from which sexuality emanates. Ultimately, both partners will feel less loved and less themselves. Love, affection, sexual desire, commitment, feeling good about yourselves as a couple, cannot survive feeling bad about yourself as a person. When partners try to balance the power, good things begin to happen almost immediately: they get along, the kids stop acting out, they grow, and their sex lives improve.

Therapy sometimes catalyzes change in men because of the enormous relief they feel in not having to use power in order to get love. They are also often grateful for not having to be in charge—and therapy may be a husband's first experience of this. Since being in charge also means being blamed when things don't turn out right, men sometimes feel unburdened and free of guilt for the first time. They may finally learn to express pain and vulnerability without feeling that they are threatening their relationship. A man may blossom simply because he no longer has to play one of the confining roles in a stagnating relationship. And finally, he may be able to get in touch with his feelings by focusing on his own emotional legacies rather than on the marital strife.

If men engage emotionally, they are less likely to use sex in place of other kinds of connection. Many women complain that "sex is the only way my husband knows to be close." Often, when men are emotionally connected, they want to snuggle and talk just as much as their wives do. Another great benefit of men changing is that when they carry the emotional burdens along with their wives, they grow more intimate. They begin to enjoy emotional support, the kind that comes from friendship, which doesn't involve sex. And, miraculously, their sexual lives become richer.

As difficult as it is for men to give up power in a marriage, they have begun to respond to the pressure from their wives. By seeing how their lives have improved since women started working, many younger men are accepting the new power balance within marriage. If men don't see how their lives will improve, they shouldn't change, because change will be superficial and short-lived. But as we'll see in Chapter 9, "Renegotiating the Marriage Contract," more and more men do experience the benefits of sharing power, and they are finally glad to have companions rather than underlings.

Fortunately, the old style of sexual dominance and submission is being challenged. This new generation may be less inclined than previous generations to accept sexual polarities. Young people who meet in school or who work at the same place increasingly base their sexual life together on their equality. My husband could never understand how our younger son, Tim, survived co-educational dorms without finding himself constantly in heat.

Our son always told him, "It's a generational thing, Dad"; he saw women as his friends, which didn't diminish his sexual interest in them. As men and women understand one another better and live more closely, they might simply become more sexually selective. Men might not be so sexually aroused by difference alone or a glimpse of naked flesh. We can only hope that eventually the culture might respond by actually producing different images for an eroticism of equality—and the social changes that would help it to last even after the children arrive.

9

Renegotiating the Marriage Contract

(Scene: Two women on their way to a divorce court in Reno, Nevada)
ROSALYN: "Can't I just tell the judge, 'He wasn't there?' "
ISABEL: "If you could say that, honey, there would only be eleven marriages in America."

—*The Misfits,* 1963

When Marilyn Monroe delivered this line as Rosalyn in Arthur Miller's *The Misfits,* she captured so much of what is sadly still true about marriages today. And as her friend points out, the marriage Rosalyn has come to Reno to end is just like a million others: her husband "wasn't there." But, presumably, he—and all the other men like him—was "there" when she married him, at least enough to have engaged her and made her feel optimistic about their shared future.

So what went wrong? What always goes wrong, I suspect. Playing the roles they were taught to play when they wed, Rosalyn embraced the marriage and her husband embraced his work, so much so that they floated further and further apart. Once married, they couldn't hold on to their identities.

Why some couples are more successful at holding on to their identities in a marriage and weathering change or even calamity has to do with what their family legacies are and whether they adequately resolved old emotional issues with their parents. That's what determines whether they have (or can develop) the maturity to negotiate. Then, of course, how much support they get from family and friends matters too, as well as how early on they tackle their problems. Sam and I had the advantage of therapy and certain positive family legacies, such as the perseverance and optimism I learned from my parents. Sam, who was an actor and opera singer, was tender enough to want to do child care and artistic enough to embrace a new definition of masculinity. I thank his mother for nurturing both of those wonderful traits.

When all is said and done, however, motivation may be the final determinant in a successful renegotiation of a marriage contract. And what does motivate partners? You can't count on love or fairness alone to make a reluctant partner want to change. Because change is often agonizingly difficult and partners resist it, staying in destructive patterns instead, sometimes even the marriage itself has to be put on the line. Yet, at times, there are obstacles to putting the marriage on the line.

Couples with small children, for example, often feel compelled to stay together even though they haven't been able to renegotiate a more satisfying contract. A man might be too guilty to raise the issue of divorce. A woman who has little or no income may feel she has no choice because alone she won't be able to support herself and her children. When such partners tell me that they've given up on their marriage but feel they have to wait to divorce until the children are grown, I tell them that's not a good idea. If you stay in a marriage you've given up on, you're wasting years of your life. You can't really put yourself on hold. Whenever you're not growing, you're stagnating. And stagnation will tear at the heart of your identity. It will wither you. Better to work once again on your marriage, or on splitting in a good way, planning for financial independence with education or training. And as one partner grows in this way, so might the other.

Money and class can be an obstacle as well. Usually, the more money a couple has, the more options, which can help them in the process of renegotiation. Money certainly helped Gary and Sharon and Gina and Dale, for example. But, sometimes, at the very top, money and the privilege that goes with it become obstacles to putting a marriage on the line.

Yvonne brought Henry into therapy because she couldn't "handle" his terrible temper. "He makes a fuss over nothing, like if I'm not there when he phones home," she said. As she talked more about Henry's "flying off the handle" when she didn't put him first in her schedule, I asked her if she felt she had the freedom to plan her own life. At this, she looked puzzled. "Of course," she said. "I just want him to understand that if I'm involved in something, he shouldn't get mad at me for that. Like when I had to drop a course I was taking to go with him on a business trip to Paris. He was furious because I got upset. I suppose I'm crazy to have a problem with a trip to Paris! Anyone I know would jump at it."

I soon realized that Yvonne, who had once been a secretary at Henry's import-export company, didn't want to "rock the boat." She wished Henry would be less irritable and more understanding, but she refused to face the implications of her complaints. Like many women who marry successful and wealthy men, she would not risk losing her marriage, which took her into a world of privilege, though not personal empowerment. Ironically, Yvonne has less power in her relationship than women in lower financial brackets, who might be more willing to press for changes and stand up for what they see as their "rights."

Henry, like many wealthy men, was so used to power he never expected to negotiate with "subordinates." "I work in a high-stress business. I don't have time to call her back three times. And I travel constantly. I want her there with me," he explained. "She's not doing anything that can't be rescheduled." What often forces a less-wealthy husband to give up his proprietary attitude toward his wife or his "I don't do housework" position is the need for her income. Also, men in lower-income brackets are much more used to sharing power and even accepting it from superiors at work. They don't expect to have unbridled power for themselves in all situations. Without these experiences, men like Henry aren't motivated to change.

When I ask partners at the beginning of therapy what outcome they would choose if they could wave a magic wand, I'm assessing whether they're committed to change or have actually given up. And sometimes I tell them that almost any couple can make their marriage work *if they are willing to do what it takes.* That's a big "if." And sometimes they don't know. They may be so busy keeping score and fueling their angers, they're glued to their positions and won't change. Ambivalence goes nowhere. Angry stalemates lock couples into misery. Movement toward renegotiation or toward divorce can always be reversed. But at least both directions involve change and are therefore hopeful. And yet, no matter how motivated a couple, change is never easy.

RENEGOTIATION TAKES MORE THAN REASON

Partners in a marriage can't just sit down and renegotiate their contract like labor and management. For one thing, when two people marry their contract is generally not explicit. Rather, it's usually a tacit understanding that the couple has signed on for shared hopes, dreams, and often unexpressed expectations of how each is going to treat the other and who is going to do what. When I ask partners what they imagined their marriage would be like, it is only then that they give voice to their unarticulated contract and, in the process, their own emotional legacies. Making the contract explicit makes it possible to change it.

When Wendy and Jordan came for therapy, he was almost silent with rage because they had lost a perfect house upstate when she "couldn't get it together to meet him and the real estate agent." He was genuinely baffled. "It was our dream to raise our children in the country. Now the baby's due in three weeks and we still don't have a house. I don't know what's going on," he said. Seeing his enthusiasm for the move and her reluctance, I asked them, "Whose dream is it, really?"

Wendy spoke guardedly. "I know how important it is to Jordan, and it seems like a wonderful idea," she said, adding, "not that I've ever actually lived in the country . . ."

"Wendy, suppose you had a different dream. Are you afraid of that?" I asked, and she admitted she was. After a minute, almost crying, she mumbled, "I couldn't disappoint him." But she had good reasons for wanting to remain in the city. She had a job she could return to if she wanted and she had friends and family. So I helped her to understand that if she tried to live Jordan's dream and disregarded her own, she'd end up disappointing him even more. We agreed to focus therapy first on integrating the baby into their lives and consider other issues about their future after they had more firsthand experience with the major change about to occur.

Like so many young couples, these partners had to learn how to negotiate so that they each got enough of what they needed to hold on to their identities. They hadn't yet realized the powerful "programming" to behave in certain "mommy-daddy" roles. That's why the first child is a trip wire, hurling the couple into a different stage that undermines their marriage contract. Their unexplored "mommy-daddy" legacies suddenly kick in. In this case, it made Jordan want to put his wife and child into the same country setting he grew up in. But until then, they'd both worked in New York City together; such a move would have radically changed their entire relationship. She'd be in the country, where she had no easy work opportunities, friends, or family, and he'd be commuting over an hour each way, every day, to his job in New York City. Her programming—to please her husband and be a good wife-mother—made her distrust her own strong desire to stay in the city, where, in fact, *she* grew up. As she was finding out, the supposed social contract—which promised her equality and a career—turns out to have a very short life. After all, there are no social supports for equality within the home once the children come. Wendy couldn't think what else to do but stay at home and raise their child.

So after these young couples realize the social and emotional pressures, why don't they just sit down and make the best new deal possible? Maybe Wendy and Jordan could have successfully negotiated for a weekend cabin so she could keep her job in the city. Or another couple with a lot of career flexibility might just decide that one of them will take off a year then the other one will, or "We'll open a bed-and-breakfast, work together, and keep the kids with us there." In other words, why don't couples just make a few logical changes in their plans? If it were only that easy. But the changes needed to renegotiate a marriage are not about finding "solutions" to concrete problems, although, hopefully, that occurs along the way.

I sometimes use words that may suggest simple behavioral and intellectual change—words like *discussion, conflict resolution, mediation, decision making,* and so on, but for *intimates* to engage successfully in these forms of negotiation, there must be *the most profound emotional transformation of the individuals and of the relationship itself.* A transformation that allows each to see and experience oneself and the other and "the problem" differently. That is what good therapy is about. And first, before they can begin, they have to let go of their anger, hurt, and disappointment.

Letting Go

Renegotiating the contract at any of the transitions requires a willingness to overcome negative feelings long enough to "try" new behaviors. It means being willing to stop destructive habits that may have taken hold and poisoned the atmosphere: constant criticism and bickering, name-calling, contempt, long stony silences, unilateral and angry decisions. Naturally, the longer the partners have been acting hurtfully, the harder it will be to change. What I often do is use specific techniques to help couples overcome "strangulation by negative feelings":

1. I sometimes begin by giving them a book to read. My friend Harriet Lerner's book, *The Dance of Anger,* helps people think differently about handling anger.
2. Then I ask them if they can agree to *behave* better; i.e., "just close your mouth," even if they don't *feel* differently yet, because feelings follow behavior as much as behavior

follows feelings. I explain that it will improve the "climate" between them if they act like friends, speak courteously to each other, and stop any name-calling so that they can discuss the "real issues" more effectively in therapy.

3. I explore with each of them their list of disappointments. Usually the list leads back to family legacies and societal assumptions. If she says, "I wanted a warm, humane man like Bruce, but I expected him to be financially successful, too" we can discuss why she expected him to be in charge of the family's financial success and how hard it is for a man to be both the things she wanted. If he says, "I wanted my wife to take charge of the household, but I expected her to stay the sweet girl I married," we can discuss where his expectations came from and if they are "reasonable."

And, incidentally, it may be interesting to point out here that women usually see the difficulties ahead and assume that they'll change their husbands after marriage but find they cannot; whereas men assume their wives will never change the positive traits that attracted them. Understanding how unreasonable such expectations are sometimes helps couples give up some of the anger about them.

4. I help clients to break down their global feelings of anger, as in "she's so critical," into specific complaints that can be addressed in therapy; for example, "It upsets me when she criticizes my way of handling the children."

When anger has been reduced but not entirely dispelled, the relationship usually becomes calmer but somewhat more distant. After all, the couple has spent some crucial amount of time using anger as a way to connect. Now if they're going to connect in a positive way, they risk and fear rejection, which they've avoided through maintaining conflict. This is the time when they have to begin taking responsibility for themselves and give up the old complaints that shift responsibility to the other: "If he loved me, he'd know what I want . . . ." or "She knows I can't stand when she talks on the phone all evening, so why does she do it?" Instead of expecting the other to change, to read your mind and give you a risk-free relationship, it's now up to each one of you to ask directly for what you want and to give—or not give—your spouse what he or she asks for.

Taking responsibility means saying what you really mean. Many partners give each other double messages. "I don't mind missing the party. There'll be others," you might say. But if you really do mind missing it, your spouse will pay, even though you appear to agree with his wish to stay home. A wife will often complain to me that "whenever I tell him about problems at work, he gives me advice." But that same wife never thinks to ask outright for the comfort or understanding she actually wants, so the husband gives what he has been taught to give: help in solving problems.

As small as these complaints may appear, they are examples of the real issue underlying global angers and entrenched bitterness. They are all variations on every couple's central struggle of individuality versus togetherness: what should I expect to get from another person, and what should I expect to take care of for myself. And they can each be worked on, one by one. Reducing the anger to specifics sets the stage for renegotiation by making each one responsible for herself or himself, not for the other.

Nonetheless, even between partners who have let go of their anger, no matter how reasonable they are, renegotiation in marriage, as I said before, is never a "reasonable" exchange of ideas. Because the investment in your "negotiating position" comes from within the emotional depths of your life, changing the organization of a marriage means exploring family legacies, fantasies, and social pressures that decide how we'll be a couple and how we'll be parents. And only if both partners change emotionally and come to recognize the social forces that make their family life difficult can they then work together on the problem instead of taking it out on each other. Only through this kind of work can they decide how they want their family to be and redefine themselves so they fit the changes they want to make. And real change, that is, abiding change that can be passed down to our children, has to reach from our innermost selves to our most public ones.

THE THREE LEVELS OF CHANGE

As a clinician, I would say that experience—and therefore change—takes place on three levels: the emotional, the behavioral, and the social. Furthermore, it is insufficient—even counterproductive—to change only one level. Yet that is precisely what many therapists counsel and many people believe.

There are currently a spate of best-sellers and marriage manuals (almost all of them aimed at women) that speak purely to a narrow aspect of the emotional level. Some counsel women to seek "the wild woman within" while others suggest loving or communicating in a different way. The implication is that if a woman changes herself emotionally, her problems will be solved. But as I said in the introduction, feeling good about yourself isn't enough—your family, your spouse, and the whole social system is out there acting on you, organizing you into roles and rules you may not be fully aware of.

But changing yourself *is* an important part of renegotiation and will allow you to interact with your spouse in a caring rather than defensive way. As I've just explained, partners must take emotional responsibility for themselves and also must give up any fantasies that the other "will make me happy." They have to stop blaming the other for "making me angry" or "pushing my buttons." Everyone is in charge of his or her own happiness, depression, anger, and buttons. Such reasoning as "they shouldn't have made me angry" doesn't justify yelling and intimidating the whole family. If I am depressed, I can't assume my partner will cheer me up or listen to me talk *endlessly* about it.

Couples also have to understand the value of appropriate emotional expression, like telling someone when you're angry or hurt instead of raging through the house or giving someone "the silent treatment." They have to know which feelings are just *reactive* emotional expression that is more a throwback to some old family issues than to a specific present event. They also have to take into consideration differences in ethnic backgrounds that allow for overplaying or underplaying emotions rather than taking it personally if this one wants to argue and that one wants to take a long walk to "get over it." And whatever the background, prohibitions on women's anger have to be lifted. Last, both partners, not just one, have to change emotionally. If a husband has been "flying off the handle" for years, yes, he has to deal with his own anger problem. But his wife will have to stop trying to "understand" his tantrums, as if she were causing them. And just as he will have to explore the real causes of his tirades, she will have to explore why she was willing to put up with them all those years.

Unfortunately, the emphasis on a sort of "feel good" personal emotional change is so popular right now that most people believe that's the only change necessary to improve relationships and change lives. But interactive behavior has to change as well so that couples can create the caring climate that produces a fair sharing of domestic and financial responsibility.

At the other extreme, some experts are only interested in behavioral change, like behaviorist therapists or some feminist social critics who propose a simple reapportionment of tasks to solve the gender problem. But they aren't taking into account that if you change behavior alone—without the emotions—the changes will be meaningless or will quickly revert.

A telling example is the father who grudgingly agrees to take care of the children for an hour but doesn't engage with them. He might just be angry about having to take care of them, or like Gary, the mostly absent husband in the first couple we met, he may not understand the legacies that keep him from being close to his children. I remember one woman telling me how her husband, brooding, walked five feet ahead of her and the children throughout their two days at Disney World. He went on the family vacation, yes, but he wasn't really there. Another frequent behavioral change that doesn't work *by itself* is women going back to work right after childbirth when doing so goes counter to their feelings. Sometimes, when a woman believes she "should" go back to work but doesn't really want to, she will have constant "symptoms" that prevent her following through: migraines, mysterious viruses, depression. A woman in this situation will have to explore her emotional ambivalence and the family and social pressures behind it before she's free to make the personal decision that's best for her.

Now I agree that behavioral change can sometimes be so dramatic that it *provokes* emotional change. That's why many family therapists begin therapy this way. A favorite saying among family therapists is "Change your behavior and you'll be amazed at how quickly your emotions change." However, we also believe that the changed emotions can and most probably will profoundly upset the system's equilibrium, unmasking underlying problems. This is especially true of changes in gender roles because they cut so deep. Let me explain.

I once suggested a simple behavioral reversal to a client whose dismissal of her husband's hypochondriacal complaints had only intensified them. She was the "overresponsible" partner in that couple, as women frequently are. She was in charge of the family, including his parents and sisters, fussing over his every problem, except his health. His hypochondria, she said, "Drives me nuts."

When she took my advice and played Florence Nightingale, her husband instantly recovered from his latest "illness," but then she found herself sobbing over what a "bitch" she'd been to withhold such a little bit of sympathy. To understand her unexpected emotions we worked over the next months to trace them back to her childhood years of caring for her critically ill mother. By pushing herself to nurse her husband she was able to experience her conflicting emotions and understand her family legacies. Only then did she realize that she didn't want to spend her life caretaking, the role she'd been trained for as the oldest girl in her family.

This is how change at the behavioral level—understood in the context of a person's family-emotional system—can be transformative. However, even when behavioral change is fortified with emotional work, the change won't last without also understanding the social context that will limit or support it. And usually even social change is also necessary.

Every time partners make behavioral and emotional changes that differ from the norm, they are making an incremental social change. That is, they're providing new models or making their business or community accommodate their change. Remember the major league football player who insisted on missing a game to be with his wife for the birth of their child! He forced the whole sports community to question whether a game was more "sacred" than fathering. And he finally got their support, though twenty years ago, he probably wouldn't have.

In our society, personal changes won't just "fall into place" when they're made as if the social level doesn't exist. That's true even within a marriage, when an issue doesn't seem socially related at all. For instance, a wife may continue blaming her husband for her being overwhelmed by child care, and her husband may distance himself angrily from her complaints, without either of them realizing that, first, the problem of child care is both of theirs, even though society assigns it to women and, second, they can't solve the problem if neither of their workplaces nor the government provides access to affordable child care.

In the same way, a husband may act as if a wife's working at two full-time jobs (home and office) is just "life in the hectic modern world," and if it's too much for her, she should "just cut back." But it's inexcusable and unhelpful if the therapy also ignores the social and economic forces that created these specific, rather bizarre, domestic scenarios where she's working two jobs and he's still only doing one.

Social context is such an important and neglected factor in renegotiating the marriage contract that partners must be aware of the "rules" that define how to be a man or woman of a particular class, religion, group, race, or sexual orientation—and how these rules restrict one's ability to define oneself differently. When you overlook any one of the social contexts of a marriage, you miss essential information.

Let's look at a couple that came for therapy because the wife believed her husband had "lost yet another job because he can't accept authority." She assumed that he "mouthed off to the boss" like he does to her and worried because her salary as a bookkeeper wasn't enough to support them. He, however, maintained that he got along fine, even with his wife, "except about the work problem." When I asked him what he did, he told me he was a manager at a printing shop. "Aren't they automating the printing industry now?" I asked, and he said they were, which meant more and more personnel at every level were out of jobs. "Then why are you two fighting instead of planning what to do about that?" I asked, and we spent the next six sessions working out a plan for his retraining so he could eventually get another kind of job. Many partners today blame each other for joblessness or low earnings because they don't understand the pressure from the economy that might require relocating, retraining, or redefining roles.

Another social factor affecting our personal interactions is our place in the pecking order. For example, if men are in charge of government and business, they don't see why women are having a problem about combining work and family. After all, they're not. And if a husband doesn't understand why his wife feels conflicted about leaving the baby in child care for ten hours a day, it's usually because he was raised to value his career above all else. And because the society places a higher value on autonomy as well, his "position" in the negotiation gets validation. Hers does not. That's why he might assume an "it's your problem" attitude. As in, "If you're going to be so sensitive, then you cut back. I have no problem with working ten hours a day." In order to negotiate the issue fairly, they'll have to learn to differentiate their own personal values from society's.

The changes a couple makes don't by themselves change society. And therapy by itself doesn't change society. In fact, unless therapists are vigilant, they risk helping clients to accept and adjust to problematic laws and customs. A couple must come to understand the social system they are part of, find their own solution within it, then challenge it when they can. Not just accommodate it.

MAKING A LASTING CHANGE

When a person changes, all three levels of experience interact at once. And that means all the unspoken signals—familial and social—kick in without their being aware of it. Change is inevitable, no matter how a person chooses to live. But for the large majority of people who marry and have children, those changes will be dramatic because each new stage of the family life cycle generates completely new individual, couple, and family tasks. In Chapter 11, "The Marital Stress Points," I'll discuss the stages of middle-class family life. For now, let me just list them: getting married, having children, raising adolescents, moving on after launching the children, and moving into later life.

Getting married, for example, requires joining two extended families, setting up a household together, making joint decisions, and working out some joint financial arrangement. This is usually a lot more complicated than setting up a small company. For one thing, so much of ourselves is on the line. The changes we make may begin with the behavioral tasks necessary at each stage, but family legacies immediately play their parts.

Family legacies create the emotional level of the change. They can be imagined both as a force flowing down through the generations of a family and as the force of the living family's "system." As a new stage is approached, the relevant legacies—the family's themes, triangles, taboos, ghosts, and roles—go to work on the subconscious, creating a new kind of anxiety that will keep a person from acting freely. Instead, the tendency will be to act in one's given role or rebel against it, as if these were our only choices.

Take the example of a female artist. If she came from a family where mothering was considered the most important aspect of a woman's life, she may feel she has to reject the role of mothering entirely in order to pursue her talents or vice versa. But if she could learn to endure the anxiety of change and differentiate her needs from her parents' expectations—as Gina did—she would then feel free to make her own choice about having children or not.

Social legacies come from our communities, whether we belong to them still or have become outcasts. The group's spoken and unspoken rules about gender, class, and culture shape the different ways people encounter the different stages of family life. A young woman growing up Baptist in a small southern city will probably leave home later than a young woman from a Brooklyn Jewish family. In the Brooklyn family, going away to college, training for a career, and setting up an independent life defines coming of age for both sexes. The young southerner may well have children earlier and more willingly accept a traditional wifely role. If she hasn't worked outside the home, her most difficult transition comes after her children are grown and leave home. Her urban counterpart, who most likely has trained for a career, might find having children the hardest transition.

Community doesn't only create different patterns of maturing. Just as often it determines whether the society will or will not support your choices. If you belong to a group that's high on the pecking order, such as educated white males, who create social policy, you're much more likely to find that society stands behind you. You may not understand the discontent of others because the society works well for you. But it works far less well for women, blacks, gays and lesbians, and the poor. Sometimes, of course, there are other kinds of supports within these groups—from a close-knit community, a church, or a political movement. Whatever your group, though, it will have a definite impact on how you deal with the changes required at each new stage of family life.

BRINGING IT ALL TOGETHER

I sometimes joke with students and clients that there are really only three basic complaints in therapy:

1. "Poor me" (individual symptoms, anxiety, etc.)
2. "If it weren't for you" (marital problems)
3. "Please fix this child without changing us" (child problems)

The therapist's job is to help the client put "the problem" (individual, marital, or child) into the larger system that it's part of. So an "individual" problem is seen as part of the marriage; a "marital problem" is seen as part of what's wrong in the extended family; and a "child problem" is seen in the context of the family. All of these, in turn, are part of the community and social system.

This means involving *all* levels of the system: emotional, behavioral, and social. If the goal remains to solve a concrete problem, the unchanged system in which the problem is embedded will continue to produce similar problems ad infinitum.

All three levels of experience—emotional, behavioral, and social—intertwine in a way that will help or hinder change. Take, for example, the primary problem in contemporary marriage: she's responsible for both home and work while he's in charge of money. We see and hear about the problem on the behavioral level: she works full-time or part-time and either does the child care and housework or arranges most of it. Meanwhile he earns, manages, and controls most of the money, "helps" around the house, and sees the kids mostly on weekends. And this couple argues frequently about both subjects; they also complain to their friends, family, and therapists.

At the level of feelings, she is resentful and emotionally exhausted. He is defensive and may also be angry at her lack of appreciation for his hard work. On a deeper emotional plane, where their feelings are connected to their family relationships, is their emotional programming. From earliest childhood, she was probably praised for her accomplishments but taught the greater importance of being a mother. Ten to one, she helped her mother with housework, cooking, caring for younger siblings, and also did baby-sitting for neighbors. Because they were close, she probably knew her mother's feelings and attitudes about "the female role," even unstated ones. Whether she wanted to be like her mother or different from her, her identity was formed by her mother.

Her husband probably learned the "male role" through observation and injunction rather than by having an intimate relationship with his father. In fact, ten to one, his father was mostly away "at work," which, in itself, was a strong message to him to focus on himself and his achievements. If his mother followed society's warnings, she backed away from him when he hit his teens "so he could become a man." He was expected not to need or want close emotional contact with either of his parents and was often lonely—although he may not have had the experience or vocabulary to identify this (or other) feelings. If he was interested in "girl things," eyebrows were raised, giggles were heard from his peers, and he was called "wimp" or "wuz."

On the social level, the separate gender roles were (and are) portrayed everywhere: on TV, in fairy tales, in movies (even Disney movies for kids), in the playground, and on the playing fields. The community, too, was and is a well-lit display of the "right way" to organize family life. Certain social "rebels" did it differently but were labeled, laughed at, and made the subject of cautionary tales: "Look at her, she got a Merit Scholarship but she's still not married" or "See how he was so involved with his children, he didn't get ahead." Many flock to movies about working mothers whose baby-sitters kill (or nearly kill) the children. And the message clicks in: "Only mother should take care of the child."

Because these same ideas about gender are learned at all levels of experience, we don't often stop to consider whether in today's world they make sense for us personally. And even if we come to think differently, those new beliefs remain on the intellectual level and don't cancel out the deeper emotional programming of our early experience. A woman may be serious about her career, but nothing in her emotional experience has prepared her for the idea that she should support herself financially for her whole life and make her mark in that career. Few "new men" have learned on the emotional level that housework and child care are as important as career success. Nothing has taught them *emotionally* that they can be real men if they aren't the main providers for their family. And yet, successful family life today requires that she also earn money and he also do child care and housework.

Since most of our behavior is automatic, we are all prone to rely on our storehouse of assumptions when we're in a difficult or highly charged situation. If we're attacked, threatened, confused or surprised (even by something as pleasurable as love), our anxiety goes up and our emotional programming kicks in, helping us to respond. It takes a lot of calm thinking and planning as well as powerful new emotional experiences for any of us to override our automatic reactions. And since we have been programmed to deal with the life circumstances our parents faced, not our own, it does seem miraculous that anyone ever changes. In fact, most people don't change their basic reactions to life and relationships until pushed or forced by events out of their control. These crucial events that lead to change often occur in our current family household, but they always lead back to the family we grew up in.

10

Going Home

It was no accident that the family therapist helping Sam and me through our second major marital renegotiation counseled us to reconnect with our original families. He could see, and he showed us, that so many of the things we blamed on each other came straight out of our old family roles—my "rebellious adolescent" and Sam's "entitled son." And how could we change them with each other if we weren't grown up enough to change them with our parents? Instead of distancing from parents (as I did) or assuming his mother's deference toward him was just "natural" (Sam's M.O.), we had to strive for more honest, significant connections.

When we saw how our relationship flowed out of our parental families, we tried what the therapist suggested—just as apprehensively and with as much anxiety as everyone else. And as we rounded some corners in our family relationships, we immediately felt the impact on our marriage. That's what kept us going in spite of how hard it was and how well we understood that this was a project we'd be working on for the rest of our lives. As for those first attempts, they coincided with the time when my father was dying, which really raised the stakes for me! But, fortunately, as I mentioned, perseverance is one of my family's traits. And it's a good thing, because going home was the most difficult part of renegotiating my marriage contract—but also the most effective.

It was March 1972 when I decided that I would try to change my relationship with each of my parents. I spent the two months before their return to New York from their winter stay in Florida thinking about the family and what I wanted to change about my position within it. I also struggled with bouts of dread and anxiety beyond all my expectations. Although my insomnia, backaches, and assorted tics tempted me to abandon the idea before I began, they also seemed to indicate that the project was more important than I realized. Drawing my family tree, making lists, and trying to organize all kinds of data gave me some intellectual distance and provided some relief and a few ideas about how to start moving. I consulted with my therapist throughout.

As I surveyed my extended family for the first time, I realized that it bore all the earmarks of a closed system loaded with strict rules and taboo topics that popped at the seams periodically with sudden death, serious illness, accidents, or breakdowns. These events were handled as semisecrets, certainly from the children, with tense, whispered conversations among adults and somewhat more open grieving by the women at funerals. They were then dropped from discussion as family members went on with their lives in the Irish tradition of endurance in the face of "troubles." My own position as the oldest was that of a typical "father's daughter"—close but conflicted toward the women in my family and warmly disposed toward, but nevertheless quite distant from the men, including my father. For the twenty years since I'd left home after college, I'd maintained polite but superficial contact with my family. There had been one brief breaking through of the facade in 1959, when I married Sam, a divorced Protestant, outside of the Catholic church. From my family, only my sister, brother, and first cousin attended my wedding. After about a year of tension, this intermarriage had been "accepted" and "forgotten" without further reference to it.

My first step in my "reentry" was to become less distant with my mother. I changed my own behavior by bringing the most uncharacteristic gifts I could think of—things handmade by me, who, it was well known, had no talent for handiwork. I concentrated on staying out of old traps (like futile political arguments) rather than doing anything in particular. But instead of staying in boring routine conversations, I asked about family history, which my mother seemed happy to talk about. Their warm response to my new behavior was the first of many occasions that made me wonder what percentage of the distance and superficiality was of my own making.

When I called a week later to follow up my "reentry visit," I was thunderstruck to find that my father had just been taken to the hospital with pneumonia and tested for recurrence of a "cured" cancer, which turned out to be extensive and irreversible. He was undergoing cobalt and chemotherapy to forestall a kidney operation. Under the stress of this news, my mother and I cried, but when my mother pulled herself together she said, "Of course, he's not to know. We'll all be brave and go on as usual." The family program was clicking in.

Now I decided I had to move straight toward my father if I were going to establish personal contact with him before he died. Although my emotions screamed for distance from this whole scene, I hoped that I could control my feelings and move in instead of out. I anticipated my family system's automatic tendency to close down under stress, as per my mother's admonition.

During the seven weeks of my father's hospitalization, I made frequent visits at times when I knew we would be alone. I made a list of subjects I wanted to bring up with him, his approaching death being the most important and the most difficult. I also wanted to bring up unspoken issues between us, such as my wedding and my entry into the field of social work, after years of hearing my father rail against all the social workers who had interfered with his own work in the rehabilitation of the physically handicapped. I wanted to know about his parents, whom he never mentioned, and what his early family life had been like after his parents split (a family "secret"). To let him know me, I planned to tell him that Sam and I sometimes had loud arguments—in spite of the family rule against open conflict—and that we'd had some very hard times—in spite of the family rule against complaining. I wanted him to know something about me as the adult I sometimes was outside the family.

Before each visit to the hospital, I chose one of these topics and planned elaborately "casual" ways of getting to the topic via some tangential and less-loaded topic. Before each visit, I also carefully prepared some remarks that alluded to his illness and approaching death, such as "I know that cobalt is terrible stuff but everyone hopes it will give you more time" or "Well, you are certainly the coolest member of the family; the rest of the family are up the walls worrying about you dying." This let him know that if he wanted to talk about it, I was available.

I further structured my visits by deciding ahead of time on the length of the visits so I wouldn't chicken out—and I'm proud to say that before the seven weeks were over, I worked them up to two hours. Although all these "precautions" sound silly, I don't believe I could have done anything without them. As it was, I once walked in and out of the hospital lobby three times before I could force myself into the elevator, and I often had to use the mirror in my father's bathroom to lecture myself before I could bring up anything on my list: "You're forty-three years old," I would say to myself, "and you're afraid to mention your wedding to your father. Are you prepared to live with that?"

My father played his part in our dance of distance. Worrying about my "safety" in that neighborhood, he'd try to chase me out almost as soon as I got there. He would launch into long discussions of safe topics like the children's activities and then suggest I run along home to them. When I jokingly said that if I didn't know I was his favorite daughter I'd think he was trying to get rid of me, he laughed, but he also stopped some of his avoidance tactics. When I persisted and brought up my issue, the length of his response was in inverse proportion to the issue's importance. When I alluded to his death, he'd say something like "Well, we've all got to go sometime."

Yet, though we were not exactly having long, easy, flowing

conversations on important emotional issues, it was clear that my father and I were beginning to make contact on other than a superficial level. He always looked brighter and perkier by the time I left, and his greetings to me took on a warmer and livelier quality. Although the visits never got easy for me, they got easier. After each one, I felt better in every way.

Once my father was released from the hospital in July, he seemed to recuperate for a while. My brother and I planned a three-generation birthday party in August for my father's, brother's, and nephew's birthdays. During the party, however, my father seemed depressed, and he stunned everyone by pretending to mistake the brand name on one of the presents for the name of a funeral home. I made some crack about black humor, and the conversation moved nervously on.

By November, my father was back in the hospital. Again, I resumed my intimate talks with him, which were easier and more natural than they had been. On my first visit, he told me that they were going to operate in a few days to remove his kidney. I started to cry and said I was afraid he was going to die. He took my hand, wiped a tear from his eye, and we went on to have several hours of the best talking we'd ever done.

My father made a kind of life review, focusing mainly on the great satisfaction he had gotten from his work—training the handicapped in marketable skills. He was himself lame from childhood polio and, as a young man, had had difficulty in getting work. I related this to my own work, and he listened and responded to me in a new way. We went on with some real ease to many family topics, some of them elaborations on subjects I'd gingerly raised during his previous hospitalization. As I was leaving that night, he smiled and said, "You've grown up, Tootsie," using a pet name he had not used with me for almost thirty years. I cried all the way home. We had two more visits like this before his operation, which he announced to me he now felt ready for, unlike during the summer, when he was sure it would have killed him. "And I'm ready for that possibility, too," he said. "I'm not as scared as I was."

On the day the operation was scheduled, my mother, brother, and I spent four hours with him before learning that the operation was rescheduled for the following day. My sister was on her way from Europe, where she lived. After the operation, when they wheeled him back into the room, semiconscious and groaning, he opened his eyes and said, "Pardon the symphony. I hope I'm on key." The doctors reported their amazement at his strength and the operation's success.

But on Christmas Day, when we called my parents from my brother's house, my mother informed us that my father had been in severe pain all day. It was a sudden turn for the worse. A few days later, she reported sadly that two doctors had confirmed her fears that "the bone pain has begun." My father was apathetic and listless. By January, sitting in the living room and watching my father tune out, the forty-fifth wedding anniversary party I was toying with for them seemed like a crazy idea. But when I mentioned it to my brother, his own enthusiasm encouraged me. He agreed it should be a surprise because otherwise they would veto it. The party was a total surprise to my parents. The doorbell just kept ringing and new people appeared, including some relatives we hadn't seen in years.

At the opening of the anniversary presents I gave a joking toast to my parents that ticked through—in reverse—a list of their attributes that used to bug me, but no longer did: "The rumor about my parents getting divorced," I announced, "is not true. Mom complains a lot, but she's trying to take better care of Dad; and Dad hates to be waited on, especially by women, but he's trying to let her do it," etc., to the accompaniment of my family's laughter.

In my various conversations, I tried to bring out and detoxify the issue of my father's impending death, which was on everyone's mind, with comments like: "Anniversary parties are more fun than wakes, don't you think so?" At that one my father laughed and replied, "Especially for the victim," and I said, "I thought you'd see it that way, Dad."

For a month or so after the party, my father was mysteriously doing well again. He started painting—his favorite hobby. For the first time since he got sick, he read with interest and fumed at the TV news. Throughout the family, acquaintances were being renewed. And when he died seven months later, not only did I know my father better but I felt more mature, and I was.

Does all this seem miles away from my marriage? It wasn't at all. Throughout the year of my emotional reentry into my family, there was a steady reduction of tension between Sam and me and between us and our children. Our children were doing better, and we were happier with them. My insomnia disappeared, along with the backaches, and I enjoyed my work again. I felt far less burdened than I had, and Sam and I planned our first weeklong vacation without the children in twelve years. We had stopped reacting to each other as the "rebel" vs. the "entitled one."

I knew there was still plenty of reconnecting to do with my family, but it was never as anxiety provoking again. By the time I had similar conversations with my mother, we two, who had walked around each other so warily all my life, had become good friends. In fact, out of the blue one evening while we were having dinner, my mother suddenly said to me, "You know, my mother didn't come to my wedding." Astonished, I replied, "Neither did mine," silently wondering if this was some weird family pattern. But since she was the quintessential "good girl" marrying Mr. Responsible, I asked why. "Well," she said, "you have to remember that in those days there was a funny attitude about the disabled." For a minute, I didn't understand. Of course, my father had been lame all his life, although I had never thought of him as "disabled." "He had a hard time getting a job," she said. "No one wanted to hire a 'cripple.' Your grandmother, who believed he'd never get work, didn't want to spoil my wedding by crying in the church." I understood that last phrase was also her apology to me for not coming to my wedding. We both had tears in our eyes, and she squeezed my hand.

EVERYBODY MARRIES HIS (AND HER) MOTHER

Although the story of my reconnection to my parents is only part of the work Sam and I did to reconnect with our families as adults, I wanted to offer it up as a heartfelt example of how difficult and how subtle an experience "going home" can be. And how vital for change. Sam and I could not have renegotiated our marriage contract that second time without changing ourselves emotionally, and that entailed changing ourselves with our original family. What I experienced and what I see constantly in the couples I treat is that talking about one's parents and reworking a relationship with them generates more emotion than any argument that occurs between the partners, which is, after all, just shadowboxing.

The profoundest change people undergo *always* occurs at the emotional level. But by now it's obvious that what I mean by the emotional level is not simply understanding what happened in the past. Understanding is the first step, yes. *But your family legacy is what is happening emotionally between you and your family now, in present time.* A person's relationship with his or her family— parents, siblings, et al.—is the very best indicator of his or her current emotional life. For how you are with them is how you are (or the exact opposite of how you try to be) with your spouse, your children, your friends and colleagues.

I've told the story of my reconciliation with my father because, as I said, his impending death made that my first priority. But since for most of us our mothers were our primary caretakers, the mother-child way of relating is generally the one that has given both men and women our blueprint for all subsequent intimate relationships. Interestingly, the idea that we "inherit" the behavior of our parents is no longer only psychological supposition. Two Israeli biologists made the news recently with their theory that humans and many other animals pass along their own learned behavior through generations without the help of DNA. Their research accounts for why people so often choose mates like their mothers. But female songbirds, they point out, seek mates with song styles like their fathers. One of the researchers pointed out that human fathers could have an equally strong influence on their young, if like male songbirds, they were equal partners in child rearing.

When we have troubled relationships with our parents, whether cutoff, distant, or overinvolved, they have to be changed into open, adult, person-to-person relationships in order for other relationships to improve and stay improved. Even if it takes lecturing yourself in the mirror, as I had to do, you must be able to talk to your mother and father about the most important emotional issues in your life if you want to grow up. I had to ask my father how he felt about not coming to my wedding. Gary had to ask his mother if she was disappointed in him. You and your parents are adults now, hard as that is to believe, and can talk as two adults, if you can give up being the child.

Most people are shocked by the idea that not only can you go home again, you must. So shocked that my colleague and friend Monica McGoldrick has seen fit to write a book called, *You Can Go Home Again* to explain why it is so important to establish healthy relationships with your original family. And I'm glad she has, since whenever I suggest someone try to improve a relationship with a parent, I invariably hear, as I did at first from Gary, "Oh, but my parents are hopeless. No one could have a relationship with them."

"Not true," I always reply with my hard-won convictions, "if you are not hopeless, your parents aren't either."

But my certainty isn't enough to convince most people, and so I hear variations on the following protests:

- But you don't understand, my mother is completely self-absorbed. All she talks about are her illnesses.
- My mother has always been emotionally abusive. I just can't take it. My father is a missing person.
- Not *my* mother. She couldn't love a plant.

To which I usually answer, "Well, if they are that terrible, how did you turn out so well?"

Talking shop, therapists sometimes laugh about clients who describe their mothers as if they were green with purple horns, so we have the mother come in, and she seems to be a lovely person, full of concern. Then we remind ourselves—"But she wasn't *my* mother!"

One of the hardest lessons of growing up is that our parents are people, just as we are. They actually have a history and a life outside of being our parents. By force of circumstance and limitations, they may have behaved in hurtful ways, and they may not have the skills to change their behavior toward us. But if we change our behavior toward them, nine times out of ten, *they will respond.* We don't believe it because we are stuck thinking of ourselves as children in relation to our parents. As children, we couldn't change our relationship with them. We didn't have a strong enough sense of self, and we couldn't have tolerated the anxiety change requires. We couldn't risk losing the system that was our survival. As a child, whenever I tried to say what I saw as the truth, someone would tell me to sit down and be quiet, like a good girl. And I did, if angrily. I had to because I was so afraid of losing my parents' goodwill. Also, intermittently, I thought their way was right. But then when I grew up I didn't shift gears—until I made myself. When parents are dead, the task of getting to know who they were as people, and changing ourselves accordingly, is too complex to explain here. But it certainly can be done.

As adults, we are no longer dependent on the system for survival. We have the power to change and to tolerate the anxiety it will cause us. You hear a lot these days about therapists' urging clients to get in touch with their "inner child." Frankly, I urge my clients to get in touch with their "inner adult."

The very act of courting a new response from your parents and accepting it when it comes is, in itself, learning to risk change. This also starts you on the path toward giving up the immaturity of your lifelong relationship with your mother, in which you blamed and resented her for whatever disappointed you.

Let's say your mother acts childishly, then you've got to give up the overresponsible position you've most probably taken with her over the years, a position that's not good for you. And, in addition, your mother will probably change in response to your change, although changing *her* is not the goal. Let's say she seems distant—the way my father seemed to me. Then, instead of remaining distant yourself, you have to express your wish for closeness, the way I did, the way Gary did, and Dale and Gina. If your father attacks or rejects you, you don't have to defend yourself, counterattack, or reject him. Instead, ask him why he thinks the two of you are constantly squabbling or so strained with each other. Remember my premise: If you can be yourself with your family, you can be yourself with anyone. And that's because when you give up blaming other people and knowing you are responsible for your own life and relationships, you've claimed your *self*.

My father and I were able to share some common ground about the work we do. It was the first time we had such a moment of mutual respect and professional identification. But I had to give up "needing" his approval, and that meant moving on from my resentment that he never asked me anything about my work or acted as if what I did mattered. It also meant risking not getting exactly what I wanted (after all, he didn't even "believe in" therapy) but being close to the person he actually was. My father wasn't going to make deathbed pronouncements or dispense the kind of paternal wisdom I've read about in novels. But what I did get from him was every bit as precious. He finally seemed comfortable being himself with me. We talked honestly. He expressed his love. And that changed my life.

No one acts in a vacuum. No husband and wife are a couple, alone. We're all part of a system and have to confront change at our system's center—where our parents are. We have to recognize the emotional and social forces that formed them in order to appreciate who they are—and who we are. Only then will we be able to understand fully the impact of those same kinds of forces on ourselves.

OKAY, I'LL TRY (OR, RESISTANCE TO CHANGE)

Whenever I suggest a change, a client will almost always say, "I'll try," which means, "It won't work." Why is it that people are so dubious? Because change creates such enormous anxiety. As in, the devil you know is better than the devil you don't. That's why men with bossy mothers marry bossy wives and the children of alcoholics so often marry alcoholics. For better or worse, they *know* that scenario and they know their own role. We might fantasize about a mate like Cosby or his wife, but in real life familiarity wins out. So we stay in dead marriages, dead-end jobs, and exasperating friendships, and we live in places we hate because we're afraid something different will be worse. Or we just won't know how to handle it. And then, if the security of sameness doesn't keep the anxiety down, we drink, overeat, overwork, take drugs, or maybe exercise to some absurd musclebound extent. Just to take the edge off.

In the late sixties, one of the most fascinating studies about the anxiety associated with change was done by two physicians, Holmes and Rahe. Looking into the frequency of medical complaints following drastic life changes, they discovered—as expected—that symptoms increased following the death of a spouse, divorce, going to jail, or losing a job. But the surprise of the research was finding out that almost as many symptoms followed the achievement of personal success—getting married, job promotion, and the birth of a child. They concluded that the stressful factor was the *degree* of change; that is, how much shifting the change requires in the emotional system—and not whether the change was positive or negative.

Furthermore, the fear of change isn't just within ourselves. It's within everyone who is going to have to adjust to any change we have to make. Remember that we tend to organize ourselves in emotional triangles to avoid the discomforts of intimacy. So if you change your relationship with your father, you'd better think ahead about who's the third person in the triangle—probably your mother. She'll feel the change between you and your father and definitely have a reaction to it. And you can rest assured that all the people around you (who make up your system) will find some way of telling you to change back! This is because they are as anxious about change as you are. How many of these "change back" responses have you heard in your life?

- You'll give your father a heart attack
- You're killing your mother
- Why do you have to stir things up
- Leave well enough alone
- You'll hurt your sister's feelings
- I'll never speak to you again

I'm sure everyone can add a dozen more to the list. And most of them, like all but the last of these, will demonstrate that there's a triangle in action. So you can see that between the voices in our heads and the soon-angry chorus outside, we're automatically reluctant to change. Yet, against all odds, we do change because—if you take the trouble to really think things through—the motivations to change outweigh (though they don't outnumber) the obstacles. Try tallying them:

OBSTACLES TO CHANGE

1. Change creates stress and anxiety
2. It means giving up being "right" or "good," giving up being a victim or an adversary.
3. You lose your excuse for why you don't do something.
4. You may have to let go of a cozy alliance with a favorite parent, spouse, or friend (remember Gina's bond with her father).
5. You'll probably feel alone at first because you're used to "comfortable" unchallenged relationships.
6. It's so hard not to want anyone else's approval or permission.

MOTIVATIONS TO CHANGE

1. You'll be more empowered in your life and relationships—especially in your marriage. The triumph over anxiety and pressure will spill over to your work and elsewhere in your life.
2. You'll avoid passing along a destructive legacy to your children.
3. You will have formed more nourishing relationships and will continue to do so.
4. You'll feel lighter, less contorted, more "authentic."
5. After changing, stress, anxiety, and many symptoms abate.

Well, of course, anyone in his or her right mind would choose to change, but choosing to and doing it are two entirely different enterprises. The obstacles are so formidable, the change-back voices are so loud, that changing requires tenacity, support, and—most important—*strategy*. If I hadn't thought very carefully about whether to follow my mother's injunction not to act with my father as if his cancer was terminal, I would never have dared talk with him about how frightened I was of losing him. And he, following suit, wouldn't have talked about his own fears and, later, readiness. My strategy, consonant with my family's tone, was to bring the subject up lightly at first, then obliquely ("the cobalt will give you time"), and finally, when the opportunity presented itself, directly from my heart.

OUTWITTING THE SYSTEM

Murray Bowen, whose therapeutic philosophy was the basis and inspiration for my own, was fond of saying that change takes three steps, but most of us dance the "two-step." We change, then we change back because the system tells us to. This is true in our own marriages and in our original families. What we're not prepared for is handling the tremendous reactions we encounter from others when we change. And those reactions, rest assured, will be as powerful as the change you are attempting to make because your spouse or the members of your family will always try to stabilize the system. Therefore, any successful plan to change your role has to include a plan to outwit this automatic family reaction through strategy, tried-and-true tactics, foresight, thrust and parry.

Of the tried-and-true tactics, two are essential for any successful change:

1. Avoid attacking the system. (This is blaming others.)
2. Do not defend, explain, or apologize for your new position. (This is giving up self.)

Avoiding these two blunders means taking an "I" position with others. Remember how Gina had to tell her mother that "this is how I want to raise my child." Since Gina was dealing with a very defensive mother, she let her know that she wasn't attacking her mother's maternal ideals. "I appreciate what a wonderful mother you were and the care you gave us." But, essentially, she then told her mother than she, Gina, was a different person, and although she loved her mother very much, she planned to do her own mothering differently.

Never confuse the calm "I" position with an ultimatum, which always sounds like "You must do this or else" or "You must support me in my decision or else." It always amazes me how many clients think that "dealing with" their parents means telling them off, giving them ultimatums, or raising old issues to "prove" they are right. These moves keep a person in the "victim" position. Other clients, fearful of conflict, want to explain and explain, which is almost as ineffective as apologizing.

The "I" position requires careful listening so that you understand what the other person really cares about. Only then can you state your position in a respectful way, as Gina did when she acknowledged her mother's beliefs and then calmly explained her own. Saying to someone "I think differently" or "I really can't do that" is far easier for them to hear than telling them something like "You'll just have to adjust."

Gina's "I" position didn't protect Gina against her mother's tears, bitterness, or anger, but it lessened the impact of all of those. Most of us don't just calmly state our position. We cry, complain, wheedle, and attack. Why? Because we don't want to risk really having to change and maybe losing whatever affection (cooperation, connection, financial support) we do have from our parents or spouse. And although there's no way around the risk, I almost always tell clients that such a risk with parents is not as great as they think. There is a bond among family members that will withstand a lot if the individual doesn't feel he's lost face, been deliberately humiliated or attacked—and, of course, if his or her thinking and emotions aren't impaired by drugs, alcohol, or psychosis. Any of these, or a history of violence, makes change a matter for professional help only.

In ordinary circumstances, when you stand your ground but also keep a loving connectedness, in most cases the system will eventually accept your new position. They may be furious at first, or cut you off entirely, but that won't last if you persist and remain connected. The familial bond—the mutual need—is very strong. And, luckily for all of us, given how hard it is to change, very small changes are perceived as significant by those close to us.

REMAKING A MARRIAGE

Once you've reconnected with your family and formed new, positive relationships, you still have to renegotiate with your spouse. Going home readies you emotionally; now the work begins.

I wish I could say that the couple bond was as strong as the familial one, but I can't. In marriages in our society, the bond may not be so strong. Divorce is deeply ingrained as a "solution" to marital problems. So when one spouse makes a change and stands his or her ground, there is a genuine risk that the other will leave. Much depends on the couple's history and the timing of the change. But if you don't risk that change, you'll end up living with a situation you resent or, worse, a life you hate. Most of us, though, can't even articulate the change we want because we're so stuck in the accommodation we've made.

If we can articulate the change, we then have to consider another vital factor in effective bargaining: carefully considering our alternatives, should the renegotiation fail. If your partner refuses to accept your new positions, and you do not have an acceptable choice for yourself, you aren't going to be able to mean it when you say, "I have to do this" or "I can't go along with that." This usually means having a viable alternative to staying together and enough money to live on. This is why it is crucial that women remain economically viable in their marriages. If they don't, they have no alternative if their partner will not renegotiate. They might be stuck in a stultifying, even an abusive marriage. Or, on the other hand, a husband may find that he can't continue in a marriage in which his wife refuses to go to work even though they can't live on his salary, or maybe she refused to have a child after having agreed to, or gets pregnant after agreeing not to. Usually however, he has the option of making this choice and still supporting himself. Considering alternatives then means just being emotionally prepared to lose your partner.

A couple recently told me the story of a young man who "house-sat" for them all summer with the agreement that he would keep the house clean. When they arrived during his last day there, his girlfriend, who had just arrived from out of state, was doing his laundry and cleaning the apartment. "Why are you doing all this," they asked, and she explained that he just doesn't clean. "If I don't do his laundry, he'll wear dirty clothes. I'd rather do it. If I didn't clean your house, he'd leave it this way."

This young girl's "solution" is all too common. What she's really saying is, "I'll give up my sense of fairness to myself to have this boyfriend." But she's not confronting what it means for her boyfriend not to have to consider her needs or play fair in order to have her. That is, if he chooses to be with her, he really should be willing to meet some mutually acceptable standard of cleanliness. For her part, when his clothes get so dirty they disgust her, she has to be willing to say—I won't go near you. I won't be seen with you. You can't sleep with me until you shower. And, yes, she has to risk that he will go in search of a girl willing to do his laundry or enjoy squalor. But what has she lost? A man she will have to "take care of" like a child. It may not feel to her like giving up self at this stage, but at the next one, when the children come, it will. She, alone, will have all the housework and the nitty-gritty parenting, and she will also have to continue parenting him or he will feel abandoned. They will become the "Angry Mommy–Naughty Boy" couple I mentioned before. Her "alternative," if he didn't choose to stay with her, is to free herself up to meet other, more appropriate boyfriends and to pursue her career without the detours and distractions such an inconsiderate boyfriend will produce in her life.

I used this example because so often a marital renegotiation is about reapportioning household chores. And usually women don't think of the domestic sphere as having clearly defined rules and standards that can be negotiated. But it does.

In a delightful article on the subject, a family therapist friend of mine, Marianne Ault-Riché, coined the term "shared laundry consciousness" to express the idea of an equitable distribution of both responsibility for and execution of domestic tasks. Like the young woman in the example, women get bogged down by the problem of a man's not caring enough about cleanliness, healthy meals, or nice clothes for the baby. At least, not enough to shop for or launder them. "He doesn't even see the dirt," she'll say. So it's *her* problem. Ault-Riché thinks differently. But, she argues, you have to raise his "laundry consciousness" to acceptable and mutually agreed-on standards. And define the tasks thoroughly. For example,

1. see garbage
2. bag garbage
3. take out garbage

Noticing the dirt is a task in itself, one that everyone can learn.

Of course, mutual acceptability in cleaning also has to take his standards into account, and that may mean if the woman wants magazines in a neat pile while he prefers a lived-in all-over-the-coffee-table look, then she'll have to pile them or accept a casual home. But if crumbs are all over the kitchen when he's finished the postdinner cleanup, she's not being finicky if she objects. Crumbs equal roaches. Food left out rots. Ordinary standards. Just as objective as putting the appropriate gas in the car and noticing when there's a peculiar thumping under the hood.

It's not enough for one partner to assign tasks to another, though to some extent they may have to, at least in the beginning. Husbands in this situation often complain that their wives "monitor" their housework, but sometimes, they're just unwilling to let their wives teach them how to make a home run. Negotiation that leads to real equality means both partners are equally aware that the laundry needs to be done, the larder needs to be filled, and children's shoes need to be replaced. That really means drawing up a list of household chores and divvying them up and then standing your ground. And really accepting the other person's style, though that may mean clothes for the kids and dinner concoctions that a partner (i.e., the woman who's used to doing it all) isn't comfortable with at first. Respecting each other's rules and responsibility for the home is a major step toward creating a full partnership and sometimes may require some pretty narrow definitions, such as public versus private space, or "my space" and "your space." In other words, a lover of clutter married to a tidy type may have to limit the clutter to his or her side of the bedroom, or the bed!

A marital renegotiation, then, requires the calmest consideration and discussion of "positions" precisely because it touches the deepest and most ingrained levels of our experience. Changing a marriage contract means altering our behavior, our emotions, and our relationship to the social worlds that have kept and would continue to keep us exactly as we are. And as strange as it sounds to most couples who hear the idea for the first time, nothing catalyzes such deep change as much as each partner's restoring a healthy relationship with his or her own parents and family.

Renegotiating a marriage contract shares some rules with collective bargaining of any kind: each party should know his or her bottom line, listen carefully to understand the other party's real investment in a particular position, take a calm "I" position about what they want, and have a clear alternative should the negotiation fail. But married partners also have to follow the rules of heart and soul. And they require a sincere search into the emotional and social legacies that created our positions, an assessment of what is meaningful to us, and an embrace of change so deep it will resound throughout our lives.

11

The Marital Stress Points

Marital renegotiations of some kind are necessary at all the major family transitions: getting married, having children, raising adolescents, launching the children and becoming a couple again, and moving into older age. Each one, while stressful to live through, provides an opportunity to grow individually and as a couple. The bad news is that at the time of these transitions, all of them times when we add or lose family members to some extent, the family system is jolted out of its usual operations and therefore can be easily stalled or derailed. The good news is that change is easier to introduce when the system is in flux than when it is moving full steam ahead.

Of course other stress points occur in some but not all marriages. These *unpredictable* stresses, such as affairs, chronic illness, or unemployment, are the subject of the next chapter. And the greatest of them—divorce (which today occurs in fifty percent of all marriages)—will have a separate chapter. For now, however, I want to map out those inevitable stresses facing couples in their first marriages and take a more thorough look at the two we have discussed in previous chapters: when the children come and when they leave home. Because these two transitions require the greatest emotional and behavioral shifts, they are the riskiest times, times when divorce rates soar. They also demand the most profound renegotiation of the marriage contract itself, not just minor amendments. While many couples manage transitions without too much difficulty, these two have become much more stressful than they used to be because of our society's unresolved "work-family" problems. But no matter which stress point a couple is facing, understanding the challenges of every transition can help couples to be as adaptable and flexible as couples today need to be.

While single-parent families, remarried families, gay and lesbian families, childless couples, and every other kind of family face predictable stress points as well, they are variations—sometimes vast ones—on the themes I'll set out here. These apply most accurately to long-term contemporary marriages.

EXCHANGING VOWS

Obvious as it is to anyone who has lived through the planning of a wedding, marriage is a major transition. By marrying, a couple joins their two families and, at the same time, commits themselves to a new family. In setting up house together, they often, for the first time, confront their different ideas of what makes a home and how it is run. Most important is who keeps it running. Also, once partners have declared their commitment to each other publicly and "officially," they often experience social and family pressure to become a traditional couple. Before, it may have been fine if they both worked at the video store, but now, Aunt Clara may say, shouldn't he be getting a real job? Shouldn't she be learning how to cook? Now partners have to negotiate carefully to set up a life that reflects their own interests and not outside expectations.

If they haven't been living together before marriage, they probably haven't realized that people can have radically different ideas about what to eat and when to sleep, when to make love, how many household chores there are, and who should do them. They may have different notions of modesty and privacy, such as whether your partner should ever see you brush your teeth or should know how much money is in your bank account. Sharing money for the first time is another challenge. An unmarried couple may have been spontaneous and haphazard before, or observed traditional "boy pays for girl" mores. But, once married, if she's earning money, he probably won't want to continue paying for everything.

I actually saw a couple professionally whose new marriage seemed to be "falling apart" because, among other things, they couldn't agree on how often the sheets should be laundered. He called her a "clean freak" and was afraid he'd be living in a "museum" for the rest of his life because she wanted to change sheets once a week. She was equally quick to generalize, refusing to live with "a pig." Naturally, they discovered that they overlapped on many of the housekeeping rules and were able to negotiate this one.

If partners have been living together before marriage, they have probably been lulled into thinking they have all that stuff figured out. So they will be shocked to discover how different the expectations will now be—not only from outsiders, but also from each other. I know one young couple who lived together for two years with a mattress on the floor and futons. They agreed that when they married they wouldn't suddenly have matching lamps and silver, but when they received such things as wedding presents, they found themselves setting up the middle-class household they thought they deplored. Then they had to confront their different responses to the "material" life. He was extremely fussy about their new "things" while she had a more casual attitude: "If we spill coffee on your mother's Persian carpet, so be it. If the china breaks, it'll break. I'm not saving it for company, like my mother did." As minor as such adjustments may seem, remember that the divorce rate for couples who have lived together is higher than for couples who have not!

Whether they've lived together or not, newly married partners may have to be concerned for the first time with how their families get along. They both might be expected to participate as a couple in family events, whereas before marriage, participation was more optional. Each of them has to renegotiate their relationship with their parents to include his or her spouse as a new family member: "Remember, Mom, he's a vegetarian." Each has to set new boundaries with their parents that preserve the couple's own agenda and other in-law responsibilities: "Mom, I know you prefer the big dinner on Christmas Eve, but that's Deirdre's mother's birthday. It'll work best for us to come on Christmas Day instead." Parents used to ordering up "command performances" by their kids will find the new constraints a "nuisance" and may resist the couple's new autonomy. But with each new choice and request, partners will be making another move toward adult individuality and coupledom.

As stressful as getting married can be, the general celebration and the fun of setting up house and being perceived as a couple are great enough to see most couples through. The negotiations aren't usually so difficult that a couple can't manage them, or learn them, especially when partners today know each other so much better than they did in the "olden days" of courting, formal engagement, and marriage. But the stresses are still very real. In fact, there's a growing number of couples who break up in the first year or two, before they have children. These "starter marriages," as they're now often called, don't survive the stress because, generally, the partners were acting impulsively. They may have married to please their parents, or to escape them. Whichever, these are "reactive marriages" jerry-built to deal with unresolved family problems and are not the result of making a considered choice of a lifetime mate.

"Leaving home," the young person's major family transition before marriage, is almost like a fingerprint, revealing the family program for handling relationship transitions. As they change status with their parents by moving out "to live their own lives," do young people have a fight with their parents and move far away? Leave everything stored at home and let their parents pay for their new apartment? Do what their parents tell them to do or the opposite? Or do they "solve" all the problems of living independently by quickly getting married? When I see a couple of any age in marital therapy, I inquire how they left home in order to give me a snapshot of their emotional programming.

Clearly, the young person who moves out without having to cling to or fight with parents, who explores work possibilities and pursues peer relationships, who becomes financially independent while staying emotionally connected to parents, has the best preparation for handling the emotional and behavioral transitions of marriage. Becoming a mature person before you try to become part of a couple has enormous advantages, which is why it can be problematic to go from home straight into marriage, as previous generations of young women had to do, or straight into living together, as many young people do today.

However, I often reassure worried parents of young people thrashing through this transition toward adulthood, that in our society "adolescence" can last until age thirty, especially in the professional and upper classes, where protracted education and family financial support are the norm. "The signers of the American Constitution were on average in their midtwenties," I tell astounded parents whose "kids" of that age are still students, "but remember, that was being middle-aged in the eighteenth century." In our own time, longevity, and all of the complex social and economic forces at work, lead to the postponement of marriage and also to impulsive reactions to that delay. But most couples stay married at least until the next far more difficult stress point: having children.

AND BABY MAKES THREE

Becoming parents is an unknown territory. Because most partners today are so poorly prepared or supported in dealing with the profound social and emotional issues that emerge, half of the time they will decide to divorce. Many other couples teeter on the edge. However, in nearly all marriages, a renegotiation could have restored the disrupted equilibrium and mutual respect that got lost with the conflicting demands of small children and the almighty workplace. Let's look at one couple who managed this transition with a renegotiation I helped them to make.

* * *

Sonya and Bob came in for therapy when Sonya was considering divorce. She made the appointment, telling me on the phone that it was her last attempt to save their marriage. And that Bob had agreed to come only because she was talking about divorce. They had never been to a therapist before, together or individually.

In the office that first evening, Bob seemed angry and withdrawn. Only his relaxed clothing—a bright blue-striped sweater, jeans, and sneakers suggested another, more easygoing side. His jaw was clenched, his gaze cast down. He was such a slender man that you could clearly see the taut muscles in his neck. But by contrast, Sonya, whose face was open and calm, her arms resting on the chair, appeared almost placid. And yet, despite their different affects, they had a similar style, both tidy and efficient, he with long sandy blond bangs cut squarely above his brows, his mustache cleanly trimmed and she, smart in her checked shirt and black sheath skirt, earrings dangling just a jot below her neatly trimmed black hair.

When I invited either to begin, Bob said, "She can go first, since it was her idea to come." He said this as if it were simply fair, and emphasized his neutrality by holding his hand up like a referee.

Sonya spoke in tones as even and calm as his, though what she said conveyed her deep upset. "I'm really—well—fed up. We hardly ever see each other and when we do, we just argue. About little things. Everything. The house, the kids . . ."

Bob rolled his eyes, sucked in his cheeks and mumbled, "It's not like I don't help with the kids when I'm home. . . ." Then Sonya, sighing, continued with somewhat greater urgency.

"I work. I take care of the house. I take care of the children. I'm trying to juggle too many things and I can't keep up without something snapping. Bob does nothing—"

"Not nothing," he rejoined, barely moving. "I travel. I'm on the road almost all week. That's my job. On the weekends, I'm with the kids as much as I can be."

Sonya grimaced.

At that point there was no trace of the glorious smile I would see on Bob's face in the wedding picture they brought in for their next session. No trace of the spontaneity captured in the snapshot of them lying on a beach, kissing passionately.

"Bob," I asked, "how do you feel about the divorce Sonya's thinking about?"

He had difficulty speaking and shook his head, then looked at her gravely. "We shouldn't have to end up like that." When I asked him what he saw as the direction to go, he said, "I've told her. I think she should quit her job."

"Sonya, how do you feel about that?"

"I don't like feeling that I have no options. I wouldn't want to feel like I have no say about what we can buy or do, or if we can go away."

"And if you could wave a magic wand and do whatever you wanted to do now, what would that be?"

Without hesitation, Sonya answered, "I'd work three days a week instead of five. That way, I wouldn't feel so hassled when I got home." And why didn't she work three days? "First of all, I have to pay the baby-sitter. I'll earn so much less working part-time, it doesn't pay to work. Secondly, I'm the office manager for a stationery business, and my boss says it's got to be a full-time job. What I'd like is for Bob to travel less."

"And Bob, would you like to travel less?"

He didn't hesitate either. "Yes," he said. "I'd like to spend more time with my children. But it's not possible. If I travel less, I don't get promoted, simple as that." He explained that he sold refrigeration systems to supermarkets and shops, and that his salary depended on the number of sales.

Now I had to discover more about what had brought them to this impasse, and that meant finding out what their life was like before the kids and what had attracted them to each other. They, too, would benefit from remembering what they had so clearly forgotten: why they were together in the first place. "Let's back up a moment here," I said. "Tell me about yourselves. For example, when were you married?"

Sonya's face softened. "In 1983," she said. Bob looked over at her fleetingly but with unmistakable warmth, and she returned his glance. Clearly, their wedding was a happy memory. In fact, throughout the story of their courtship, they revealed the warmth and closeness that was obviously still there beneath their anger.

It was Sonya who explained how they'd met. At the time, she was living in Pittsburgh with her family. Another secretary at her office invited her to a party. Her friend's boyfriend, who managed his family's supermarket, brought Bob, who had been in town selling their store new equipment.

"I liked him immediately," Sonya said. "He dressed well. He was smart and had a good sense of humor. He was reserved, but I could tell he was responding." Bob was grinning, looking at his knees while she spoke. "He was very fair-minded. I liked that."

Bob nodded, breaking in. "I liked that about her, too. How reasonable she was." Then he added, flirtatiously, "And, of course, I thought she was really pretty. I still do."

That week, Sonya said, they saw each other twice. He interrupted to add, "I actually extended my trip by switching my accounts around so I could see her again." Sonya looked at him, surprised. "I guess I never mentioned that," he added and finished the story: for that year they dated whenever Bob was in town. Then Sonya came to visit in the spring for a week's vacation. She stayed with a cousin but met Bob's family, too, and liked them, especially his mother who, she said, was so accepting and sweet. By the end of that week, they decided to marry the following fall.

Bob was now thirty-four and Sonya thirty-three; they had a five-year-old girl, Trisha, and a two-year-old boy, Evan. They lived in their own house, though the mortgage was high. When they told me that Sonya earned $36,000 and Bob earned $45,000, I said, "That's hard in the New York area, given today's economy, when you have two children. And yet, Bob, you think Sonya should quit work?"

Again he held his hand up like a referee and said, "We can live without extras."

"My salary doesn't just pay for extras," she said. "Plus, if we could never go out together, why stay married? We *do* still go out occasionally." This she said to me but then looked at him to confirm it.

Bob's face lit up, "No, I wouldn't want to give that up. We don't *always* argue," he said.

Now that Bob had let down his guard, I wanted to try to help him open up more emotionally. "Tell me, Bob, is traveling lonely?" I asked him.

"Yes," he answered, "night after night in those motels is really no life at all."

"And where did you learn that a man's lot in life was to be stoic and endure?"

"From my father. He taught me, even if you're sick, you get up and go to work."

After Bob explained that his father had also been a traveling salesman and was always gone five nights a week, I asked him if he thought his father had been lonely on the road.

Bob said, "Speaking from experience, I know it."

"Have you ever told Sonya how lonely it is on the road?" No, he hadn't. When I asked why, he cocked his head, perplexed.

"I guess because she has enough problems of her own. She doesn't need mine." The whole time he spoke about his life on the road, Sonya stared at him as if he were a stranger, and was clearly moved.

"Bob, how many years did your father travel?"

"About forty," he said.

"And is that what you want for yourself? Can you endure that much?"

"No," he said softly. "It's already getting to be a drag."

"Do you want this life for your son?" Again, he shook his head. "And did you ever talk to your father about how he felt on the road? If he has any regrets?" No, he never had. "Would you be up to trying?"

"Well, it would be a very strained talk," Bob said. "You see, we're very much alike. I really love my Dad, but we don't really talk about anything."

"And would you be willing to make a change?" I asked him. "I'm thinking about you and your children. Do you want it to be different with you and your children? If you can have a different relationship with your father, it might be easier for you to have a better one with your own children."

"Yes," he said. "Okay, I'll try." His ready acquiescence was unusual. I attributed it to his fear that Sonya really would divorce him if he didn't change.

In the next sessions, as I did Sonya and Bob's genogram, I learned that Sonya was the oldest of four children. Her parents divorced when she was eight. And while her father remarried twice, her mother never married again. Both her parents and Bob's were recent Eastern European immigrants. Bob had an older brother and a younger sister. A couple of years before, when Trisha was two, Bob's mother had died of breast cancer.

Neither Bob's nor Sonya's families encouraged their children to get any higher education. However, Sonya's mother regretted giving up working when her children were born, particularly in light of the divorce. She urged Sonya to keep working so she wouldn't find herself "without anything" later on. Although there were many other significant facts, these had contributed strongly to their tacit contract, as I saw as soon as I asked them both what they had thought their lives would be like with children.

Sonya said, "I don't really know. Except I assumed it would be different from when I grew up without a father. You know. Like Bob would tuck the children into bed and they'd run to greet him at the door every evening. It never occurred to me that he'd hardly ever be there. As for work, I always expected to work, but I don't think I understood how little time I'd have with my kids if I worked full-time."

Bob said, "I just assumed Sonya would raise the children, like my mother did. I never expected to actually take care of children. Maybe make Sunday barbecues and go to soccer games."

"Well, it sounds like you each had a different marriage contract in mind, and neither of you mentioned it. And isn't it strange, Sonya, that you ended up feeling many of the burdens and disappointments your mother felt after your father left?"

"That's really true," she said.

"We re-create our patterns, don't we?" I pointed out. "Bob's version of your marriage contract came straight from your family, right?" He nodded. "So maybe now's the time to ask how the talk with your father went."

"It was short," he laughed. "I asked him if traveling had been hard on him and he said no."

"Well, that his style, isn't it?"

Bob agreed. Then I suggested he try a different approach. That he might begin by talking honestly about how hard it was for him, Bob, and what stress it was causing in his family. Like most men, Bob tried to convince me of the "uselessness" of having a "real" conversation with his father. And like most, he felt too awkward and constrained to try. It's always necessary for me to connect such talks with results important to the men, like having a better relationship with their own children or avoiding divorce. But once they've made up their minds to do it, they are often less distracted from the task than women, who really do worry that they may "hurt" the other person or damage their relationship.

Bob did try and eventually his father responded, telling Bob honestly how much he regretted missing out on the family and how hard it had been to come home on the weekends and feel like a stranger. Even though he'd make a big fuss about cooking pancake breakfasts, he felt as if he didn't know his family as well as they knew one another. Finally, he even acknowledged to Bob that he had lived a terribly lonely life.

In one of our later sessions Bob said, "I would never have imagined my father would talk like that. Never." He was shaking his head, as if he'd seen a ghost. He felt "almost honored" to have his father confide in him. It gave him a new confidence and inner pleasure.

"How about your mother?" I asked. "I know that she died several years ago, but do you know how she felt about your father's traveling?"

He had no idea. She never talked about it.

"To you," I said. "But she may have talked to your father or your sister. Would you be willing to ask them about her feelings?"

"More talking," Bob said in mock annoyance, widening his eyes.

We all laughed. Sonya nodding encouragingly, despite the

fact that that she still talked as if divorce were the most obvious option. She did admit some of the strain had lifted and Bob was more willing to help with the housework, but her admission came only in response to my questions. Yet Sonya was clearly pleased when Bob reported back that his sister, who was the child closest to his mother, had told him how much his mother admired Sonya for working, and that as much as she'd enjoyed raising the kids, she'd said that she'd had cabin fever a lot of the time.

Bob's father had also been forthcoming about Bob's mother's feelings. "My mother actually told my father that she was sorry when I'd gone into sales. I never knew that. She'd never said a word to me. I thought it was what they both had wanted," Bob said.

As Bob was making progress toward understanding his family legacies, he found new understanding for Sonya's need to work. Once she felt more trusting of him, I broached the subject of Sonya's dilemma about work. I asked about her vision of her future, when the kids were grown. She was taken aback, she said, she'd never thought of work that way. But two weeks later she said she was very good at business, and having nearly run the stationery business for her boss, she felt she could run her own. "After all, women can get small business loans, why not me?" She also considered taking some marketing courses to fill in areas she didn't yet know about. Bob agreed that she probably could run a stationery business.

A few sessions later, once Sonya felt more certain about having a future career, she decided that it *would* be better to cut back at work for the present. She spoke again with her boss, who suggested then that she hire a replacement for herself and switch to a part-time job in the accounting department. With an eye to her own business, she was even happy about the chance to learn how an accounting department was run. And two weeks into her new schedule, Sonya came in beaming. "We're not fighting anymore," she said.

Some family therapy stops here, once the partners feel close to each other again. But this crisis provided an opportunity for Sonya and Bob to really renegotiate their marriage contract, preventing another breach later on. They had made a few adjustments, but they hadn't yet reorganized their system: Bob still felt tremendous pressure to earn the family's living—even if it were just for the present—and Sonya was still primarily responsible for child care. In fact, ironically, they had now moved more in the direction of the breadwinner-homemaker marriage. And that meant that Sonya, who now earned less, could also lose the very power she now had to challenge their arrangement in the first place. This was an inequality that had to be addressed. So I pressed them further, asking what they wanted to work on.

"Well," Sonya said, as if she'd rehearsed her proposal, "now I'd like Bob to cut down on some of the travel and be home more. If I can change my work, he can change his."

I reminded Bob that he said he wanted to travel less and asked if he'd have a talk with his boss about the problem. "Nothing ventured, nothing gained," he said with new optimism.

The talk was a success. His boss said he could travel less if he transferred to technical support, although that would require retraining. Bob thought it over and agreed, commenting to me that it was hard to give up his white-collar job. But he accepted the reality that he could earn as much money fixing refrigeration as selling it, and spend more time with his family as well.

Now that they both said things were "terrific," I said this was the time to work on the hardest problems. And Sonya said, "I'd like to talk about dividing up the housework more fairly."

Bob made a mock gesture of surprise, throwing up his hands. "You mean we're never done?" he yelled, then quickly took Sonya's hand and they both laughed.

In order to renegotiate their marriage contract, Sonya and Bob had to look even more closely at the family and social forces operating on their marriage, and they did. Both of them were open to reevaluating their inherited ideas about women's and men's roles. Both of them spent a great deal of time considering their parents' values in the light of their parents' own experience and heritage. By doing so, they were able to come to their own conclusions. They both changed their relationships with their family members. Although there isn't space enough here to trace Sonya's reentry into her family, she did learn to stay close to her mother while maintaining her own different ideas about marriage. This, plus reconnecting with her distant father, gave her the confidence to rethink her own goals. Bob learned to talk more openly about his feelings and therefore connect more deeply.

Once they understood the social context of their marriage, they both made very different choices from their earlier, more automatic ones. In the end, Sonya and Bob both took less prestigious jobs in order to have a happier family life. This may have been easier for them to do than for Sharon and Gary, the first couple discussed in this book, because they weren't so locked into the materialistic upper reaches of the American Dream. Being middle class rather than upper-middle class, Sonya and Bob hadn't expected such affluence in life. So when they had to relinquish some of what they had attained and even reduce their income, their self-image wasn't as threatened. As I stated earlier, having less to lose materially can sometimes facilitate change emotionally.

Sonya, of course, was in a special bind, as most women are. From the beginning, she recognized the power of money in her relationship, and yet she still had to cut back at work to make her own life manageable. What made this possible was actively planning for a satisfying and viable financial future. Her decision to complete her business education in small doses and eventually to start her own business seemed entirely reasonable. Sonya understood that the outside world had made their ideal arrangement impossible at this point. However, awareness, open communication, and planning helped to keep power equal when income was not.

"WHAT HAPPENED TO OUR KIDS?"

If a couple has survived raising small children, the next transition is the children's adolescence. This requires that the parents make their family boundaries far more flexible than they were in order to allow for the children's growing independence. Children will now be moving in and out of the family system, often in unknown ways and sometimes in frightening ways with people *they* choose. When we were adolescents, our parents didn't have to worry about gangs and guns in our schools. And although drugs and teen pregnancy have been around for a while, they are far more prevalent now—in every community.

When children reach adolescence, many middle-class parents now face what poor families have always faced: TV, peer groups, and the streets have more influence over our children than we do. Especially if Mom and Dad can't agree on rules for teenagers. And for many parents, the new worry about the kids precipitates or coincides with a midlife crisis of their own.

Partners will have to resist the impulse to focus entirely on the adolescent problem, to become reactive, resentful of weirdly shorn hair, rap music, or whatever the child does to assert his independence from his family. In addition to pulling together in their parenting, the couple also has to stay focused on themselves and their own relationship, and assess the impact of having more independent—even sexually active—children.

One family came to therapy because of an ongoing conflict between the mother and the seventeen-year-old daughter. "She doesn't fill out her college applications, she comes in any time she wants and stays at her boyfriend's house when no one is there. If I say anything, she curses at me," said the mother, Marie. Stewart, the father, and their daughter, Lisa, rolled their eyes. Fourteen-year-old Peter stared at the floor.

I soon saw that Stewart and Marie disagreed over the rules ("she's too strict; he's too lenient"). And Stewart had gathered both children into an alliance with him against Marie. Marie, however much she yelled or complained, had no system of consequences for breaking the rules. She really expected her husband to enforce them.

"The inmates are in charge of the asylum," I told the parents in a session with just the two of them. So the first part of the therapy was about getting the couple to negotiate and mutually support a system of rules and consequences, such as not letting Lisa use the car or the phone if she behaved in an unacceptable way. Although it was difficult for Stewart and Marie to believe it, what I told them turned out to be true: even teenage werewolves get into line if both parents agree.

When this new regime was started, even tenuously, the therapy shifted to the "real" problem: Marie's anger about how little Stewart earned as the administrator of a senior citizen center and Stewart's feeling that Marie was too bossy. The reason that they couldn't agree on disciplining the children, of course, was that through the battle over the kids they were fighting out these marital complaints rather than facing each other directly. And it is this covert emotional battle of the parents that prevents common-sense disciplinary solutions from succeeding.

MIDLIFE CRISIS: FACT OR FICTION

Midlife crisis has probably received the most publicity of all life stresses. But not everyone has a midlife "crisis." Basically, there is a tendency around midlife for people to notice that their life will not be endless and to make an interim evaluation of how they're doing so far. If they score low on this Life Report Card of theirs, they will have an emotional crisis, which might trigger wholesale reevaluation or panicky overthrow of several of their life structures: marriage, career, family relationships. Or they may act out their distress with ill-considered or sudden life changes—affairs, a first child, another child, walking out on a job.

In one sense, this kind of crisis is useful in that it opens up the person and the couple to the need for radical change, which most of us prefer to avoid. It is always wise to see "sudden, crazy behavior" of a spouse as a wake-up call. Time for change. Big change.

Although midlife crisis—if there was one—used to coincide most often with children's adolescence, nowadays it is a movable marker that can coincide with almost any of the transitions or stress points: getting married or divorced, having a child, or launching the children. Therefore it can be quite a different phenomenon. Now, when women may have their children at any age between their adolescence and their midforties, midlife crisis might coincide with the arrival of a first child. The child may be a partial resolution of that crisis or may bring on the crisis in one or both of the partners. Another couple may face the stress of midlife reassessment when the children leave home or when the parent's own parent gets sick or dies.

Our primal response to loss is to react to all the losses in our lives. With our family system threatened, we have to come to terms with the kind of family we now have and whether we want to belong to it. And our scrutiny always raises questions of our membership in every other emotional system we belong to: our jobs, marriage, our original families, our communities. Do I really want to live in this town or city? we'll ask ourselves. Do I want to keep giving my life's blood to this corporation or should I open up a little restaurant like I've always dreamed of? We worry that if we don't resolve things with our parents, one or both may die before we have a chance even to try. Is this the person I want to grow old with? we ask ourselves about our spouses.

Also, it's important to remember that midlife crisis comes at different times for men and women. Men generally experience it connected to their age, usually in their early forties, while women go through it between forty and fifty-five, whenever their family relationships pose a serious dilemma: children coming or going, parents dying, or their marriage not working.

Obviously, the crisis will be different for men and women because society values men and women differently, and because their life experience is so distinct. Meryl Streep is considered "over the hill" as an actress, although she's younger than Robert Redford, Paul Newman, and Clint Eastwood, all of whose market value increased with their age. Pulitzer prize–winning novelist Annie Proulx, who began writing after she was fifty, talked about being able to gather so much information unobserved because no one notices older women. Many older women experience this. But while some women find that new invisibility a relief, others are hurt by it. Men, who can still reproduce later in life, can begin new families; women cannot do that. On the other hand, some women report feeling a new sense of strength and entitlement "now that they don't have to please others." In other words, they feel liberated from being in the "sexual marketplace." Some find their voice and finally feel listened to or taken seriously, particularly in their professional lives. I heard somewhere that Margaret Mead used to refer to the "joys of PMZ"—postmenopausal zest, the stage at which a woman cares more about speaking her mind than about the approval of men! I love it.

So many factors contribute to whether people have a midlife crisis or not and what form it takes. But the greatest single factor may be whether partners have confronted the issues between them throughout their marriage and renegotiated their contract as they went along.

ALONE AGAIN: MOVING AHEAD AFTER THE CHILDREN LEAVE

In 1983, our son Tim turned eighteen and went away to college. Bennett, who was twenty-two, was still living at home but only until he saved enough to move out. Both Sam and I felt that between working full-time and socializing with friends on weekends and evenings, he might just as well have been gone. And wasn't that great: at last, our child-rearing years were coming to a close. Those were our official sentiments, but something was wrong.

Instead of drawing together to plan our coming "freedom," we were increasingly irritable and withdrawn with each other. Sam also had physical symptoms, frightening attacks of rapid heartbeat (fibrillation) that incapacitated him for days at a time and often required hospitalization for various tests. Although his attacks scared me to death, I sometimes felt annoyed instead of sympathetic—as if he were doing this to me. Hoping to blot out the anxiety, I turned to my work. Meanwhile, Sam seemed more focused on complaints about his work than on our life together. What had happened—and when? I couldn't figure it out. Of course, I knew intellectually that profound change of any kind produces enormous anxiety and "symptoms," but knowing this didn't make me feel better. In addition, as happy as we were that our "boys" were moving on, we were unprepared for how much we would miss the daily involvement in their lives. So off we went—for the third time—to couples' therapy.

Our first therapist had been a neighbor we both knew and

respected. I'd chosen our second therapist because he seemed like me (Irish, with a good sense of humor) and had a theoretical orientation I admired. I chose our third therapist for Sam (I must have considered Sam to be "the problem"). The therapist was a kindly, nice guy with a southern accent, like Sam. Perfect. Like most therapists when they are clients, I was trying to stay in charge. But he was a really good therapist as well as a southern gentleman, and I soon left the driving to him.

It was 1984—that ominous date. I was fifty-five years old; Sam was fifty-nine. Although we began therapy with complaints about each other, we each were soon thinking and talking about ourselves. I was feeling overworked and resentful about it, as if someone else were making me do it. I also felt guilty now that the kids had grown. Had I worked too many evenings while they were young? For his part, Sam regretted that he hadn't had a longer singing career and wondered if he had settled too soon for that regular paycheck. Had he given in to family needs? Although he had won a Grammy award as a record producer, he wasn't sure he'd been successful enough. We were each able to talk like that to the therapist, but we hadn't been talking straight with each other for some time. When we tried, I cried and Sam acted bewildered and that was that.

I went back in my mind over the decades of our marriage: In the sixties we had renegotiated our brand-new marriage contract after experiencing more than the usual stress in starting a family. Then, in spite of the special worries we'd had about the children and not having enough money, we had moved along briskly. Looking back, I skipped over the enormous pressure of those years and our life then seemed very rich. We had wonderful friends; we were active in the civil rights and antiwar movements, and Sam and I had both gone back to graduate school at different times.

In the early seventies, as we both launched new careers, we renegotiated again to bring more balance to our work-money-family responsibilities and to stop restricting each other's outside activities. That's also when we brought our extended family back into our lives. But since then, life seemed harsher: we had moved, we'd both been working like demons, I had cofounded a family therapy institute, Bennett had left home for boarding school and returned, Tim had gone through adolescence, I had had a crisis over my fiftieth birthday, and both of our mothers had died. Now, twelve years after our last therapy, we were somewhat out of touch, tiptoeing around land mines of distance and resentment.

For us, this third renegotiation in the mideighties was about clearing out the old angers that had been buried during the mad-dash years of careers and child rearing. Only then could we each sum up and share the successes and regrets of our younger years and plan ahead as a couple again. I have come to realize that this kind of reevaluation and negotiation is a necessary task in long-term marriages. Neither of us had learned in our families to express anger directly, but Sam and I did it well enough to move on.

Over our next few years, we ventured into new territory. I still clearly remember the signposts: Sam's heart fibrillations became rare occurrences. We planned his early retirement from his now unrewarding work. We had a "launching party" to celebrate Bennett's move out on his own. I stopped working evenings. Tim became self-supporting. We sold our big old family home to move to an apartment near my office and bought a converted barn for a weekend home in the Berkshire Hills of Massachusetts. That had been a dream of ours for fifteen years. At the end of the eighties, we joyously celebrated our thirtieth anniversary (and my sixtieth birthday) with the biggest party we'd had since our wedding.

And the ripples continue: After Sam retired, our usual division of responsibilities shifted *without* any specific negotiating. I was still working almost full-time and he wasn't, so he began to do the marketing and cook dinner. More astonishing, he slowly began doing both on his own recognizance, without consulting me to make a list and plan the meals—and took to cleaning up afterward. Then we found ourselves in a rhythm where he does the laundry and cooking during the week while on weekends in the Berkshires we share the work.

I sometimes laughingly tell my young women clients, "Don't give up. If you insist and persist, if you negotiate now, there's no telling what he'll be doing around the house twenty or thirty years from now! Or how intimate a relationship you'll have."

Like Sam and I, most people are unprepared for how much more tension there might be *without* their children around. Once the children leave, they think life will be smoother, easier, and therefore happier. All that time together, finally. Delicious solitude. But fifteen minutes after the last child settles into his or her new life, every unresolved issue and buried resentment a couple has shoots back up in their faces.

If you have never renegotiated before, the issues that surface are enormous. They may push you into parallel lives with mutual criticism and a feeling of great estrangement. Or they may make you openly hostile. Sometimes I think—with a degree of horror—that if Sam and I hadn't had our earlier negotiations, how angry I would have been when the children left home. Remember, divorce during this period is very common. This is the time when stories abound about how "One day he just up and left" or "He's having an affair with a woman young enough to be his daughter" or "She's left him to concentrate on her career." All such sudden breakups after so many years of marriage are signs that these partners never negotiated when they needed to.

Not long ago, a couple married for thirty years with three children came to see me. Their marriage was unusual. She was an upper-middle-class woman who worked as a children's librarian. Her husband, who had come from a working-class family and had only a high school diploma, worked in the post office. Her family hadn't approved of the marriage. In their WASP thinking, she was "marrying down." But she had successfully quashed their protests so that everyone got along fine all these years even though they never approved of him. Now, the minute their youngest child left, the couple came to therapy because of her complaint that he was nasty to her family who, in response, was now furious at him.

In their case, the buried issue is glaring: the family triangle that had been there throughout their marriage resurfaced. She'd begun to reconsider that maybe her family was right all along. Look at how nasty he is. But taking the long view, I tried to help her see that she could consider the problem as part of their stage of life. That is, if she had married him to rebel against her family and stayed married because of the kids, she now had to decide if she wanted to stay married to him. And why now had she suddenly reconnected to her family's class values? Why had he "turned nasty" with them now, when they had gotten along so well all these years?

By the end of their therapy, she decided that she had married her husband to rebel but had come to love and respect him. She was happy with him, and she let both her mother and father know that she expected them finally to accept him or else, regretfully, she would be seeing them a lot less. As soon as *she* asserted herself with her parents, *he* stopped provoking them. But it wasn't a coincidence that the unsettled class issue between them came back to haunt them once they were on their own.

GROWING OLD TOGETHER

When younger women fuss about their "looks"—as I used to—I smile in the smug wisdom of advancing age and think: Don't they know that the only thing that matters is health, strength, full use of your faculties, and a boundless horizon? My conversation with my contemporaries nowadays is full of jokes about our failing memories and genuine concern about health. Everyone's routine checkup is a source of worry. Now we don't think of every illness as curable, and we realize how much a continuation of life as we've known it depends on our health. And we talk constantly about retirement: when, where, how are you doing it?

Retirement is an extremely complex milestone in the life of a couple. A man who feels he wasn't successful in his work may either refuse to retire, even though work brings little satisfaction, or he may retire and then become depressed or physically ill. "Workaholics," successful or not, usually suffer because they haven't developed other interests or talents. A man who retires with a sense of satisfaction and with financial resources may find that his wife is not ready to retire with him. As with every transition, life is more complicated now that women no longer automatically make whatever adjustments keep a relationship running smoothly.

Money also looms again as a major problem, and the income gap between men and women only widens as women collect lower amounts of Social Security, reflecting their lifelong lower incomes. Even couples who have had large incomes will face a greatly diminished cash flow unless they've saved enough, which most couples can't do. Couples now have to worry about a major health crisis or long-term care that will wipe out what savings they do have, since adding income is no longer possible. Such worries, lifestyle reductions, and hard realities can drain the life blood of a relationship unless partners can work together on the problem and accept the help from others they may sometimes require.

But the major negotiation for the couple facing (or not facing) retirement years is planning a new life structure. Up until now, work structured the days and years. Everything else— children, travel, friends, and even each other—happened "after work." However much we complain about overwork, we depend on work to keep us going without a new decision every day about how to spend our time. Without structure, people are at the mercy of transient moods and feelings, anxiety and depression. Then, too, if both partners don't retire at the same time, and usually they do not, they still have to negotiate whose schedule is "free" and whose isn't. Free to do what? Do they *both* want to move to the Sunbelt and live a life of leisure? Do they both like to travel? Where? Do they both want to just stay home, volunteer, and see the grandchildren?

This past week I saw a couple in their early sixties. Irene and Charlie had enough money in investments to "think big." But she still worked as a paralegal in the same office where she had worked for twenty-five years, while Charlie had been retired by law as an airline pilot three years before at age sixty. He said, "I feel like I'm just marking time waiting for her to retire."

"Retire to do what?" was Irene's question. "I hate golf and cards. Every step of our lives has been about taking care of the kids and then the grandkids. Now I want my own life. *Our* own life—just to suit us. I'm not talking about excluding the kids but just not focusing our life on them. What I really want is to sell everything and do whatever we feel like. But Charlie says that would just plunge us into chaos."

"Well, Charlie," I said, "you don't have to take her too literally. Why not just brainstorm a bit?" Actually, I almost lost my concentration thinking, She's right. Life just to suit the two of them. I can't wait to talk to Sam tonight.

What Irene and Charlie worked out for themselves isn't really important. With sufficient money, couples can always find some mutually satisfying plan. The important point—the one that electrified me—was Irene's proposal that they create a life *just to suit them* and not designed around the needs of others. Perhaps that seems such a novel idea because Sam and I are at that very stage when, like Irene and Charlie, we've lived life according to the obligations of earning and parenting for so long, we can hardly imagine any other. And "parenting" gets trickier and trickier as children and parents grow older. It's true that you're always your children's parents, but you have to renegotiate that contract too, changing the job description as the children grow. You may have been a "caretaker" and "director" of young children, but it's important to shift to "adviser" of adolescents (with occasional directing thrown in where necessary) and "consultant" to young adults.

By the time the "kids" are married and into their thirties, you should be trying to do your half of having an adult-to-adult personal relationship with them, even though you think they're awfully young and imprudent, and they think you're getting stodgy and stuck in your ideas. At this delicate transition in the life cycle, we're missing an important ritual. I tell clients and students only half jokingly that grown-up "kids" ought to give their parents a "retirement" party (and maybe an appreciative gold watch) to mark their retirement from "active parenting duty" and the passing of the torch to the next generation. Then some of the automatic parent-child behavior could be questioned. "Keeping in touch" could be shared equally by the generations, instead of becoming a dutiful one-way street in either direction— which it often does.

One forty-year-old client of mine complained that her retired parents had "taken me and my family up as their hobby. They

visit without notice, they give me unsolicited advice on everything
from money to child care, and they're driving me nuts."

On the other side, a client in her sixties recently told me that
she'd heard about someone who was going to put a message on
her answering machine to respond to calls from grown-up off-
spring:

> If you require financial assistance, press one; if you are in
> emotional turmoil about a romantic partner and require a
> few hours of sympathetic discussion, press two; if you are
> being treated unfairly at work or school and wish to displace
> your anger onto us, press three; if you are telephoning to
> ask about our well being or pass a few moments of pleasant
> conversation, you probably have the wrong number.

With the proper approach, the generations—parents and
their adult children—can share their lives in a spirit of caring
rather than obligation. And why hasn't a useful ritual "naturally"
developed to help parents and children move into this new
stage? Do you think it has something to do with the difficulties of
giving up power and the equally hard assuming of responsibility?
Of course, but the day may also come when the final shift must
be made and adult children must become the "advisers" and
"consultants" or even the caretakers of their elderly, ill, or frail
parents. However, even this shift will not be so drastic if the renegotiations of the relationships have been made along the way.
Sound familiar?

As for planning a new life structure for our retirement years, Sam
and I, like Charlie and Irene, have not yet confronted the second
aspect of the plan: dealing with each other on a twenty-four-hour
basis.

There's an old saying among women, "For better or for
worse, but not for lunch." What it refers to is the burden many
women feel of having their formerly busy husbands with them all
day long. Not only is it literally "too much togetherness," but
often the women feel their husbands are "meddling" in the
kitchen, reorganizing the house, computerizing accounts they

were once in charge of. Partners will now have to renegotiate "domains" and responsibilities. They will also have to continue to cultivate their separate lives as well as their shared ones. And here we see the final struggle between the voice of "togetherness" and the voice of "autonomy," although just to keep life interesting, the genders may switch roles at this stage, especially if the wife has finally fought her way out.

The stresses of older age can be enormous. Declining health, dying, and death may be constant issues. Ruth, a woman in her midseventies, tells me she and her husband go to another funeral every month. They make hospital and nursing-home visits regularly. "It's so hard not to be depressed," she says. The losses of old age are certainly pervasive: friends, siblings, co-workers may all be "dying out," as many elderly people put it. Not only may the symbols of "their time," such as movie stars, writers, and politicians, die, but their obituaries may mean nothing to the younger generations. There is a terrible sadness in watching one's peers and one's era pass away.

And yet, that sadness doesn't have to mean constant depression. Ruth said it's hard *not* to be depressed, but, in truth, she's not. "Old age is not for sissies," as they say. Few get by unscathed by illness, infirmity, or bereavement. But loss is not the only experience of old age. Ruth and her husband moved to a smaller house in a sunny place they both feel terrifically lucky to live in. Their involvement with their children and grandchildren keeps them "caught up in life." And even in their shrinking circle of friends, there are joyous celebrations: an eightieth birthday, a friend's remarriage at age seventy-three, the birth of a great-grandchild. And also, their involvement with each other is "better than it ever was," they both say. How is it possible? They have retained separate interests and pursuits; they have continued the emotional tasks begun in the preceding life phase, increasing their intimacy by sharing regrets about the past and reminding each other of earlier triumphs. They have maintained their sexual connection, dealing tenderly with reduced energy or libido.

In older couples, the death of a spouse is a grave loss, for it means losing someone at whose side you have "always" walked.

His death may signal your own impending one. And even so, this does not necessarily mean endless grief. It is the greatest challenge of old age to weather a partner's death and design a final new identity for yourself as a single person. I remember the day my mother said to me—several years after my father's death—when she was in her late seventies: "I woke up one day last week and said to myself, As long as I'm still here, I might as well live. I might as well have some fun." Whereupon she embarked on a series of travels with my aunt or my brother and seemed like her old spunky self again—right through her own final illness in her eighties. And yet, her favorite poem of those years was one by Robert Burns that begins, "We clamb the hill t'gither" and described, for her, her life beside my father.

The paradox of older couples is that the harder they have worked on their relationship, the more genuinely intimate they have become, the more self they have developed, the more surely they will withstand the death of their spouse, but the more painful it will be. It's true, old age is not for sissies; neither is growing old together.

12

Dealing with Adversity
Unexpected Marital Stresses

In addition to the predictable transitions of the family life cycle, there are the unexpected problems, "the slings and arrows of outrageous fortune" that can disrupt and even paralyze a marriage. A couple's reaction to the stress of challenges such as intermarriage, infertility, infidelity, unemployment, or in-law conflict may be enormous. Graver misfortunes like chronic illness and the death or disability of any family member sometimes devastate them.

Typically, partners handle adversity according to temperament and learned gender roles: the woman pursues and the man distances. The wife, who feels responsible for dealing with emotional upsets, will try to reduce her anxiety by making emotional contact: She wants to talk about the problem and her feelings, do something about it, maybe plunge into action. But she may also feel abandoned if her spouse doesn't go on "red-alert" with her. Meanwhile, the husband, who has been taught to "remain calm," withdraws under stress. He tries *not* to think about the problem any more than necessary to make practical decisions. Instead of plunging into action on the problem, he plunges more energetically into work. He may even appear to ignore the problem altogether. Trying hard to avoid the people, conversations, and situations that might set off his own tightly controlled emotions, he'll be bewildered if his wife gets angry at him for "not dealing with this."

When our family system is calm, these styles feel complementary. The pursuer is called "lively, spontaneous, warm" while the distancer is regarded as "dependable, practical, and reasonable." But under stress, the couple often polarizes, exaggerating the different styles and even taking on either an overly optimistic or pessimistic role. The pursuer may then get called "hysterical and controlling" and the distancer "stony cold." Depending on whether the pursuer's or the distancer's style prevails, the partners may either get caught in their emotions or in an angry shutdown. If couples take the behavior personally instead of recognizing it as socially programmed, frustration and anger will escalate and prevent them from working effectively on the problem.

The threat of death, the greatest taboo, may leave partners struggling separately, alone. With severe illness, partners tend to triangulate around medical decisions, which raises anxiety. With divorce, they may vent feelings through money and custody battles. Whatever the stress, if it is big or enduring enough, it will hit every weak spot in the family system. Regardless of a family's presenting problem, I scan the families I see for stress. A child's arrest for shoplifting is understandable when I learn that the child's grandmother just died. A couple's talk of divorce is understandable when I hear that one of their children is severely impaired. "It's certainly not fair," I tell them, "but now that there is such severe stress, you have to roll up your sleeves and work harder than ever on your ordinary problems." There's no way to get through life without adversity. The key is to use it as an opportunity to grow.

A note on addictions, violence, and psychosis: I could write a book on these adversities alone, but writing a section on them would be misleading. It might suggest that you can deal with them yourself—like other adversities. You cannot. Trying to do so can be dangerous to your entire family. You need to get professional help or advice from a self-help organization specializing in the problem. Such disorders fall beyond the bounds of the "renegotiation" that partners can undertake with the unexpected marital stresses that follow here.

INTERMARRIAGE

If you met me and Sam, you wouldn't immediately think "intermarriage"—two white, Anglo, middle-class professionals. But remember that my devout Catholic parents considered my marriage to a divorced Protestant such a problem that they didn't attend our wedding. Luckily, they didn't go so far as to cut us off, as many parents do. In fact, in the relatively short span of a couple of years, especially after Bennett's birth, Sam was fully accepted into the family. The funny part of our situation was that we ourselves never experienced difficulty over the difference in our religious backgrounds. But we do to this day still wonder at the totally different customs in Brooklyn and Chattanooga, Tennessee. Sam swears that for ten years he couldn't get in a word edgewise with my family. He'd been taught never to interrupt while others were speaking! I always laughed at him for that and his other "quaint" ways, but over the years I've come to appreciate his soft-spoken courtesy, and to complain about its absence around New York. As for Sam, when I do something "pushy," like plunge into New York traffic to nail a taxi, he laughingly says of me, "You can take the girl out of Brooklyn, but you can't take Brooklyn out of the girl." And then he's glad I got the taxi.

Contrary to conventional wisdom, opposites don't generally attract. The 1994 University of Chicago survey of sex in America reports that 63 percent of couples met through mutual friends or at a gathering place for like-minded folks, like a church or a political group. According to the researchers, the more similar the couples were in cultural background, education, and age, the easier it was for them to share their lives.

Over the years, I've seen plenty of conflicts caused by the dissimilarity of partner's backgrounds. And I often see marital conflicts rooted in the expectations of different sibling positions. So I would agree that intermarriage does make a couple's life more difficult; similarity makes it easier. But easier doesn't necessarily mean richer, more rewarding, or happier. When partners from different backgrounds take the time to think about their differences and help their families understand them, they have a chance really to accept their differences and to incorporate the enjoyable features of each into their family life. The challenge is to resist giving up your own heritage to accommodate your partner. Even religious conversion works well only if the partner who converts wasn't really attached to his or her own religion. When partners can hold on to their own heritages and enrich themselves with another, it can be a growth experience for everyone.

The problem is that most of us aren't looking for growth experiences. We're too anxious about differences. That's why intermarriages are more stressed than others. Because the original families so often disapprove of racial, ethnic, religious, and class intermarriage, there is a tendency for the couple itself to form a "united front" against "the enemy." Then, instead of exploring their differences, there's a possibility that the partners will ignore differences, opting for togetherness over intimacy. And remember my adage: The opposite of growth is not stasis, it's stagnation.

INFERTILITY

In the bad old days, when a couple didn't have a child in their first couple of years together, the woman may have had a checkup and paid more attention to the time of the month, but if nothing happened, the couple either accepted their "fate" or adopted. Nowadays, with all of the new medical technology, a couple trying to conceive has more hope, but also a lot more heartache as they undergo treatment after expensive treatment provided by a billion-dollar growth industry.

In a report to our staff on their study of the impact of infertility on couples, my friends and colleagues Ronnie Diamond and Margo Weinshel brought to our attention that, far from being a "woman's problem," men and women are each responsible for the infertility 40 percent of the time. They also emphasized how there is a danger that the couple will identify themselves as damaged or stigmatized, isolating themselves socially, creating stress, conflict, depression, and paralysis. We found this to be all too true.

Lynn and Keith came to our clinic because of their constant fighting. Their analysis was that "she's too bossy" and "he's always away at work." Several sessions passed before the therapist asked the question that explained their stress: They'd been undergoing infertility treatments for six of their eight married years. Lynn had become pregnant and miscarried three times, the last being a few months before. Keith just wanted to stop the treatments. Lynn said she'd stop only if he agreed to adopt, which he didn't want to do. So they continued with their insemination program and fought over every detail of their lives.

It took Lynn and Keith many months before she could resolve the emotional reasons for her persistence "against all odds'" and before Keith was able to think about his automatic rejection of adopting. It turned out that she didn't think that they had a "real" marriage if they had no children, and her parents agreed with her. Having grown up in midwestern farm country, Lynn was used to big families. She was one of six siblings, and the other five already had from one to three children each. Keith, on the other hand, could accept a childless marriage rather than "risk an unknown" in adoption. Before this couple was able to handle their problem, Lynn had to make a trip to her parents' Nebraska farm and visit her siblings before she could recognize how her family's blind insistence on the need for children had kept her locked into her struggle.

After several tearful talks with her parents and grieving about her infertility, she realized that she was free to make her own decision. Once Lynn was clear that she wanted to stop the treatments, Keith could examine his own prejudices, which were, as he finally said, about "male pride." Although women today are more flexible about how they become mothers, there is still some primitive taboo against adoption that is communicated to men. Maybe the "insult" of "another man's seed." Finally, Keith was able to let his fear go. Of course, once they decided to adopt, they then had to deal with the many stresses of *that* difficult process. But by then they were "on the same side" instead of taking out their frustrations on each other, and their marriage began to thrive.

JOB CRISES

Especially in today's perilous economy, everyone understands that a man's unemployment causes financial and emotional stress. But do we understand how much? Recent research has shown that although black men between twenty-five and thirty years old are four times as likely to be involved in violent crime, *employed* black males and employed white males have almost the same level of violent behavior. Clearly, unemployment is far more destructive than common wisdom tells us. And that may be why a wife's expectation that her husband will provide can so debilitate a couple facing employment problems outside the man's control. You saw this in the case of the husband trained in the printing industry whose wife thought he "couldn't hold on to his jobs because he was mouthing off all the time."

Unemployment is so anxiety producing that often the partners blame each other instead of pulling together to make the difficult decisions their situation requires. In fact, poverty causes such excessive stress on marriages that poor couples divorce twice as much as comfortable ones. But like all crises, unemployment can also catalyze growth, particularly for men who have defined their lives in narrow traditionally male ways. One such transformation in a troubled traditional marriage came about when Terry, a fireman in his thirties, was injured severely enough in the line of duty that he had to retire. Their "endless fights" brought them to therapy.

Before the accident, Terry worked long hours, moonlighted, and spent free evenings out drinking with other firemen. When he couldn't work and his disability provided less than $25,000 a year, they became "stuck." Both Terry and Diane believed in the traditional roles. As a result, they couldn't adapt to their situation, which required that they both work at something outside and take care of their home and two young children together.

Diane made unusual children's furniture, hand-painting inexpensive items she bought secondhand. But she only earned a couple of thousand dollars a year from it. According to Terry, their problem was that Diane could earn more if she sold to the fancy department stores instead of just going to community fairs, but Diane wasn't interested. Diane said they fought because although Terry cooked dinner and put the children to bed— neither of which he had ever done before—"he leaves the housework for me."

They focused their energies on finding work for Terry, which meant borrowing money to open a consignment craft shop he thought he could do well with. It never occurred to either of them that —even temporarily—Diane could work full-time as a dental hygienist, which she was trained to do, while Terry handled the housework. Since the role reversal was so alien to their backgrounds, we called them family "pioneers" in therapy.

Gradually, they warmed to the idea of making a new kind of marriage and soon agreed that full-time work for Diane was the best way to earn and save money. Terry accepted that it would be up to him to learn housekeeping. Ten months later, they were both working part-time. Diane was still working three days a week in the dentist's office and also painting children's furniture, but now Terry, who had learned carpentry, was making the furniture. Although they hadn't yet begun to sell to the department stores as they planned, they were selling in their own craft shop and had also gotten their first commission to make a complete bedroom set for a child's room. Terry had become a true coparent and was doing half the housework. What he said was, "I'm so grateful for the life my accident pushed me into."

This, of course, is the story of adversity ending in growth. However, it is worth noting that it was the husband's employment problems that motivated the partners. Everyone takes men's unemployment seriously, but we're far less aware of the stress caused by a woman's job problems. So much so that couples routinely relocate so the husband can take a better job, even though it means the woman may end up with no job at all. I'm currently seeing a couple who moved constantly with his job for twenty years, bringing her career aspirations to a halt. The wife now wants a divorce. Also, even though women today still face far greater challenges in the workplace than men do—often suffering the rejections, losses, and disappointments of sexism—a woman's job crisis rarely mobilizes a couple the way Terry's crisis did. The husband may gladly support his wife while she's unemployed, even taking on an extra job to do it, but he may be far more hesitant than she would be to relocate or regroup as much as Terry did once he was forced to by his injury.

Unemployment for either partner, like all these unanticipated crises, is a crucible for a couple. Ignoring the issue, refusing to change or adapt, or blaming the other may destroy a relationship. On the other hand, responding to the problem together can only mean knowing each other better and making an even deeper commitment to the marriage.

IN-LAW TRIANGLES

A Son Is a Son Till He Gets Him a Wife,
A Daughter's a Daughter for All of Her Life

Although two young people getting married usually imagine that "their" wedding is all about joining the two of them, it is actually the far more complex joining of two families, probably strangers, now designated by the dubious kinship label: "in-laws."

I've already said that the greatest stress in a family is from the addition or loss of a family member. Try adding five or ten new members all at once, and all already organized into their own way of doing things!

Marital therapy resounds with complaints about in-laws: their intrusions, their indifference, their values, lifestyles, and politics. Among the favorites are these:

Money. "Everything they give us has strings attached."

Social class. "They act like John married down, snubbing me and my family."

Lifestyle. "They're more interested in trips around the world than getting to know their grandchildren." "They can never just sit and talk. They've always got to be watching some moronic TV show."

Proximity. "Every time I turn around his parents are in my kitchen, criticizing my cooking or my kids." "Her mother phones every day. I'm not exaggerating. Every day."

To the degree that either of the marital pair does not have a good working relationship with his or her own family, the issues will be fought out between the couple, or between the in-laws, where they can never be resolved. I usually say to couples, "Your job as a daughter-in-law or a son-in-law is to get along with them. Whatever it takes, just get along. If there's a problem, it should be handled by the one of you whose family it is, *not* by the in-law."

The problem behind almost all in-law triangles is that wives get "assigned" the job of dealing with family emotional and social matters. It's as if husbands wrap their families in a huge ribbon and present them to their wives as a wedding gift. The wife looks at this assortment of strange people, with traditions and habits that probably differ from her own, and she sighs. Suddenly, it's her job to know what gifts to buy them, what to cook when they visit, what to talk about, what not to talk about, and to phone regularly. Most intimidating of all, her new and tenuous position of authority on all matters domestic must stand up to the scrutiny of that older woman who has heretofore been in charge, her husband's mother. The two women eye each other warily, and the mother-in-law triangle is established.

It is no accident that the most contentious and problematic relationships in families are often the ones involving the women: mother-daughter; mother-in-law—daughter-in-law; sisters-in-law, and stepmother-stepdaughter. Sister-in-law problems are generally a sign that a husband doesn't deal directly or effectively with his own sisters, and so his wife steps into the vacuum, where her efforts are seldom appreciated. In families where the father plays a strong patriarchal role or where there are a lot of issues about money or work, in-law triangles may involve father and son. Otherwise the women are expected to handle all family issues. If there's an emotional problem, women in the family are trained to try to resolve it. It takes mothers and daughters many years to get the hang of this with each other, but when you get relative strangers rushing at the family problem, each imbued with the feeling that she must "fix it," you get your basic "wicked step-mother" or mother-in-law problem of song and story.

We should note that although mother-in-law jokes are told by men about their wives' bossy or impossible mothers, in my office, "mother-in-law problem" is invariably about the *husband's* mother. And while his wife and mother fight, he "stays out of it." It's impossible to stay out for long when conflict involves people so close to him, so the husband soon finds himself in the middle, explaining his wife's position to his mother and his mother's position to his wife. Or he joins his wife in arguing with or distancing from his mother. Or he joins his mother's position emotionally, telling his wife to stop criticizing his family. He does everything he can think of except take a position on the issue with either of them.

If the wife's mother causes a problem, it is usually handled, well or poorly, by the wife, as it should be. The husband, trained as men are to run for cover at the first sign of an emotional problem, typically withdraws from that conflict. It does not become a triangle unless the couple fight about her on their own or unless the wife has either a stormy or distant relationship with her parents, in which case she might draw him into the conflict—on her side.

It's the unusual young man who, against all cultural injunctions, has managed to maintain a close enough relationship with his mother to be able to conduct an *active* role of married son with her, sharing his new family life with his mother and helping her to know where the new boundaries are around him and his wife. My friend and colleague Olga Silverstein wrote a whole book on the subject, which should be required reading for mothers and their grown sons. For if a man conducts his own relationship with his mother, she will not feel his marriage as a loss and his new wife will not experience his mother as a burden and/or a threat to her. After all, they do have something important in common: They love the same man. Complex as an in-law relationship may be, it will be an enrichment of the marriage itself if handled well. And the most valuable wedding gift that newlyweds can give each other is maintaining a good relationship with their *own* parents.

AFFAIRS

I have never known a marriage where an affair did not cause an extremely painful crisis. I have never known a couple where affairs were "accepted," even if they were an open secret. Movies, television, magazines, and songs give out the false impression that affairs are common, "no big deal." But they are not common at all, as the 1994 survey on sex in America showed. On some level, most couples do understand what a "big deal" an affair really is and refrain.

When I hear about an affair in my office, I have to try to evaluate whether it is a cry for marital help or a signal that the marriage is over. It can be either. One of the telltale signs is how an affair is discovered by the partner. If the "perpetrator" confesses it or leaves some obvious clue in his partner's path, it's usually a cry for help. On the other hand, a long-standing, discreet, well-hidden affair may be a sign of a fading or defunct marriage.

Although affairs have been called the "eternal triangle," they are no more "eternal," inevitable, or enriching than any other emotional triangle. Like all triangles, they are simply attempts to manage differences in a marriage by detouring rather than dealing with them. They allow partners to "act out" their conflicts rather than resolving them, which usually requires that they change. Although people will sometimes say that affairs "improve" a marriage, they do not. They merely quiet the conflict by sweeping issues under the rug.

Of course, no marriage can compete with an affair for excitement. What can be as thrilling as the illicit? However, all this excitement has nothing to do with love. Basic divorce research indicates that although one partner in most divorcing couples was having an affair, only a fraction of those partners went on later to marry their lovers. And when an affair is a cry for help rather than an exit sign, the "competition" and subterfuge can make it the most difficult triangle to undo.

Putting an affair behind them so they can work on their own issues is often a protracted and stormy ordeal for a couple. The sense of betrayal is strong in the "wronged one," along with the anger of having been deliberately "driven crazy" by the inevitable lies, evasions, and subterfuge. If others knew about the affair and "covered" for it, all the worse. The left-out partner will feel humiliated in direct proportion to the number and closeness of the "coconspirators." However, the strongest fuel for the emotional roller-coaster ride that typically follows an affair is simple sexual jealousy—the feeling that you have been irrevocably damaged in the most vulnerable area by your most intimate friend. "How can I ever trust you again" is the real stumbling block to renegotiating a marriage contract.

In the days and weeks after an affair comes to light, the pendulum swings wildly between open, honest, long-overdue communication, and heartbroken expressions of betrayal and guilt. And it swings between depressed resignation and raging anger at (depending on which partner is talking) the loss of "innocence" or the loss of the lover. And even when both partners want to move back to their own issues, the affair tends to haunt them. Remember Adam from Chapter 8 who took his wife, Sasha, to their honeymoon inn in Vermont hoping to "forget" her affair with an old boyfriend only to find the old boyfriend seemed to be in the room with them. As much as Adam understood that their real problem was the traditional roles they'd fallen into, he was too depressed and angry to move on.

"I think I know what you mean," I remember telling him. "Your mind says to let go, but your emotions are frozen. You can't just tell them what to do. They have a life of their own." When he nodded glumly, I said, "Let me try this idea on you. I've seen it work for others at this impasse." I then told him about a woman who was similarly "frozen" when she discovered a love letter her husband wrote to another woman. After weeks of talking about it, she finally hit on the idea: "Maybe I could forgive him if he wrote *me* a love letter!" So her husband did, with tremendous feeling, and when he read it aloud to her in my office, all three of us cried. "That's when she forgave him," I said.

Having Adam's full attention now, I also told him about the man who'd been left with the kids while his wife went on her "overnights." "I'll forgive you," he told her, "if you make breakfast in bed for me every Sunday for as many times as I made the kids breakfast while you were with your lover."

Looking more animated than he had in weeks, Adam turned to Sasha and said, "I want you to take me to every fancy restaurant and hotel you went to with Robert. I want to replace him in every place you went." Sasha smiled in relief. "That's perfect," she whispered. "I would love to do that. To erase him with you."

Then, as they worked out the details of this plan, Adam realized he wanted *her* to pay for it all, and when she nervously wondered out loud how she would do that, I thought, Absolutely perfect. Not only does the "cure" relate to the affair, it relates to the real problem—that Sasha gave up on her own life and money when she married Adam. Which is how the ritual ultimately "cured" them: Sasha worked like a demon at her modeling job for the money, but afterward—after Adam had forgiven her and was ready to move on—she wanted to talk about some better way to earn a living than "posing and strutting all day."

Therapy trainees are sometimes mystified by why such rituals work. "Is it some cosmic sense of fairness, or retribution?" they'll ask. I tell them that I think they work because they touch the most profound level of our emotional lives—the level deeper than thoughts or words. All the religions in the world know this, and they have all created rituals and ceremonies that go where words are not enough. Even some secular institutions, like graduations and legal proceedings, for example, try to capture some larger sense of awe and majesty to lend weight to their message. As my friend and colleague Evan Imber-Black, who has written a book about rituals in daily life, points out, sometimes a private ritual—such as the one Adam designed—is the only way to move the emotions to restore the awe and majesty of married love when an affair has "tarnished" it. In the process, partners can also deepen their lives with new understanding, acceptance, and renegotiation.

"IN SICKNESS AND IN HEALTH": MARRIAGE, ILLNESS, AND DEPRESSION

Most of us are happy to vow our love "in sickness and in health," but few of us really know what we're promising. A friend of mine, family psychiatrist John Rolland, whose excellent book covers the ideas outlined here, has made a special study of families and illness because of how hard it is for partners to manage emotionally in the face of a long-term affliction. This is one of those "slings and arrows" that calls for a complete change of the marital system, which is why a couple's successful adaptation will depend on their stage in the family life cycle, whether there are children, and how the partners previously divided tasks.

Under the terrible stress of serious ongoing illness, partners tend either to pull away from each other or cling together. Their communication system may virtually shut down or become very selective as they try to avoid discussing the implications of the illness. They may isolate themselves from their family and friends, showing them only a stiff upper lip or even bravado.

How partners respond to the crisis and to taking on new roles will depend in large measure on their emotional legacies. What was the family attitude toward illness? Was it used as a weapon to gain power? Did it bring rights and privileges to the invalid or was it shameful and weak to be ill? Were you supposed to "fight it"—even to the point of denial? Or was it okay to "succumb" and let yourself be taken care of? Was it okay for women but not for men? Family, ethnic groups, and culture all teach us the "meaning" of serious illness and can make us feel it is a sign of "saintliness," for example, or even just deserts. Freighted with feeling, touching our deepest fears, serious illness can threaten the most solid marital commitments.

To cope successfully, partners will have to join together "against the illness," making it a "couple problem" rather than an individual one. They'll have to face the limitations of their situation but still find ways to grow and live a "normal" life. The patient needs room to grieve and express frustration, just as the caregiver must plan for some respite from the rigors of that role. Women, who are expected to be "natural" caregivers, frequently fail to protect themselves from the physical and emotional overload. Whereas male caregivers are usually comfortable about hiring helpers, female caregivers may try to do it all themselves and feel "guilty" about taking much-needed breaks.

It's easy to see why the partners' communication about their practical, intimate, and sexual lives needs special attention. Yet at the same time they must be careful not to spend all their time together on "problems." If the roles of caregiver and patient become their chief or only connection, they'll become more like parent and child than partners. Maintaining a marital partnership in the face of burdens, fears, and pain will take more honesty and courage than couples must usually muster. That, of course, can also mean greater depth and intimacy.

Family and social support help couples enormously. Not only can they relieve the caregiver, their company can "normalize" the couple's life, bringing gaiety and news of the outside into the home, which shouldn't become solely a "place of illness." That's one of the reasons why the stigma of an illness like AIDS is so pernicious. And why the physically handicapped, who often refer publicly to themselves as a minority group whose special situation is not shared by the rest of the family, can feel such loneliness in their struggle.

I find it hard to imagine any situation in which a couple could better use good counseling than when a spouse has a chronic illness, especially a stigmatized one, or a physical handicap. Yet I think they should "shop around" carefully to be sure the counselor is experienced and comfortable dealing with serious illness, which arouses anxiety in medical and mental health professionals just as it does among family and friends.

Long-term depression in a spouse can be as isolating as any illness, particularly because it can be hidden. It can also be mistreated or ignored by professionals. Depression has always been overdiagnosed in women and underdiagnosed in men by therapists and by the partners themselves. In the past, women's "depression" was seen as the primary cause of the couple's difficulties rather than the result, and she was sent off by her husband to "get cured." Meanwhile, as my friend, psychologist Ron Taffel describes it, an irritable, withdrawn, or erratic man would be considered just "difficult" rather than depressed, and he'd probably self-medicate with alcohol.

Today, the women's movement has given credence to women's complaints, so therapists are more likely to address women's real problems. However, the depression problem persists. For one thing, men's depression is still rarely recognized, even by the man in question. And when it is, when, perhaps, he goes for therapy or goes on Prozac, many families—including my own, I can tell you—would forever consider him a "nut case" or a weak person. And there are also marital upheavals caused by a formerly depressed spouse's renewed interest in life.

For example, one husband whose wife had been depressed and apathetic for years insisted that the new medication had made her "aggressive" and "intrusive." It turned out that she had started to participate in the decisions and routines he had gotten used to controlling while she was "out of it." Sometimes, too, the caregiver can only express the anger and distress felt during the illness once it's over. So, once again, the couple has to communicate carefully, rebalance themselves, and maybe even use a personal ritual to move beyond the depression.

Another friend and colleague, Peggy Papp, who has undertaken a study of depression and gender, found that men usually become depressed because of job failure or loss of status, whereas women's depression more often results from distance, problems, or cutoffs in close relationships. As caretakers of a depressed spouse, men try problem solving to help their wives—and become angry, even abusive, if their tactics fail—whereas women tend to protect, placate, and appease depressed husbands, often blaming their depression on themselves.

Papp has also found that connecting depressed men to their spouses immediately relieves their isolation and depression. Since the men often don't know how *they* feel, she gets them interested in the feelings and emotional stress of their wives. However, women's depression is relieved by inviting them to talk about their own feelings, which they usually do readily.

Some people resist help for depression because they feel it puts them "one down" in the marital power struggle. "You're not going to send me to a psychiatrist," snapped one husband in my office. "I'll never hear the end of it. All of our problems will be blamed on *my* craziness." As it turned out, when this particular man did go for a consultation, he was given lithium to control his manic depressive illness. Yet as helpful as that was, medication by itself doesn't solve emotional problems, and their marriage then needed much emotional work and another renegotiation.

In the fine-tuned, hair-trigger marital system, stress comes with any change, whether it is the illness itself or the cure. As does growth. Couples confronting a partner's illness often find themselves able to focus on what's truly important to them. They'll sometimes be able to communicate about life's deepest questions and their own complex feelings in a way they never have before. Not only is illness a reminder of the preciousness of life, it is usually a shocking reminder of the preciousness of our partners, for both the sick and the well one.

FACING FINALITIES: DEATH, DYING, AND DISABLED CHILDREN

It's not surprising that death of a spouse is the top of "the stress scale" I spoke of before. When you think of how much of ourselves and our dreams we invest in marriage, you understand that a spouse's death is the end of that investment.

While the death of a spouse in old age is a serious loss and a signal of one's own impending death, it is at least an expected, inevitable event for which there has usually been some degree of preparation. The death of a spouse in the prime of life not only shocks and betrays the hopes of the surviving spouse but also leaves an enormous number of essential family functions to be shouldered.

Bereaved spouses have to rouse themselves from their own grief to help their children, whose resolution of the loss depends largely on whether it is resolved by their surviving parent. At the same time, the survivor has to figure out how to replace the dead spouse's income, child care, and household functions so that the family can restabilize and move on.

Isolated from the previous social life revolving around couples, and perhaps finding it hard to be with the dead spouse's grieving parents and family, the bereaved spouse may feel trapped in a tunnel of grief, worry, and work. Traditional men, lacking outside friendships and unused to solo parenting, may jump into a hasty marriage to provide "a mother for their children," while wives earning little or no money may do the same thing to survive financially. Or they may do the opposite—

refusing to date others even years after the death, finding the beloved one irreplaceable and the thought of a happy new life disloyal. Family therapy would offer help in both situations, lest the family be haunted for decades or generations by the ghost of a beloved young spouse whose untimely death made it difficult to let go of him or her.

The death and dying of a parent will usually also have a profound effect, as I indicated in the story of my reconnection to my own dying father. It will have an especially profound effect on the adult child's own marriage. When a client tells me about a parent's serious illness, I always declare this a "true family emergency" and explain to the couple that they have an opportunity to give a boost to whatever issues they are in therapy to work on. If the relevant partner improves relations with his or her dying parent, it will automatically improve their marital relations. Conversely, if the parent's death or the death of any family member leaves everyone with a lot of unresolved issues, the death may be followed by what Murray Bowen called an "emotional shock wave" of symptoms, accidents, illnesses, or divorces throughout the family.

I recently saw a woman on the verge of divorce a year after her mother's death. And although her two brothers had divorced earlier in that year, no one in the family connected these divorces to the death. According to Bowen, such a shock wave operates underground in the network of family and couple emotional dependency. People don't like this theory because no one wants to think that others, even our parents, could have such a life-and-death effect on us. But they do.

Sometimes the death of a parent pushes a young person precipitously into marriage, as if losing someone important means you have to grab on to someone else in a hurry. Or if a parent's death occurs shortly after a new marriage, it can derail the switch of loyalties and upset the process of renegotiating boundaries with the original family, especially if the new spouse feels neglected because of the partner's grief. A similar pull in opposite emotional directions happens to partners whose parents die around the time they have a child. If the couple doesn't understand the confusion, it might play itself out as conflict or over-concern about the child.

Couples who have not been able to support each other through mourning may struggle for generations with the issue of separation. It will flare up whenever children leave or the couple faces another death. A similar legacy plagues families that have suffered catastrophic losses in war or natural disasters. As a society, our dread of death and dying seems to grow greater with each passing generation. The "death industry" encourages us to deny that death is a part of life. I have met people who have never seen a dead body or attended a funeral or let their children attend one, no matter how close the relationship of the dead person. Funerals are immensely important, taking us—as rituals do—where words cannot, helping us to absorb the meaning of the death and move on. Two excellent books about death and dying have been published recently by colleagues: *Families Facing Death* and *Living Beyond Loss*.

The death, dying, or disability of one's children is another category entirely. Parents are immediately and profoundly affected. When a child dies, the divorce rate doubles. It is as if the parents cannot bear to see their own suffering constantly mirrored in the eyes of their spouse. Or perhaps the circumstances are such that one spouse blames the other for the death. Or they blame themselves.

And terrible as the unexpected death of a child is, the serious impairment of a child's functioning is also a loss of expectations and dreams—as well as a summoning of young parents to a terrible task. They must set aside their own feelings, if they can, and pour all their resources into the nurturing, training, and planning for the special life of their wounded child.

On the day of his birth, Bennett, our first child, scared us to death. He developed severe jaundice, which required a transfusion of his entire bloodstream to rid it of the killing antibodies developed in response to my RH-negative blood. Now, of course, there are simple treatments to prevent fetal RH disease, but there weren't any in 1961. Once this birthday operation was done, however, the baby was as good as new—or so the doctors told us.

I still don't know if this traumatic event played a role in Bennett's later diagnosis as autistic, but the literature on this neurological condition is replete with traumatic birth events. In 1964, however, when Bennett, at age three, was diagnosed, autism was considered primarily a psychological condition. It was supposedly caused by the parents, particularly the mother. Imagine contemplating your catastrophically dysfunctioning child, and then being told that you caused it! On that score, we were luckier than most. We took him to a leading New York child psychiatrist who said, "He's autistic, and you didn't cause it." However, my ignorance of the condition—indeed of the word *autistic* itself (I thought at first she'd said "*artistic*) was so great that it wasn't till later that her consoling follow-up became a life raft in a sea of accusatory psychiatric literature.

Most psychiatrists then believed that autistic children were "empty fortresses" trying desperately to "develop a self" in spite of "cold, domineering, self-interested parents" who had crushed their spirit. That's what I read sitting in the New York Public Library, too shocked even to cry.

I don't know whether it was the extreme nature of Bennett's condition—he didn't answer to his name, didn't let anyone except us touch him, and couldn't have a verbal exchange with anyone, although he could parrot our speech perfectly and sing songs as complicated as Gilbert and Sullivan's "I Am the Very Model of a Modern Major General"—or whether it was the extreme descriptions of the parents, but somehow, most of the time, I was able to believe Bennett's psychiatrist and disregard the opinion of the rest of the profession. Still, I was not yet a therapist myself, and so I had a layman's exaggerated belief in their expertise. Naturally, their pronouncements crept into my thoughts in the middle of the night. Could we have caused this? "Well," I would answer myself (judge, jury, and defendant), "for him to be in this shape, I think we'd have had to lock him in the basement, chained, for a year or two, and never touched or spoken to him."

Fortunately, Sam and I helped each other overcome the guilt

and organized ourselves into a "treatment team." We invented games and exercises to try to teach Ben to pay attention. Sam used flash cards, songs, stories. I "invented" behavioral conditioning, using M&M's to get through a trip to the supermarket with him. I also became an expert "arm twister," explaining to nursery school teachers, school principals, camp counselors, and baby-sitters that their efforts with him were saving his life, which they were. And so a group of dedicated teachers kept him in the public school, surrounded by normal children, all the way through fourth grade! Remember that there were no special classes at that time and no programs for autistic children, so we had to create our own.

The worry was constant: would Ben recover sufficiently to live independently later on? (95 percent didn't, the statistics said). Were we doing enough to help him be in the 5 percent? Did anything we did matter, or was it physiologically predetermined? The strain on our relationship—Sam's and mine—was enormous. I had started arguing with Sam about going back to work before Bennett's diagnosis (perhaps Ben's unresponsiveness and "peculiar" play rituals had been an added incentive, though I steadfastly denied to myself and others that there was anything "wrong with him.") When we understood that his condition was severe, chronic, and of uncertain outcome, I was more determined than ever to work part-time as a respite, and Sam, more than ever, thought I was "needed at home."

Also, the unremitting vigilance and worry frayed our nerves and made us short-tempered with each other. Silence and distance crept into the scene as we tried to keep our most depressing thoughts to ourselves. Or conflict erupted over some desperate statement, like the time I said I thought it would be easier if Bennett were "just retarded" and we could plan for the future. Guilt overtook either of us whenever we lost patience with Bennett and yelled at him. The major problem between us, in addition to the stress of the daily struggle with the "forces of darkness," as I had come to think of it—was the fact that we had both summoned all of our resources and had built a front of "competent coping" that allowed us to carry on in an unendingly difficult situation. We were afraid to let down, even with each other, for fear we wouldn't be able to gather ourselves back again to cope. If I ever start crying, I used to think, I'll never stop.

The therapist who helped me believe that it was okay for me to work also helped us to soften our "stiff upper lips" and cry with each other. And not only about Bennett, but about our whole dream of family and future, because in 1963, a year before Bennett's diagnosis, I had had a stillborn baby, another victim of RH disease, only this time it had taken hold before he was born. While we were trying to recover from that loss, Ben was diagnosed, and our full attention shifted to him.

As we found each other again through the clouds of grief and worry, the next logical question arose: Shall we adopt a baby? And, of course, I immediately thought yes, and Sam thought no. We argued, not much though. Sam wanted another child, too, and soon we agreed—one of the best decisions we ever made. That's how we started the search that led us to Tim, our second son, who came home to us straight from the hospital, five days old, in 1965.

The other best decision we made was to work like crazy to teach Bennett and to get him into whatever programs looked useful, even a special boarding school for older children. Today, although he has some learning problems, Bennett is a high-functioning, well-rounded, warm and friendly young man who works, drives, and lives on his own. He has his own friends and activities and has won many medals in Special Olympics contests. He probably mobilizes more of his resources than the rest of us do to get through life, but he does it with good cheer and few complaints (there's my family legacy again).

Sam and I know how close we came a few times to buckling under the stress, but it was always somehow inspiring to see the indomitable spirit with which Bennett climbed over hurdle after hurdle—and I think we realized that we had to expect as much of ourselves. At one of Ben's schools, the graduates—including him—sang that popular song from *Man of La Mancha* about dreaming impossible dreams. In the audience, Sam and I reached for each other's hand and both started to cry. Not only for Bennett—his struggles and triumphs—but for our own. This is the kind of "sling and arrow of outrageous fortune" that, if it doesn't break you apart, brings you closer together. It's one of those experiences that you two had together and no one else really knows how it was.

As you can see, all adversity, even those that seem the most unendurable, give married partners an opportunity to grow—together and individually. No matter how much stress the problem inflicts on the partners, it inevitably demands honesty, communication, focusing on what is truly important, confronting life's most serious issues, and appreciating the preciousness of one's beloved. If partners can work together on the problem, adversity will call forth what is deepest and best in the marriage.

Divorce

The Ultimate Renegotiation

Dear Jesse,

I guess you'll be surprised to get this letter from me about our marriage, of all things, almost two years after the fact. But I don't want us to go on being polite enemies, and I assume you don't either.

I'll begin by confessing that in spite of how cool I was during our divorce, I was so depressed by it I couldn't even date that next year. Since then, I've felt mostly anguish trying to figure out what went wrong. Finally, after a lot of therapy and tears, I have some ideas.

The main thing is that I don't think we knew how to talk about having children. Yes, you told me when we first got serious that you didn't want any part of parenthood. I should have listened to you. But partially I believed I could live without children and partially I assumed that you would just wake up one day and want kids. When you didn't, I thought it was because you didn't love me enough. Like my father, I guess, who just left. I've done a lot of work on that one in therapy. I see now how a lot of old stuff made me deaf and blind to you, and I guess the same was true for you.

Instead of getting to the bottom of things, we just argued and hurt one another. I do regret that we couldn't find a way for both of us to change or at least part with love and understanding. I certainly had some of the happiest times in my life with you. And I don't want to throw all that away by denying it.

I know you're living with someone now and I'm happy for you, Jess. I've just started to see someone I like. I wish for both of us that we use our experience to make it work the next time. Call some time.

Warm wishes to you,
Chloe

Even when no children are involved, divorce is an emotional process, not simply a legal event. As this letter, written by one of my clients, suggests, there's a lot of emotional work to do—on the behavioral, the emotional, and the social levels of experience—before a person changes enough to move on and, if desired, form a better relationship.

Of course, few people *want* to do all this work. It's much easier to assume you picked the wrong person. Or *he* wouldn't change. In so many divorces, both partners blame the other: "If only he or she . . . " But it's never *only* the other person's fault. Even if a woman *is* involved with the unresponsive, insensitive "absentee" she thinks she is, she will still have to take responsibility for choosing such a man and for not having negotiated to get her own needs on their joint agenda.

If you don't learn to negotiate and change your relationships (most importantly, the relationship with your parents), you forever play out the same roles. Take the man who believes his former wife is "she who must be obeyed." Nothing compelled him to obey, except his own fears and expectations. If he doesn't confront them, he will forever pursue the same kind of woman or her polar opposite—Ms. Compliant. Ms. Compliant might feel to him like blissful relief at first, but in the long run she won't provide more satisfying companionship than wife number one.

I knew a man who married during college and had two children right away. His wife had strong leftist political convictions and a commitment to living simply. When they married, he admired her convictions. He was proud of the modest brownstone they fixed up for themselves in Brooklyn, near where he grew up. And he was proud of the new cultural magazine he had started with a friend. Although he wouldn't have recognized the resemblance, his marriage quite accurately reflected the marriage of his parents, who were both educators, committed to culture and family: the father "charming," the mother, "strong." However, his parents' stated values were different from their unstated ones. They also resented their pinched lives and envied "the rich."

Without exactly knowing why, several years into his marriage, my acquaintance grew resentful of his wife's "bossiness" and her "disapproval" of his growing desire to live well, now that he could afford it. He wanted and got a divorce. Shortly after, he began living with a very different, deferential woman—a dancer who made her living as a masseuse. She was thrilled to drive his new sports car and fix up his new East Side apartment with him. He complained that she was nonverbal and didn't fit into his circle of educated friends, but, he said, she was teaching him to enjoy dance and music. All seemed stable until five years later, when he discovered she was having an affair with a choreographer. Just as their relationship didn't satisfy him, it didn't satisfy her either. As it turned out, she resented both his domination and his lack of real respect for her.

End of story? Not quite. His third wife is a dead ringer for his first, except that *her* strong political convictions are consumer capitalist. They now live in one of New York's poshest suburbs, where he belongs to an exclusive golf and tennis club. He doesn't see his old friends, none of whom travel in his new circles. But to all reports, this wife approves of him. Angry Mommy/Naughty Boy has become Contented Mommy/Good Boy. And this third marriage now reflects the *unstated* values of his family of origin.

Unfortunately, as long as this "boy" bases his relationships on an approving "mommy," his relationships will stagnate. But since he has remained a "boy" in relation to his own "strong" mother, whom he alternately shuns and showers with expensive gifts, he will not change. Until he remakes his relationship to his own parents and sifts through to find out what his own values are—a process made more difficult by his parents' confused legacy—he'll be stuck forever in this reactive "marriage—divorce—countermarriage" pattern.

My acquaintance's story is typical in two important ways. First, he blamed the marriage's problems on the other person—her personality and her politics—thereby avoiding having to renegotiate and make changes in himself. And second, he fled from the intensity of the painful postdivorce feelings by immediately jumping into a new relationship. And "rebound" relationships, we know, just don't work. Everything from Aunt Agnes's clichés to country western songs warn us that as soon as the passion ebbs, the newly divorced lover will find himself (or herself) feeling the same grief, regret, and fear that he tried to leave behind.

Many couples will divorce and marry several times. Like the couple in the stormy marriage who develop a pattern of breakup and reconciliation, these couples do the same but change partners as they do, making the emotional impact even greater. And as it turns out, gender, money, and the power of the traditional model of family all play a role in this pattern. Like my acquaintance, men who have serial marriages are usually looking for the "right" wife and have little understanding of what they themselves contribute to marital problems. In the unusual case where they have custody of their children, they are probably looking for a "mother" for their children. But women are motivated somewhat differently.

Poor women remarry in greater numbers than financially solvent women; women with sons feel social pressure to find a "father" for them; and single mothers with no time for a social life think that "settling down" will provide them with companionship. However, our society doesn't teach people the difference between the nuclear family and a remarried family—which I will explain in the next chapter—so these remarried families are often disasters. Newly remarried couples too often try to re-create the mother-father roles of a first marriage, which alienate the children and eventually break up the relationship.

There's another problem, too. Children introduced to a series of mother's boyfriends or husbands become increasingly reluctant to connect to someone who may soon disappear. And, again, money and gender play a role. Most children live with their mothers after divorce. Their fathers are far freer to date or live with as many women as they wish without disrupting their children's lives. And, of course, more affluent women can hire baby-sitters or nannies so their children aren't exposed to too many of their casual relationships. Without such help, many women feel forced into the only "solution" that society offers: marriage. And, as we know, marriage undertaken to solve economic or social problems doesn't work.

The way that someone divorces is always a reflection of their relationship to their family of origin. In fact, I always ask divorcing partners how each left home as a young man or woman. How you left your parents is probably a blueprint for how you are leaving your spouse. The youth who moved to the other coast, feeling he "escaped" his family, is going to have a hard time negotiating a divorce that doesn't end in a similar cutoff. The person who finds another relationship immediately is often someone whose sense of self is weak, someone who wants to be taken care of— emotionally or financially. Like my acquaintance, these people may have jumped into marriage early, never having given themselves the time to live on their own. They may never have learned to be themselves in the presence of their parents. Divorce is the time when all this unfinished business resurfaces, creating enormous anxiety.

I don't mean to suggest that divorce always involves operatic misery. The extent of people's suffering will depend to some degree on what divorce means in their families or religions, how much support they get from their social milieu, how mature they are, and how much economic change is involved. Furthermore, the more divorce is seen as a possible additional stage of the family life cycle rather than a "tragedy," the easier it is to adjust. The more it is understood as a transition with particular emotional and practical tasks to accomplish, the better prepared spouses will be to tackle the project.

In my experience, divorce *is* always painful, but it need not be a disaster. You are not "dooming" yourself or your children. If the emotional tasks are worked on successfully, everyone will recover—exactly as they do at every other marital stress point. The problem is that the emotional work is often *not* done. Instead, divorce is handled as a cutoff because the tasks are daunting, as anyone who has divorced will recognize. If an emotional recovery is to take place after divorce *one must stop blaming the other and retrieve the self.* In this latter process, one takes the hopes and dreams invested in the marriage and reinvests them in oneself.

Divorce is not about having chosen the wrong person. It's about oneself in relationships. As such it provides an opportunity to go back and redefine the self. And this, of course, means reworking your relationship with your parents, which is how you will have better relationships with all intimates in the future, particularly another spouse.

IF DIVORCE IS THE ANSWER, WHAT IS THE QUESTION?

Divorce, like marriage, is a Ping-Pong game. If you talk to only one player, you hear only one side: the pong, but not the ping. At the time of divorce, I always hear that the other one is "crazy." And what partners tell their friends, family, and therapists will often sound like madness on the "opposing" side. But I guarantee you, it is usually not the case (unless there's a serious history of psychosis, violence, or substance abuse). So whenever I hear about "that maniac" (bastard, bitch, child, idiot) from one partner, I always question my client about the interaction between the two. And if I ask the right questions, I almost always hear about the "ping" that accounts for the supposedly crazy "pong." Let me explain.

One man made an appointment to get my help in "handling" his ex-wife. "She is so crazy," he told me, "that on Christmas Eve, when I came to collect the kids as planned, she threw the children's presents out of a second-story window at me."

When I questioned him closely about all of the details, I learned that though they had *just* separated, he pulled up Christmas Eve in a brand-new car with a gorgeous blonde who draped herself against the fender while he rang the bell. He hadn't told his wife that he'd bought a car or was seeing someone and intended to bring her along when he picked up the children: ping (outrageous provocation)—pong (ballistic reaction).

Now it's true that neither husband nor wife behaved very well, but neither was "crazy," as each claimed. They were acting with the rage and hurt that is generally very high at the time of divorce, making it extremely difficult to renegotiate. What's worse, each partner will engage family and friends to see "their side," which only reinforces their "ping" view of things, escalating the blame and anger that prevent a real retrieval of self and a good negotiation. That's why I always encourage couples going through divorce to keep up joint sessions and discussions as long as possible.

I've come to believe that most decent divorces are made by couples who spend a long time trying to work things out. In the process, they begin to understand *their* part in marital problems, their partner's point of view, and the willingness or unwillingness of either of them to change. Women especially often feel unable to let go of an unsuccessful marriage—or suffer from intense guilt if they do—unless they feel they did everything possible to work the marriage out.

THE SHARK AND THE BARRACUDA

If I had to name the single most harmful aspect of divorce American style, I would say it is the way divorce law is practiced. Divorcing couples too often expect their lawyers to fight a war with the spouse's attorney, and "win." So, given a hurt, angry, and emotionally vulnerable couple, the typical divorce lawyer pours salt on the open wounds in the form of provocative and threatening letters, unreasonable demands and ultimatums, all the tactics of war on behalf of one spouse against the other. The only "bargaining chips" in the war are money and children. So the couple, fueled by the hurt and anger that can never be resolved in the legal system, end up using their "chips" as the battle escalates. Formerly loving fathers refuse to pay their children's college tuitions even when they can afford to; formerly loving mothers sue for sole custody or threaten to move far away with the children. And the spouse countersues. And so on and so on. The longer it takes, the more of the money goes to the lawyers, the less to the ex-spouse and children. By then, everyone is so angry that child support may be withheld and visitation blocked.

Emotional problems can't be solved in the legal system, and the legal system is set up to defend individuals from their enemies, not to mediate disputes among family members. Which is why I spend a lot of time explaining divorce mediation to clients. And why some states mandate parent education programs for divorcing parents—an excellent (and free) alternative to family therapy. And why a mediator is far better than lawyers for divorcing partners.

Divorce mediators, who may be lawyers or therapists, think of the whole family as their client and assume that the practical differences are rooted in the emotional issues between the partners. While mediators aren't actually doing therapy, their understanding of the role of emotions in the divorce process can help couples move on.

Unless there's a history of spousal abuse or intimidation, divorce mediation makes so much sense that it's a pity it's not used more often. People are sometimes afraid of it. Men with substantial assets believe they need their own lawyer to "protect" their money, and women often don't feel skilled enough to "argue their own case." However, both these positions are based on the misinformed idea that you are alone in making your case with the mediator. Both spouses can and should have as many advisers as they feel necessary—lawyers, accountants, therapists—to go over any plan the other spouse proposes. At its best, mediation is a family-friendly framework for renegotiating the marital structure. Even if they have advisers, both spouses fully participate in restructuring their family. They are looking each other in the eye, standing up for themselves, providing what's best for their children, and helping themselves to overcome the enmity they may feel. And to grow.

Divorce is never "the answer." It is only rarely inevitable. But it is unfortunately often necessary when one spouse changes and the other does not, or when change comes too late to make a marriage work. In that case, divorce has to be understood as the ultimate renegotiation of the marriage contract. Because this is a change of great magnitude, it will generate enormous anxiety, uncertainty about the future, and feelings of loss and failure even for the one initiating the divorce. It is also very much a literal renegotiation—the working out of finances, visitation, and custody—in addition to an emotional renegotiation. As with all the stress points in the family life cycle, the more mature a person is—the more self-reliant and emotionally connected—the easier it will be to grow through each of the inevitable stages of divorce.

THE STAGES OF DIVORCE

The extensive research of my friend and colleague Connie Ahrons has created the categories we all use to study and describe the divorce process:

1. decision
2. revelation
3. separation
4. reorganization

Decision. In my experience, this first stage can actually take the longest because partners are often quite unsure about "whether things will straighten out" or how unhappy they really are. They might assume their unhappiness is just normal; for example, if they have just had their second child and find themselves fighting about home and work or why they can't make ends meet. If, unlike Sonya and Bob, they don't go to therapy to try to renegotiate, they might "stew" in their misery for years before they decide to divorce, especially with a man like Bob, who was trained "to endure," and a woman like Sonia, who may not have another viable alternative. Ambivalence is the earmark of this stage, and when people are ambivalent it is best to air doubts and problems rather than keep silent or "threaten divorce" in every argument.

Keeping silent and coming to a solitary, unilateral decision to divorce is unfair to one's spouse and oneself. Doing so prevents a shared understanding of crisis and the need for change. The opposite, endlessly threatening divorce, will either be discounted as meaningless or will engender so much anxiety and reactivity that the real problems in the relationship are obscured. Acting out in a way that provokes the spouse to make the decision, with drinking or affairs, for example, or rude or stonewalling interactions, is failure to take responsibility for one's position.

As important as it is for the decision to be mutual, it seldom is. The usual process is a long period of conflict or silent emotional withdrawal during which one of the spouses shuts down, lets go, and decides "this is it." "This" may be a single word or a dramatic incident, after which the deciding spouse stops looking for ways to negotiate and angrily starts building his or her "case." The time between the internal click and its revelation to the spouse may be a minute or ten years. But after this "click" all attempts by the spouse to negotiate change will usually be fruitless. The initiator generally feels the need to stay angry so that he or she can go through with the divorce.

To avoid the guilt and angry defensiveness that fuel the "bad divorce," it is important to avoid the extremes of silence or endless conflict and go for help while there is still a genuine chance to negotiate change.

Revelation. Revealing one's discontent to the spouse, hopefully, is a part of the decision-making first stage. But however unilaterally or mutually the decision is made, a usually irrevocable step toward divorce is made when the decision is revealed to family and friends. How and what to tell the children is the first and most crucial plan that should be jointly made, if possible. Here is the first of many crucial negotiations that the two hurt, angry, and maybe guilty spouses will have to make. And they have to tell the children "the truth" without blaming or bad-mouthing each other; they have to respond rather than react to the children's upset; they have to reassure them without giving them false hopes.

Telling parents, siblings, and friends may be even more ticklish because of the hope for support and the fear of disapproval or disappointment. The more the partners have worked through the decision together, the easier it will be to present it to their world.

Separation and reorganization. These are really overlapping, not separate, stages.

There are two aspects of separation for divorcing couples, and each requires extensive renegotiation. The physical separation, requiring a decision about who moves out and who stays, if anyone, has both emotional and financial ramifications. Gone are the days when it was "understood" that the husband moved out and the wife and children remained. As more and more wives initiate divorce, more husbands challenge this arrangement. "If you want a divorce, then *you* can move out." Actually, in most middle-class families, the house is often the only asset and has to be sold to support the two households. "One divided by two does not equal one," I often have to remind divorcing partners arguing over their future arrangement.

The emotional process accompanying the physical separation resembles the response to death, the only loss that scores higher than divorce on the stress scale. That's why I suggest that it involve everyone's participation, as a funeral would. I advise against a father's moving out when everyone else is visiting grandma or when the children are at camp. Everyone should be there, help with the packing and moving, and be allowed to experience and express the grief that they feel. Most people shrink from this, but those who go through it recover faster. Especially the children, for whom it is a nightmare to have a parent just "disappear."

The other aspect of separation is legal, and this is the first legal part of the divorce. In many states, a "no fault" divorce can be obtained automatically a certain number of months after the "legal separation" is filed. This document requires that all of the final financial and child custody arrangements of the reorganized family be signed, sealed, and delivered. As such it actually belongs to the reorganization stage of divorce. Part of the turmoil of divorce comes from the fact that the couple often has to negotiate their reorganization before they are emotionally separated, assuming, of course, that they *ever* actually achieve an emotional separation.

How long does separating and reorganizing take? The answer is longer than most people think. Divorcing couples, their children, and the grandparents need time to adjust to this new stage of family life. Studies suggest this takes *at least* two years—and that's only if everyone is working on it. That can seem like a very long time in an impatient society such as ours. And it's important to realize that time—alone—doesn't heal all wounds. Newly separated people have to use the time to do the necessary emotional work. If they try to rush through the experience, they merely have to work out the overlooked problems later on, when they may be more difficult to face. Some people, men more than women, try simply to "jet" out of the painful middle stage, fueling themselves on a new passion or burying themselves in work. Treating the divorce as a financial and logistical event, they delay feeling its full impact.

Women, on the other hand, usually feel the full emotional impact immediately, and then slowly get over it. And while we're discussing this gender difference, I want to mention an important related finding based on a 1987 study that found a substantial group of non-remarried mothers, but few non-remarried fathers, doing exceptionally well six years after divorce. And that was true despite the fact that most men are much better off financially after divorce while women are worse off! That study may reflect which spouse was suffering more in the marriage. But obviously, it pays to consider divorce a growth opportunity, spending whatever time it takes to "heal" and become a whole person on one's own.

I always try hard to engage separated spouses in the work of redefining themselves in their relationships with their parents to enable them to become "whole." For women, becoming whole usually means developing their autonomy: financial independence and decision-making skills. For men, it can mean creating a home and a social life—on their own. For both, it means figuring out your part of the marital failure and changing yourself accordingly. A recent news story reported that women, especially, are making this postdivorce adjustment so well, they are more reluctant to remarry. Men have a harder time and remarry much more frequently. In the best-case scenario, whatever the new life, it will include the former spouse to some extent. My husband, Sam, maintains friendly relations with his former wife, although they never had children. And I've always believed we are all richer because of it. This brings us to the reorganization and the most complex renegotiation of all.

DIVORCE DOESN'T END A RELATIONSHIP, IT RESTRUCTURES IT

As soon as children are involved—and they usually are—divorce takes on another layer of meaning. For no matter what, these divorced partners will *always* be the coparents of their children. That is, they will always have a relationship, whether it's managed successfully or not. Even if one of them disappears, from a child's point of view that inadequate or missing parent is still "my father" or "my mother," however disappointing. And from each ex's point of view, no one else except the former partner will probably ever share the parents' depth of connection with that child.

Unfortunately, without joint custody, and sometimes even with it, fathers tend to drop out of the family picture. According to a study on the subject, "paternal visitation" is still the dominant arrangement for divorced families, and "half of noncustodial fathers gradually lose all contact with their children." The study notes the cruel fact that after their parents divorce, most children aged eleven to sixteen have no contact with their fathers. And, perhaps crueler, these were largely fathers whose "attachment to their children was strong before the divorce."

At least part of the reason why this happens is because the parents divorced in anger and could not successfully renegotiate their contract to restructure their family. Of course, another reason is the gendered expectation that the children will stay with their mother and their father will "visit." But it turns out that even the most common arrangement—Wednesday night dinner with father and every other weekend—just isn't enough to keep a parent and child sufficiently connected. Sometimes, also, men have no experience in how to stay emotionally connected, or they want to blot out the pain of the divorce and, hence, turn away. Sometimes the woman wants to take the children away and begin a new life without him. However, when either parent cuts off, everyone suffers.

Shari and Randall came to me in the final throes of their marital breakdown and soon decided on divorce. Shari wanted to move upstate where her parents lived and where she'd been offered a job teaching in a private school that would accept their son, Brandon, on scholarship, when he reached school age. Randall protested bitterly, since he was bound to New York City because of his job with the Urban League.

I told them the statistics on father-child disconnection after divorce and explained how harmful it is for a child to lose a parent. I strongly recommended that they live close to each other so both of them could remain involved in Brandon's life, know his friends and his school. After a lot of discussion and protest on Shari's side, she decided that she would stay after all. Because Brandon was only three, they decided he would live primarily with his mother. But Randall, who moved around the corner from them, came every day to take him to school and spent one or two evenings during the week with him. On the weekend, Brandon stayed at his father's house, where he had a bed, clothes, and toys. Shari and Randall changed this schedule when either one needed to be away, but they preserved the sense of free access to their son and plenty of time with each parent.

Of course, Brandon had to get used to two homes. There is no such thing as a perfect custody plan. But almost any plan that both parents are happy with, the children will adjust to. If either parent is unhappy, then the children will be as well. Three years later, Shari sent me a Christmas card with a picture of Brandon and a note to tell me how well he was doing. "As much as I wanted to move, I can see now that this was the best decision for my son."

At the end of a successful divorce, the reconfigured family will be parents living separately, with the children living as full members of both households, moving between them as frequently as parents decide, based on their ages. Joint custody means that both parents remain fully involved in decisions about their children's lives; it doesn't mean the kids have to spend the same number of minutes with each parent. Both parents must have full access to the children, full involvement in decision-making, and full responsibility. Parents also have to have their finances worked out fairly. And, finally, they need to maintain their relationships with their former in-law family to insure their children's continuing relations with all significant extended family members.

What I've described is a tall order. You can see the enormous renegotiation of the contract involved, and redefinition of self. Because divorce involves continued parenting with the ex-spouse and mutually acceptable arrangements, there will need to be an adequate emotional divorce. Enemies cannot coparent, nor can they move on successfully to their own new lives. The extent to which there is continued uproar or animosity is the extent to which the emotional process is incomplete. Unfortunately, it usually is. According to Connie Ahrons's research, which is described in her book *The Good Divorce*, five years after divorcing, 12 percent of ex's were "perfect pals," 50 percent varied between angry and furious, and only 38 percent were cooperative colleagues, which is what ex's are if they've separated emotionally.

Clients don't want to hear all this when I talk about it. "If I wanted to put all this energy into this relationship," they tell me, "I wouldn't have needed a divorce." Indeed. It's a paradox that it takes as much goodwill and hard work to get a decent divorce as it does to have a good marriage.

DIVORCE: IN A CHILD'S EYE

Divorce, in itself, needn't damage children irreparably. Particularly when it is accepted by their parents as a new stage of life rather than a "tragedy." And certainly, children today generally don't feel like pariahs, since half their peers are also children of divorce. So when children do have behavioral and emotional problems after a divorce, a recent issue of the journal *Science* reported, they usually had them before the divorce as well. The study they reported, involving 17,000 families, concluded that if there is marital conflict, the children will be adversely affected whether the parents divorce or not.

In itself, divorce doesn't harm children. What harms children are three specific things:

- poverty
- losing a parent
- having embattled parents (married or divorced)

Unfortunately, it's rare that a child of divorce doesn't suffer one of these torments.

Lamentably, joint custody is not the most frequent choice for couples, especially if they are very angry. Yet, when both partners are good parents, it is the arrangement that is best for children. Many divorced women in America today are "left" with the children, and with little or no child support. Often, there are good intentions, but as the father's emotional involvement flags, so does his financial contribution. Sometimes, he refuses payment as a way of "punishing" his wife. As I mentioned at the beginning of the book, the average in child support is about $2,000 a year. According to government agencies, twenty-four *billion* dollars remains uncollected annually, and that's just on cases where the women have made complaints. Nevertheless, as a society, we blame the mothers for their poverty rather than finding an effective way to collect the child support that's owed them.

The crisis in the American family is this: We have few models and little support (emotional, financial, or social) for "the divorced family," and that's what it is—a restructured, dual-household family that must continue to function as a family for the sake of everyone involved. And so it must be accepted as a bona fide family form if we really care about family values. Given how things really are, when a couple with children tells me they want a divorce, I ask the wife how she will support herself financially and I ask the husband how he will stay connected with his children. If the woman has no support of her own, she will remain dependent on her ex-spouse, and this is not financially or emotionally wise. If the man doesn't vigilantly sustain his relationship with his children, he will feel ever more peripheral to their lives.

Very often a man will move out into a one-bedroom apartment or, worse, a studio. "Where will your two children sleep?" I have to ask. Then I suggest that he work out an entirely different plan that includes a room or rooms for his children. And that's the easy part particularly if this is a man who hasn't ever taken care of his children by himself. He will need a lot of training and support and honesty if he's going to do more than "get through a weekend alive" with his children and do this without turning the children over to his girlfriend, his mother, or the "normal" family next door. "They want *you*," I often have to remind the fathers. "They want to know that you'll always be their father and that you love them and will take care of them."

Women, especially those without good jobs or skills, will have to create a realistic budget for themselves and a plan that will make them financially viable, whether or not their ex-husbands support them at first. When such a plan involves a radical change for a woman, it may take a long time to work out. And often, at first, her greatest emotional task is accepting that she may remain permanently single. *Single in a Married World* and *Flying Solo* are two recent books by family therapist friends of mine addressing this fear. In any case, if a woman doesn't develop her autonomy, her chances for a successful second marriage are not good. That's why I focus on helping women to create a short- and long-term plan so that they have some immediate income and can soon begin to get the training necessary to support themselves later on.

Children rush the stages of divorce in one way. The former partners have an obligation to move beyond their bitterness and feuding as quickly as they can so that they can negotiate effectively for their children's welfare. Not only will their children be very needy emotionally for a while, but the parents will also have a lot of touchy new situations to figure out right away, such as, will they both go to the parent-teacher conference? Will they be together for the child's birthday party? For Thanksgiving and Christmas? The best research on the subject tells us that what makes these new coparent relationships successful are not the specific details that the ex-partners decide on but their having clear and mutually agreeable boundaries. A lot of anger and tension lingering over the years is a clear sign that the divorce may have taken place legally, but it has not happened emotionally. Until it does, ex-partners are not emotionally ready to move on.

THE PENDULUM SWINGS

I often warn clients that they have to be careful to protect themselves from whatever social trend happens to be popular at the time they are making their own crucial life decisions. Marriage, divorce, large families, small families, living together, or staying single all have their fifteen minutes of fame as the "right" way to live. As a matter of fact, the popularity of the choice of the moment usually reflects social, political, and economic forces that remain largely hidden.

In the expansive sixties and seventies, focused as they were on questioning old rules and institutions, the divorce rate surged. Popular culture characterized divorce as "no big deal," and lots of people divorced who just wanted to be "free." Even worse, therapy at that time was seen as a means to this end. In fact, and it is my own personal favorite, there was a particularly ditzy-looking woman therapist in one of the first movies to treat the subject, *An Unmarried Woman.* She looked and sounded like a gypsy fortune-teller and, if I remember correctly, sat on the floor during sessions—reflecting, I suppose, the same "freedom" she was helping her client to get. Meanwhile, my office and that of every therapist I know, was jammed with couples and women alone going through the pain of discovering that divorce is a *very* big deal.

In good therapy, people get help solving their own problems and therapists—at least family systems therapists—are trained to keep themselves out of the person's or the couple's decision-making process. The biggest difficulty we have in training new therapists is teaching them that their job is neither to "hold a marriage together" nor to advise a couple to split. Few therapists in training want to advise a split, but many beginners, consciously or unconsciously, try to "save the marriage," pasting the couple together, giving them advice and "solutions," downplaying their differences until these tactics boomerang and explode in the couple's separation or hasty departure from therapy.

"You have a big enough job deciding on your own marriage or divorce," I tell my trainees. "You can't make decisions for other people." The therapist's job is to help the couple explore their differences, look into their emotional legacies and blind spots, and change themselves accordingly—and to help them see whether their social circumstances are creating problems for them and can be changed. Weighing the degree of change necessary and finding the motivation to do it—or not—is the job of each of the partners.

This training of marital therapists to avoid being triangled into the couple's decision making has become even more important in the "conservative nineties," as the pendulum of social opinion has swung back to being and staying married. Now popular culture warns couples that divorce will ruin their children's lives and they should stay together "for the children." But what on earth can children learn about marriage in a family where the partners are simply "resigned" to the marriage and are sacrificing their happiness for the children's sakes?

Every day, my mail contains "expert reports" and newsletters from newly organized institutes and councils on the family, labeling and stigmatizing "the culture of divorce" and "children of divorce." They want to put the toothpaste back into the tube: making a first heterosexual marriage the only "right" kind of family; making divorced, remarried, unmarried, and "fatherless" families "wrong"; and don't even mention gay and lesbian families. In this kind of thinking, everything that goes wrong in the life of a child whose parents are divorced is attributed to the divorce itself—as if divorce were a terminal illness from which there was no recovery. And as if staying in a marriage full of unchanging anger, bitterness, contempt, violence, or emptiness could be better for children than a decent divorce.

And, again, hidden backstage are the current problems of the larger system that have produced this swing of the pendulum, almost all of them economic: fewer jobs, especially for the uneducated and technically unskilled; lower wages for women and minorities; and a general feeling that we can't afford to support the education, training, and child care that would help with the real problems—poverty and the myth of traditional marriage. Does any of this mean that I think divorce is good? Or that children don't need loving parents? Not at all. I have worked for twenty-five years with parents and children in pain because of family conflict, distance, or complete cutoff. My point is that what matters are the relationships—working out the emotional problems in the relationships—and this is necessary whether the couple is married, divorced, remarried, unmarried, or gay. *And whatever the family form, helping children stay connected to all their family members* (assuming that they are responsible, available, and caring people).

I suppose that the people who propose "reinstitutionalizing marriage" (that's what they're calling it!) are well intentioned, wanting to help neglected children and estranged or cutoff fathers. But they are ignoring the fatal flaws in the institution of marriage that cause the problems in the first place. They are mistaken to think the institution of marriage can thrive in today's world without serious repair. And they are mistaken to think that economic problems or social breakdowns are caused or can be "fixed" within the family.

14

Remarriage
Reinventing Family

When Roger and Cassie came for therapy, it was ostensibly because the youngest of Roger's three sons, eleven-year-old Benjamin, was suspended from school for breaking another boy's arm in a fight. He'd been such a behavior problem all semester that the school counselor referred them to me. Both Roger and Cassie acknowledged Ben's hostility, describing how he treated Cassie and her five-year-old son, Shawn, rudely and continually threatened to run away from home. But as a newly remarried couple, they blamed Roger's ex-wife, Louise, for turning the boys against Cassie and for "abandoning" them to return to Canada where she was from.

I addressed Cassie separately, though she and Roger were leaning against each other, Roger's arm around her shoulder, her hand resting on his thigh. "Cassie, did you expect to live with Roger's boys when you married?"

"Not really," Cassie said, her cheeks suddenly flushed. She

seemed a "spunky," athletic woman, muscular with a healthy glow on her freshly scrubbed face. "I thought they would visit for weekends and holidays. I mean, their mother really loved them. She was always doing homework with them, talking about their grades or something smart that one of them had come up with. I never thought she'd walk out."

As I had learned from the school counselor who referred them, Roger and Cassie, who had been the family's baby-sitter for three years while she was training for a license in electrolysis, had been having an affair with Roger while he was still married to Louise. Roger was forty-four, a periodontist; Cassie, twenty-eight, was a single mother whose ex-husband "took off" two months after Shawn was born and had only very sporadic contact with them. He might stop by around Christmas with some present for Shawn or take him out for dinner when he visited his mother, who lived nearby, but that was all.

Louise's claim that she returned to Canada because she couldn't support herself and the children was probably true. Roger had kept their home because his practice was built onto an extension in the back. Louise had taken a house nearby so the boys could continue at the same school, but rents are high in that district and Roger's child support payments didn't begin to cover the real costs of raising the boys. She had to stop studying for her Ph.D. and take a full-time job. In Canada, she told them, she'd have free tuition, health care, and could live with her sister until she got on her feet. The older teenagers refused to go because their friends and activities were *here*. She did take Benjamin, but Toronto was "too far away" for him. He returned two months later. As soon as Louise left, Roger moved Cassie and her son into the home he had shared with his wife and within six months had divorced Louise and married Cassie.

"And if you had known from the beginning that Roger was a package deal, three sons included?"

Cassie sighed. Her cheerful face puckered as her gaze flitted here and there while she thought. Then looking down into her lap, two tears fell from her eyes. Roger, a handsome strong-jawed man whose black hair and mustache accentuated his confidence and clarity, took her hand in both of his. I could hear him whisper, "It's going to be all right, baby. We'll get through this." Then, to me, he said, "It's been very hard on her." I would never have guessed at this point that these two would go on to do as complete a job as anyone I've ever worked with on the many complex issues involved in creating a successful remarried family. But they did.

When I asked her to tell me about Roger's sons, she glanced at him. Fidgeting with her billowy blonde hair, the buttons at the neck of her white blouse, the interlocking ringlets of her gold wedding band, Cassie was clearly not as sure of herself as Roger was of himself. But Roger nodded, encouragingly, and she said, "It's just that I can't take being the wicked stepmother anymore. Ben is so nasty to me, telling me to 'shut up' all the time, calling Shawn a 'mama's boy.' I can't even protect my son. And here I thought . . . " Her tears flowed now. But when I asked if she had hoped Roger would be the father Shawn never had, she stopped crying, looked straight at me, and said, "Yes, I did."

This is when we began a long discussion that would continue through many sessions, the gist of which is in this exchange: "Cassie, tell me, what's wrong with your son's having mostly a mother in his life? You're not a good enough person to be a model for him? Do *you* think he's not going to be a 'real boy' because he's with you too much?"

"Well, yes. Like when he was little, he'd say he was going to grow up to be a girl, like Mommy."

"But that was when he was a toddler," I told her. "He soon learned he was a boy, didn't he?" She conceded that he did. "I know that society tells you you'll ruin your son if you're too close to him, but you don't have to buy into that nonsense. It's ideal for children to have both parents, but women are perfectly able to raise sons by themselves if they have to. And it's important to be close to all of our children, boys and girls. Besides, no one can become 'instant dad.' And it sounds like Roger has his hands full with his own kids. It's going to take a lot of time for Roger and Shawn to develop a relationship. And then he won't ever be his father. Shawn has a father, even though he's not doing his job."

Cassie smiled, wiping her tears with her fingers. Now she and Roger were sitting apart, Roger leaning back on the two rear legs of his chair, as if to give Cassie the floor. "I guess I never thought about it like that. I thought it would ruin Shawn—a boy not having a father around. And then when I married Roger, I was just so disappointed because I had thought we would be one happy family. But we have a dividing line between *your* family and *my* family. If *his* kids start in on me—and Ben does it all the time— Roger says I should just handle it or leave the room. I'm the grown-up, don't get down to their level. But I can't leave the room if I'm cooking, let's say. Or if I'm watching a program, Ben will just turn the TV to his show without asking me. Then what am I supposed to do? Go and tell Roger, like I'm a child running to complain about the other children? It's humiliating."

"Do you think Roger appreciates how difficult your position is?" I asked. She shrugged. "I do and I don't," she said. "I just feel like he loves his kids more than me."

In almost every remarried family, this question arises: Who do you love more—me or your kids? It's not a fair question, I tell them, because it puts the children and the marriage on the same level, and they shouldn't be. I explained that Roger had been the boys' parent much longer than he'd been Cassie's husband, and the bond was therefore stronger, at least at this early stage in the marriage. In addition, the love and responsibility a parent feels for his children is completely different from what he or she feels for a spouse. Since Roger was nodding in agreement, I invited him to join in and tell me what he thought the problem was.

Smiling, Roger rocked forward in his chair, crossed his legs, and said, "You know, the boys were crazy about Cassie when she was their baby-sitter. They'd roughhouse with her, tease her, get all excited over the cakes she made. She's a great baker. Then when the boys were living with Louise, Cassie made their weekend visits so special. We were always busy—amusement parks, movies, we went skiing once. So when Louise left the boys with us, I thought, It's going to be like 'The Brady Bunch.' Cassie would be 'Mother Number Two' and everything would stay the same. I was raised to think mothers believe the sun rises and sets on their kids. So I was caught completely off guard when Cassie began complaining about how Ben's rude to her or the older boys ignore her. Or she'd make dinner and get furious because the boys didn't come home on time—"

Cassie broke in. "You want 'The Brady Bunch' and there I am, making a great big homey dinner so everyone would sit down together, and you don't even care when they don't come home. You won't stand up to them and say, 'Look, Cassie made southern fried chicken and a chocolate layer cake. You make it your business to get there.' Instead you treat me as if I'm getting riled up about nothing—"

"Roger," I interrupted, "I'm interested in your position in the middle. Cassie says that you're not strong enough with the kids, you don't insist they treat her with courtesy or respect. How do you plead?"

Roger, his face dead serious now, said, "I'm really afraid they're going to be more hostile if I'm hard on them. Especially Ben. He tells me, 'You don't love me. You don't care about us anymore.' I'm scared, really."

"First of all, it sounds like you have at least one very upset boy. Ben's squeezed into the middle position too, you know. His father wants him to love his stepmother, but if he does, he feels like he's betraying his mother. If he loves his mother, he's 'killing' his father. Then you also have to realize that Ben's angry because before Shawn came on the scene, he was the 'baby of the family.' Our sibling position is like our name or our fingerprints, and changing it precipitously is a big deal, particularly for someone like Ben, who has a lot to deal with. And so do you, Roger. I think you're too tenderhearted. That's why you're caught in the middle. You feel for Cassie, but you care deeply for your children, too."

Roger pointed his finger at me. "That's it," he said. "I feel like I'm standing with one foot on a ski pointed uphill and the other on one racing downhill. And I feel guilty."

Now *his* eyes got teary, and he nodded. I could see from the pain traveling across Roger's eyes that he was terribly conflicted. He loved Cassie, but he hadn't taken time to work out the emotional divorce from his first wife or his guilt toward her and the children. "You're so afraid of alienating them, or of having them accuse you of hurting their mother, that you can't allow yourself to tell them how to behave." When Roger reminded me that Ben threatens to run away, I told him, "The school counselor thinks that's just blackmail. Your kids know you love them. And even though it hurts you to press them, they need a much stronger message from you about how to treat Cassie. They might complain, but I doubt that they're going anywhere."

As the session ended, the two of them standing up and talking about what had come up, Roger said to me, "I guess if we stopped arguing about the children, we could think more about ourselves."

"Roger," I said, applauding as I stood, "that's a very good thought. Let's talk about *that* next time."

It took quite a few more sessions before Roger truly understood that Cassie could never replace the boys' mother. He also slowly realized that he wasn't disciplining the boys because, in addition to guilt, he wasn't used to that job. Louise used to discipline them. That's why he was so annoyed with Cassie for not being able to "handle them better" (read: be a better mother to them). Once he accepted his responsibility for disciplining his children, he did begin to take some risks with his sons, insisting they behave decently to Cassie and Shawn. But his change wouldn't have gone as well as it did if he hadn't also made the first moves to give up his battle with Louise.

Once, after Roger got through listing his grievances about his ex-wife, I asked, "Why are you still so emotionally involved with her? When are you really going to get divorced?" I told him that being "enemies" is a close relationship, whether it's out-and-out vengeful or just fighting over money. When he finally opened the lines of communication with her, first by letter, then by phone, his children, especially Ben, seemed to calm down immediately. The change in Ben's behavior was so dramatic, Roger was able to see that Cassie wasn't to blame for Ben's problems, nor was Louise. "Thinking back," he told us, "I realized I'd made a terrible mistake. One time when Ben asked me if I ever had good times with Mommy, I told him no, never. Now I understand how devastated he was by that." Now Roger was determined to confess to Ben that he was just angry then, and all the other times when he criticized Louise to the boys. Laughing, he added, "I'm going to think of at least ten times we were all happy as a family, even if it kills me."

I assured him it wouldn't kill him at all. Quite the reverse. "Facing the truth—and the truth is you were happy sometimes—can only improve your life, and your new marriage." Since that's just what happened, he was encouraged to work more and more with Louise. At the beginning of therapy, he had refused to pay for Louise to visit the boys or for them to visit her. "She has her own money," he told me, citing a trip she made to visit a friend and a "fancy new coat she was wearing the last time she was in town." But gradually, as he talked more with her by phone and they exchanged several letters, he found himself ungrudgingly paying for the boys' visits to Canada, including a ski trip for Louise and the boys that Christmas. "I was just too angry at her before to give her a cent more than I absolutely had to, even if it meant making the boys unhappy. I was cutting off my nose to spite my face." And as he saw how happy his sons were when he treated their mother respectfully, Roger understood how his affair with Cassie while he was married had angered them and turned Cassie into their "enemy." Later in therapy he even mustered the courage to apologize to the boys for that.

As for Cassie, difficult though it was for her to give up her bond with Roger against the "enemy" Louise, she seemed to understand that if that didn't change, neither would their new family relationship. And, oddly enough, Cassie was a help in this process because, as she said, "Louise and I always got along really well. I liked her. I respected her." After all, Cassie had worked closely with Louise as caregiver to Louise's children. She did know her and was often able to "correct" Roger's picture of Louise, which had become distorted by his anger.

For example, Cassie said, "What Roger says is true in a way. Louise isn't a 'fun' person. She's the serious type. But she has a good time in her own quiet way, with books and music. She'd always have her music on while she studied." At first, when Cassie said things like that, Roger would either smirk or make some sarcastic crack like, "If I had to sit through one more symphony . . ." But when his anger abated, he'd say such things as, "I guess I just resented her for not enjoying what I did."

Finally, as Roger changed his relationship with his parents and understood his family's tendency to cut off anyone who challenged them emotionally, he actually warmed to Louise's plan to move back to their town when she got her degree. "It'll mean everything to the boys," he said. "And it will certainly cut down on my phone bill."

Cassie also had her own work to do to overcome her anger at Shawn's father. I questioned her closely about him and determined that he was neither violent, crazy, nor addicted, then stressed to Cassie how important it would be for Shawn to have a connection with his biological father and his father's family. "No one ever replaces a parent," I had to say many times before she was convinced enough to accept my proposal that I invite him in for a session alone to discuss Shawn with him. Since Shawn's father was now living in Hartford, over a two-hour drive away, it took a few weeks before he was able to get in to see me.

When I finally met him, Robbie defensively blamed Cassie for keeping him away from Shawn. But when he realized that I wasn't blaming him, a much more complex picture emerged. He said that Shawn was an "accident." He'd been twenty-four at the time, a college dropout, and mostly out of work. "So I panicked," he said sadly. "That's probably why I got involved with another woman and drifted away. It was easier. But naturally that didn't work out. I was very young, and stupid," he said regretfully. "I didn't consider taking Shawn for a day. My girlfriend didn't want to baby-sit, and I didn't have a clue about babies. By the time I was alone again, I just thought that Shawn was better off without me."

"Well, he's not," I stated unequivocally. "Children never give up on their parents. He'll always wonder why you didn't keep in touch with him, and it will hurt him all his life." By this time, I could tell from how his eyes glistened that he understood how much Shawn needed him. And he did, despite the fact that I meant what I said to Cassie about her being perfectly capable of raising her son successfully. One parent, male or female, can certainly give a child all the love, guidance, and family life a child needs; however, they cannot easily make up for the hurt of that child's loss when that child knows his or her father exists somewhere and just doesn't care. The rejection will always be there. And Robbie clearly hadn't meant to reject Shawn. When he saw it that way, he changed his attitude.

"I would like to be there for him," Robbie said, "but Cassie—"

"Never mind Cassie," I responded. "You were both very young five years ago. But now you're mature enough, so it's time to work something out for Shawn's sake. And your own."

Meanwhile I coached Cassie about not letting her animosity get in the way of Robbie's reconnecting to Shawn. "It's not your fault that he gave up fathering," I told Cassie, "but there's no sense giving him an excuse to quit again by making it harder for him." So Cassie gritted her teeth for Shawn's sake and was civil enough to Robbie to make the reconnection possible.

Of course now Roger's fears had to be quieted, too. But I was able to convince him that his and Cassie's own life together would be greatly enhanced if Cassie worked out the past with Robbie just as Roger was doing with Louise. That way the children could all have their respective parents, leaving the space and freedom for Roger and Cassie to be husband and wife, and friend to each other's children.

I saw Robbie alone a few more times, helping him work out a fathering plan and also to reconnect Shawn with his grandparents and the rest of Robbie's family, who'd gotten "lost." Robbie, who was doing well in his business, agreed to go to a mediator with Cassie to work out the specifics for child support and a new joint custody agreement.

The hardest part of this emotional work for Cassie was to explore the circumstances surrounding the separation from Robbie. Until now, Cassie had seen herself purely as the victim, unable to "get anything" emotionally from her first husband, who had abandoned her with her baby. But she began to see that she never asked him for anything either, that she was someone who was afraid to make her needs known. She was quite surprised when she began to ask—if only on Shawn's behalf—and this supposedly indifferent, selfish man drove over two hours in a snowstorm once so he wouldn't disappoint Shawn, whom he had promised to visit. Once Cassie became more assertive with her ex-husband, her own parents, and Roger, her own position in her remarried family improved. It wasn't long before Cassie let Roger know that she wasn't really comfortable living in "Louise's house," and they decided to find a new house of their own.

Moving into a new home was difficult for Roger and Cassie. They had a hard time selling the first house, and then Roger had to rent an office. But as I explained to them, a different house is terribly important if it's financially feasible. Whoever used to live in a house—like Roger's children—feels invaded; the others—like Cassie and Shawn—will always feel they are outsiders. I wasn't surprised to learn having a new house of their own helped Roger and Cassie to set up their *own* new family instead of trying to keep things just as they were. Once they were moved in, Roger was even more ready to take equal responsibility for their "home life" instead of turning it over to Cassie, as he had been doing. And she was no longer trying to create one big happy family with inappropriate (although well-intentioned) gestures like expecting the teens to turn up regularly for "family dinner."

Once Cassie, Roger, and the children agreed on what things they would do together and what not, Cassie began to understand that teens routinely resist the kind of daily family rituals she was trying to establish, and they do that in intact families too. Together, everybody set up the house, decided who would get which room and what new things they needed. Roger proudly told me he was a part of every decorating decision and that he'd personally gone with the boys to pick out whatever they needed for their rooms. He had learned the difficult lesson that turning the kids' lives over to the "woman of the house" is the surest way to keep Cassie in the "wicked stepmother" role. In their new house, *he*, alone—though with Cassie's support—was his children's parent, and that meant disciplining them, making decisions about their daily lives, and helping them to settle into their new surroundings. That let Cassie return to her old role as the children's friend. Cassie still baked wonderful cakes, but as she said, she and Roger would have theirs at dinner with whoever showed up; everyone else could have what was left in the fridge.

During their last session, Roger said things were going much better. "We may not be 'The Brady Bunch,' but the 'war' is over."

"THE BRADY BUNCH," OR "WHAT'S WRONG WITH THIS PICTURE?"

"The Brady Bunch" indeed! It is remarkable to me that in our times, when *the remarried family is quickly becoming the fastest growing family form,* we have no models for just what that might be except for a silly sitcom from the seventies that shows *his* and *her* family happily blended in their new "nuclear" home. Of course, both the "new mom's" and "new dad's" spouses are conveniently dead, so there's no conflict, no divided loyalties on the children's parts, no back and forthing, logistical arrangements, financial feuds, or any other of the problems *real* remarried families face. And heaven forbid Mr. or Mrs. Brady ever ask the quintessential remarried family question: "Who's number one—me or your children?"

However unlike real life "The Brady Bunch" is, nearly every remarried couple who came into my office during that time wondered why their family wasn't like them. Without a workable model for a remarried family, they attempted to create a new "instant" nuclear family along traditional lines, and that's always a disaster.

Remember how hard getting married was the first time, when only two families were involved? Remarrying may seem as if hordes of people are making demands and judgments, arguing and vying for attention in the midst of which the new couple is just trying to find some time to have a relationship—which they had while they were going out on dates or spending weekends together. The children were then very much in the background.

Now, instead of growing gradually into shared parenting, one or both partners may suddenly be plunged into multiple roles, as in the case of a woman who has never been married before becoming a wife and stepparent of three or four kids at the same time. If both partners are parents, they may find themselves juggling two very differently organized households or trying to integrate two families at different stages of the life cycle. Cassie and Roger are typical of this struggle: one parent with a five-year-old and the other with adolescents. Yet, bringing teenagers from different families together under one roof also requires a lot of supervision and communication. Remember, the incest taboo is not instantly operative with two newly combined family groups and won't develop until those involved feel more like family. Also, since teenagers are trying to get away from the family they already have, it confuses them to be asked to deal with new family members, and they often respond by acting out or getting angry. Given all these tensions, marriage—the second time around—can be very complex.

Statistically, second marriages are more precarious than first: the divorce rate is quite a bit higher—57 percent and as high as 62 percent for younger couples. The more children, the likelier the redivorce, and divorce happens sooner—at four rather than seven years. Remarried couples have to find room for themselves among the children, former spouses, and multiple sets of extended families. *However, many divorced couples do remarry and manage to be successful.* Remarriage is not inherently unstable, except at the beginning when the parent-child bonds are stronger and longer than the new couple's. When the couple tries to create an instant new nuclear family, it means interfering with ties to the children's first families, which is a nightmare for the children, and brings about behavior problems, depression, or acting out on their part.

Although there is a role for someone to "step" into to replace a dead parent of young children, children after divorce are understandably unwilling—actually unable—to substitute the new "parent" for their lost one. Nor should they have to. Their relationship to their own father or mother must be honored, or they will inevitably reject the stepparent and even try to destroy the new marriage. While Roger watched without understanding, Ben was well on his way to turning Cassie, someone he had liked as a baby-sitter, into a wicked stepmother. From his point of view she was now usurping his mother's place.

Toward the end of therapy with remarried families, I always ask the children to describe the relationship they would like to have with their parent's new wife or husband. They usually describe some friendly relation, *but not another parent:* a basketball coach, an adult friend, an aunt or uncle. Such positive involvement of children and their parent's new spouse is one of the crucial ingredients of a successful remarriage. But children in remarried families aren't seeking new parents. They are mostly concerned about how their own parents are treating them. One six-year-old boy, when asked by his teacher to introduce her to the people who brought him to school, said, "This is my mother and this is . . . my Lloyd." His own father was a violent man whom his mother had had to flee, but the child was accurate. He had a father. This man, whom he loved, was someone else.

That loyalty often takes the irritating form of anger at the new spouse. One of the greatest difficulties for remarried partners is letting their children express the full range of negative and positive feelings toward all four adults involved in their lives, but it's necessary to do this. This is especially hard when the newly remarried spouses, who may tend toward "mandatory togetherness" after the divorce wars, are threatened by the children's rejections or comparisons. Name-calling should not be tolerated, but you may have to fasten your seat belt and accept a child's stated wish that his or her "real" mother or father were here instead of you.

THE MYTH OF THE WICKED STEPMOTHER

Another fatal flaw destabilizing remarriage is applying traditional gender roles. If men turn the parenting over to the new wife, either because they don't know how to parent or they think the children need a "mother," the children will act out against the "impostor" for fear of losing their real mothers. Or they will become completely confused by two mothers trying to rear them often with a competitive or hostile edge. Traditional roles are also impossible to apply to a remarried couple's finances, which may include collected or uncollected child support, alimony or support of multiple households, previous debt, etc. In remarriage, the fact that what's mine is *not* yours should be much more apparent from the beginning. Nevertheless, they may both still expect the new husband to be the household's main financial provider, even if he has to reduce or withhold financial support from his first family. The golden rule—whoever has the gold, rules—is all the more galling for a woman with children who may not accept this stranger's authority, even if he puts food on the table. The children will resent him all the more and be infuriated by their mother's (and therefore their) dependence.

Also, to the extent that partners expect the other to relieve them of their unresolved feelings about their ex's, the new relationship will flounder. As I explained in an essay on the subject, "overtrying" by a "new" parent in remarried families is often related to guilt about a first marriage. For example, a father who has cut off the child of his first marriage may be compensating by trying to be a terrific dad to his new wife's children. But the children may not want his intense attention, which challenges their loyalty to their own dad, or they may not "believe" it. A woman who sees the misery of her stepchildren may try to love them as much as she loves her own children when, in fact, she cannot. Her need to see herself as a good mother may make her unable to admit that she doesn't like them, finding them "spoiled" or too demanding.

One of the worst problems remarried partners face is being cast in the role of wicked stepparent. In our culture, the term "stepparent" is nearly synonymous with "wicked." This scapegoating of one member of a complex and poorly understood system inspired one of my colleagues to rewrite that archetypal tale of remarriage, *Cinderella,* from the stepmother's point of view. A digest of the humorous new twist goes something like this:

> I'd been so lonely I was easily swept off my feet by Cinderella's father, marrying him when we hardly knew one another. Once we did, I saw that he was still obsessed by his dead wife. He blindly adored Cinderella and spoiled her so badly that she had not even been expected to help out around the house. He lavished gifts on her and not my daughters, who were understandably jealous. They also resented the fact that they had to clean and cook while Cinderella refused. Whenever I tried to straighten the poor motherless creature out, she had a tantrum and went running to her father, who always took her side against me. And when the poor man died suddenly, I couldn't control Cinderella. She was out all hours. Next thing I knew, she had eloped with the prince

(who was a source of worry at the palace) and they told re-
porters that he had "saved" her from virtual slavery in her
own home.

This amusing reversal of the famous fairy tale makes the serious
point that every family conflict has another version. For every
ping, there's a pong. Furthermore, the underlying assumption
that the stepparents should automatically love their partners'
children as much as they do their own can't help but catch them
up short. That assumption alone has created more wicked step-
mothers than almost any other factor. And why is it a step*mother*
with grown daughters who always plays Grimm's greatest family
antagonist? Because elder daughters, as it turns out, are their
biological mother's greatest protectors, her most loyal torchbear-
ers, and so, inevitably, they will be their stepmother's greatest
provocateur.

PIONEERING THE NEW

The very term "remarried families"—instead of blended families
or stepfamilies—suggests to me a new kind of family, one that
avoids the impossible dream of "blending" and the stigmatized
"second bestness" implied by the prefix *step*. I also like the term
because it emphasizes the marital bond that brought the separate
families together in a new constellation. And a new constellation
is what the remarried family must be.

Because our society doesn't really support or promote any
kind of family except the traditional first-marriage nuclear family, remarried couples are left to invent their new family on their
own. But it shouldn't be this way. Social scientists of all disci-
plines—and members of successful remarried families themselves—know enough about what constitutes well-functioning
family relationships to be of great help, if their messages were
picked up and publicized in the broader culture, such as television portraying a real remarried family instead of "The Brady
Bunch." Remarried families shouldn't have to wait until pain
and failure drive them to therapy to learn what will help their
complex system work, and what tears it apart. When that does

happen, the family therapist has a double job, *education* as well as therapy. That's why I sometimes sound like a teacher when I'm working with divorced or remarried families.

The remarried family will have to tolerate more permeable boundaries than they may have ever had before, including "weekend" children into the private life of the family and fostering open lines of communication between themselves and children's biological family: cousins, grandparents, aunts, and uncles on "the other side." This is often an immensely complex logistic and emotional feat, undertaken while the new remarried family is also seeking a stability of its own.

They'll have to parent and pay according to their relationships with their biological children, and not according to the prescribed roles. And that may entail a man who cooks little Molly's dinner and buys her a birthday dress, no matter how much easier it may seem for his new wife to do both. No matter what the partners' backgrounds are, if it is "her home" and his children make a mess of it, the fighting begins.

Instead of fighting that losing battle with her husband's kids, a woman must resist the tendency to take over the domestic scene and instead support her husband's learning how to be more of a day-to-day parent to his children and how to make a household run. Similarly, only the parents' joint participation in earning and managing the household finances will resolve the competing claims to the family resources. Even when women don't earn as much as men, which is usually the case, her serious contribution to the finances can help to solve his dilemma about how to fulfill his financial responsibilities to his first family while they manage to stay ahead of the bills in their new family, even if her ex-husband's child support payments are "iffy."

The issue of money in remarried families is played out again at a later stage when the couple is older and the time comes to make wills and decide which children get what. The more money there is, and the more it "belongs" to one parent or the other, the greater the potential for a will that tears the family back into its original component parts. A reverse version occurs when an older affluent parent plans to remarry and the grown children create an uproar for fear their inheritance will go in part to the new spouse. As it sometimes does.

Last, remarried families must accept a very different emotional atmosphere from the idealized Brady Bunch. Second families carry the scars, the loose ends, and the commitments of their members' attachments to their first families. Everybody must be allowed the time and space to mourn the loss of that first family and to give up their fantasies of a reunion. The children must be allowed their ambivalence. Where there are two sets of children, they may live more or less separately for however long it takes them to connect, and depending on their ages and other factors, *they might not ever connect.* The research shows, however, that even though additional children add to the complexity—"his, hers, and ours"—having children born to the remarried couple pulls everyone together and enhances remarried family integration and stability.

Finally, if and when the remarried family does feel a sense of cohesion, it generally takes about three to five years! That's a far longer time than couples imagine. "Family feeling" grows in remarried families with time and positive experiences. So if the children are young and the "stepparent" is wise, he or she can slowly graduate over the years from stranger to Mom or Dad's spouse, to children's friend, to baby-sitter, to the position of loved and respected adult. If the children are teens or older when the remarriage occurs, the "stepparent" may have to settle for children's friend. Is that so bad?

Toward the end of my work with a particular remarried family, I often suggest creating new rituals to help define their new family. For example, I might ask how each former family used to celebrate Thanksgiving or Christmas, then help them plan out a different celebration that suits their new needs and interests. If some of the children spend Christmas Eve and morning elsewhere, maybe they all could go ice-skating on Christmas afternoon and open presents when they get home. If the children are older, maybe the whole family agrees on a play they'd like to see together during Christmas vacation or a ski trip they'd enjoy. I also suggest setting up "picture day," when children bring albums, videos, and memorabilia of what their life was like before and show them to the children from the "other side" or to their father's new wife if she had no children. This helps remarried families understand one another and acknowledge and accept the history and other facets of their members' lives.

Rituals serve different functions. But all rituals—from "grandparent" day (when all the grandparents are invited) to "negotiation night" (when all the new family members get to air their grievances and work out a resolution)—help remarried families to become connected in ways that suit their unique group.

Divorce and remarriage are the ultimate renegotiations of the original marriage contract. And because of the stress involved in this degree of change, they warrant our maximum social support and guidance. Instead, in many powerful segments of society, divorce is automatically stigmatized and dismissed, while remarried families get perfunctory lip service support (after all they *are* organized around a married man and woman, and that's the only kind of family we acknowledge). This "support" of remarried families, however, fails to include accurate and educational models that would teach people the few essential do's and don't's, unless the remarried couples form their own support groups or connect to stepfamily organizations.

When remarried family members do get the right help or figure it out themselves through painful trial and error, it is often the case that they have learned to tolerate ambiguity, to include "outsiders" into the very heart of the family, to form a full joint partnership of husband and wife, to heal and reconcile the wounds from the past, and to enlist children in active participation in their family relationships. Through all of these intense, complex emotional negotiations, the members of remarried families may emerge more tolerant than the rest of us. That's why, in reinventing family—mixing the old with the new—the successful remarried couple often works out a degree of flexibility that could serve as a model for the next generation. Which is a good thing, for it will also be a major American family form of the twenty-first century!

15

The Future of Marriage

> *Anyone, therefore, discussing the future of marriage has to specify whose marriage he is talking about: the husband's or the wife's. For there is by now a very considerable body of well-authenticated research to show that there really are two marriages in every marital union, and that they do not always coincide.*
>
> —Jessie Bernard, *The Future of Marriage*

NEW ROLES—OLD RULES

The problem with contemporary marriage is that the lives of men and especially women have changed dramatically, radically, in this century, but the rules about marriage have *not*. So contradictory expectations exist side by side until the tension explodes in conflict:

Men think:

   1. We're equal and we both participate in decision making (but I make most of the money, I'm in charge of it, and I have more say—or at least veto power).

2. I do much more child care and housework than my father did. My wife and I are partners at home (but my work comes first—as a man's work must— and there are certainly limits to the kind of scut work I'm willing to do. Anyway, she does it better. And she's better with the kids when they're cranky or sick).

Women think:
1. I want an equal relationship and I expect to work and earn money (but I expect him to support me financially if I feel I need to cut back or stay home with the children).
2. I expect my husband to be an involved father and to share in the housework (but I want to be the children's primary parent like my own mother was and to control the home as a good wife should).

Is it any wonder that marriage today is more complicated than ever? Bringing marriage into line with our *actual* lives and *real* expectations requires the most scary change of all—giving up the old expectations related to gender roles and changing our behavior and our communities accordingly.

Partly because of economics and partly because of the women's movement, women's behavior has changed drastically since the sixties. The vast majority of women are now in the workforce and half of them are providing as much or more of the family's income as their husbands. But men's behavior has changed far less. For personal, social, and economic reasons, they have not accommodated themselves to women's working by participating equally in the home. Although they now "accept" that a woman will work, they also "expect" her to be a homemaker. It is this lag in men's role change (combined with women's ambivalence about insisting on greater change) that results in contradictory wishes that weaken so many marriages.

Ironically, today's couples have a better *chance* of a good marriage than ever before: the possibility of true companionship and a contract tailored to them personally, not simply one shaped by social expectations. But the territory is uncharted and the external pressures are even worse. When both parents work, the wife also does a "second shift" at home while the husband feels her resentment and is angry about not having the kind of "wife support" his own father had. Meanwhile, the partners have no time for either each other or life's pleasures.

In addition to blaming their husbands, women in this predicament often blame the women's movement for "taking away their 'right' to stay home." Instead of joining with other women to find support and solutions, they join the backlash that paints feminism as the enemy of men and family. They may lose themselves in the excesses of the self-help movement, focusing on their "codependency" or their "inner child," as if these were the *real* problems in their marriages.

Men in these harried marriages also blame women. Instead of helping men to become more involved with the daily emotional and practical lives of their families, the men's movement blames contemporary women for "making them marginal." Spokesmen encourage men to take back their rightful place at the "head" of the family, becoming the "essential male link between the child and the community." As my colleague and friend Marianne Walters points out, the men's movement is about "male bonding" against women's "domination," not about developing men's capacities for emotional connection with wives and children and adjusting to equal partnership. Yet if men don't learn to negotiate with their wives as equals, their wives will continue to divorce them. If they don't learn to stay connected with their children after divorce, they will continue to lose their children as well.

The changes women have made by coming into the world of work and politics have been a step up for them, a gain of power. For men, however, family involvement seems like a step down, a loss of power. This stall-out reflects our continued valuing of power over connectedness and the continued association of power and money. Yet men have everything to gain by being more emotionally engaged in their lives.

THE GOOD FATHER: CHANGING MEN'S LIVES

Most American men say that family is the most important facet of their lives, and at least half say that fatherhood is their most satisfying accomplishment. Why, then, don't more men willingly embrace child care and household work? Because they fear that doing so would impede their achievement at work, which they have been taught to believe is their most important goal. (And because it's tedious and unpaid work.)

While the traditional definition of masculinity is surely being challenged, it still holds sway in most men's lives. Remember Dale, the computer programmer who feared being a househusband? He was hardly your typical workaholic, but still he said, "Society will judge me not by what kind of father I am, but by my work." And the rules for "man the provider" are still very slippery. Is his wife fully committed to being a coprovider for life, or will she suddenly decide she has to stay home with the children? If his children are a priority for him, will he be penalized at work for taking paternity or family emergency leaves?

Men are also often afraid of the intimacy of family life. They are afraid they don't know how to be intimate, and they're afraid of their own feelings, which they've been taught to suppress. Intimacy and connection have traditionally been the feminine sphere. Recognizing that "feminine" part of themselves threatens a man's identity.

Unfortunately, avoiding intimacy also means men cut themselves off from their deepest feelings, from their spouses, and from their children. Remember Bob, the traveling salesman? He was lonely and hopeless about his own happiness but wouldn't ever tell his wife, Sonya, about it. Remember Gary, the workaholic lawyer, who only recognized his anger at his wife's family but not how hurt he was by his own distant parents. Men who don't "feel" are as haunted and unhappy as women who aren't autonomous. They might grin and bear it, drink, gamble, have affairs or become TV zombies, but escape is never satisfying. The demons are there when the high or the numbness wears off.

Among my clients, men lose their children because they

haven't developed the skills for having a relationship with them, and then they don't persist against the obstacles to maintain one should the family break up. It's not my experience that divorced wives block their fathering. But when fathers are upset by arguments with their ex-wives over money and child care (the very issues that undermined the marriage), or when their new significant others resist the complications of dealing with their children, many men give up.

What does finally motivate men to change? Recognizing their own pain. Most men I work with begin to realize how much they suffered because their own fathers were distant and overworked. In their own longing and pain, they find the will to be a different kind of husband and father.

What motivates men to change is also the prospect that their wives won't be angry at them, won't be complaining all the time. That they won't have to be solely responsible for the money their families need. Very few men, it turns out, are really happy with the breadwinner-homemaker division of labor. They often feel like drones. Paradoxically, they often feel powerless. They are usually aware, if only vaguely, of their isolation. And they usually wish that things could be different between them and their children. Finally, the real relationship that can ensue between men and their children does, in itself, change men even more. Children provide a deep emotional satisfaction, an overflowing of love that most men hadn't hoped for from anyone except their wives.

This is what men have to gain from changing: love, connection, and emotional fulfillment. Furthermore, if men expand their ideas of masculine identity to include nurturing children, and most importantly, if they put children and family on the same par as career, they would still be able to be successful fathers and family members even if their marriages fail. And with these new masculine identities, they might eventually support or even press for the changes in our society that would allow the family to thrive.

Men's reluctance to change has certainly been an obstacle to family life today. But to a large extent, society hasn't allowed them to change. It certainly hasn't helped them. If there is a villain in the contemporary marriage problem, it is our society. Women at work and men in the family are this century's revolution *and problem*. Society pays lip service to equality and to marriage, but there has been so little support of the two-paycheck marriage that I've come to think of the American workplace as the iron vise squeezing the life out of otherwise resilient, viable couples.

BUSINESS FIRST

"We have done better at playing according to the men's rules than changing them to our own."

—Susan Estrich, first woman president of the
Harvard Law Review

On those particularly long hard days I used to have building my practice—when it could take five tries to get out of the office and I may (or may not) have eaten a quick sandwich at my desk, someone would invariably say to me, "Well, that's why they call it work." And I would invariably think of those leisurely lunches when all business closes down and even executives strolled around the square . . . *in Italy*. Now, *they* know how to live, I would think—as if it was the nature of Italian life to leave time for enjoyment and the nature of American life to work as frantically as you can all day, then collapse.

It's taken me a lifetime to realize that how we live and work as a nation is our own choice. And mostly I feel as if we don't even *try* to make our lives better, though it wouldn't be so very difficult to do so; we did it in the early part of the twentieth century by legislating an eight-hour day and workplace safety standards. But now, women—who suffer most—don't dare challenge the status quo for fear we might sound "unrealistic" or "unable to make the grade in a man's world."

Remember the 1993 Family and Medical Leave Act I mentioned in Chapter 3? It sounded good, but it didn't actually change our lives. In the first place, the legislation only applies to companies with more than fifty employees, while most Americans work for smaller ones. Second, employers can exempt "key employees," so women and men who want to take parental leave can kiss the best jobs good-bye. Third, the provision is for three months of *unpaid* leave with the birth of a child or a medical emergency. If parents need the income, they can't take off. But still, we don't join together to challenge the workplace rules that leave no time for family. And one thing we need, desperately, is more time with our families.

The real reason most parents don't take sufficient time off when a child is born or a family member is ill is because they are afraid of losing their jobs. Justifiably. As much talk as there has been in the business community about the "work-family" problem, there's been precious little action. Why?

• Because the large majority of companies surveyed *believed* that work-family programs were too costly, *even though it has been proven that companies don't actually lose money.*

• Because most bosses are male (95 percent of CEOs have wives at home), they just don't see what the problem is. Or if there is some problem for working mothers, their bosses believe it's up to the mothers to solve it.

• Because women don't yet have enough power in the business community to change the work-family conflict. A quarter of the female Harvard MBAs dropped out of the business world because they felt companies were "blatantly hostile to them" and that "they had been forced out of the best jobs once they became mothers." And the women were prepared for top jobs.

Add to these problems several more: the large majority of working women still earn less than $25,000 a year; child care is expensive and often of very poor quality; there are few after-school programs, no elder care for infirm parents, and no coverage on school holidays. And giving in to economic pressure, or careerism, or greed, parents work so much overtime that they often can't be home to put their children to sleep, let alone eat dinner with them.

OUR BEAT-THE-CLOCK LIVES

Like most of us, the couples in this book are all caught in a no-win transition. In the past, the puritan work ethic caused no conflict because the wife was the homemaker. Now that nearly everyone works, home life is often as hectic as work.

Work has become the center of our universe, our raison d'etre, even though most salaries today no longer buy either the free time or the upward mobility enjoyed by our parents. We have lost the economic prosperity that supported those breadwinner-homemaker marriages, and we are not likely to get it back. Today both partners usually *have* to work just to stay in place. But—and here's the shock—most don't really have to work as hard as they do.

It is always remarkable to me that couples so rarely consider trading status and money for leisure, or better put, personal time, even when it is clear that they would be happier if they did. We don't want to be a workaholic society, but we can't seem to stop ourselves although this frantic work pace puts our marriages, our children, and our lives in jeopardy. Now, at the close of the twentieth century, we are actually working *more* than we have since the legislation of the eight-hour day!

Harvard economist Juliet Schor points out that *the average American is now working the equivalent of two months more each year than their German or French counterparts.* Yet, given our productivity, "we actually could have chosen the four-hour day. Or a working year of six months." Instead, we choose to work longer hours to have more consumer goods. We are driven both by the voices within us and by the society outside.

Most Americans are in love with *things*. Nowhere else on earth do people have our material living standard. Even in Switzerland, Germany, and Scandinavia, the richest countries in Europe, people have on average only three-quarters of our incomes, less housing space, and fewer cars. Every conceivable home appliance, two televisions, and two cars are now assumed "necessities" for middle-class families. Shopping has become Americans' major leisure activity. This is a relatively recent corruption of the American Dream, which used to mean having steady work and benefits enough to own a home, get medical care, educate our children, and even have a car. Most of us achieved this dream and then failed to move on to a less materialistic and more spirit-enhancing vision of "the good life." We are no longer helping those on the lowest rungs to achieve the basic dream.

But it's not that we're just crass materialists. In *The Poverty of Affluence,* one economist theorizes that our luxuries now supply our main sense of security. They make us "feel strong and expansive rather than small and endangered." Once, however, community gave individuals that feeling. Now we have more individual freedom but, "we have no reserved seats. We must *win* our place."

And so here we are, striving so fiercely and working such long hours for security only to find ourselves feeling lost in an obsessive concern with marketplace values and an out-of-control whirlwind of activity that we don't know how to stop long enough to take care of our relationships.

Whenever asked, we *say* that family life and betterment of society are more important than having a nice home, car, and clothes. Clearly, our beat-the-clock lives are not in sync with our deep belief in family and community. The result is that not only do we suffer from overwork, we also betray ourselves daily. Overworked Americans cannot raise their children well, cannot contribute to their communities, and cannot sustain the companionship they once found in their marriages. They also can't live according to their expressed values; they just don't have the time.

Society also drives us. We don't want to be workaholics, but we just can't stop. In a *Time* magazine survey, half the men said they would forfeit a quarter of their salaries to have more family and personal time and they would refuse a promotion that involved sacrificing family time. The problem is they can't work fewer hours or refuse the promotion and hold on to their jobs.

Even more women than men would give up money and status if they could have more family time. But they can't. In a recent study of over nine hundred female Harvard graduates in business, law, and medicine, all the women would have preferred to work less, but instead they either put in their grueling hours, dropped out, or went into business for themselves. These were "the best and the brightest," and even they couldn't make the system support them as parents.

The lucky few can work shorter hours if they let themselves. Gina and Dale, who both essentially work for themselves, are examples, as are Terry and Diane, both talented crafts people, who went into business together. The average couple, though, has to work outside the home at inflexible jobs, confronting a terrible choice between work and family. Clearly, sweeping changes are necessary.

FAMILY-FRIENDLY BUSINESSES

What would make the workplace work for people who also want fulfilling personal and family lives? In the last several years, social critics and workers have come up with a list of suggestions. These are the most frequently cited:

1. *On-Site Day Care.* It's usually better quality and cheaper, since the company subsidizes it. Parents can commute with their children, see them on breaks, and know their playmates. Second best: subsidies or discounts at child care near the workplace.

2. *Flextime.* This allows employees to choose their hours and days. A 7:00 to 3:00 schedule, for example, might mean one parent can pick up the children at school while the other parent, with 9:30 to 5:30 hours, can drop them off in the morning. *Compressed workweeks* help, too, especially when there's a long commute. The Corning Glass factory offers a four-day week of ten-hour days that is quite popular.

3. *No Mandatory Overtime.* If workplaces respected people's need to be home for dinner, they could arrange meetings and events for office hours and have business lunches instead of dinners. Workers wouldn't be penalized for refusing overtime.

4. *Family Leave.* What would a really supportive plan look like? Sweden's. Swedes are guaranteed six weeks of *paid parental leave*, three months paid leave for sick children,

eighteen months of unpaid parental leave to men and women, and the right to work part-time without losing your job or benefits until your children are seven! If it sounds fantastic, IBM offers up to three years' maternity leave. Executives say it's better for the company. There's less turnover and retraining.

5. *Telecommuting.* Many companies are now experimenting with employees working at home two or more days a week. IBM now has 20,000 employees telecommuting and finds it boosts morale and productivity. Some companies go a step further to the "ultimate flexibility" of the *virtual office.* With laptops, E-mail, cellular phones, and beepers, people can work wherever they work best.

Companies that institute these family support programs see "a significant drop in absenteeism," says one Prudential Insurance VP. A third of the *Fortune* 500 companies offer some form of flex-time and telecommuting. At Bell Atlantic, an executive who helped create such programs said employees are less stressed and more productive. And not just women employees. Polls show that men are just as concerned with family problems as women are, and they are just as unlikely to handle work challenges well when they are worried about their children.

Given how much better family support programs could make the lives of today's men, women, and children, wouldn't it be wonderful if the men's movement turned its energies to advocating such programs? Instead of beating drums and bonding to reclaim their lost "masculine" power, men could bond by sharing fathering problems and the challenges of their new roles. Men's groups could explore the work-family problem to see how business today might support them as fathers and equal partners in their marriages. Finally, men could use the very real power they have to campaign for changes in the workplace.

Wouldn't it be wonderful if we as individuals all asked ourselves what our own companies and workplaces might do to make family life easier? Once my clients have made a personal change, many of them do try to help their colleagues at work. Gina, for example, was very aware of how privileged she was to be able to cut back to a three-day week. "What would I do," she said toward the end of therapy, "if I didn't work for the family business?"

"Well," I said, "that's an excellent question. What do the other men and women in your company do when they have children? What provisions are there?"

That began Gina thinking and investigating. She soon found that many of the women employees dropped out when they had children rather than returning to work full-time. And when she inquired, she found that the majority of them would have liked a part-time option. Although I don't know what actually happened, my guess is that Gina, who was an excellent organizer and a most diplomatic executive, found a way to institute the part-time option throughout her father's firm. And that, of course, not only sends a signal to other businesspeople she and her company deal with, but it also makes life better for that many more American families.

FAMILY FRIENDLY GOVERNMENT

We're on the brink of a new world we don't yet understand. And as we change we need public policies that don't throw the baby out with the bathwater. What legislation could enormously improve family life? Legislation for subsidized child care, a six-hour day or four-day week, improving education, and maintaining adequate poverty supports—just to name a few.

Poverty may be the greatest challenge to the American family, for the poor are the most vulnerable to social and business policies, have the least flexible lives, and the fewest options. As our country changes, we need leaders who can address the pain, fear, and insecurity in our lives without scapegoating the poor. Poverty, not alternative family structures, destroys families. The noted pediatrician Penelope Leach has recently declared that poverty "is the biggest risk of all" to children. She calls for government programs to support them.

IT TAKES A WHOLE VILLAGE TO RAISE A CHILD

This African proverb recognizes that child rearing is a task too complex for any individual family but requires family-rooted-in-community. Thus, a nurturing family structure requires at least one loving parent or parent figure, with an adequate income, who is supported by the involvement of several other adults from the extended family or friendship network. These "others" also provide some of the love and support the family needs.

When the children's mother and father are both people with positive values, caring equally about each other and deeply involved with their children—and are also rooted in a supportive network of family, friends, and community—then so much the better; perhaps this is ideal. But when one or both of the parents are very self-involved, abusive, or emotionally unstable, absent or addicted, the children can still be successfully and happily nurtured by other loving adults.

Although having a two-parent family can be ideal for children—and virtually all marriages start out with this ideal—the two-parent structure alone doesn't insure successful family life. If those two parents are isolated, depressed, and angry with each other, their children may be at far greater risk than the children of an emotionally well-adjusted single parent or a gay or lesbian couple or a remarried couple. Once the basics of survival are assured, it's the emotional and social texture of family life, not its structure, that are the crucial ingredients for success.

When people belong to a community, everyone benefits— parents as well as children. The clients who come to my office to try to repair their marriages and family relationships want to believe that their lives have some meaning beyond their own narrow self-interest. Caught up, like the rest of us, in the scramble and the individualism of the competitive marketplace, they nevertheless readily acknowledge that "there must be more to life than this." Then they think, someday . . . when I've established my career or when the kids' college money is set or when I've retired. Then what? Then, we'll start to live? I guess it's this kind of hedging that produced the saying "Life is what happens while you're planning something else."

The positive side of any crisis that brings a couple to therapy is the opportunity to reflect in just this way: Is my life meaningful? Do my relationships work? Are we teaching our children what they need to know? Do I like my work? Is money as important as I thought it was? Do I have caring connections? Do I belong? Among my clients and friends, some search for this kind of meaning or spirituality through religion, but many seek it through a connection with others in a positive, mutually helpful way. That is, by being part of a caring community.

To thrive, a married couple has to repair their deep emotional connections to their original families and also put out new shoots into the various levels of community, whose support may make a life-or-death difference to their marriage. So few people seem to understand how interconnected the personal and public levels of experience are. So few couples make the time to invest themselves beyond their circle of family and friends, beyond their own personal ambition and pleasure. And most couples I see suffer because they don't. Ending the isolation of marriage is as important as changing the emotions and behavior within it. We have overloaded the marital circuits by expecting to get all of our needs met through this one relationship.

As one of my clients told me: "When we were first married, I thought happiness was standing facing each other, looking into each other's eyes. Now I think happiness is standing side by side, our arms around each other and the children, looking out at the world—to find and make our places there, and to help change what needs changing there." When so many people today go to therapists because they feel their lives are meaningless, it is up to the therapist to help them recognize that the meaninglessness they feel is actually disconnection from family and from something larger than their own interests and pleasures.

A routine part of my therapy with divorcing men in particular and other men who are cut off is to look into their social network and discuss with them the ways they could become more connected, less isolated. And very often, the therapy I do with couples concludes with some work that helps to "de-isolate" them as well.

As part of my regular inquiry, I asked Dale, the computer programmer who worked at home, how he managed to meet and be with other people. This was particularly important, since life with an infant can be very homebound. He told me that he was just talking with Gina about this problem the other day. The mayor had invited her to join a task force to help place teens and young high school graduates in apprenticeships and internships with local businesses. "Nobody remembers about people who work at home, like me. I'm a business, too. I could teach someone my business." I then asked Gina why she didn't suggest that Dale join the task force with her to represent "home-office" businesses? "Well, I wasn't even sure I wanted to do the task force, with the baby coming," she said. But when I asked her how she'd feel if Dale did it with her, she smiled broadly. "Then, yes," she answered, "I'd definitely do it."

Gary and Sharon, the couple who lost themselves in supporting their extravagant lifestyle, were able to begin to orient themselves toward their relatively new Scarsdale life near the end of their therapy. They had reduced their expenses and cut back at work. Sharon, however, expressed her concern that Gary had no friends or outside interests. When Gary acknowledged this, I suggested he join one of the men's groups offered at Family Institute, which he did. Then, urged by a physician in the group who was troubled by cutbacks that had endangered several of his critically ill patients, Gary got involved in political activism for the first time. "Well, that's great for Gary," Sharon remarked as he reported this, "but *we* have no couple friends." She was angry that Gary had refused to accept an invitation to join a monthly culture group. He reasoned that it was "easier" to go to the theater on their own. "He really doesn't get it," Sharon said. "Why should we go with these lovely people and have dinner with them, too?"

We all laughed, including Gary. They did join the group, which they enjoyed, and Sharon ended their last session by teasing, "If I can just keep his work hours down enough, I might even be able to socialize him."

"WE'RE ALL IN THIS TOGETHER": CHANGING OUR COMMUNITIES

If children cause the crisis in couples' lives, they also provide the strongest experience of community and hence the greatest opportunity for social change. It has been said that love takes the couple out of the society; children bring them back. Therapeutically speaking, children provide an opportunity to bring out three levels of experience together and to experience ourselves as part of the larger system. The couple with children is suddenly connected to other parents, to schools, to civic issues on the local, city, state, and national level.

While it's certainly true that one couple's transformation doesn't change the world, it can make a difference in our communities. Because parents today desperately need social and institutional support, they might yet find a way to challenge our consumerist work-centered values and create a more family-friendly society, one with some of the amenities the Scandinavian and other European countries have.

Some social critics believe that Europe's generous social services have caused the decline of those European economies. But if you look into the details, you'll find that family support is a tiny portion of their economy; its cost is negligible compared to Europe's very generous pensions, early retirement, and lifetime unemployment benefits programs. In fact, I should think we can learn from Europe how *little* child care and parental leave cost a country and how much better it would be for most of us to work less.

It may seem odd that a family therapist should issue a call for social and political involvement, but it is precisely the misaligned connection between marriage and society that has put marriage in such jeopardy and will continue to do so if the social contract isn't repaired. We must recognize the degree to which we are all interdependent. Just as we benefit from understanding how a family functions as a system, we can benefit from understanding how society functions as a *system* and how, as individuals and couples, we are all inextricably a part of it.

I teach my therapist trainees that it is their job not only to connect the client's complaint to what is going on in the family system, but also to what is happening in the social system they live in. A truly systemic therapy encourages clients to question their role in every system they belong to. Alienation, cynicism, and despair poison relationships, whether their source is the family system or the larger systems of society, or, typically, both.

Now that the "greedy eighties" are over, it is easier for people to understand how we have overprized autonomy. As a culture, we have begun to understand the importance of connectedness and what we have lost by devaluing it. This is one of the reasons why the issue of "family values" strikes home for so many people. But family values need not be defined according to a notion of rigid family forms and traditional sex roles. Real family values are more appropriately defined as parents who are as involved in their marriage and their children as they are in their own achievement. Real family values are reflected by a family's involvement in society and by a society that supports the needs of its families. And American families today are made up of two-paycheck marriages, single-parent households, remarried couples with their children, and gay and lesbian couples with their children. Today, a very small percentage of families with children have traditional wage earner-homemaker partners.

The problem with the so-called family values debate now raging in America is that it has become a code phrase to signify support for the traditional family structure of yesterday. But wage-earner father/stay-at-home mother is a family structure few of today's families want or can afford. Nor do women want the contemporary variation on that structure that "allows" wives to work if the family needs the income but preserves the traditional roles of husband-money manager and wife-homemaker. We cannot turn the clock back to a marriage contract meant for a different social system. But we can certainly uphold family values. Who could possibly be against "family values" if it means what it always has: adults caring about each other and teaching their children to be loving, responsible, productive people. Bad values, an equal opportunity problem, can be learned from family or peers in the slums, in the heartland, in school, in the corporation or the country club.

The traditional family structure led to a 50 percent divorce rate and certainly produced at least as much alcoholism, drug addiction, incest, and physical abuse as any other family structure. It could exist only through the sacrifice of women's autonomy. Better we should strengthen the family values in the actual present-day structures of the American family. We should support the best in who we really are. And this view was upheld recently by the men and women interviewed in a national survey. The vast majority of them did not define family values as having a traditional nuclear family. Nine out of ten of the women said, "Society should value all types of families." And the families that make up these new structures must in turn make their voices heard in their local communities and in the American polity.

That may sound very grandiose, but as Madeleine Kunin, three-time governor of the state of Vermont, has said, "The difference between community activities and political action is merely one of scale." As Kunin organized to better her children's lives, she took the next obvious step and got involved in local politics. But she never deviated from her family focus. The result of her efforts and the efforts of so many idealistic young families that settled in Vermont during the sixties and seventies is that Vermont was ranked the number one state for environmental policy, children's services, and mental health. And Kunin was rated one of the nation's top ten education governors. I am reminded of my favorite quotation from Margaret Mead: "Never doubt that a small group of thoughtful, committed citizens can change the world. Indeed, it's the only thing that ever has."

The more that men are involved with the daily workings of family life, the easier it will be to get legislation that supports family needs. And the more women learn to translate their personal needs into political action, the more that public policy will reflect real American values. There has seldom been a time when we have so urgently needed to return an ethos of caring about others to the American dialogue. We need a new vision of communal life that we can relate to—one that calls forth our caring, not our fears; one that describes more than the "information superhighway" that lies ahead. And this new vision should include an extension of family values into the larger society, such values as taking responsibility for ourselves and being responsible toward others, particularly those in need. As someone once said, we are not here to see through each other, but to see each other through.

Real people make real changes in our collective lives. Some of them are the ones you've gotten to know throughout this book. I always help the couples I see to "get involved," just as I've helped them to renegotiate their relationship. They help others while helping themselves: What goes around comes around.

Not long before Sonya and Bob finished therapy, Sonya commented on how bleak their local day care center was. "I think that more than anything makes me sad to leave the kids there." After talking about how *they* might actually help to do something about that problem, Sonya and Bob joined together with the other parents to plan improvements.

Jerry and Denise, who had more time for themselves once Jerry cut back at work, were talking about putting some of that time into the church. Both of them had strong religious backgrounds, and this was the natural place for them to begin reaching out. They also wanted to make their neighborhood better for kids. After one such discussion, Denise got together with other mothers of toddlers to see if they could begin a preschool program at their church. Jerry, who worried about the teenage gangs and drug dealers on the rise near their home, thought he would talk to his minister about starting a chapter of "Mad Dads," an organization of African-American fathers who "took back" their neighborhoods. "I read that Mad Dads started in a church," Jerry said, "so maybe my church would sponsor a chapter."

We would all benefit from similar involvement. We all suffer to the extent that our lives are limited by rigid gender roles. Because we aren't changing society to support our changing needs, we all pay a high price in overwork, alienation, and divorce. Yet we also suffer from pessimism about the possibility of change.

Since family, work, and community seem to be the best social institutions we've managed to create, why not remake them so they support our children and ourselves? The American ideal of individualism seems to have convinced us that we caused our own problems and must solve them ourselves.

It isn't so.

Last June, our son Tim and his fiancée, Jennifer, were married in our garden in a ceremony that reflected their important social and emotional connections. Sam and I stood beside Tim's two groomsmen—Bennett, and Tim's friend, Jeff—and Jennifer's parents stood beside her bridesmaids, representing, as the clergyman said, "the traditions and families from which Jennifer and Tim have come." At one point in the service, the minister said to our assembled family and friends: "We have come together because a new family is established in our midst. Therefore, I ask all of you: Will you affirm your love and support of Tim and Jennifer as they grow in their marriage: Will you offer them the best of your care and counsel in their times of struggle and your celebration with them in their times of joy?"

And we all answered loudly each time, "We do—we will." Tim and Jen then completed their vows, promising to support each other "through all of life's surprises" and to "treasure and respect" their differences.

Sam and I smiled at each other. Whatever renegotiations the future might hold for them, this was a wonderful beginning.

Notes

CHAPTER 1

BACKSLIDING INTO TRADITIONAL MARRIAGE

14. **"they want traditional weddings . . ."**: from a private interview with editor in chief of *Modern Bride*, 1994, Cele Goldsmith Lalli.

14. **earn the same money as their husbands**: Ibid.

16. **Fifty percent of American marriages**: statistics on divorce from Arthur J. Norton and Louisa F. Miller, *Marriage, Divorce, and Remarriage in the 1990's,* U.S. Department of Commerce, Economic and Statistics Administration, Bureau of the Census, October, 1992.

16. **And couples who have lived together**: according to Robert Shoen, Professor, Department of Population Dynamics at Johns Hopkins University, who is doing current research on the subject.

CHAPTER 2

THE MOTHERING PROBLEM

35. **study done by a Yale psychiatrist**: Kyle Pruett, M.D., cited in *Working Mother,* July 1994, 32.

35. **"men become mothers . . ."**: Kathleen Gerson, *No Man's Land: Men's Changing Commitments to Family and Work* (New York: Basic Books, 1993), 240.

36. **"insist on, or fall into, primary parenting"**: Rhona Mahony, *Kidding Ourselves: Breadwinning, Babies and Bargaining Power,* (New York: Basic Books, 1995), 102–109.

39. **two sociologists determined**: W. Keith Bryant, Ph.D., of Cornell University, and Cathleen Zick, Ph.D., of the University of Utah, cited in *Working Mother,* July 1994, 35.

40. **children are happier**: Pepper Schwartz, "Me Stressed, No Blessed," *The New York Times,* Nov. 17, 1994, C1, describes study done by Dr. Rosalind Barnett at the Center for Research on Women at Wellesley.

40. **And recent studies on work, family, and stress**: Ibid., describes research done by sociologists Tobey Parcel and Elizabeth Menaghen of Ohio State University.

40. **"power moms"**: Alicia Swasy, "Stay at Home Moms Are Fashionable Again in Many Communities," *The Wall Street Journal,* July 23, 1993, A1.

42. **a *Modern Bride* survey**: according to editor in chief. See note, Chapter 1.

42. **men are . . . doing about a third**: *No Man's Land,* 7.

43. **When David Williams**: Sam Howe Verhovek, "At Issue: Hold a Baby or Hold That Line?" *The New York Times,* Oct. 19, 1993, A1.

43. **"After having dutifully puffed . . .":** Colin Harrison, "Here's Baby. Dad Stays Home. Dad Gets Antsy," *The New York Times,* August 31, 1993, A17.

44. **"I've been a man with a rocket ship . . .":** Benjamin Cheever, *Lear's,* August 1993, 81.

45. **"When I became visibly pregnant":** Tricia W. Atallah, "So I Became My Own Boss . . ." *Women's News,* Westchester and Rockland Cty, Jan. 1994, 3.

47. **One sociologist discovered:** Arlie Hochschild with Anne Machung, *The Second Shift* (New York: Viking Books, 1989), 3.

CHAPTER 3

WHY ISN'T MARRIAGE FIFTY-FIFTY?

58. **"Why Are Men and Women Different?":** *Time,* Jan. 20, 1992.

58. **he saw his fifteen-month-old daughter flirt with men:** Christine Gorman, "Sizing Up the Sexes," Ibid., 44.

58. **"in the final analysis . . .":** Ibid., 51.

59. **"men are defective: . . .":** Richard A. Schwader, *The New York Times Book Review,* Jan. 9, 1994, 3.

62. **many women and men today are similarly deluded:** *The Second Shift* documents the way in which couples delude themselves in order to believe in their equality.

CHAPTER 4

DISCOVERING THE GOLDEN RULE:
WHOEVER HAS THE GOLD MAKES THE RULES

66. **At most divorce hearings:** for a full discussion of the subject, see Marcia Millman, *Warm Hearts and Cold Cash: The Intimate Dynamics of Families and Money* (New York: The Free Press, 1991).

71. **"The Person Who Has the Gold . . .":** Marianne Walters, Betty Carter, Peggy Papp, and Olga Silverstein, *The Invisible Webb* (New York: The Guilford Press, 1988), 237.

72. **"I wouldn't go that far . . .":** Ibid., 240.

76. **"Whoever Controls the Purse Strings . . .":** Henry Weil, *Bridal Guide,* Jan.–Feb. 1994, 32.

80. **"When you have got a woman in a box . . .":** quoted in Michael S. Kimmel and Thomas E. Mosmiller, eds., *Against the Tide: Pro-Feminist Men in the United States, 1776–1990* (Boston: Beacon Press, 1992), 364.

CHAPTER 5

THE SEARCH FOR INTIMACY IN MARRIAGE

88. **"Despite the limited development of his individuality . . .":** Michael E. Kerr, M.D., and Murray Bowen, M.D., *Family Evaluation* (New York: W. W. Norton, 1988), 70.

CHAPTER 6

MATRIMONIAL DUETS: POWER GAMES AND POWER PLAYS

109. **power over . . . power to:** this distinction was first made by psychologist Jean Baker-Miller in her 1981 lectures. She also wrote about the terms in "Women and Power: Reflections Ten Years Later," in Thelma Jean Goodrich, ed., *Women and Power* (New York: W. W. Norton, 1991). Adrienne Rich also made this distinction in *Of Woman Born: Motherhood as Experience and Institution* (New York: W. W. Norton, 1986), 67–68.

110. **"this generation would rather be a workaholic wife . . .":** *Esquire*, Feb. 1994, 67.

116. **pursuit and distance:** these terms were coined by Thomas F. Fogarty, M.D. in "The Distancer and the Pursuer," *The Family*, vol. 7 #1, 1975, 45–50.

CHAPTER 7

EXCEPTIONS THAT (DIS)PROVE THE GOLDEN RULE

135. **One of the most famous recent studies of American couples:** Philip Blumstein and Pepper Schwartz, *American Couples* (New York: Pocket Books, 1985).

135. **"make a conscious effort":** Ibid., 55.

135. *partners who feel they have equal control:* Ibid., 89.

138. **"when lesbian couples become parents . . .":** Valory Mitchell, Ph.D., "Two Moms: The Contribution of the Planned Lesbian Family to the Deconstruction of Gendered Parenting," *The Journal of Feminist Family Therapy*, Special Double Issue Vol. 3 & 4 (1995), eds. Robert Jay Green, Ph.D. and Joan Laird, Ph.D.

138. **In the same study on American couples:** *American Couples*, 74.

141. **Nancy Boyd-Franklin:** *Black Families in Therapy: A Multi-Systems Approach* (New York: The Guilford Press, 1988), 232.

142. **"Black girls are taught self-reliance . . .":** Audrey Chapman, *Entitled to Good Loving: Black Men and Women in the Battle for Love and Power* (New York: Henry Holt, 1994), 25.

147. **". . . we must viciously compete with one another":** bell hooks, *Yearning: Race, Gender, and Cultural Politics* (Boston: South End Press, 1990), 75.

147. **"many of us believe . . .":** "Financial Affairs: Can Money Really Buy You Love?" *Essence*, Feb. 1994, 79.

147. **Many young black educated women feel despair:** Sam Roberts, "Black Women Graduates Outpace Male Counterparts: Income Disparity Seen as Marriage Threat," *The New York Times*, Oct. 31, 1994, A12.

147. **" 'One day I'm going to have . . .":** *Waiting to Exhale* (New York: Viking Books, 1992), 30.

148. **"he had a series of fits . . .":** Ibid., 33.

149. **recent widely publicized studies:** cited in editorial, "The Rich Get Richer Faster," *The New York Times*, April 10, 1995, A24.

150. **So concluded a federal commission:** Peter T. Kilborn, "Women and Minorities Still Face 'Glass Ceiling,' " *The New York Times*, March 16, 1995, A22.

CHAPTER 8

EROTIC EQUALITY: SEX AND POWER

159. **"a subdued picture . . .":** Tamar Lewin, "Sex in America: Faithfulness in Marriage Thrives After All," *The New York Times*, Oct. 7, 1994, A1. The survey cited

was conducted by the National Opinion Research Center at the University of Chicago and published as: John H. Gagnon, Edward O. Laumann, and Gina Kolata, *Sex in America: A Definitive Survey* (Boston: Little Brown, 1994).

160. **women, when they become wives, abandon their sexuality:** for a full discussion of this theme see Dalma Heyn, *The Erotic Silence of the American Wife* (New York: Random House, 1992).

163. **Many prominent feminists have argued:** most notably, Nancy Chodorow in *The Reproduction of Mothering: Psychoanalysis and the Sociology of Gender* (Berkeley: University of California Press, 1978).

164. **says psychiatrist Ethel Person:** *Dreams of Love and Fateful Encounters: The Power of Romantic Passion* (New York: W. W. Norton, 1988), 68ff, 137ff.

165. **"wall socket sex":** discussion taken from his lecture, "Constructing the Sexual Crucible: An Integration of Sexual and Marital Therapy," Oct. 2, 1993, SUNY, Purchase. The title is also the title of his book (New York: W. W. Norton, 1991).

CHAPTER 9

RENEGOTIATING THE MARRIAGE CONTRACT

178. **Harriet Lerner's book:** Harriet Lerner, Ph.D., *The Dance of Anger: A Woman's Guide to Changing the Patterns of Intimate Relationships* (New York: Harper and Row, 1985).

CHAPTER 10

GOING HOME

197. **Not only did I know my father better:** This story appeared in an earlier, longer version in Froma Walsh and Monica McGoldrick, eds., *Living Beyond Loss* (New York: W. W. Norton, 1991).

198. **Two Israeli biologists:** Natalie Angier, "Heredity's More Than Genes, New Theory Proposes," *The New York Times*, Jan. 3, 1995, B13.

199. **You Can Go Home Again:** *You Can Go Home Again: Reconnecting with Your Family* (New York: W. W. Norton, 1995).

202. **Holmes and Rahe:** T. H. Holmes and R. H. Rahe, "The Social Readjustment Rating Scale," *Journal of Psychosomatic Research*, vol. 11 (1967): 213–216.

207. **"Shared Laundry Consciousness":** Marianne Ault-Riché, "Sex, Money, and Laundry: Sharing Responsibilities in Intimate Relationships," *Journal of Feminist Family Therapy*, vol. 6 (1) (1994): 69–87.

CHAPTER 11

THE MARITAL STRESS POINTS

232. **the income gap between men and women only widens:** Tamar Lewin, "Income Gap for Sexes Is Seen as Wider in Retirement," *The New York Times*, April 26, 1995, A19.

CHAPTER 12

DEALING WITH ADVERSITY: UNEXPECTED MARITAL STRESSES

239. **opposites don't generally attract:** Jane E. Brody, "Making It Work When Opposites Attract," *The New York Times,* Nov. 23, 1994, C7.

242. **although black men between twenty-five and thirty years old:** cited in "A Symposium of Black Intellectual Leaders on the Plight of Black Men in America," *The New York Times Magazine,* Dec. 4, 1994, 74.

242. **poor couples divorce twice as much as comfortable ones:** Robert Pear, "Poverty Termed a Divorce Factor," *The New York Times,* Jan. 13, 1995, B1.

247. **basic divorce research:** psychologist-researcher Mavis Hetherington notes that although 75 percent of the divorcing couples in the group she studied were having affairs at the time they split up, only 15 percent went on later to marry the person with which they had the affair. See E. M. Hetherington, "Modes of Adaptation to Divorce," a study done at the University of Virginia, 1982, and presented in a lecture at Georgetown University, March 1983.

249. **Evan Imber-Black:** Evan Imber-Black, Ph.D., and Janine Roberts, Ed.D., *Rituals for Our Times: Celebrating, Healing, Changing Our Lives and Our Relationships* (New York: HarperCollins, 1992).

250. **family psychiatrist John Rolland:** John S. Rolland, M.D., *Families, Illness and Disability* (New York: Basic Books, 1994).

251. **psychologist Ron Taffel:** Ronald Taffel, "The Politics of Mood: Depressive-Caretaker Relationships," *Journal of Feminist Family Therapy,* vol. 2, nos. 3/4 (1990): 153–179.

254. **an "emotional shock wave":** Murray Bowen, M.D., "Family Reaction to Death," P. J. Guerin, Jr., M.D., ed., *Family Therapy: Theory and Practice,* (New York: The Gardner Press, 1976), 338ff.

255. **The two books about death and dying:** Elliott J. Rosen, *Families Facing Death* (New York: Lexington Books, 1990). Froma Walsh and Monica McGoldrick, eds., *Living Beyond Loss* (New York: W. W. Norton, 1991).

CHAPTER 13

DIVORCE: THE ULTIMATE RENEGOTIATION

263. **divorce and marry several times:** Susan Chira, "Struggling to Find Stability When Divorce Is a Pattern," from a series on "Fractured Families: Dealing with Multiple Divorce," *The New York Times,* March 19, 1995, A1.

263. **Poor women remarry in greater numbers:** Betty Carter and Monica McGoldrick, eds., *The Changing Family Life Cycle: A Framework for Family Therapy,* second edition, (New York: The Gardner Press, 1988), 402.

266. **the typical divorce lawyer:** an excellent article on the subject appeared in *The New York Times,* May 13, 1995: Jan Hoffman, "An Adversarial Relationship: Divorce Can Mean War, Especially for the Lawyers."

267. **some states mandate parent education programs:** Tamar Lewin, "Now Divorcing Parents Must Learn How to Cope with Children's Needs," *The New York Times,* April 24, 1995, A10.

268. **Connie Ahrons:** Constance Ahrons, *The Good Divorce* (New York: Harper-Collins, 1994).

270. **this takes *at least* two years:** Constance Ahrons, "Redefining the Divorced Family," *Social Work,* vol. 25, (Nov. 1980): 437–445.

271. **a 1987 study:** E. M. Hetherington, "Family Relations Six Years After Divorce," K. Pasley and M. Ihinger-Tollman, eds., *Remarriage and Stepparenting Today: Current Research and Theory* (New York: Guilford Press, 1987), 185–205.

271. **men have a harder time:** Jane Gross, "Divorced, Middle Aged and Happy: Women, Especially, Adjust to the '90s," *The New York Times,* Dec. 7, 1992, A14.

272. **"half of noncustodial fathers gradually lose all contact with their children,"** Edward Kruk, "The Disengaged Non-Custodial Father: Implications for Social Work Practice with the Divorced Family," *Social Work,* vol. 39, no. 1, (Jan. 1994): 15.

274. **the journal *Science* reported:** cited in Jane E. Brody, "A New Look at Children and Divorce," *The New York Times,* June 7, 1991, A18.

275. **the average in child support:** Robert L. Griswold, *Fatherhood in America: A History* (New York: Basic Books, 1993), 232.

275. **twenty-four *billion* dollars remains uncollected annually:** Tamar Lewin, "New Tools for States Bolster Collection of Child Support," *The New York Times,* June 15, 1991, B1.

276. **The two books on being single:** Natalie Schwartzberg, Kathy Berliner, and Demaris Jacob, *Single In A Married World* (New York: W. W. Norton, 1995) and Carol Anderson, *Flying Solo* (New York: W. W. Norton, 1994).

279. **"reinstitutionalizing marriage":** from "Marriage in America: A Report to the Nation," published by the Council on Families in America (March 1995): 13.

CHAPTER 14

REMARRIAGE: REINVENTING FAMILY

290. **the remarried family . . . the fastest growing family form:** according to the U.S. Bureau of the Census, remarried families are now 21 percent of American families—nearly a quarter—and that's a significant rise from 1980, which was only 16 percent.

291. **second marriages . . . the divorce rate is quite a bit higher:** *Marriage, Divorce, and Remarriage in the 1990's,* p. 6.

293. **Cinderella, from the stepmother's point of view:** Edwin Friedman, *Friedman's Fables: An Address Delivered to the National Association of Family Therapists by Cinderella's Stepmother* (New York: The Guilford Press, 1990), 149.

296. **having children born to the remarried couple:** L. Duberman, *The Reconstituted Family: A Study of Remarried Couples and Their Children* (Chicago: Nelson-Hall, 1975), 428.

CHAPTER 15

THE FUTURE OF MARRIAGE

299. **as much or more of the family's income:** Tamar Lewin, "Women Are Becoming Equal Providers: Half of Working Women Bring Home Half the Household Income," *The New York Times,* May 11, 1995, A27.

300. **blame the women's movement:** see Sherrye Henry: *The Deep Divide: Why American Women Resist Equality* (New York: Macmillan, 1994).

300. **"essential male link between the child and the community":** *Marriage in America*, 12.

300. **Marianne Walters points out:** "The Codependent Cinderella Meets Iron John," *Networker*, (March/April 1993): 60.

301. **Most American men say:** *No Man's Land*, 181.

304. **companies don't actually lose money:** Although there are no studies on the subject, companies that institute family support programs note reduced absenteeism and turnover as financial compensation. See Mary Granfield, "The Case for On-Site Child Care," *Working Mother* (Nov. 1994), 40.

304. **95 percent of CEOs have wives at home:** Frank Edward Allen, "What Problem?" *The Wall Street Journal*, Supplement on Work and Family, June 21, 1993, 16.

304. **"blatantly hostile to them":** Deborah J. Swiss and Judith P. Walker, *Women and the Work/Family Dilemma: How Today's Professional Women Are Confronting the Maternal Wall* (New York: John Wiley and Sons, 1993), 220.

304. **the large majority . . . less than $25,000 a year:** Sam Roberts, "Women's Work: What's New, What Isn't," *The New York Times*, April 27, 1995, B4.

304. **child care is expensive and often of very poor quality:** Susan Chira, "Care at Child Day Centers Is Rated as Poor," *The New York Times*, Feb. 7, 1994, A6.

305. **"we actually could have chosen the four-hour day . . .":** *The Overworked American: The Unexpected Decline of Leisure* (New York: Basic Books, 1991), 2.

306. **"feel strong and expansive . . .":** Paul Wachtel, *The Poverty of Affluence: A Psychological Portrait of the American Way of Life* (Philadelphia: New Society Publishers, 1989), 65.

306. **"we have no reserved seats . . .":** Ibid., 62.

306. **Time magazine survey:** cited in *No Man's Land*, 254.

306. **In a recent study . . . Harvard graduates:** *Women and the Work/Family Dilemma*.

307. **Corning Glass:** *Working Mother*, Oct. 1994, 34.

308. **IBM now has 20,000 employees telecommuting:** Ibid., 46.

308. **"ultimate flexibility":** Phil Patton, "The Virtual Office Becomes Reality," *The New York Times*, Oct. 28, 1993, C1.

308. **"a significant drop in absenteeism,"** *Working Mother*, Nov. 1994, p. 32.

308. **At Bell Atlantic:** Ibid., July 1994, 24.

308. **men are just as concerned:** Sue Shellenberger, "Family Woes Worry Men as Much as Women," *The Wall Street Journal*, Jan. 5, 1994, A1.

309. **pediatrician Penelope Leach:** *Children First: What Our Society Must Do—And Is Not Doing—For Our Children Today* (New York: Alfred A. Knopf, 1994), 188.

315. **"Society should value . . . families":** cited in Tamar Lewin, "Women Are Becoming Equal Providers," *The New York Times*, May 11, 1995, A27.

315. **"The difference between community . . . of scale.":** Madeleine Kunin, *Living a Political Life: One of America's First Woman Governors Tells Her Story* (New York: Alfred A. Knopf, 1994), 28.

315. **top ten education governors,** Ibid., 29.

316. **"Mad Dads":** *Family Life*, March–April 1994, 21.

Index

Betty Carter, M.S.W.   **Joan K. Peters**

BETTY CARTER, M.S.W., is the cofounder and director of the Family Institute of Westchester, where she conducts a clinical practice. She has written numerous professional articles and books, received several professional awards, and is often quoted in *Redbook, Family Circle, Cosmopolitan,* and other national magazines.

JOAN K. PETERS is the author of *Manny and Rose,* a novel. Her stories, reviews, and articles on travel, motherhood, and politics have appeared in *The New York Times, Ms., Family Life,* and other publications.

The Tinsel
and the Hay

By
Harold Kohn

tidings

1908 Grand Ave.
Nashville, Tenn. 37203

FOREWORD

To read this book at one sitting may be a mistake. It was prepared to be read with imagination and time for reflection. Taste it. Feel it. Reflect upon it. Enjoy each one of the essays as you would enjoy a piece of hard candy. And when you have finished the book go back to your favorites, read them again and again. Each time you will get a new glimpse of truth into the nature of Creation and of the Creator.

Dr. Harold Kohn writes from personal experience—his own intimate knowledge of the Creator and the world in which we live. In page after page of this book he gives evidence of his faith in the living God. Sentence by sentence he opens our eyes and ears to the presence of God in the world around us.

The author has been a source of strength and courage to all who have been fortunate enough to know him personally. With unusual clarity his life exemplifies the honesty, integrity and the grace of one who walks with God.

November 1968   Rueben P. Job
Nashville, Tenn.   Editor, Tidings

To
LUCILE BERNARD
of
PINEYRIE
and
BILL AND ESTHER FREEMAN
of
Birchbluff,
with
affection and gratitude

ACKNOWLEDGEMENT

The author and the publisher express thanks to S. George Little, Rex Barley and Ed Grade of General Features Corporation, the Newspaper Syndicate, who first distributed to newspapers across the nation several of the essays in this book, and by whose permission they are printed here. Editor Curtis A. Chambers and publisher Donald A. Theuer of *Church and Home* Magazine have been kind in permitting articles that first appeared in that publication to be printed again in this book.

As always, the author is deeply indebted to his wife, Marian, for her encouragement and grateful for her assistance in reading manuscript and her gentle criticism, and he is appreciative of the efficient and eager help of his most excellent secretary, Twilla Kayner, who typed manuscript.

Open-Hearted Moments

Here we are in December.

This is not so much another month as another state of mind. Wherever the story of the first Christmas has been told, and wherever the coming of another Christmas is celebrated, people will be different from what they were in November or in any other month of the year.

December is a month of Christmas melodies, Christmas decorating, Christmas planning, Christmas buying, Christmas giving. For eleven months some folks suppress their best impulses and splendid sentiments. They would feel self-conscious and a little silly singing the joyous songs of Christ's coming, decorating their homes so gaily, saying the kind, appreciative word and performing the gracious deed any other time of the year. For eleven months they attempt to hide their best selves. But now, in December, they seek a way to reveal their hidden feelings. These are man's most open-hearted moments.

For these few December days we dare to be openly tender and kind in ways that would have seemed awkward a few short weeks ago. Some feelings are a little like twinkling out-

5

door Christmas lights of blue and gold, red and green. Many people hide warm friendliness, kindness and generosity away all year in some dark attic of their souls. As Christmas draws near the tender feelings are brought out and openly expressed. December is different: it is filled with open-hearted moments.

Besides revealing the hidden splendor God has fashioned within us, the Christmas season manifests what life should be like all the time. Of course, this does not mean that daily life should ring with Christmas carols or shine with Christmas lights or be loaded with Christmas gifts. But the open-heartedness of Yuletide month should distinguish all our days.

For instance, at Christmas time we offer gifts to those near and dear to us with a holy kind of carelessness: we do not give according to the merits and worthiness of our families, nor do we receive according to our just deserts. Does any parent, at Christmas shopping time, meticulously calculate the relative merits of his children and accordingly estimate how much money should be spent on each gift, following some mathematical scale of disobedience and obedience? Does any husband or wife try to total up the times the spouse has given smiles or scowls, thanks or complaints, pleasure or disappointment and then purchase a gift that reflects the mate's merits. Hardly! Instead, in December, we are caught up in a holy heedlessness concerning what those near us are worthy of receiving. Now there is an openheartedness about us, and it lets a little of God's grace flow in and out of us so that we give as God gives, not what is deserved but what expresses our love.

Isn't this what life should be like, always? Should we not always serve the world according to our love and the world's need, rather than according to what we determine others deserve from us?

Again, at Christmas time, when we are at our best, we care less about what we receive and care more about what we give; care less about our own happiness and more about the happiness of others. What a year it would be if that Christmas spirit were allowed to break its December bonds and flood and saturate the other eleven months.

What the world needs is a less spectacular Christmas celebration and a more enduring Christmas spirit.

When "the Word was made flesh and dwelt among us," He came not merely for Christmas Day, but forever.

6

Life Is More Than It Appears to Be

Now across much of North America autumn slowly dissolves into winter. December poverty possesses the landscape. Hardwood trees are bankrupt; every leaf has been wind-driven from their limbs. Grasses are withered and brown; their last greenness has been spent. Summer flowers have shriveled and fallen, and the landscape is thus color-poor. Seeds sleep beneath the first light snows of this season, a blanket too flimsy to keep them warm. (But the blanket will soon thicken.) If some observers were to choose appropriate music to accompany these days, it would surely be some solemn December dirge.

But look more closely. Look closer still! Winter has not yet officially arrived, and already there are small signs of spring! Scrape away the snow and leaf-litter near any maple tree and you will see sprouting seeds, next year's shoots and the next century's giants in their cradles. Carefully examine the twigs of shrubs and trees, and you will find the tiny buds of next spring's leaves and blossoms already forming. Look around you and you will see life in seed, root, bulb and shoot, life in bud and cocoon, life hidden and asleep in burrows, under crystals of ice and beneath drifts of snow and in the bottoms of brooks and ponds. Every lawn, every hillside, meadow and forest, every stream, pond and lake testifies in little ways that spring is already on its way, even before winter begins.

Of course, to the casual eye there is no spring here, but only the bleakness of winter. Average minds see only the obvious. They have sight without insight. Winter trees *look* dead to them, so they must *be* dead. Earth is clothed in a funeral shroud; therefore it must be devoid of life. But the perceptive observer is not deluded by the obvious into believing that winter has made a final conquest. Even while he shivers under his woolens, he is aware that spring, as well as winter, is on its way. The obscure signs of spring remind the insightful person that the world is not forsaken by the sun. Sap will again flow in the maples. Swallows will return. Wild flowers will bloom, and lilacs will perfume the moist air of another April. Even in December he believes in springtime.

Faith knows that things are not what they appear to be.

THE TINSEL AND THE HAY

Beneath all dull obviousness lurks God's glad surprises. The plain, the commonplace and ordinary things of life only thinly disguise God's great wonders and are waiting for some perceptive person to draw aside the veil and let the glory out.

Christmas teaches that there is something more to life than meets the eye, something that reaches beyond appearances. It was patently clear that first Christmastime that righteousness was weak and evil was strong. The Jews, the lovers of God, were the virtual slaves of the Romans, the worshippers of military might. Soldiers who slaughtered innocents ruled the earth. What chance did the Baby and Joseph and Mary have against Caesar and his hordes? Anyone that prattled about a baby born in a manger having any prospects of saving the world would have been considered an empty-headed, honey-coated sentimentalist. And the "realists" would have laughed him off the streets of Bethlehem. After all, it was obvious that hatred, not love, ruled the world, and conquests must be made by the sword, not by lovely words and kindly deeds, and never by a cross.

But, behold, what wonders lie hidden beneath the surface appearances! The Baby, and not Caesar, held the secret to the world's future. The riches, pomp, war banners, clanking arms and armor of Caesar's reign possessed a loud, ostentatious greatness that commanded the world's attention. But Christ would claim the world's love at last. Caesar's forces were noisy, while Joseph and Mary, the humble strangers from Nazareth, kept in their tender care a Power as restrained as Joseph's shy tears of joy, as gentle as Mary's caress, as quiet as the Baby's breathing.

Two thousand years on the far side of the first Christmas, when "Caesar" would be but a dusty, corroded, cob-webbed name, millions would proclaim the Christ their living Lord and celebrate His birthday. All of this was far from obvious, but it was true. And all that men thought most obvious on that Holy Night was not true at all. How God reverses our human values!

How should we live, then, in the kind of world that Christmas reveals? The Wise Men offer us some clues. They rejected the obvious signs of power as being delusions. They paused briefly at Herod's glittering palace and then passed on toward Bethlehem, refusing to be intimidated by bigness, by big buildings, big budgets, big armies, big successes, big names. They were not overawed by pomp, show and noisiness. They found God near and real in a humble place, and they saw His power and glory revealed in the Small Wonder that lay in the manger. Where do we look for God? Are we understanding enough to recognize the power of the Eternal where it appears in commonplace surroundings, in lowly garb, in feeble disguise? Can we be that wise?

We can look up, and the Wise Men did and faithfully follow such light as God gives us until we come to His Gift, hidden in some unexpected place.

We can think of Christ and be glad about God, as the Wise Men did. For if God is Christlike, which is the central meaning of Christmas and of Christianity, then the world and our own little lives are governed by the Lord of Love. Our worst fears, frustrations and despairs are unrealistic if the Christmas story is true, and if the Wise Men were really wise.

Christmas reminds us, then, as it did the Wise Men, that God's goodness comes to us in surprising ways. It prompts us to recall that God always has some glad springtime hidden beneath bleak winter, His bright hope for the world obscured by a covering of darkness, His Gift of love concealed behind a stable door.

Wise men dare to believe it. And the wise know where to find Him.

What Can We Expect of God?

God does not beat drums or blare trumpets to announce His presence among us. The Divine prefers to come to us unobtrusively, as gently as cattle breathe in a Judean manger, as silently as starlight falls upon Bethlehem, as quietly as the love of Mary and Joseph reaches toward the newly born Baby in the cattle stall.

God loves to make His appearance in unexpected places that seem unworthy of Him, as does a hay-filled trough from which cows and sheep and donkeys feed in a shabby out-building with a dirt floor. But the Christmas story teaches that revelations of God occur in the most unlikely places, and for this reason the world often misses the coming of God into our midst.

It is particularly true that God's grace and work are revealed in the most unlikely people. We expect to find signs of God's presence in the lives of the heroic spiritual giants of the race—Abraham and Moses, Saints Peter and Paul, Saints Augustine and Francis of Assisi, in Kagawa of Japan and Schweitzer of Africa. But if we look for God only in the lives of such rare souls, we miss the Divine who is nearer than we guessed.

The Nativity Story reminds us that God surprises us by revealing His presence through unlikely people, such as a peasant girl and her carpenter spouse, whom the world did not recognize as saints or benefactors, although through them the Eternal Goodness came among us, and through them the Greatest Gift was bestowed.

Even the non-religious sometimes show surprising signs of God's presence and work in their lives. In the old Testament God speaks to Cyrus the Persian through the prophet, Isaiah: "I am the Lord, and there is none other, besides me there is no God; *I gird you, though you do not know me . . .*" (Isaiah 45:5). The prophet says nothing about Cyrus' character, whether it is good or bad, and nothing about Cyrus' religion, excepting that he is not acquainted with the true God, but Isaiah sees Cyrus as God's instrument for the accomplishment of God's purposes. Without knowing it, Cyrus provides the means by which God's work is done, for it is through Cyrus

that God's people are released from bondage and are returned to their beloved homeland. Thus, the prophet illustrates what men of faith have always believed, that the sovereign God of the universe uses all sorts of tools to achieve his ends, and the instruments of God's will may be wholly unaware of the God they serve.

For a modern example of God's grace at work in one who made light of conventional religion consider Henry L. Mencken, the author, critic, student of "The American Language," social historian, and long-time editor of the *Baltimore Sun*. He seemed to pride himself on cynicism and agnosticism. A controversial character, he was widely and thoroughly hated by those who felt the painful barb of his sharp tongue and pen. But, while he was detested by many who knew him slightly, Mencken was adored by those who knew him well.

Although to the general public H. L. Mencken was notorious for his acid criticisms and his roaring invictive, to his intimates he was known as conspicuously polite and incomparably considerate and kind. Everywhere Mencken went he seemed to touch the humble, needy and lonely with unusual grace.

One Italian woman claimed Mencken saved her business and pushed her toward prosperity by his kindly interest in her. When she first opened a small restaurant Mencken urged her to junk the juke box, stop featuring spaghetti and begin advertising more exotic Italian dishes. Otherwise she would be running merely another spaghetti joint, of which Baltimore already had a great plenty. She followed his advice and had more business than she could handle.

Mencken invested two afternoons each week calling on the sick and lonely in hospitals. Doctors and nurses trooped after him as he visited hospital rooms, watching him distribute armloads of books and listening to his words of cheer, gay quips, and his clownish, farcical lectures on medical topics.

Near the end of his life Henry L. Mencken eagerly waited for school to dismiss each day, and intercepted neighboring children on their way home from school and visited with them about their lessons, their problems, hobbies, friends, wishes, hopes and plans. And the children never guessed that the old gentleman who was fascinated by their excited chatter was one of America's foremost men of letters.

Mencken loved animals and was genuinely concerned about

their welfare. He took nuts to a certain squirrel that lived in a little park across the street from Mencken's home. Once when several days passed without Mencken seeing the squirrel in his old haunts, this man who was known to the world as hard and capable of withering scorn, insisted that a thorough search be made for the animal, and explained his command, saying, "He may be sick!"

What do you make of a man like Mencken? Religiously he was unorthodox, to say the least, and irreverent at his worst. But in behavior he sometimes came close to Christlikeness. We know little about what Mencken thought of God, but it is easy to imagine what God thought of Mencken. If godliness means reaching beyond conventional religious doctrines to perform the God-like deed, Mencken was distinguished by a depth of godliness that would put many orthodox Christians to shame.

God is in no way obligated to live only where men look for Him—in His heavens; in the breath-taking beauty of nature; in the solemn splendor of vast cathedrals, or the quaint loveliness of little churches; in the enlightened conscience of those who love Him and seek to serve Him, or in the souls of recognized saints.

Christmas celebrates the glad Gospel of God's surprising grace in appearing where we least expect to find Him and in the most unlikely people. This is why the life of faith is venturesome and exciting: the faithful expect God to do the unexpected, and wise men now, as at the first Christmas, look for the Eternal where others would hardly guess His presence.

Christmas and Christian Realism

Whether or not we wish to look long and hard at the Bible, the Bible looks hard and long at us. It does not flatter us, telling us only what we wish to read and hear, nor is it maudlin sentimental about the condition of the world we live in. It ruthlessly tells the painful truth about man, as well as the splendor of man's possibilities under God. It shows the depths of sin to which man can sink, as well as the heights to which man can rise. The Bible depicts man cursing as well as praying, engaged in lustful self-indulgence as well as in selfless love, in massacre as well as in humble service.

We ordinarily think of the Christmas story as one of almost uniform beauty. But the Bible does not picture the first Christmas that way. Beauty is there, to be sure—star light, shepherds on the hills, angel voices proclaiming good news, Joseph and Mary tenderly caring for the newly born Christchild.

But the Christmas story in the Gospels also describes the ugliness of the world situation that first Christmas time. Caesar's warring legions marched over much of the known world, and people cowering in fear of their crushing cruelty. Jealous, apprehensive Herod had heard of the expected Messiah and was ready for him—with swords and spears. So the truthful treatment of Christmas, from the standpoint of Biblical realism, sees the world that first Christmas as both beautiful and ugly, filled with the sound of tramping soldiers, but blessed with the songs of angels over Judean hills; on the one hand Herod's harshness and arrogance, and on the other Mary "so tender and mild"; a world both godless, and God-touched, God-loved.

The Christmas season is an appropriate time to re-examine the meaning of realism. We frequently hear self-appointed "realists" begging idealists, "Let's be realistic," when they surely must mean, "Let's be cynical." They see the world's worst side and call that "facing the cold, hard facts," and "being realistic." But, in the interest of supporting their cynicism, they neglect the warm, gentle facts which are also parts of the human story. "Just look at Herod's treachery," they cry. "What chance do the faithful have aginst the power of Roman paganism?" When they have made such indictments against the world, they feel they have been realistic. But they miss the tender truths such as starlight and stable, lowing cattle, manger hay, a Baby's breathing, Mary and Joseph's joy, quiet pride and boundless love. These are real, too.

So at Christmas time in the modern world. Greed is real, and there are some people who are looking for how much they can get for Christmas. It may be true, as the realists profess to believe, that selfishness is a trait native to human nature, a taint on man's soul from birth to death. Post office authorities declare that December mails are exceedingly burdened with letters from little children to Santa Claus, each letter pleading for gifts for Christmas. But rarely do the post-Christmas

13

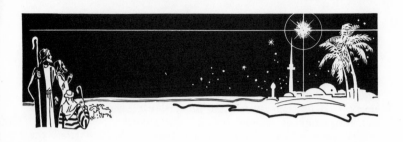

mails carry a "thank-you" note from a grateful child, expressing appreciation for gifts received. Do we begin life, and end it, with such a give-me stain on our souls. Some say, "Let's face it. That's human nature!"

But what about this? Several years ago a thirteen-year old lad who attended Mohawk Central School at Paines Hollow in New York heard an appeal for contributions for Santa Claus Anonymous, a group that provides gifts for unfortunate children that otherwise would go without Christmas presents. The boy struggled to acquire and save a few pennies for this purpose. On the Friday before Christmas vacation he had fifteen cents, and planned to turn in this small treasure at the school that day. But a furious blizzard blasted the area that Friday, and the school buses could not run. So the boy waded a considerable distance through deep snow to give his fifteen cents to the school principal.

The principal found it difficult to control his emotions as he accepted the gift, for the youngster was one of the destitute children listed to receive a Christmas present from Santa Claus Anonymous.

While selfishness in the world is real, that boy, too, is real. So is that spirit of self-denial real at Paines Hollow, and everywhere that the story of Christmas is told.

All right, then, let's face the facts of life. And they are often ugly. But we can never be real realists without taking into account characters like the poor little rich boy from Mohawk Central School, and Bethlehem, a certain starlit night, a manger stall, simple, travel-weary parents huddled around a little Child wrapped in swaddling clothes, and shepherds and wise men kneeling in awe-struck reverence near his crude cradle.

The real realists will recall that the dust of centuries had

14

not dimmed the memory of that Baby, and the armies of the world have not been able to crush the Prince of Peace, nor could a cross destroy him.

The real realist will remember "what a difference a day makes"—if that day is the first Christmas—in our thinking about God and the world and the value of human nature in God's sight.

The true realist will remember that no conquests by emperors have ever been so effective and far-reaching as the victory of that Child in winning our hearts.

And the real realist will remember that, in spite of Caesar's vaunted power, it is not Caesar-mas we celebrate in December, but CHRISTMAS.

A Prayer as Christmas Draws Near

Our Heavenly Father, another Christmas rapidly approaches, exciting our thoughts, warming and gladdening our hearts. And another Christmas will soon be gone, leaving us little better than we were before, unless we find some way of keeping Christmas.

LET US KEEP CHRISTMAS, O GOD: LET US KEEP THE PEACE OF CHRISTMAS.

Grant us the inner peace of knowing that we are serving a purpose worthy of the sons and daughters of God; that there will be light enough for the next step of our journey; there will be strength enough for each day's tasks and testings; there will be Redeeming Love enough to cover all our frailties and failings.

Bless us with the peaceful confidence that all unexplained mysteries have their answer in Thee, and all evil can be overruled by Thee for good, as was Herod's evil will that first Christmas time.

Bring loving goodwill among all the sons of men. Show us how we may better follow the Prince of Peace so that the quarreling of nation with nation, strife amidst races and conflicts within our own breasts may cease. Hasten the day when nations will need no armaments, and national boundaries will need no patrols, and Thy sky above our heads will not be blemished by bombers and missiles. Rid us of unfeeling selfishness and greed, and fill us with mutual helpfulness, that plenty of the world's goods may prevail everywhere, and contention for life's barest necessities will be no more.

Let us never forget, between one Christmas and the next, that "In Thy will is our peace."

LET US KEEP CHRISTMAS, O LORD: LET US KEEP A SMALL SANCTUARY OF CHRISTMAS STILLNESS IN OUR HEARTS.

Amidst the hurry of busy time and toil may we reclaim the quietness of that "silent night" of long ago. Let us be still enough, detached enough from the world's noise, its ceaseless cares, complaints and vain desires, to hear the heavenly voices proclaiming good tidings of hope and gladness in a dark world.

Let us find some moments as hushed as a darkened hill, as silent as starlight, where we can weigh our thoughts, cleansed from the dust of yesterday, and clarify our vision until eternal things become real to us again. In such undistracted stillness we trust Thou will steady and reaffirm our faith, strengthen our hope and refresh our souls.

Between Christmases may we dedicate an occasional hour for resting in a quietness hallowed by thoughts of Thee, Thy greatness and goodness, Thy love and care for all the world, and what Thou hast done for us in sending Christ to earth.

LET US KEEP CHRISTMAS, O LORD: LET US KEEP IN MIND ALWAYS THE GLORY OF COMMONPLACE THINGS.

Forbid that we forget Bethlehem where the glories of heaven are strangely mixed with common things of earth. Celestial light falls on a sleepy small town, undistinguished for size or power. A hillside becomes a touch of heaven when plain men there listen to angel voices. A cattle stall becomes a shrine when wise men worship there. A hay-filled manger becomes a holy of holies, more sacred than golden altars, when Christ is there. How splendor-filled the plain things are at Christmas!

Not only at Christmas, but in all our common days, let us expect Thee to work wonders through commonplace things and imperfect people. May we attempt to achieve great purposes with ordinary talents, tools and powers. Preserve in us an appreciation for the durable, homely joys of fireside and friendship and family ties. May we never forget the Christmas lesson of doing ordinary things with uncommon grace to make people extraordinarily happy.

Let us ever remember between Christmases how often the Highest is revealed in the lowliest.

LET US KEEP CHRISTMAS, O GOD OUR FATHER: LET US KEEP ITS TENDER KINDNESS.

Let the remembrance of the Christ Child, and the Savior he became, soften our severe judgments of others, dissolve our harsh hatreds, break our sharp envy, conquer our unyielding greed and hard bargaining for position and advantage.

Like Mary and Joseph's gentle care for their child, may we care for the world's helpless ones within the reach of our voices, our hands and our gifts and sacrifices. Let every human being whose life touches ours be our chance for a kindness, without any thought of whether he deserves our love. May we never consider trivial the little, unremembered acts of helpfulness that Thou alone dost recall.

Let Christmas kindness not be lost when Christmas Day is past. Let us keep kindness.

LET US KEEP, CHRISTMAS, O GOD: LET US KEEP THE CHRISTMAS FAITH.

At this holy season we remember how all impossible things are possible with Thee. Now dawns on our minds the wonderfully unthinkable things the Christmas story tells. Thy promises come true amidst unpromising circumstances; the power of mighty Rome is pitted against that "helpless" Infant, and Rome declines while the Baby grows and conquers the heart of the world.

In Christ the far-off, transcendent God comes into our midst; the unseen becomes visible in Bethlehem's manger; the Almighty is expressed in frail flesh like our own. Through Him our hopelessly stained lives are miraculously cleansed.

If the first Christmas can be believed, nothing is too difficult for Thee. Let us keep that Christmas faith, O Lord.

We will not keep Christmas trees and wreaths and glittering ornaments for long, O God. Soon trees will be discarded and ornaments will be put away. But let us keep the spirit of

17

Christmas with us always, that Thy kingdom may come nearer, that Thy will may be done constantly, that the world might be fairer and life on earth brighter.

In the name of the Christ Child. Amen.

Pauline

Power in the Silences

Life's least important activity is often noisiest and its most significant activity is frequently quietest. From where I sit just now I can hear a clock tick and a dog bark. In the far distance a freight train rumbles down icy tracks. At the same moment, from this desk I can see, but not hear, the waters of Lake Charlevoix lying serene beneath the wintry heavens, snowflakes drifting lazily toward the earth, and sunlight struggling through leaden, overcast skies.

The noisy things in my environment are far less meaningful than the quiet ones. The clock is not as important as its rhythmical boasts suggest. The clock cannot "give the time"; it but measures time. Our time is a gift from above, and not from clocks. Dogs are lovable, companionable creatures, but it is not their frenzied barking that endears them to us. Rather, it is their quiet, agreeable company that we enjoy. Our great-great-grandfathers could remember the day when the hollow roar of a freight train had never been heard upon the earth. As methods of transportation change, such a time may come again without undermining man's welfare. The noisy things, ticking clocks, barking dogs, thunderous trains and all the rest are not the world's most meaningful factors.

The most elementary matters are nearly always quiet. Water, like that in our neighboring lake, is a mighty mercy pervading all of life. Where water is noisy it is least necessary, as when it tumbles over rocks and cascades down falls. But where water is silent it is most significant, as when it is swallowed by thirsty soil and avidly absorbed by dry roots, where it oozes into springs and wells, where it is co-mingled with other components of man's blood and mixed into the tissues of every living creature.

18

THE TINSEL AND THE HAY

Snow falls with no discernible sound, bringing with it from above such fertile elements as nitrogen and sulfur. It is gentler than pattering rain, less erosive to the soil. Snow insulates some of earth's crops against winter's frost. And all snow's gifts are given silently.

Silent sunlight sifts down through millions of miles of space before it graces the earth. Scientists tell us that earth receives only a twenty-millionth part of one per cent of the sun's total output of energy. Yet, this infinitesimal amount is enough to warm and illumine the earth, to manufacture the food of all earth's creatures and make life here possible.

All man's loud implements and the sound of man's exertions make it seem as if our inventive ingenuity and our efforts are the most meaningful elements of our existence. But we would be helpless without the beneficence of silent powers that ceaselessly work on our behalf.

The Christmas story reminds us that real spiritual power is found in life's quiet happenings. In his Christmas carol, "O Little Town of Bethlehem," Phillips Brooks expresses the significance of silence:

> "How silently, how silently,
> The wondrous gift is given!
> So God imparts to human hearts
> The blessings of his heaven.
> No ear may hear his coming,
> But in the world of sin,
> Where meek souls will receive him, still
> The dear Christ enters in."

See the sharp contrast between the silent and the noisy elements in the Nativity Story. Saint Luke tells how Mary "brought forth her first-born son, and wrapped him in swaddling clothes and laid him in a manger, because there was no room for them in the inn." A crowded inn is a clamorous place, but little of lasting worth happened there that night. But in the stable where all was quiet, save for the gentle breathing of the cattle and the tender whisperings of Mary and Joseph, history was being recast. There was power in that quietness.

Any casual observer in Palestine on that first Christmas night would have said that the real might of the world was represented by Emperor Caesar Augustus and his soldiers, by the thunder of horses' hoofs and the clatter of chariot wheels as the militant hosts of the Roman Empire rode through

19

Palestinian streets. But all of this was an attention-getting, noisy show that would soon be over. Real, durable power lay quietly in a manger.

It is still true that power and quietness belong together. Spiritually, we move farther forward in a moment of reverent stillness than we ever can in frantic haste, and we are never so much alive as when bowed motionless in silent awe before our God.

Noisy babblers and constant chatterers seldom inspire us. The people who have the best effect upon us influence us quietly, more through the inaudible testimony of what they are than through anything they say. They possess more power in their silences than others do in loud exhortations and unsought advice.

The quiet acts of God and the frantic busyness of men are still starkly contrasted, and God's wondrous workings and the eternal values are missed amidst the noises of our hectic haste. Only those who, like ancient shepherds, are familiar with silence will hear messages from Above. Today's wise men, like those of yore, free themselves from life's fuss and fretfulness and find God performing wonders in quiet places.

God's wondrous gifts are silently given. Learn to be still.

The Tinsel and the Hay

Two of our common Christmas decorations serve to remind us of the meaning of Christmas. Tinsel, glittering on the Christmas tree, is symbolic of a superficial celebration of this holy day, while hay in the manger of the créche, where lies the figure of the infant Savior, signifies the essential significance of Christmas.

Tinsel represents the glistening, showy things of the world, and stands for shallow values and superficial riches, fanfare and loud trumpetings, gaudy displays of power that dazzle and astound. Tinsel represents Herod and Caesar Augustus and all those of Jesus' day and ours whose first interest is surface glamour. This is the world of secondary matters, the world of

20

incidentals that overlooks elementals, of powers that time erodes, the world that comes and goes while Christ comes to stay.

It is the world we see today in artificial icicles and artificial snow that are pretty, decorative and impressive, but non-essential and so secondary that we can pack them away in boxes when Christmas is over and label them "Christmas decorations" and store them away to use but once each year.

The deeper meanings of Christmas are represented by hay in Bethlehem's manger, the commonplace stuff of life. Hay is natural and basic to life here. It symbolizes the elemental matters upon which all of God's creatures depend, for it comes from the earth and is composed of fabric spun from rich nutriments of the soil and from golden rays of the sun. Hay, which is any of the family of grasses, dried and cured for fodder, is the miraculous garment worn by meadows, pastures, lawns and glades. While it clothes the earth, it is also food for many of earth's children, such as those four-legged creatures that witnessed the wonder in Bethlehem's cattle stall that long ago first Christmas night. Nearly omnipresent, and so familiar that man has foolishly taken it for granted, this dried grass feeds the animals that feed men, and it strengthens the animals that, through the ages, have carried men, hauled their chariots and wagons and borne their burdens.

The Christmas tradition tells us that it was a humble, hay-filled manger that the Holy Child was laid in swaddling clothes, soon after his birth in Bethlehem. Yet, from that bed of hay have come our highest thoughts about God, our noblest estimate of man, our standards for living as God's children, and the power we need to live by those standards. And from that manger bed has come One who has demonstrated that, living, or dying, even on a cruel cross, it is possible to trust in "spiritual forces," which is man's weak way of saying we can utterly and unreservedly trust in the goodness of God.

Gioacchino Antonio Rossini, the Italian composer who had a special genius for writing joyous melodies, once said, "Give me a laundry list, and I will set it to music." The glad gospel of Christmas is composed of material almost as prosaic and unpromising as a laundry list: crude, unlettered shepherds and their sheep, a manger stall filled with hay, and a baby born to a peasant girl. If it were not for that very special Baby, His incomparable life and redemptive death, we would have heard little of Bethlehem, and nothing at all of the shepherds, the sheep, or of Mary and Joseph.

Nothing about that first Christmas was glamorous. It seemed so commonplace that the townspeople and guests in the next-door inn did not notice what was going on. The glory of God was among them, and they knew nothing of it. And the shepherds would have missed the event had it not been for angel voices that called their attention to what had happened in Bethlehem. Even the Wise Men had stopped off first at Herod's palace, as if to search among the glitter for the infant Christ, before they moved on toward the humble cattle stall and found Him in a manger.

The Gospel of Matthew declares "And His name shall be called Emmanuel, which being interpreted is, God with us." This is the essential note of Christmas. Each year the celebration of Christmas freshly declares that God has come into our midst, that God has reduced Himself to human size and human terms, taking on Himself ordinary flesh like our own, walking under the same skies that cover us, soiling His feet with the dust on which we sojourn. The great, good news that Christmas proclaims is that God is lowly enough to dwell among the lowliest of us, that He prefers mangers to palaces, and He has a greater affinity for hay than for tinsel.

A Power that has a liking for quietness and a preference for the ordinary is still working wonders in the silences and amidst the commonplace. We are still more likely to find His Spirit revealed amidst the common than amidst ostentation. Ask yourself where, in your own experience, God makes His presence known. It is in some event as flashy and rare in appearance as the flash of Haley's comet across the sky, or is it as common as sunset, dawn and starlight?

Is God most clearly revealed to us in the singular splendor of some rare saint who may appear on earth once every century or so, or do we catch better glimpses of God's goodness in the kindliness of everyday saints whose thoughtful, gentle deeds remind us of Christ?

Some people have a humble, ordinary way of doing good that puts to shame all our committee-contrived, highly publicized, glittering charities. Their person-to-person kindnesses may be as unglamorous as hay—and just as essential to life on earth.

THE TINSEL AND THE HAY

A meeting was held in a small church for the announced purpose of praying for a local family that was in serious financial straights. There was insufficient food for the many children that thronged the bare, unheated floors of the shabby home. While a committee of the devout were offering fervent prayers for God's mercy and blessing upon the destitute family and for relief from this terrible want, steps were heard entering the church. The small son of one of the church elders made his appearance and announced, "Dad couldn't come to the prayer meeting, but he sent his prayers in my wagon. Please help me bring them in." Dad's prayers consisted of a sack of potatoes, a quarter of beef, several bags of assorted vegetables, a large bag of flour, a basket of apples, several jars of jellies and other staples. The prayer meeting was immediately adjourned.

The man's "prayers" were as crude and humble as Bethlehem's manger—and as lovely, for Christ was there.

One busy father, who had spent little time with his growing son, placed an envelope for the lad upon the Christmas tree. In the envelope was the man's written promise to give the lad his dad's companionship for at least one hour of each weekday of the year, and two hours on Saturdays and Sundays. The boy was overjoyed, and the father kept his promise.

It is far easier to give a child a new bicycle, an increase in weekly allowance, a radio or television set for his room, or almost any other material gift, than it is to bestow the gift of time. Time is elemental, for time is the stuff of which our years are made. It is an unglamorous gift, without glitter, but basic—more like hay than tinsel. And it was the gift of time the shepherds brought to Christ when they came to spend awhile at his manger bedside.

Might we not make the world better, and capture the significance of Christmas if we all abandoned tinsel-giving, and gave kindness-filled time to those who want nothing so much from us as the gift of our undistracted selves for a little while?

In God's plan the little things are really the big things. The weak things presage powerful things. Commonplace things are most extraordinary. And the obscure, easily overlooked things are most important. The birth of the Savior— little and weak, hidden in a manger in an obscure town—tells us so.

Here, then, is a rule for measuring both wisdom and religious devotion: how and where do we look for God? Eagerly and patiently as did the Wise Men, and joyously as did shepherds? And do we search amidst the little, weak, commonplace and obscure things, as did both Wise Men and shepherds?

And when we become aware of the God who reveals himself in our midst do we pause to adore, as did shepherds and Wise Men?

If Christ Were Born in Our Town

A few days ago I was asked, "If Christ were born in our town this December 25, in what ways would His coming contrast with His birth in ancient Bethlehem?" My answer? "There would be hardly any contrast at all, at least not in the important things."

To be sure, there would be little differences. Wise Men would arrive from the East by jet airliner rather than on camel-back. Instead of shepherds coming into town from starlit fields to adore the Holy Child, a few factory and office workers would gather to do Him honor. The crowded inn of Bethlehem would be replaced by some local motel where a sign flashed. "No Vacancy." And, since we don't have cattle stalls in our town, Mary and Joseph would likely settle down for the night in the empty stall of a two-car garage. But these matters are all trifling in comparison with the real essentials of Christmas.

In all important regards the birth of Christ in our town would compare, rather than contrast, with the event in Bethlehem nearly twenty centuries ago. This is so because God has not changed either His character or His way of accomplishing His purposes. God is the same. Furthermore, it is so because human nature has not basically changed. Our material advancement in these two thousand years has been astonishing and has outdistanced spiritual progress by far. We have improved on Bethlehem's sheep, but not on the devotion of shepherds. Wise men can travel farther, faster, more comfortably now, but are they better men, wiser men, than those of yesteryear when they reach the end of their journey? And is the purpose of today's traveling any improvement over that of the Wise Men of the East, or could it ever be?

Are we not much like Bethlehemites of old, crowded together, excessively busy, preoccupied with secondary things, too conscious of trifles, and generally unaware of what God is doing among us? Doesn't the passage of two thousand years leave us in the innkeeper's predicament? Our accommodations are crowded. We are too full. And modern man's most familiar excuse for turning away the Highest and Best God sends our way is still, "I'm too occupied!" So God's glory passes us by and goes elsewhere, and we miss it, because our attention is absorbed with lesser things.

But if Christ came to our town now, as on that first Christmas night, there would be some who would be sensitive enough to feel the brush of angel wings, quiet enough to hear the angel song, attentive enough to listen to the heavenly messenger break the good news, "Unto you is born this day . . . a Savior." There would be those who would excitedly say, as did the shepherds, "Let us go . . . and see this thing which is come to pass, which the Lord hath made known unto us." They would find Mary and Joseph and the Babe.

There are still wise men and women who would travel any distance at any cost to find the Christ and bow at His cradle. Times have changed, but we have not, and our need of Him has not. Wise men still come to Him and find Him in the most unexpected places.

Phillips Brooks, the Boston minister who wrote the Christmas carol "O Little Town of Bethlehem," was widely known as a man of kindly manner and splendid influence. One day this note about Dr. Brooks appeared in a Boston newspaper: "Yesterday opened cloudy and unpleasant: but about noon Phillips Brooks came downtown, and everything brightened up." The presence of that good man made life in Boston take on a different hue.

One who is far greater than Phillips Brooks, or anyone else who has ever walked the earth, came to our world one glad night long ago. His presence made a difference in all who knew Him and loved Him. Mary and Joseph, the shepherds and the Wise Men were never the same after they looked upon Jesus.

He will make a difference in us, too, if we really are aware of His coming, and welcome His presence among us, and live by the Good News He proclaimed.

"Would You Like to Hold the Baby?"

One of God's good gifts to us is that rare moment or occasion when we are freed from some of our foolish and sinful inhibitions that stifle God's grace within us, so that for an instant we are as thoughtful, as tender, generous and loving as God has meant for us to be all along. Perhaps pianos can serve as a parable of these moments of driving impulse and holy action. Pianos have "soft" and "loud" pedals to regulate the volume of sound. Actually, the "loud" pedal does not increase the volume of music as does the volume knob on your radio or television set. Instead, the "loud" pedal device simply lifts dampers from the strings of the piano so that the strings can vibrate in a free, uninhibited way.

Many of us are like strings on a piano that seldom have their dampers lifted. Therefore, our spirits seldom sing as they were meant to do. Then, someone or some occasion finds our "loud pedal," and sweet chords within us, that we hardly knew we had, begin singing. Babies do this for us. We may pride ourselves on being hard-headed, coldly reasoning creatures, with our emotions under rigid control. No soft sentiment can move us. Then we see a baby or hear its cry or its first laughter, and we are surprised at our own tenderness. Before we can catch our words, a whimsical petition escapes our lips, "Do you mind if I hold the baby?"

I remember that as a sixteen-year-old boy I hitchhiked many

miles to see my older sister who was confined to a hospital, having given birth to her first child, a daughter. After I reached the hospital room and had visited briefly with Gildreth, the infant was brought from the nursery to her mother. I stood at the bedside, lost in awe and wonder at this pink, nameless little creature, marvelling that the button nose, tulip lips, dark eyes, shell-like ears, fragile fingers and toes were all in their proper places. Then the child's mother suddenly asked, "Would you like to hold the baby?" Surprised and with misgivings concerning my teen-age clumsiness, I took the infant in my arms and held her close to me. It was one of the most memorable moments of my youth, an instant seasoned with a touch of fear and tinge of fascination and mystery, and thoroughly blended with joy.

Since that day I have sometimes wondered if the shepherds who visited Bethlehem that long ago holy night may have had one among them who shyly asked of Mary and Joseph, "May I hold the Baby?" Or, do you suppose one of the Wise Men from the East relaxed his oriental reserve enough to ask, "Please, would it be asking too great a favor if I held the Baby?"

Or did gentle, gracious Mary, sensing a shepherd's yearning, mixed with reverent awe, or a Wise Man's longing, mingled with worship, form the question for him, asking, "Would you like to hold the Baby?"

Be that as it may, whether a visitor to the manger made the request, or Mary made the offer, or whether the question never advanced further than an unspoken desire, this is the question that comes to all of us this Christmastide, and always—"Do you want to hold the Baby?" And we are likely to respond in surprise and perhaps with pleasure, "Oh, may I?"

Let us look at this vital matter. *Babies need holding.* Child specialists, such as Dr. Benjamin Spock, have long known of this need and have emphasized it. But it was always so, since the first human baby was born; babies have needed to be held. They derive feelings of security and a sense of worth from being wanted and loved and from the warmth, closeness and support of being tenderly embraced.

Even the strongest, mightiest of men once had to be held. It is difficult, isn't it, to imagine our towering heroes as nursing babies, unknown to the world, weak and utterly dependent upon a parent's care, crying in the night like millions of babies before them. Washington, Lincoln, Lord Nelson, Winston Churchill, Albert Einstein, Albert Schweitzer and all the world's other men of power were once tiny morsels of flesh, frail, needing constant care. The strongest once could not walk. At one time the most eloquent could not speak. The most brilliant at one time were dim of mind and blinded by the newness of the world into which they had emerged. All the world's greatest once lay helpless in a parent's arms.

And, of course, at Christmas time we remember the Infant that Mary held. Like all other babies, his tenderness required the shelter and support of a parent's embrace, and Joseph and Mary were doubtlessly pleased and proud when others, too, wanted to hold the Holy Child.

What we have said about the Infant Jesus is true of all of God's gifts: they need to be held. They cannot be left suspended in the world without support. This is so concerning the loveliest abstractions we know, such as beauty, truth and goodness; they must be held by something solid and strong. See how true this is. Attempt to retain the word "beauty" in your thoughts for two full minutes without attaching it to any specific beautiful thing. You cannot do it. Before the moments pass the word "beauty" becomes associated with some splendid thing, a starlit sky, or freshly fallen snow that spreads white blankets on the fields and white shawls over the trees and puts white stocking-leg caps on every stone and stump and post. Or you remember the face of someone near and dear. You see beauty not as an unsupported abstraction but as loveliness held by the form of something in particular.

When someone says "truth" in your hearing, your mind at once associates the word with a specific verity that means much to you or with a certain truthful person whose genuineness you have learned to trust.

Hear the word "goodness" and your thoughts quickly fly to some scene where unselfishness or helpfulness is held in the embrace of a certain generous deed or a particular gracious person. When one little lad was asked where his dad was, he replied, "I don't know, but I'll bet he's somewhere helping someone." Goodness was no vague abstraction to that boy. Goodness was a virtue made visible and real, held in the care of a man with his dad's face, voice, stride and helpful hands.

This is the nature of all of God's good gifts: they cry out to be held. They need human support and warmth and love.

So Christ held the idea of God and the character of God for the disciples. The Eternal could be described in many ways, but the disciples said the best way to picture God is to say, "God is in Christ." He is compassionate as Christ is compassionate, patient as Christ is patient, loving as Christ is loving, forgiving as Christ is forgiving. As John put it in the Fourth Gospel, "The Word became flesh and dwelt among us, full of grace and truth." The Word was never grasped by man until it was held in Christ's flesh. As the Baby grew the Word was expressed in feet that walked and ran, in lips that spoke and hands that worked at a carpenter's bench and blessed little children and touched the sick with a healing caress.

How could Christianity ever become the dull affair some people imagine it to be when it carries such exciting news about God—the Creator of the vast immensities we call "the universe," the Fashioner of stars beyond the stars we see and world beyond the worlds we know, coming to lowly Bethlehem to be expressed in baby flesh and to be held in a poor woman's arms? This is the most astonishing story ever told about God, or man, or babies.

Here the Good News again! God has come among us in the person of Christ! Christ has made use of our humanness. He wants to do it again. If Christ is to live in today's world it will be in us.

He will speak through our lips.

He will walk with our feet.

He will perform His wondrous works of mercy with our hands.

Shall we give Christ that chance?

Would *you* like to hold the Baby?

What Is Your Forwarding Address?

As we approach the gateway of a new year we are confronted by countless uncertainties. What new excitement of great joy will be our successes, disappointments and failures in work, business, health and character? What new knowledge and wisdom will we lay in store? What troubled nations will stir the world's anxiety? What world events will change our lives? We do not know.

But we can be sure of one thing: we will change.

In this universe all things change in time. The scientists tell us that their observations are not recordings of everlasting facts. Instead, they are merely snapshots of a rapidly changing universe, caught at a certain instant. For example, I burn today's newspaper in the fireplace. What is that burning newspaper? It is matter in transition. Telescoping its long history into a few hours, I observe that last week it was a seed, then a tree; yesterday, a mass of wood pulp in a paper factory. This morning it was a clean sheet running through a rotary press. This moment the printed sheet is being reduced to ashes. Tomorrow the ashes will be dumped, and they will mix with the soil where lie more seeds from which more trees will grow. So the circling change continues.

And what is true of paper is true of the distant stars and the entire universe. And it is true of you. An essential difference between you and all other parts of the universe is that you can determine the direction of change. Unlike a scrap of charred newspaper, blown by the wind wherever the wind "wills" it, you can set your destination. You can determine to be better rather than worse. You can choose to be more considerate of others next year than you have been in the past, more efficient in your business, more faithful to your church, more dedicated to God.

God has so fashioned us that we cannot stand still. We go forward, or we slip backward. It is sometimes said of a likeable person, "He's a good egg!" But no one can be a good egg for long. An egg either hatches into something other than an egg or it rots. It changes from egg to chick or it spoils. "Spoiled" people are folks who have not moved from one stage to another as they ought. They are the adults with infantile emotions. When frustrated they behave childishly, whimpering, sulking, indulging in tempestuous temper tantrums. Or they may be the perennial teen-agers, immersed in romantic fantasies, who never know a mature love and loyalty, and throughout their lives they go from one flirtation to another, from one mate to another. They were once good eggs, but now rotten eggs because they never hatched into maturity.

Well, where are you going? In what direction are you moving?

If you have ever moved from one town to another, you likely went to the post office and arranged to have your mail forwarded to your new address. A clerk gave you a form to fill out, and you wrote your old address and the address to which you were moving. Now, as an old year comes to a close and a new year begins, it is a good exercise of mind and spirit to determine what your forwarding address will be. Where will you be spiritually at the end of January, in the middle of June, when December of next year reaches its close?

We can decide now the kind of accommodations we will move into. At our new address let us have more spacious minds. Let there be room for new truth, no matter how offensive it may be to our old prejudices; room for disagreement without bitterness or rancor; a place for leisurely reflection, for reading the best books, for listening to the best music, for enjoying and absorbing the most beautiful sights. Provide room for recollections of the towering heroes of the human race and the saints who have blessed the world; room for contemplation of God's works and His great goodness.

Let us move into roomier spiritual abodes. May there be capacity for all kinds of people in our love and prayers, room for giant beliefs and greater compassions; a capacity for play with little children and for visits with the lonely and the aged. Let there be a bigger place for reverence and frequent worship. Make room for God.

One of life's most exciting events is making an advantageous move to a new address. What will your new address be?

May God go with you.

Happy New Year!

We Thank Thee For the Coming Year

Eternal God, who as the ages come and go, abidest ever the same, we thank Thee for the coming of another year, like a new leaf torn from eternity, fresh and clean, unstained by sin, unblotted by failure.

We thank Thee for bringing us through the many changes and testings of the past year to this moment when in faith we face forward toward the unknown.

For failure and sin forgiven we thank Thee. For guidance out of dark confusion; for meaningful work to do; for joys and strength shared with us by friends; for love we have received and given; for loneliness lifted by an awareness of Thy presence; for sorrows made bearable by Thy comfort; for radiant memories of good that illumine dark days; for hopes that shine brightly down the uncertain future, dispelling shadows of anxiety; for these and all other mercies shown us, we praise Thee, our Father.

Purge now our hearts both of shallow self-sufficiency and foolish fear, so that we may know that without Thee we can do nothing, and with Thee we can do all things needful.

Free us from fretfulness that compels us to hurry through our days, overlooking wayside blessings, unaware of nearby opportunities for good.

Let us trust Thee and Thy slow pace and patient working through the years, remembering that sin must succeed in a hurry, but Thou art the inseparable Ally and Lord of time.

Forgive us for complaining that we are of no use to the world because we have so little time, when, as long as Thou givest us breath, we all have the same amount of time—the same number of weeks in each year, and days in each week, and hours in each day, and minutes in each hour.

Forgive us for merely spending time, when we could *invest* it, and draw rich dividends. Let us invest time: a moment of our presence and undistracted attention with the lonely; a few minutes sharing our quiet joy with the cheerless, lighting lamps of faith in life's dark places; an hour with those weighed down with trouble and grief, easing their burdens; occasional quiet moments in quiet places for quiet reflection on the meaning of our existence.

THE TINSEL AND THE HAY

Let us employ time in sacrifice of instant pleasure for the sake of long-range achievement; in the pursuit of worthiness rather than happiness; in multiplying the number of people we love and help; in enriching the quality of life rather than merely extending the length of it.

Let us devote time to knowing what is good and doing it; to remembering what is beautiful and appreciating it; to seeking the truth, speaking it boldly and living by it courageously; to righting wrongs; to spreading goodwill and working for peace among all men; to worship, where we meet with Thee and are reverently sensible to Thy nearness.

Teach us to be timely, to say the timely word of encouragement and cheer precisely when it is needed most, to speak the timely word of honest appreciation and praise, to offer the timely hand of help.

Teach us, too, to be timeless, to live by everlasting things, things which time cannot corrode and the years cannot spoil, and to live now and evermore for Thee, Eternal Father.

We rest our souls in the glad confidence that this new year, like all our years, like all eternity, is Thine, O Lord, and in Thy capable, kindly hands. Do with it what is best.

In the name of Christ, who in all things trusted Thee.

—Amen

Trouble Is a Revelation

Stripped "to the bone," now, are most of our hardwoods. The maple, elm, birch and poplar are bare. So are the ash and apple tree. These most plentiful hardwood trees of Hidden Brook can no longer hold the secrets they have so carefully kept all summer and into early autumn. The long-concealed nests of thrushes and robins, of scarlet tanagers and purple finches, indigo buntings and their many neighbors are plainly revealed. So are the scars left by broken limbs and the wounds left by woodpecker bills. And the strengths of the trees are clearly seen now, too—the massive boles and the stout, knobby limbs that seem to send their anchors far down through the great trunks to where groping roots are intimate with rock. The frost and wind have wrenched confessions from the complaining trees as to where lie the secrets of their weaknesses and strengths.

Is this not one service trouble renders for us all? Unlike lush comfort, prosperity and summery success that sometimes hide what we are, trouble bares our souls, disclosing our frailties, and our powers.

Trouble is a revelation.

34

On Facing the Future Unafraid

The Creator has fashioned His world in such a way that ongoing life is normal and good. Retarded life soon becomes an evil thing.

Attempt to arrest the beauty of a rose by plucking it at the peak of its loveliness, and the rose soon dies.

If I try to capture and hold in a bucket a bit of the lively little brook that skips and sings past my study door, that bucketful loses its gaity and song, and soon becomes no more than a few gallons of stagnant water.

We foolishly try to keep our youngsters mere children by objecting to their struggles to break their mother's apron strings, and we become disturbed and anxious when they show some measure of independence. Parents sometimes say of a child, "If only he would always remain so young, innocent and charming!" But a child that remains a small child in intelligence, insight and emotional development is one of the world's greatest tragedies.

Many people resent the passing of their own youth, the onset of middle age, and are depressed with feelings of forboding about the coming of old age. There are few sights so pathetic as that of a person who desperately tries to halt the passage of time and pretends to be many years younger than he really is, and thus misses the peculiar glories that belong to each season of life. Aging gracefully is the art of anticipating changes the years will bring, sensing that every era of one's life has its own unique adventures, pleasures and contentments, and then moving into each phase of life gladly, with faith in God's goodness and with high expectations.

We always lose life's charm and miss its meaning when we try to stop its onward flow or shrink from necessary change. And we look eagerly toward the tomorrows when we sense life's venturesomeness and step out into the unknown, confident of the accompanying presence of a loving God.

However, such a confident attitude toward the future means more than a simple, generalized trust in God. In particular, it means an awareness that uncertainty and risk-taking are parts of God's plan for the world. Without risks there could be no character, no courage, no faith, for there would be little need for them, and there would be no testings upon which they could develop and grow strong. The ancient faith of the Hebrew people was founded by Abraham who left the comfortable familarity of his homeland for the uneasy unfamiliarity of a strange land and a strange people. Of Abraham the book of Hebrews says, "By faith Abraham . . . went out, not knowing whither he went." Risk-taking was not evil and faith in God good. But risks and faith belonged to each other. The changes Abraham took demanded a growing faith and at last vindicated it.

America was founded and developed by those who faced the chancy future unafraid of risks. Explorers and pioneers pushed across oceans and wildernesses full of unknown perils. The first businessmen who financially supported our early, insecure national government risked failure. Our national history has been blessed by thinkers unafraid of new thoughts, scientists courageous enough to accept truths never before apprehended, statesmen who were brave enough to make courageous, venturesome, risky decisions. All of these knew that risk-taking is a necessary part of the good life and belongs to progress.

Finally, the courageous risk-takers of history have been those who had some great, central certainty, such as Columbus had about the world being round and Louis Pasteur had concerning the existence of bacteria and the preventive treatment of fermentation and infection and Christ had about the love and Fatherhood of God and the redeemability of man. In algebra we find the unknown in any equation by using the *known* to get at it. And this is a valid method of arriving at the answers to life's elemental problems. Of one thing the man of faith is certain: there is an everlasting steadiness at the heart of things, a reliable love and care that we call "God."

A little girl who had enjoyed an exciting Monday with her family and playmates was heard to pray, "We've had a lovely day, dear God. What do you plan for Tuesday?" Those simple, childlike words express essential elements of faith: the recognition of God's hand in today and curiosity about the future, with an awareness that God has plans for tomorrow and for all our days. We dare to ask what the plans might be, and yet we are half-glad that God's usual answer is a kindly, "Wait and see!"

Growing Every Day

Now, in winter, when trees are stripped of their foliage, the bark on their trunks shows clearly how greatly trees expand as the seasons come and go. On most of our common trees, such as the maple, oak, elm and ash, the bark splits to allow the trees to grow. The "healed" cracks make a textured roughness on the trunks of these giant plants. The elastic bark of white birches has no such vertical breaks in its surface. It simply expands with the growth of the trees. When the bark finally snaps, it falls in long banners that flutter in the wind.

What I admire most about a tree is that it continues to grow until it dies. All creatures change from day to day, but all change is not growth. Decay, too, is change. The botanists tell us a tree grows as long as it lives, daily adding breadth and height to its stature. Daily its roots draw sustenance from the soil, and daily it drinks moisture from the air and absorbs light and energy from the beneficient sun. Wind, rain, snow and ice contribute to its tough character.

The Psalmist said of the righteous man, "And he shall be like a *tree* planted by the rivers of water." The expression is apt, for a chief characteristic of a tree and of the life of faith is perpetual growth.

America's greatest folk hero, Abraham Lincoln, was not always heroic. Once he was nearly as unprepossessing in personality as he was physically ungainly. As a young man he was easily depressed, moved to morose glumness and to sullen silence. He made serious, though sincere, mistakes which he later regretted. But Lincoln grew.

There was a time when the sensitive Lincoln could not have shrugged off the misunderstandings, name-calling and slander that fell upon him during his Presidency. When a member of his cabinet was reported to have called Lincoln a fool, the President replied, "He must be right; he is a very smart man." As a young man Lincoln lacked the grace to respond habitually with such ready tolerance and forgiveness. Early in Lincoln's life he could not have felt, let alone spoken, the imperishable words of his Second Inaugural address, "With malice toward none; with charity for all . . ." He was not always good enough, wise enough, great enough to feel or think or speak that way.

Lincoln stood tall in spiritual stature as a youngster. He

was taller still as a young congressman, and a giant when he was nominated for the Presidency of the United States. But Lincoln was never spiritually tall enough to please Abraham Lincoln. He grew all the days of his life.

What are the conditions of growth? How is spiritual growth encouraged?

Dissatisfaction with self, when it is creatively used, is a growth stimulant. Growth comes from the recognition that we do not know everything worth knowing, that we have not achieved everything worth achieving, and that we have not become what we ought to be.

Growth comes from a certain openness, a porousness, like the roots of a tree that absorb nourishment from the surroundings. Growth rises from hospitality to beauty, truth and goodness that are not our own, making them into our own. This means careful consideration of viewpoints that are new to us, and that differ from ours. It means a willingness to be disturbed, upset, changed. All conversion starts here, and all growth.

We grow when our spiritual income exceeds our expenditures.

Growth in spiritual stature and strength is encouraged by association with other people who are also seeking to grow, just as trees are strengthened, and stabilized and stimulated by intertwining their roots with the roots of neighboring trees.

Accept big responsibilities. They tend to excite growth that is sufficient to handle them.

Without fear, resentment or self-pity accept your share of this world's troubles. The art of growing is not one of dodging trouble, but that of using it as food for growth.

We grow as we improve our habits, substituting bad habits for good and still better habits for good ones. The holy habits of regular, set times for meditation, private devotions, public worship, writing notes of encouragement, making visits that bring cheer and help to the needy, all of these, and more, add to our stature.

We need a standard against which we measure our growth. A molehill must seem great to an ant. Little hills appear to be big until we see the mountains looming beyond them. Mountains seem great until we measure them against the stars. A Christian may feel sufficiently tall while standing back to back against his neighbor. But let him stand face to face with Christ and he recovers his spiritual perspective.

Before the father of William the Conqueror left for the Crusades he compelled his barons to swear allegiance to his young son. The barons protested, "He is but a child." The father answered, "He is little, but he will grow." The Christian is a mixture of humility and hope. He knows he is little. He is sure he will grow.

Winter Hardiness

Deep winter weather tests the physical reserves of plants and animals in the northern section of our nation. In the tall, shadowy timber around my study, last summer's lush ferns lie dead beneath the bitter-cold, blue-white silence. In gardens and flowerbeds the begonia, California poppy, cornflower, marigold, morning glory and snapdragon have long-since succumbed to the first waves of cold that swept over the land.

While many plants died with last autumn's frost, and others have perished since, some hardy plants survive winter's most withering blast, their roots insulated by heavy blankets of snow and autumn's comforter of fallen leaves. Most of our shrubs and trees will endure the tests of frosty winds, blizzards and ice storms. And when blithe May arrives there will be flowers aplenty to afford a gay welcome.

Horticulturalists define hardiness as the ability of a plant to endure winter outdoors, in cold climates, without man's protection. There are "hardy chrysanthemums" that can survive sub-freezing weather and many other perennial plants, such as anemone, aster, bellflower, clematis, iris and some grasses that emerge from the hardest winters alive and green.

Not only do many organisms endure the cold of winter, but some *require* it in order to develop properly. Scientists have discovered that a period of severe cold is absolutely essential for germination of some kinds of seeds; without frigid temperatures the seeds will not sprout when springtime comes.

Even the eggs of a few species of insects (the Rocky Mountain locust, for instance) require severe, cold weather for hatching.

39

So, in bleak weather life abounds beneath the snow and above it, in hollow log and cedar thicket, in seed of plant and insect egg, in hiding snowshoe hare and browsing deer—hardy life that winter's severity cannot discourage and often only succeeds in stimulating toward fulfillment. In plant and animal, hardiness is the capacity to endure a crisis and use it for future growth.

Hardiness is also a quality of the life of faith. Hardiness is the courage to hang on when you would rather let go, to go ahead when safety lies in retreat.

Hardiness is the holy habit of private prayer continued through those cold periods the saints have known when a petition seems to rise no farther than one's head, and answers are long in coming.

Hardiness is Brother Lawrence, caught in the deadly routine of a French monastery, spending his waking hours among heaps of soiled cooking utensils and dirty dishes, yet learning to "practice the presence of God" until the kitchen becomes a sanctuary and the kitchen table an altar.

Hardiness is faithfulness to the Church even when we are not fond of the minister, and the sermons are unimaginative, uninspiring and uniformly dull, because we know the Church is much more than any minister and has proven its divine origin by surviving centuries of human incompetence.

Hardiness is goodwill toward members of another race after they have quit their docile acceptance of social wrongs and have begun to demand justice, even through lawless rioting.

Hardiness is the patience to suffer verbal abuse and to leave the hard, hurtful, vengeful word unsaid.

Hardiness is undiscourageable love, love that "suffereth long, and is kind," that "beareth all things, . . . endures all things." It is unlimited loving concern for others when we do not agree with them and when we are disturbed or slighted or purposefully, cruelly embarrassed or profoundly and lastingly hurt by them. Supremely, hardy love is Christ on his cross praying, "Father forgive them. . . ."

Hardiness is persistent trust in the goodness of God when existence seems unbearably evil, when tragedy strikes like a blizzard, blotting out the glory of life, chilling our hopes. Hardiness is tenacious trust when long loneliness follows sudden grief, when sickness and pain find no relief. Hardiness is the blind poet, John Milton, declaring, "It is not miserable to be blind; it is miserable to be incapable of enduring blindness."

Nearly anyone can believe in God's goodness when life is comfortable, healthy, prosperous and radiantly bright. But bleak spiritual weather demands a hardy and enduring trust.

The Springtime of the Spirit

Earth will not renew itself this spring. It will be revived by a power beyond itself. The Northern Hemisphere of the earth will be warmed as the North Pole leans toward the sun so that the sun's rays can strike us almost directly, rather than obliquely—as they have done all winter. Now, as March draws to a close and April approaches, the sun rises earlier each morning and stays a little longer in the sky. Coldness yields to the sun's persuasion, and the days are milder.

Down at the root of things life begins to awaken, yawn and stir. There is sap-flow in the trees. A new amber glow appears in the willow tips. Buds on shrubs and trees begin to swell. Shrivelled grasses on south slopes, along brooks, rivers, and lakes become greener. In root, branch and ting twig, in grass, in animal, bird, and every crawling creature, and in the mind of man, life is renewed. The miracle of spring occurs because earth turns to a position of receptivity, and responds to powers beyond itself.

The best things in the world are never produced by strenuousness alone, but by moving toward resources of strength that are greater than man's best efforts. Every springtime of the body and spirit, all renewal, comes from placing ourselves in a position where help, strength, and inspiration can come to us.

The man who lives as if he were wholly self-sufficient is crazy in a literal sense. Our word "crazy" comes from the German word "krazen" which means "broken." The crazy person is one who has broken relations with reality. The self-sufficient suffers from the illusion that he came to life un-

41

aided, has been sustained by his own unassisted ingenuity, and can go on and on without vital connection with any power other than his own. But in reality he was created by Another, with the assistance of parents. He was nursed through days of helplessness by the tender care of others. And every moment of his precarious existence he will be dependent upon the soil, sun, and rain, the seasons, the produce of the good earth, the air that bathes his lungs—and hence upon the generosity and mercy of the Eternal Goodness, from whom all things come.

The man who "lives off" his stocks and bonds may feel a little less dependent upon the wheat, and soil, and sun, and shower and the Father's Will than does the farmer whose livelihood seems to rely more directly on Heaven's beneficence. But let the person of "independent means" try eating bonds for breakfast instead of cereal, or stock certificates for dinner instead of steaks, and he will discover before long how pitifully reliant he is upon fertile fields, the smiling sun, the gentle grace of falling rains, the plants and animals that feed upon the good earth, and the ceaseless energy, benevolence and compassion of a kind Creator.

Sanity, then, has this religious meaning: sanity signifies that we are in touch with Ultimate Reality. Among other things it means we are aware of the Power beyond our limitations, conscious of the graces and mercies beyond our human efforts. It does not matter that "our daily bread" comes to us in a plastic wrapper from the corner grocery; we are still cognizant that the inexhaustible activity of God produced the light, warmth, fertility and seed that yielded the wheat that was made into flour that was baked into bread. The petition for "daily bread" in the Lord's Prayer is a humble acknowledgment that the essentials and benefits of life need not be traced far before we run headlong into the goodness of God. So the words used there signify more than a single request for a specific necessity of life. They denote a corrective for our egocentricity, our boasted self-sufficiency, and they express an attitude essential for keeping a sane perspective, and for achieving some peace of mind. The petition counsels us, "Remember, you were never intended to be self-sufficient. Keep ever in mind that your sufficiency is in God."

A man of prominence was being interviewed by a newspaper reporter. During their discussion the reporter said, "I am told, Sir, that you are a self-made man." The eminent gentleman replied, "Yes, I suppose I am what people call a self-made man." Then he added wistfully, "But if I had life to live over again, I would call in a little help!"

The man of faith knows that no one is self-made or self-sustained. He calls in help and is aware of the Help that has been with him since before he uttered his first cry, and will be with him forevermore. Every time his attention turns in the direction of that Strength beyond his own powers, another springtime comes to his spirit, and he is renewed.

An April Prayer

O Lord of all creation
Maker of heaven and earth,
We thank thee for the joys of being alive—
Especially in April.
We praise thee for bright hours, green with promise,
When everything around us seems flushed with faith
And bursting with hope,
   and
All creation seems to sing a resurrection song.

By the sacrament of springtime reminds us
That death is not fatal
To those things we love most;
That beyond every bleak winter of the soul that loves thee
There will be resurrection of hope and gladness.

By the glad gospel of springtime
Thou hast written across the earth
Remind us once more
   that
All tombs are sealed in vain.
As surely as
New life buds within the barren bough
   and

43

THE TINSEL AND THE HAY

Urgent growth prospers beneath unfruitful-seeming sod,
Thou hast given us
A quality of life
That cannot "winter-kill."

Not only now
When spring breaks the tight bonds of winter
May we expose our souls
To thy creation,
But in all seasons
And on all days
Let us delight in thy handiwork.
Thus may the joy of springtime days
Be spread
Across the years.

Teach us to immerse our thoughts
In thy springs and streams,
The lakes and the sea
Until they are cleansed
Of fretfulness and worldly care.

Teach us
To look to thy heavens,
To the sun, moon, and stars,
Until the splendor of the sky
Soaks into our thinking.

Teach us to stretch our thoughts
Across thy fields and forests,
Across thy hills and mountains
Until our thoughts are roomier
    and
Have far space for thee and thine.

Teach us to saturate our souls
In thy greatness and goodness
Until all that we think,
All that we do,
All that we are
Is drenched with the eternal.
In Christ's name. Amen.

44

Homemade

You have likely opened and examined a wormy hickory nut, and could find no hole in it through which the worm could gain access to the inside of the nut.

How did the worm get there? Here is the answer to the mystery. In April or early May, before hickory trees are in bloom, little insects with sharp stinging instruments visit the trees and drill holes in the tiny hickory buds. They then deposit their eggs in the holes. During the spring and summer there is hardly an outward sign that these buds have been afflicted. Buds grow and develop. Nuts form from the buds. But when the kernels in the nuts become fat and good to eat, the insect eggs develop into worms that feed on the nut kernels. Then, if no one harvests the nuts and interrupts them, the worms eat holes in the shell and emerge.

In a similar way evil gets its start in our lives, by being introduced when we are but budding human beings. In our most tender years, when we are most impressionable, evil makes its subtle unnoticed entrance. Impatience, a tendency toward temperamental tantrums, selfishness, petty dishonesties, prejudices against other races, religions and nationalities, all these evils, and more, gain unseen admittance and start secret growth in our delicate years. They then develop and emerge when we are older and have taken our place in the world.

Have you ever heard a provoked parent exclaim, "What has got into that youngster, anyway?" Of course, something bad has got into the child, or nothing bad would come out. For badness and goodness are acquired, and more often than not from the home environment.

Character and morals are largely homemade. The child's first instructions on what is right and wrong are received in the home. And the instructions are more often given by example than by precept. The parent's own conduct is the first standard of behavior the child knows, and the child's own actions generally become patterned after the parent's standards, at least until the youngster is old enough to compare the parent's standard with those of other people. (But by the time he is old enough to recognize better behavior patterns, the impressionable child has already made the parent's behavior his own. He is habituated to that kind of conduct, and finds it difficult to change in favor of a higher standard of behavior.)

Mental health and mental sickness are mostly homemade. Children are emotionally crippled by parents who are inconsistent with them, making unpredictable changes between over-indulgence and spiteful rejection. Children suffer from parents who "give in" to their every want and whim, who break their promises to them, constantly threaten them or quarrel with them over trifles. Parents who reproach children unjustly, who are stingy with praise and indications of affection or indifferent to their attempts to please, parents who refuse their harmless requests, mention to relatives or friends the children's faults and discuss their misbehavior in the children's presence, parents who infuse the children's minds with their own neurotic anxieties, worries and superstitions, parents who make uncomplimentary comparisons between their children and other children, parents who neglect, bribe and embarrass their children or lie to them, or teach by word and example a timid, fearful, or dishonest, deceitful, or self-centered philosophy of life, such mothers and fathers make their children less fit than they should be to face the realities of human existence. Such parents stunt the emotional growth of their children, for the children imitate the immature behavior of the parents. And the children have no incentive to grow toward adulthood because they already behave as well as these adults whom they know best.

But there is great, glad gospel as well as solemn warning, in the fact that morals and mental health are largely homemade. The best gifts God gives us usually come through the home. Even religious faith is homemade. Nearly always parents awaken within the child the first awareness of a Higher Power, place the name of God on the child's lips and teach him his first prayers. Saint Paul, writing to his young friend Timothy referred to ". . . the unfeigned faith that is in thee, which dwelt first in thy grandmother Lois, and thy mother, Eunice and I am persuaded, in thee also." Paul was convinced that Timothy's faith and character were largely "homemade." Most religion is. Few people of strong religious faith come from homes where there is indifference or opposition to religion.

If it is in a bad home that a child learns to hate those who differ with him in color of skin, or religious creed, or national allegiance, it is also in the home that children are taught to love others and it is there they learn to hate, and work to destroy, the things that hurt men's souls and bodies—such as ignorance, disease, abject poverty, political tyranny, war, materialism and all kinds of injustice. It is here, in the good home, that they learn what is worthy of indifference or contempt and what is worth wanting, respecting and loving.

An eminently successful sheep farmer was asked by an acquaintance how he managed to produce such splendid specimens of sheep for his flocks. The simple answer was, "I take care of my lambs." The future of all humankind depends upon the care we give today's children. We who are parents will not be here forever. All that we have treasured most in the way of religious faith, ideals, moral standards, character, all of this will be in the hands, and at the mercy of, the next generation. For this reason we should regard our children, and all children we influence, as our highest achievement, and give them the best possible training, environment and example, and let them know we love them and enjoy them.

Everything we care about most depends, at last, upon our influence upon our children.

All that matters most is homemade.

When Home Is a House of God

The home is deeply rooted in instinct. Animals as well as human beings have a generous supply of home consciousness. Dogs and cats have been known to walk hundreds of miles to return, emaciated and worn, to their old homes after a brief separation. Home, to a pigeon, may be but a roosting place in a barn loft or a nesting box barely larger than the bird itself. Yet, so highly treasured is that single spot that pigeons will make their way in swift flight over many miles of strange country, buffeted by wind and storm, drawn irresistibly by the mystical attraction of home.

The whitetail deer possess a keen consciousness of home. If food and water are within easy reach, a deer may spend weeks or months within a circle less than a mile in diameter. One authority, W. J. Shoonmaker, writing for the *New York State Journal of Mammalogy*, has told of closely observing a certain buck and doe deer throughout an entire winter. So far as Shoonmaker could see, these animals never once crossed a nearby road, and seldom wandered more than a quarter of a mile in any direction from a special small knoll where they often slept. This authority concludes, after much observation of many deer, that the home range of the whitetail is small, and, except for the rutting season and heavy hunting pressure or food scarcity, most deer prefer a home area no more than half a mile square.

A deer's home is replete with comfortable familiarity. He knows every sun-splashed forest aisle, every lakeside pasture opening washed by damp breezes, and the soft singing of every small stream. He is familiar with places where winds tune up their music on pine boughs, and he is intimate with coverts where he can lie secluded, surrounded by dense foliage and thick silence.

The point of the foregoing instances is that an instinct for home is one of this world's elementals. Since the instinct is rudimentary in human nature, as well as in our animal neighbors, we need to recognize the significance of home and make the most of it. With our increased mobility, furnished by the automobile and airplane, and a growing trend toward travel, there is real danger that our modern restlessness may stifle our recognition of the value of home and frustrate the realization of its benefits.

Aware that many of the services of the home had been supplanted by other institutions, one modern young woman asked a real estate agent, "What do I need of a home? I was born in a hospital and educated in public schools and a college. I was courted in an automobile and married in a church. I live out of a delicatessen, tin cans and paper sacks. My mornings are spent at the hairdresser's and on the golf course, my afternoons at the bridge table and my evenings at the theater and at movies. And when I die I will be sent to the undertaker's. A home? All I need is a garage!"

But home is much more than a place where part of the family waits until others bring back the car. Home is the "Beginners' Department" of life, where we learn the principles and the spirit by which we shall live. There we learn responsibility, cooperation and sacrifice, or we are unlikely ever to learn them at all.

Home is much more than a house, built of brick, stone or wood. A home is constructed of sturdier stuff. A home is walled with love and truth, loyalty, helpfulness and trust in each other and in God. A home is warmed by companionship and cheer, and blessed by frequent, fervid prayer.

A good home is both incentive and reward for much of our labor and striving. It is the place where we usually grumble most and are treated best. It is a great leveller, making the great seem small and the small seem great. Home is the place where we are loved not only because of what we are, but often *in spite* of what we are.

Home is where the biggest failure can know he is a success, if he has made a woman love him, respect, admire and trust him, and if little children there want to be like him, and if the goodness of God is revealed through him.

A home is a house in which people live happily. Robert Rainy, the great churchman, was plagued by general misunderstanding and was tested by carping criticism. One day a friend told Dr. Rainy that he could not understand how Rainy could bear the burden of so much opposition, and Dr. Rainey replied, "Ah, but then, you see, I have a very happy home!"

A chief privilege and responsibility of every one of us is to make home such a place of resource and strength that from it every member can confidently go out to face any testing that life can hurl at him, and then return with expectation of finding peace and joy.

Such a home, like a church, is a house of God.

—KOHN—

New Roots in Old Root Channels

Foresters have discovered that pine trees grow better in forested land than when planted in open meadows or abandoned fields. Pines started on uncleared forest soils achieve greater size and hardiness to withstand winds, because their roots follow old root channels and strike deeper into the ground. As roots of a young tree grope toward the heart of the earth the tip of the tree stretches farther heavenward, and as roots penetrate into old channels and expand in the roomy space previously prepared for them by trees long-gone, the entire tree is strengthened and stabilized against days of adversity and testing.

One of the many advantages of knowing the history of our faith, being thoroughly acquainted with the Bible and the creeds, the lives of the heroes of ancient Israel, with the Gospel stories of Christ and the saints of the early Church, is that such knowledge, rightly used, enables us to send the new roots of our souls into old root channels. Our thoughts burrow into the big questions that confronted men of old: "Where is thy God?" "Canst thou by searching find out God?" "Where is thy brother?" "If a man die, shall he live again?" "What shall it profit a man if he shall gain the whole world, and lose his own soul?" "Is it lawful to give tribute to Caesar?" "What think ye of Christ?" "Why seek ye the living among the dead?" We discover how God's people answered the searching questions, and we learn what they did with their anxieties, tensions, guilt-consciousness, lostness, loneliness, their feeling of frail finitude and brooding death-consciousness. We discover how they found answers, and *the Answer,* to their problems and needs. And we search in these likely places for the satisfactions they found. When our roots penetrate old root channels our spirits grow to an extent otherwise impossible.

Using old root channels does not mean we believe Biblical truth is stale or static, and that new revelation is unavailable to us. And it does not mean an unthinking acceptance of our inheritance from the past, a casual, mindless acceptance of creeds and catechisms at their face value. Indeed such careless assent is irreligious, rather than devout, for it ignores the commandment to "love the Lord your God with . . . all your mind," as well as "with all your heart, and with all your soul

. . . and with all your strength." (See Mark 12:30.) The words of the Bible and the witness of the Church should never close our minds, but open them. They should not do away with individual investigation, but stimulate it. When we come to some new understanding of the Word or the creeds our exclamation should never be "I have arrived," but a restless "I must be on my way!"

Attention to the witness of the devout souls of ages past means rediscovery of what has made life most worthwhile to the best of men of all time— an experimental awareness of the greatness and goodness of God. In the history of our faith, then, experience has preceded doctrine. Then, through doctrine, the faithful have attempted to announce, define and explain experience. For example, Pentecost, with the coming of the Holy Spirit into the lives of the apostles, is the root of Church teaching about the Holy Spirit. We should always remember what the early apostles so well knew, that while it is important to have the right *opinion* about the Holy Spirit, it is possible to have the correct opinion and none of the *power* of the Spirit. And we are more likely to celebrate Pentecost than to experience it. Using

51

old root channels means plunging our souls deep into the experience of Power and Abiding Presence that the early Church called "Pentecost."

Walt Whitman illustrates our thought. One time "the good, gray poet" listened to an astronomer's fact-filled address about the heavens, the location of the planets, the stars and their constellations and the glory of a starlit night. "I began to feel tired and sick," Whitman said.

> "Till rising and gliding out,
> I wandered off by myself,
> In the mystical moist night-air
> And from time to time,
> Look'd up in perfect silence to the stars."

Life offers no satisfying substitutes for that kind of knowing. Information about the stars will greatly enhance and deepen appreciation of the night sky, but no lectures on astronomy or learned books on the subject can take the place of a star-bath, when the soul is cleansed of earth's dust by soaking in the vast stretches of God's universe. Such an experience is radical. It goes "to the roots," rediscovering for oneself what thoughtful, reverent men have always felt when they have stood in the star-drenched silences and have thought of the baffling distances, the wondrous beauty, the littleness of man and the greatness of God.

So we should always be restless with mere information, opinions, doctrines and creeds about God, as important as they are. There must come times when we rise and "seek His face," and sit at the feet of His Son, and feel the surge of His Power. Then we are "radically" Christian in the best sense.

Then our roots find old channels, and the soul can climb to towering heights.

A Meaningful Memorial Day

At the end of World War II a law professor at Harvard University hung a group of photographs on his classroom wall. Each picture showed a former law student dressed in his military uniform. Beneath each picture was inscribed the date the boy was killed. And under every photograph were the framed pages of a biographical essay the lad had written before leaving law school to serve his country. These pages expressed the boy's purposes and hopes, what he planned to do with himself and what he was eager to do for the world.

This display was eloquent with hope and tragedy, soaring aspirations, high purposes and death. Young faces spoke from beyond their graves of hopes that died with them on foreign fields of battle.

What do we owe such men? How can we best honor their memories? Are Memorial Day parades, speeches and decoration of their graves the only appropriate memorials to the sacrifices they have made for the world? How can *this* Memorial Day be more meaningful?

A BRIEF HISTORY OF MEMORIAL DAY

Memorial Day was begun to commemorate the deaths of men who fought for their nation. Shortly after the Civil War Southern women chose a day in early spring to decorate the graves of soldiers of both the South and the North. This kind, generous gesture was noted in Northern newspapers, and appreciation for the thoughtfulness of Southern women helped heal the terrible emotional wounds of the recent hostilities.

In 1868 General John Logan, Commander-in-Chief of the Grand Army of the Republic, formally proposed a Memorial Day, and ordered that every army post should hold suitable memorial exercises and decorate with flowers the graves of their dead comrades. Logan concluded his order with these words: "Let no ravages of time testify to coming generations that we have forgotten as a people the cost of a free and undivided Republic." This original order now extends to commemorating the deaths of men and women in all wars. Before many years had passed the custom of decorating graves on Memorial Day became an occasion of family commemoration, when the graves of family and friends were visited and beautified.

But are flowers, monuments and ceremonies at cemeteries and bands playing stirring music the most valuable and fitting ways of remembering those who have dangerously lived and heroically died for others? In addition to our Memorial Day customs, could we not honor those who have fallen in battle by giving fresh thought and renewed dedication to banishing war from the world?

SOME REASONS FOR BANISHING WAR

In memory of our dead let us rid the world of *the terrible waste of war*. Isn't it the height of stupidity to continue paying huge installments on wars fought decades ago, sacrificing mightily to keep a present war going and making other vast payments on weapons-development for future wars we don't want, while all the time we are making comparatively meager investments and sacrifices to study how to wage peace? Economists have estimated that the dollar-cost of World War II would build for every family in the world a six-room house and purchase a car, and provide for every community of five thousand or more a new and adequate hospital and a modern, well-furnished high school. Is the continued squandering of economic resources a fitting memorial to young men who fought and died in a "war to end war"?

But the greatest sacrifices we make in war are not economic, but in wealth of talent and character. Every war levies a drain on undiscovered talent in the boys who are killed. Who knows what gifted minds, what budding scientists, what spiritual and intellectual leaders were snuffed out in the last war and are perishing in present conflicts? Generations to come must build as well as possible without the contributions these dead might have made. How much greatness we have denied ourselves by destroying potential genius in war no one can ever guess. While it takes about twenty years of peace to make a man, one second of modern war can destroy him! Let us fight courageously and stubbornly against the war system that impoverishes the world by misspending talent and skills and by swallowing up all manner of possibilities for good.

Moreover, war erodes morals. War warps and twists our ethics. Millions of kindly people of all nations, who in peacetime would not hurt anyone for anything, suddenly in wartime give their consent and support to the annihilation of entire cities, including the mass murder of women and children. If someone argues that war also permits expression of courage and self-sacrifice and other noble traits of character, I heartily agree. But this is one of the abominations of war—any war: *it puts man's best to the service of his worst;* it employs courage, self-denial, loyalty and other worthy virtues to serve the ends of fear and hatred.

Usually war restricts the very freedoms men hope to save through war. While war may be begun to "save freedom," before war progresses far freedom is greatly curtailed, and intellectual regimentation is imposed, and freedom of expression and dissent is necessarily suppressed. So war "to save democracy" is a contradiction, for democratic freedoms are suffocated by war itself.

Finally, war is like a forest fire, easy to start, most difficult to control, and almost impossible to stop at will. And all the solutions involve dirty work and grave risks. The conflict in Viet Nam is illustrative of the nature of war. Both the "war hawks" who want to step up the war and the radical "doves" who want to withdraw our troops oversimplify our situation. Each advocate sees his proposed solution as "a good thing to do." But there is no "good thing" that can be done, once a conflict is of these proportions. Our choice now is between two *evils:* we can pursue the war more heatedly, killing more soldiers and more innocent civilians and risk world-wide conflagration, or we can compromise our position and commitments by withdrawing. Any choice we make will be an evil choice, and we can only select the lesser of evils. The agony of our national leaders is one of choosing between evils, when they would rather choose between a good and an evil. This is terrible torture for any ethical soul. But we must expect this kind of awful trial if we are to have war at all, for the nature of war is essentially evil.

Is perpetuation of this evil an appropriate memorial to those who have died for the sake of a better world?

Let us, together with all men of goodwill, push toward an ethical international equivalent of war. Let us express our innate aggressiveness and hostility by destroying the things that destroy men, rather than destroying men themselves. If we are incurable fighters, then let us combat disease, famine, poverty, all manner of injustice, and fight against violent, brutal methods of solving international differences. Let us work toward sufficiently strong agencies of international law,

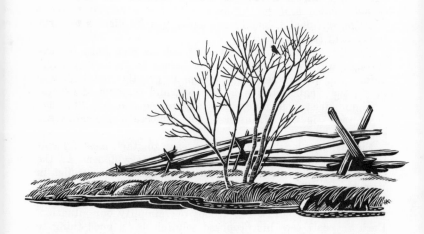

world courts, and international police force mighty enough to discourage and destroy the germs of war before they can grow and spread and sicken, and kill. In our generation let us destroy the great destroyer—war itself. Wouldn't such a victory over war, bringing about its end, be the most fitting memorial to those who have died in past wars?

When Ramsay MacDonald was Prime Minister of England, a friend said to him, "The desire for peace will not insure it."

"I know that is right," MacDonald replied. "Neither does the desire for a meal satisfy your hunger, but it does start you moving toward a restaurant."

At present the desire for peace is strong in the world. Could there be a more appropriate memorial to those who have died to end war than this—to make bold moves toward permanent peace, and to establish lasting peace in the names of those who have died believing they were making it possible?

All Thing Are God's

In our home library we have an embosser that we use for marking books. The plate on the embosser reads, "The H. E. Kohn Family Library." When we purchase a new volume we slip the lips of this instrument over a few pages of the book, one page at a time, and press the handles, which operates like those on a pair of pliers, and the embosser prints on the page, in raised letters, "The H. E. Kohn Family Library."

We do this because we lend a large number of books, and we like to spread a broad hint across a few pages, indicating to the borrowers where these books actually belong. (Our experience has led us to believe that a "bookkeeper" is less a person whose profession is that of keeping business accounts, than it is a person who borrows a book from the Kohn library; a "book collector" is a person who has borrowed several books from that library; and a "rare book" is any book that is returned when the borrower is through with it! Now that men have learned to cross-fertilize plants to improve their resistance to disease, and to heighten the beauty of their flowers,

57

and have crossed donkeys with horses to get mules, I wish some geneticist would cross books with homing pigeons!)

When books from our shelves go forth into the community, embossed with the name of the owners, there is no doubt who owns the library. But also, there is a certainty that the owners of the whole library, also own each individual book; those who care for the whole library care also for the parts.

See, now, the lesson of this parable. The Owner of life is also owner of the details of life. The Creator and Sustainer of the details. And—for those who have eyes to see—His mark of ownership is on all the details.

CONSERVATION IS CARE FOR GOD'S PROPERTY

Here is the highest motivation for the conservation of natural resources: they are God's, not ours. The distinctive mark of God's ownership is upon them.

The devout soul looks to the forests, to the soil, to the vast riches of precious minerals and metals hidden deep in the earth, to the enveloping air and the waters, in wonder and reverence, for they are the Creator's handiwork. God alone could fashion them. We cannot duplicate them. They proclaim His artistry and beneficence and exclusive title to all that is in the universe.

When we despoil the earth, it is an insult against God. The destruction of forests without replacement, the erosion of soil, pollution of air, the poisoning of lakes, streams and seas are ways we vandalize the good earth that has been lent to us as our temporary home. This is God's world. Man is a privileged visitor here, and God is his host. The reverent person would no more erode the soil or ruin any other natural resource than, when visiting his parent's home, he would throw rocks through the windows and set fire to the carpets.

While there are abundant secondary reasons for the conservation of natural resources (such as the fact that their destruction is always disastrous to human welfare, and we exhaust them to our detriment or extinction), the principal religious reason for conservation practices is that this is God's world, not ours. And it should be treated with the respect due to Another's property.

ALL PERSONS BELONG TO GOD

All abuses of our fellowmen are sins against God, for all men—whether or not they are aware of it—are God's children, and bear the marks of His ownership. When we judge members of another race, nation, religion or class as essentially inferior to ourselves and treat them as such, we repudiate a basic essential of our faith—that they, like ourselves belong to God, and should be treated like God's children, and like our brothers.

Forcible segregation in the Church violates the basic nature of the Church and is an intolerable self-contradiction. It means exclusion from the "House of God" those who are the children of God, and therefore belong in God's House. The primary issue for Christians is not whether they like the practice of racial equality and racial justice and whether such practices suit their taste. Rather, the issue is that these practices are consistent with the Christian principle that all people are God's beloved children, and should be treated like it.

WAR IS VANDALISM

The worst evil of war is not its inevitable dislocation of the ordinary conduct of our lives; nor is it the vast, inordinate expenditure of money, national treasure, and lives. The essential wrong of war is that it brutally compels us to treat God's children as if they were not God's, and precious in His sight, as if they were trash. If all hope of averting war vanishes, and a nation must defend itself against unjust attacks, its Christian citizens will recognize they must choose between two evils, submission to aggression and killing in self-defense. But honest men will not call the evil of killing "good" simply because it is self-defense. Christ said, "Love your enemies," while war compels citizens to kill them. When we are trapped into contradicting an essential element of our faith, let us at least confess the betrayal of our principles. War is vandalism of the worst kind, the destruction of what is God's—His children.

Everything on earth, and every person, is a trust from God. We show our integrity of character, as well as our religion, by the way we treat what is God's.

JESUS: A Man of Nature

From the day of his coming to earth to the time of his departure, Jesus was a friend of nature. A star signaled his birth. During the silent years of his childhood and youth, he worked with timber in Joseph's carpenter shop, and came to know the appearance, aroma and feeling of the grains of all the common woods of Palestine. He chose the solemn quietness of a wilderness as the appropriate place to think through his public ministry before beginning it. Flowers, birds, fish, seeds and winds, and all manner of natural things, were used as object lessons in his teaching. When his ministry was finished, he was slain upon a cross of such timbers as he had sawed and planed on the work-bench at Nazareth. Then he was buried and rose again in a garden. After cheering his disciples and giving them final instructions, he departed from them into heaven, from "the mount of Olivet." From his coming to his going, he had an affinity for nature, for stars and seasoned wood, for wilderness, flowers, seeds, for gardens and mountains.

ENJOYMENT OF NATURE

Jesus enjoyed the world of nature. This was his Father's world, and he looked upon it with appreciation and enthusiasm. Our Lord addressed God as "Father, Lord of Heaven and Earth." The farthest stars were God's, and the birds of the air and the flowers of the field were his, too. Our word "universe" Jesus never used, but the meaning of the word is implicit in his teaching: "Universe" literally means "turned into one" or "the wholeness." All the multi-form things of earth belong to one great design, saved from chaos because God draws all together under his creative craftsmanship, ownership and care. It is all one because it is all his.

So Jesus found delight in the natural world as a child finds joy on his father's farm or in the products of his parent's skillful hands. He joyously called attention to flowers and birds saying, "Behold!" which is an equivalent of "Just look!" Frequently he pointed to some new touch of splendor amidst the commonplace things of earth and said that the humblest flowers of the field teach the most meaningful lessons concerning God's care.

60

Although Jesus held no deed on any piece of land, his appreciative eyes owned all the landscape they surveyed. Nearby pastures, where grazed the sheep, distant ranges of hills, sunsets and sunrises and the shimmering sun, itself, were his—claimed by the gladness in his eyes.

He was as familiar with rich soil and gently waving grain as he was with the table where he dined or the bench at which he worked. With his fishermen friends he sailed the little seas of Palestine, peering into the strange mysteries of their depths, telling the men with nets where better fishing could be found.

Jesus beheld nature as others did not see it, with the spirit as well as with the eyes. He saw what others saw, but he also beheld more than they, because he came to nature better prepared. He was spiritually ready to see. Nature did not so much bring Jesus closer to God as Jesus brought his love for God close to nature, and interpreted nature in the light of all he knew about the Heavenly Father. For example, Jesus believed in the faithful love of God for his children, and in nature he saw evidence of that faithfulness. The good earth showed a remarkable dependability, always bringing forth wheat from wheat seeds. Many people look upon rich soil and fertile seeds without remembering God's reliable goodness. Jesus remembered.

He brought much away from his nature adventures, because he took much with him on his walks in the fields, amidst hills and under the panoply of sun's radiance and star's friendly light. He took along his faith. Our Lord never substituted a prayer in a garden for worship in synagogue or temple. But he brought the habitual experience of reverent reflection to the garden and thus made it, too, a place of prayer. So with other places of natural seclusion. Typical of Christ's search for solitude is Mark's expression, "And in the morning, a great while before day, he rose and went out into a lonely place, and there he prayed." Matthew informs us that "After he had dismissed the crowds, he went up into the hills by himself to pray. When evening came, he was there alone . . ." Noises of crowds and villages, the congestion of community living, fought against the undistracted listening to God which is prayer. But hills and open fields, woods and gardens called him, with utmost urgency, to private replenishment of spirit. He augmented public worship with lonely vigil under the stars.

Then, too, perhaps the fidelities of nature comforted him. Men could be unstable and undependable, but without exception, each morning the sun rose in the east; each evening it settled in the west. With unfailing regularity and in dependable order the seasons flowed, always returning at their appointed time. Stars held to their courses in the heavens, unaffected by man's impulses and whimsies. Men rebelled against God, but nature is "the realm of perfect obedience." To One who found his dearest friends changeable and inconstant, the faithfulness of nature must have been consoling. It was a sacramental reminder of God's constant concern and his unfailing love.

THE OUT-OF-DOORS, A CLASSROOM

Nature was Jesus' classroom. Much of Christ's teaching was done in the out-of-doors. "Seeing the crowds, he went up on the mountain, and when he sat down his disciples came to him. And he opened his mouth and taught them. . . ." A mountain side for a classroom! Again, as he sat by the sea, crowds gathered around him "so that he got into a boat and sat there; and the whole crowd stood on the beach. And he told them many things in parables . . ." So the seaside served as schoolroom. Perhaps only the out-of-doors could accommodate the crowds that came to hear him. But then again, when his class consisted of but one pupil, such as the woman by the Sychar well, or Nicodemus on the housetop at night, the natural world seemed to be a favorite place for teaching.

A TEACHING AID

Jesus used nature as an aid to teaching. He dissolved hard truth in simple parables so that it would be more palatable to the mind and more easily absorbed by the spirit. In this way he made men more conscious of nature in order to make them more aware of nature's God.

His teachings overflow with parable. "With many such parables he spoke the word to them, as they were able to hear it; he did not speak to them without a parable . . .", said Mark of one discourse. And many of Christ's stories were drawn from the natural world. Remember them? The parable of the seed that sprang up while the landowner slept; the story of the tares sown amidst the grain; the parable of the soils; the story of the barren fig tree, and others were taken from wild nature or domestic scenes.

Sometimes Jesus' nature lesson was more of a brief simile or metaphor than a story. How memorable are his few phrases about sparrows and God's care. In Luke's narrative we hear Christ saying, "Are not five sparrows sold for two pennies? And not one of them is forgotten before God. . . . Fear not you are of more value than many sparrows." The words hang like shafts of light in our memories, dispelling our despair by assuring us of our individual worth to God. We are remembered! Jesus did not say that each sparrow is spared from pain and death, but that it is "not forgotten before God." It is remembered. This is what we need to know, not how earth's anguish can be avoided, but that Heaven's help and love are with us in the midst of trouble. "Not forgotten!" Once our minds are saturated with that certainty, any bird becomes a winged reminder of where we stand with God.

"I am the vine, you are the branches," Jesus said. "He who abides in me and I in him, he it is that bears much fruit, for apart from me you can do nothing." The folly and futility of trying to be Christians without Christ are vividly, unforgettably pictured there.

In like manner, using short, luminous phrases that expressed his experiences with nature, Jesus spoke of fox dens and birds' nests; springs of water; the mysterious, invisible winds playing in the night; sand and rock foundations under houses; rains falling and floods rising; and sheep that wander from the flock. Each expression was intended to cast new light upon some meaning that had been obscure or altogether unknown to his listeners.

JESUS WAS NATURE'S MASTER

Jesus was nature's Master. That was the way the disciples remembered him, and that is how he is pictured in the Gospels. No attempt is made to explain *how* his mastery of natural forces can be harmonized with his obvious acceptance of many of the limitations of our human nature. Instead of explaining, the writers simply cite the events, describing them with wonder still untarnished by the passing years.

Read again the New Testament stories of "the mighty works" which shone brightly in the memories of eyewitnesses. Recall the simple recitations of events that were passed from Christian to Christian before the first New Testament books were written. Narratives of the healing of sick bodies and of the raising of the dead daughter of Jairus and the deceased son of the widow of Nain and the story of the resurrection of Lazarus are preserved for us by the Gospel writers because these were significant signs of the Savior's power over nature. To the early Church, often threatened with extinction, they spelled "hope." These memories of his power had a radiance that illumined their way through dark, discouraging days. Those who belonged to him were safe in the care of One to whom even sickness and death were subservient.

Yet, it is significant that he did not heal *all* the sick or raise *all* the dead and that he, himself, did not escape pain and death. This, too, is written in the Bible, as if to teach us that sickness, pain and death are here for some purpose, but they must never be permitted to frustrate the will of God. Where they threaten to do that, Christ will take care of them!

Moreover, not only was he Master of nature as it is expressed in human bodies, but he was Lord of trees and water, wind and storm. An unproductive fig tree withered when he spoke harshly to it. One time when the disciples were in distress on the sea, Jesus came walking to them upon the waves, Matthew tells us. The incident is preserved in the Scriptures to give Christ's followers evidence of the Divine help that is ever near us in peril as well as in joy.

Again, a sudden storm arose on the Sea of Galilee while Jesus and his disciples were crossing to the other side. Jesus reproved the wind and demanded of the sea, "Peace! Be still!" And the waves were calmed. The disciples asked of each other, "Who then is this, that even wind and sea obey him?" The disciples never forgot that Christ could bring peace to stormy lives and calm to a turbulent world.

No matter how we try to interpret such miracles, whether narrowly or broadly, this conviction is inescapable: those who knew Jesus best believed he was not nature's slave but its Lord. And they consistently pointed beyond the miracles he *performed* to the miracle that he *was*—the Resurrected Christ —as the ultimate evidence of his mastery.

They would have found it easy to sing wholeheartedly the "Crusader's Hymn":

> "Fairest Lord Jesus,
> Ruler of all nature. . . ."

NATURE, AS SEEN THROUGH CHRIST'S EYES

In our time, through the miracles of modern surgery, "eye banks" and cornea transplants, many people have gained new sight and are looking at the world through the eyes of another. Christians will value life here more if they behold their Father's world through the eyes of Christ.

Sails and Anchors

In the peaceful harbor city where I spent much of my ministry, we see ships coming off the Great Lakes, into a sheltered channel, and thence into port. This city, famous as a resort town, is a favorite harbor for sailing yachts, and much of the year the skyline is colorfully decorated with the tall masts and fluttering flags of sailing vessels of every make and style. Here ships are anchored, and here ships and their crews rest from their voyages, deliver goods and passengers, make needed repairs and take on supplies. Then anchors are lifted, and the ships sail forth again, moving beyond the safety of this place, out onto the deep on many an adventure, visiting many a port, feeling the splash of white spray, the decks resounding with the thunder of whipped sails.

In a sailing vessel we have an apt parable of the nature of human existence. We are somewhat like such a ship, fashioned for venturing on life's seas. But, if we are to sail far, we need anchorage, too. We must find some place of refuge from life's heaviest, most brutal storms, a place where we can make repairs and take on supplies.

Some people have great sails, but possess no anchors. They want to be continually on the go. They are venturesome, but

they soon fail in life, because they have not taken time in harbor to anchor, to make needed repairs, to stock up on supplies.

Others have anchors, but no power of propulsion, no sails. They love the safety and security of harbor, but shun adventures on deep and dangerous waters. So they never get anywhere. The best ships possess both sails and anchors.

We must be anchored in self-discipline if we are to venture successfully in freedom.

We need to anchor in some quiet, restful refuge from the world's hustle and haste if we are to be prepared to engage in the world's busy activity.

Especially, we must be anchored in love if we are to venture into a life of human helpfulness. If we are to become deeply involved in human relationships, we will need some silent sanctuary of the soul where we can take on vast supplies of human concern for the needy and the troubled. In a day when we are frequently warned, "Stay out of trouble. Do not get involved!" men of goodwill need to remember that the real benefactors of the race have always delighted in getting involved with human need.

When a visitor found that his doctor was not at home, he asked the doctor's small son where the doctor might be found. The

66

lad replied, "You will have to look for him someplace where people are hurt or sick, or something like that. I don't know exactly where he is, but I'm sure he's helping someone somewhere." Thank Heaven we all know someone who, at almost any waking hour, is certain to be found helpfully involved with someone in need.

But to live like that demands spiritual resources. One must be prepared to be troubled by people, distressed by their distresses and hurt by their hurts. Furthermore, one must be strong enough to have one's motives and methods misunderstood, and to have one's help go unappreciated, without becoming bitterly disillusioned or discouraged.

Some people do not have the spiritual wherewithal for such involvement. Their affections are so meager that there is barely enough to spend on themselves. Others have only enough for themselves and their immediate families. Those who serve their fellowmen must unreservedly have taken on vast supplies of love and concern for others, and thus can venture forth and lavishly spend affection on others, because there will always be more love where the last came from. Their supplies are well-nigh inexhaustible.

If we are to risk sailing forth to touch other lives helpfully —the crying child, the discouraged employee, the confused teenager, the invalid old woman, the senile old man, the destitute neighbor, the limping dog, we shall need some quiet harbor of the soul where we take our supplies and become spiritually reconditioned. There old woes and slights are discarded. There the wild nerves are quieted, and the vexed mind is calmed, and the spirit is filled to brimming with confidence, trust and love.

So anchor for awhile, regularly, in public worship at church, frequently in private devotions in a quiet place to your liking. Anchor in quiet reflection, examining your own spiritual condition, taking inventory of life's real and highest values, filling up on God's patience, kindness and love, listening to what God has to say—which only the silent person can do.

Then, from such anchorage, set sail into meaningful human relationships where you spend your cargo of spiritual resources in human helpfulness.

The Meaning of Humility

Now, in midsummer, heads of wheat are heavy with grain, stalks of corn are weighted with ears and boughs of apple, peach and pear trees begin to bend under the burden of ripening fruit. The heavier the fruit, the lower stoops the stalk and limb.

Bending low is the habit of fruitful people, too. Truly great people seldom feel great, and the smallest people seldom feel small. The pipsqueak who accomplishes little is likely to boast a great deal about his little achievements, while the wise and good benefactor of mankind sees what he has accomplished as far too small in comparison with what he would like to do for the world.

Throughout the Bible, and secular history, too, we see signs that humility and greatness belong to each other. When God called Moses to lead his people out of captivity, he answered, "Who am I, that I should go into Pharaoh? I am not eloquent. I am slow of speech." When Jeremiah was summoned to become God's prophet he asked to be excused, pleading, "Ah, Lord, I know not how to speak: I am nothing but a child." What do you make of Paul writing to Timothy, "The saying is sure and worthy of full acceptance, that Christ Jesus came into the world to save sinners. And I am the foremost of sinners." Albert Einstein said of his remarkable contributions, "Many a day I realize how much my own outer and inner life is built upon the labors of my fellow men, both living and dead, and how earnestly I must exert myself in order to give in return as much as I have received." It is a strange fact, revealed in the history of greatness, that the better a man is the worse he seems to be to himself, and the greater he is, the humbler he is in his own eyes.

Humility, like other virtues, is easier to preach than to practice. The employer thinks it a good quality in the employee. Parents expect it of children, teachers in their pupils. The layman hopes to find it in his minister, and the preacher advocates it to his parishioners. And humility has always been regarded as essential to Christian faith. Saint Augustine declared, "Should you ask me, 'What is the first thing in religion?' I should reply, 'The first, second and third thing therein is humility.' " But what is humility in precept and in practice?

HUMILITY IS THE GRACE FOR FEELING AWED AND REVERENT BEFORE THE MYSTERIES OF GOD'S WORLD. It is the recognition that the universe is far bigger than our meager minds, and that no matter how much we know our knowledge is not enough to make us proud. Sir Isaac Newton, the illustrious seventeenth and eighteenth century scientist and natural philosopher and discoverer of the "law of gravitation" said not long before he died, "I do not know what I may appear to the world; but to myself I seem to have been only like a boy, playing on the seashore, and diverting myself by now and then finding a smooth pebble or a prettier shell than ordinary, while the great ocean of truth lay all undiscovered before me." The world's vastness, complexity, richness of meaning and its mystery defy our attempts to completely encompass it or penetrate it with thought and understanding. Reverent wonder is an expression of humility.

HUMILITY IS AWE IN THE PRESENCE OF HUMAN GREATNESS. An American college student, while travelling in Germany, visited the home of Ludwig von Beethoven at Bonn. She stood for a moment quietly looking upon Beethoven's piano. Then she asked the guide whether she might play on it. With evident reluctance the guide granted permission. After playing a few bars from the "Moonlight Sonata," she said to the guide, "I suppose all the great pianists have played on this instrument when they visited here." "No," the guide replied. "Two years ago Paderewski was here, but he said he was unworthy to touch it." The great are always awed by greatness.

HUMILITY MEANS AVOIDING A SEARCH FOR PREFERENCE OVER OTHERS. Many years ago a gala festival of music was held in Milan, honoring the composer Verdi. Several famed conductors were invited to participate in the event, among them Toscanini and Mascagni. Mascagni, noted for his great "Cavaleria Rusticana," was jealous of Toscanini's fame and popularity, and he would agree to conduct the orchestra only on condition that he was paid more than Toscanini. He declared he did not care if it was only one lira more, but his pay had to be larger than Toscanini's. The management of the festival agreed to Mascagni's terms. At the close of the festival Mascagni collected his pay. It was only one lira. Toscanini had conducted without fee.

HUMILITY IS THE TENDENCY TO STOOP TO SERVE WHEREVER A NEED ARISES. It is said that George Washington one day rode past several soldiers who were hoisting a heavy log on top of a fort. Believing the load was too heavy for the soldiers, Washington returned to help them. The general saw a corporal standing idly by and asked him to assist. Not recognizing the Commander-in-Chief the soldier replied, "Sir, I am a corporal!" Dismounting from his horse, Washington helped lift the log in place. Then he turned to the corporal and said, "Corporal, when you have another such job to do and not enough men to do it, send for your Commander-in-Chief. He will come and help you." Small men find humble tasks beneath their dignity. Great men never do.

HUMILITY IS THE RECOGNITION OF OUR OWN LIMITATIONS while being trustfully aware of the power of God, and humility denies total self-sufficiency while resting in the sufficiency of God. It is awareness that we do not produce power: we merely appropriate it, using what God has produced. We can sow seed, but we cannot compel a harvest to grow. We can practice health measures, but we do not produce health through them. Health measures give God's power its opportunity for expression. We do not invent truth, although we can "tell the truth." All truth is of God. So with all the power and good in the world, it does not come *from* us, but *through* us.

Joseph Haydn expressed the spirit of humility when, after composing the great oratorio, "Creation," he exclaimed, "Not from me, but from above it has all come." Genuine humility does not demurely deny the good within us. Instead, humility

is the recognition that the good within us is not self-made; it comes from above and beyond us, from God.

Centuries ago Lao Tze said, "The ocean by lying low receives all things into it." Could this be why the really great are so full of good things, because they are lowly enough that God's descending goodness can flow into them?

Shallows and Depths

Most bodies of water that delight our eyes vary greatly in depth. Our little brook gaily races over amber, sun-drenched shallows, lightly ripples over stones, playfully teases the whirligig beetles and water striders that play on its surface, trying to upset them with a frenzied burst of speed. But the brook also has somber, quiet depths where brook trout and rainbow trout lie, where ducks pause for a morning swim, where birches and balsams are reflected in tranquil pools.

Mighty Lake Michigan, one of the world's largest lakes, lies off to the west of us only about five miles away from where I write. Is Lake Michigan shallow or deep? It is both. Along the shore of this great body of water there are places where the water is only inches deep, water lilies hold their clean cups to the sun, little waves whisper secrets concerning timeless things, and carefree breezes play tag among the sedges. Then, again, midway across Lake Michigan, and just opposite the entrance to Green Bay, a deep, dark pocket indents the bottom of the lake, plunging to 923 feet beneath the surface. Lake Michigan is shallow and deep, depending upon where you look, and its variety of depth is part of its beauty and charm.

So it is with human nature. Some people derisively say of a person, "He is so shallow," or exclaim admiringly of another, "He is such a profound person." Such judgments are only partly true, at best. Few people are entirely shallow, having no deep desires whatsoever, no profound loneliness, no abyss of mystery.

And no one is equally deep all over, any more than is our brook or Lake Michigan. Even the best person, like the deepest ocean, has his shallows, his moments of humor, light laughter and musing—when his mind is at play. God made his children, as He fashioned the waters of the earth, with a variety of depth—ranging from shallow to profound.

It is a primary concern of the devout soul that he does not confuse the shallows with the depths. The profoundly troubled Psalmist, remembering how the snows of Mount Hermon melted and dashed down the steep walls of the mountain, likened the echoing and re-echoing of the waterfalls to man's questioning and God's response, to man's prayer and God's answer, to God's call to man, and man's reply: "Deep calls to deep at the thunder of cataracts." (Psalms 42:7) This is true, as every man of faith has found; the depths do cry out, and from the Depths a response does come. Man prays. God replies with ready help. Or God speaks to the sensitive soul through Scripture, a disciplined conscience, the Word spoken from the pulpit, through historical events, through nature, through a disciplined conscience, through the wisdom or example of a friend, and the attentive soul makes an appropriate response.

But it is just as true that a similar communication occurs between the shallows in man and the shallow things of life. A humorous situation, or a story related by a friend, strikes us as funny and we laugh. A trashy drama appears on television and we give it little thought. Silly commercials on television, radio and billboards get only a superficial consideration from us. Golf, baseball, swimming and other forms of recreation have their places in our lives, but—if we are well balanced—no sport has a prime importance, taking the place of family or God. Recreation is a secondary interest, eliciting a secondary response. One of the worse things that can happen to a person is to mistake the call of the shallows for the call of the deep, and to give to superficial matters a whole-hearted, devout response.

And another tragic response is that of answering the call of the deep with a shallow reply. Marian Evans Cross, the most distinguished of English women novelists (whose pen name was George Eliot), was very much attracted to the sociologist and philosopher Herbert Spencer. For years Spencer toyed with the woman's affections. Finally he took a coin and flipped it. Heads he would marry her, tails he would not. The coin came down tails up, and Spencer did not marry the lady. That superficial response to marriage labels the man as shallow where he should have been deep. One of the curses of modern society is that when the profundities of life's most intimate human relationship call, many men and women answer from the shallows.

So with our treatment of children. A society that is more concerned about the horsepower of its automobiles than the character of its children, a society that shows more concern for gleaming teeth than for shining souls, is one that has its shallows and depths confused. A society that gives first-rate attention to second-rate matters and second-rate loyalties to first-rate causes desperately needs to ponder and heed Christ's one-sentence sermon on values: "Render to Caesar the things that are Caesar's, and to God the things that are God's."

That which chiefly distinguishes the life of faith is its different and courageous valuation of things. What the world holds dear—money, fame, sensational pleasures, freedom from responsibility—the dedicated spirit sees as secondary, at best. And that to which the world is indifferent or lukewarm, or sees as secondary, the devout soul holds dear—the search for God's truth, wonder at the beauty and mystery of the universe and the goodness and grace of God—the devout soul holds dear.

Perhaps the way God measures us is by our responses. When the shallows call do they receive the shallow answer they deserve? When the deep calls, does it get a worthy response—from the depths?

The Peril of the Inconspicuous

Now begins the dry season of the year, increasing the danger of forest fires wherever trees are plentiful enough to furnish abundant fuel. Conservation departments and the forestry services will issue warnings to campers to be certain that fires are thoroughly extinguished and caution smokers not to throw away lighted cigarettes, cigars, or live ashes from pipes. Such warnings are good and necessary, since a careless camper or smoker can destroy more trees through a moment's neglect than nature can grow in hundreds of years.

If the average person were to be questioned as to what ruins the greatest number of trees in America each year, he would likely name any one of three causes: forest fires, the woodsman's saw and axe, or epidemics of diseases which sweep over vast tracts, blighting and killing millions of trees. All of these ravages are serious and important, and all of them are spectacular. The devastation is obvious and often makes headlines in the newspaper. But forestry experts say that most tree losses result not from forest fires, or lumber cutting, or from phenomenal epidemics that occur periodically and affect large areas of the forest population. The worst destroyers are inconspicuous diseases that are constantly present in timberlands and subtly kill off this tree and that one until an appalling number are destroyed. They reduce the rate of wood production, and they damage the wood by slow decay and disfiguration. A fifth of all the wood grown each year in this country is destroyed by slow, subtle, and almost imperceptible causes.

Ruin in human life is worked as it is in forests—not so much by spectacular disasters as by inconspicuous factors that toil unnoticed. One reason for human failure is that we look for danger in the wrong direction. We warn our children against life's big temptations for fear they will succumb to them. But a child's greatest danger is not that a great temptation will prove his undoing, no more than man's greatest peril is that he will be killed by a spectacular stroke of lightning. Just as most people die of infections caused by invisible viruses and germs or by the breaking of a small vessel or the forming of a little blood clot, so small defects and subtle ones are more apt to bring a person down than will some dramatic moral catastrophe. The little irritations will make him fretful. The small fears will make him anxious. The little failures will drain his confidence. Petty dishonesties and what seem like insignificant moral compromises will weaken his integrity. We say when a scandal breaks around a man and he is proven guilty, or when someone is jailed for a crime, "Now, he's ruined!" Quite to the contrary, he has merely fallen like a rotten tree. He was ruined earlier, or he would not have collapsed.

What destroys marriage? Usually not a conspicuous act of unfaithfulness. Such obvious disloyalty is like the resounding crashing to earth of a tree in the forest. The fall itself is not the real tragedy, but rather the climax of it. It is the end result of diseased attitudes. Marriages that fail finally fall because of little things going wrong that finally make the big things go wrong, too. Petty selfishness eats at the roots, with each partner demanding what he can get rather than contributing what he can give. Often an almost imperceptible withering is caused by imperfect people insisting upon another's perfection, and the life of the marriage is sometimes slowly starved for want of mutual appreciation and honest praise. Then comes the big testing, and sometimes the shameful failure of one partner or another to be true to his vows. But before the marriage collapsed with a sickening thud, it was ruined by the gradual penetration of unobvious enemies.

Seldom does anyone lose his job because of one big blunder. Usually it is because of many little mistakes, omissions, and neglects.

We do not wreck the lives of children under our care by a single false step in training them but by countless little oversights, slips, wrong methods of teaching, and unwholesome attitudes that are hardly discernible to the persons who are at fault.

But there is glad gospel here as well as warning. Fortunately, the elements of good work just as inconspicuously and steadily as the germs of evil, the greatest and best things in this world being accomplished in an unspectacular fashion little by little, by little people, each in his own limited way and in his own limited sphere, so that at long last, even though some trees and people fall from the attack of little evils, the world is replenished and gets a new chance through the scattering of little seeds of goodness.

God has ordained that all the big things in this world depend upon the little things.

Where God Can Be Found

When Chateauneuf, Keeper of the Seals for Louis the Thirteenth, was a lad of nine years, he was questioned on religious matters by a bishop and gave prompt and intelligent answers that amazed and pleased the prelate. Finally the bishop said, "I will give you two oranges if you will tell me where God is not."

One of the fundamental declarations of the Bible is that God is everywhere and altogether inescapable. The Psalmist expressed this faith, saying, "Whither shall I go from Thy spirit? Or whither shall I flee from thy presence. If I ascend up into heaven, thou art there: if I make my bed in hell, behold, thou art there." God is the abiding Presence, the persistent Love that will not let us go. Wherever we move, He follows us. Whatever we do His care broods over us, glad when we do good, tortured when we do evil.

Many a sensitive soul experiences the wish to escape the Inescapable. Francis Thompson, the Nineteenth Century English poet, was for many years a drifter and an opium addict. But, although he sought to evade responsibilities and to run from his fears, he could not escape the pervading consciousness of God that plagued him. This awareness he described in his poem, "The Hound of Heaven."

> "I fled Him, down the nights
>   and down the days;
> I fled Him, down the arches
>   of the years;
> I fled Him, down the
>   labyrinthine ways
> Of my own mind;
>   and in the midst of tears
> I hid from Him, and under
>   running laughter.
> Up vistaed hopes I sped;
> And shot, precipitated
> Adown titanic glooms of
>   chasmed fears
> From those strong feet that
>   followed, followed after."

We may resent God's presence because He seems to intrude upon our freedom to be what we want to be and do what we want to do. His absolute holiness shames the evil in us. His great love makes our own lesser love seem shabby and incomplete. In His presence we are embarrassed by our petty disloyalties and disappointing disobediences. The book of Genesis vividly pictures man's condition when it shows Adam and Eve, having disobeyed God, covering their nakedness and attempting to hide from God in the Garden of Eden.

But God is constantly confronting us, more often with glad surprise at His nearness and goodness than with shaming accusation of our sin. We think we have escaped from God, but then we walk through a shadowed wood and see a shy wild flower, or we hear a hermit thrush in evening song. Or we witness the orderliness of the universe, the lack of haphazardness that pervades the natural world from the tender blossoms at our feet to the most distant constellation of stars, from the design of every cell of the smallest plant and animal to the way mountains are formed and the course of the earth as it silently circles the sun. Questions arise. How is it all done? Why does it happen that the universe is dependable rather than fickle, planned rather than capricious? And if it is planned, who is the Planner?

We see beauty in softly falling snowflake or in blazing sunset, and we are startled by a loveliness that no materialism can explain. We cannot account for it all if no one designs the design or orders the order or beautifies what is beautiful.

Again, we may imagine we have escaped from God, and then we come upon an inescapable goodness in some human being that leaves us bewildered and confused if we try to leave God out of the situation. Whence comes the goodness if there is no Source of the absolutely Good. In the depths of the depression of the 1930's a government agent visited the Smoky Mountains in Tennessee. The federal government was making small allotments to impoverished farmers for stock and feed and necessary equipment. The agent came upon a mountain woman who lived all alone and tried to grub a living from two acres of land. She had no floors in her cabin, save the packed earth that held a few sticks of homemade furniture. Daylight streamed through chinks in the cabin wall. The agent looked around him and then asked, "If the government gave you two hundred dollars, what would you do with it?" The woman weighed the question for a moment and then replied, "Reckon I'd give it to the poor." How can we account for that kind of human goodness? Where does such unselfishness come from? If human nature is nothing but a slightly elevated form of animal nature, how does a Divine Love get expressed through it?

Again and again our consciousness wanders far from God and then, suddenly, we find God is near in the life of someone who expresses God's kindness, generosity, love. As long as we live among such people, God is inescapable.

The answer to the Psalmist's question, "Whither shall I flee from thy presence?" is "Nowhere at all," for wherever we go His surprising goodness is already there.

A Zest For Permanence

The realm of nature is a strange mixture of change and permanence. Look at the month of June, for instance. Junes will vary from year to year, some being hot and dry and others being cool and damp. But there is a permanent quality to June, the sun always being a "June sun" in the time of its rising and setting, and never a "January sun."

June flowers come and go, trilliums, violets, lilies, lady slippers succeeding each other, but there will always be wild flowers in June. We can depend upon that, as long as there is a bit of wildness to nourish them.

Look at the heavens. See the Polestar. Polestars change from age to age, at one time being Thuban and at another time being Vega of the Lyre. But stars remain.

Nature is full of change, but draw back the veil of transformation, and behind it are the trustworthy, enduring permanencies.

The great men and seers of all time have been conscious of change, but they have been aware, too, of the strong stabilities upon which man can rely. Events of the moment could prove upsetting, but they saw them in relation to the long-range certainties upon which they could depend. They were well aware that this world is a mysterious mixture of change and changelessness, but they searched for the dependable, permanent elements on which they could fix their trust. Furthermore, they attempted to build into their character and reputations the kind of durability they found in nature. They had a zeal for permanence.

Still standing in the eastern part of our country are seventeenth- and eighteenth-century homes with foundations far deeper and thicker than necessary. Barns are there that were built in George Washington's day. Bordering the fields are rail fences built when Lincoln was a lad. Those barns and fences are mementos of an enthusiasm for durability that has become rare in our hurried world, where the highest compliment that can be paid a product of man's labor is that "It will last for a lifetime!" Merely one lifetime? Not nearly enough.

Have we Americans lost our early zeal for durability? It appears that way. We erect too many homes that will merely "last as long as we live." We have too many hit tunes and too few lasting melodies. We have too many sensational, instant successes in fashions, styles, theater, in books and art and automobile design, in business, politics, in romance and marriage, and we have too many bankruptcies in these areas shortly following the "instant" successes.

Perhaps the prevailing uncertainty of our times has made for our short-time attitude toward living. Our annihilation hysteria may be partly to blame. If we are afraid that the world may be blown apart at any minute by man's ingenius, diabolical instruments of destruction, why think of the distant future? There is an answer to that question, and it is this: our salvation rests in a zest for permanence. We need not be afraid of the decisions of statesmen who are patiently planning for a better world in the next century and for centuries thereafter. Those who imperil the welfare of mankind are the impulsive, make-shift diplomats, and those who seek the immediate advantage rather than the long-range good of all men. The dangerous leaders are those who think only of the next crisis or the next election rather than of stable, durable, long-lasting solutions to world problems.

From international diplomacy to the individual handling of our private, everyday affairs a change is needed in our mental and spiritual climate, where we worship haste rather than admire dependable workmanship, where change in fashions so completely rules our lives that there is little time to test anything as to whether it is lovely or ugly, comfortable or unpleasant, strong or frail, good or bad. Before anything is proven, it is discarded in favor of "the newest" and "the latest" thing.

A restoration of a zeal for permanence is overdue. But where can we begin to restore permanence in everyday life? Try some simple things.

Build a stone planter or a garden wall that will outlast you.

Plant long-lived trees that will bind your generation to the next, and the next and the next, where leaf-rich boughs will shelter birds and shade wayfarers you will never see.

Live with, help, and influence for good, little children who will greet many a dawn following your last sunset. Support worthwhile causes that will ease loads burdening lives not yet conceived. Above all else, through daily meditation and prayer cultivate fellowship with the Eternal God, so that His nature can leave its imprint of everlastingness upon you.

Live Above the Animal Level

A significant difference between man and other members of the animal kingdom is man's power to use his reason to restrain or direct his conduct in the light of his basic principles and ideals.

Animal life bears out this picture: each stimulus tends to get a direct and immediate reaction. The fox spies the rabbit, leaps upon it and devours it. The great horned owl sees the ruffed grouse roosting on a limb and instinctively dives upon it, kills it and then eats it. Accidentally step on a dog's tail and he at once growls and snaps at you. Every creature in its natural, undomesticated state, is an instinctive, impulsive reactor.

But man at his best tempers instinctive reaction to a stimulus with reflection, careful judgment, with understanding and compassion. He does not react impulsively and excitedly to the slightest slur or insult by calling his offender humiliating names or by bashing him in the nose. The mature person has ideals and principles that enable him to control impulses toward a "natural" reaction.

James Whitcomb Riley, the beloved Hoosier poet, knew how to accept criticism with good grace. He did not become alarmed or self-defensive. Often his critics felt frustrated by Riley's charm and his disregard of their harsh judgments. One time, after the poet had given a reading of his homely poems, a well-known foreign writer criticized Riley's work unmercifully, claiming he was corrupting the English language with the Hoosier dialect.

Someone asked Riley, "Why don't you strike back?"

"Oh, I did," answered the poet. "I hit him with a huge chunk of silence!"

Silence in the face of sharp, severe criticism is not natural; it is a sign of highly disciplined self-control. It means that a person has standards of conduct that permit him to live above the animal level. He is not a mere automatic reactor to stimuli. He chooses his conduct in any situation according to his ideals.

One ailment runs across the face of many troubled marriages like an ugly scar: each marriage partner is a *reactor*, rather than an actor. Each person waits to see how the other will act, and then simply responds. Thus, one woman excuses her nagging by saying that it is her natural reaction to her husband's laziness and neglect of chores around the house and yard. Another wife's alibi for her emotional coolness is that it is an inevitable reaction to her husband's clumsy ardor in the first weeks of their marriage. A husband excuses his flirtations with women by saying it is his natural response to his wife's neglect of her appearance. Another confesses adultery, but assumes any man would behave the same with a wife like his, who has killed his love by too much fault-finding. Each lets his or her behavior depend entirely on the conduct of the marriage partner.

Not only in marriage but in all their human relationships some people are reactors, working hard or cheating their boss, depending upon how well the boss treats them; speaking to a newcomer in the community, if he speaks first; smiling if another smiles first; kind to those who show kindness, rude to those who are rude.

When we are mere reactors, we place our manners in the control of others. If they treat us politely first, we will then react with politeness. If they speak first or smile first, we will respond by speaking or smiling. But if they snub us, we will snub them. They, not we, determine whether we will be gentlemen or barbarians.

Moreover, when we are mere reactors toward others, rather than the initiators of our own behavior, we place control of our happiness under the command of other people, and we become their obedient slaves. If they treat us nicely, pamper and praise us, we respond with appropriate warmth and appreciation. But if they are indifferent to us, or critical of us, we are emotionally crushed and miserable.

As for me, I refuse to be emotionally enslaved by anyone. I will not let anyone control my every action and determine my every mood. Being a mere reactor would rob me of my freedom, manhood and human dignity.

We cannot control everyone's behavior toward us, but we can, by God's grace, control our reaction to their behavior.

We are not responsible for everything that happens to us, but we are responsible for how we *respond* to whatever happens to us.

The Sacrament of Laughter

While there is much terror and sordid ugliness in the world, there is also a stream of health, cascading like a clear mountain rivulet of melted snow through human experience. This stream is the flow of wholesome, spontaneous laughter—one of the most delightful sounds of earth—God's gift for refreshing and renewing our souls.

A life lived with little laughter is like land devoid of springs, streams, lakes or ground water; there are some things such a life cannot grow. Good companionship can hardly thrive there, for what is friendship without sharing an occasional comic moment? Objective self-analysis cannot prosper there, for we cannot take ourselves seriously if we cannot occasionally take ourselves lightly, laughing at our less serious foibles and blunders.

A penetrating philosophy of life can hardly flourish there, because a wise understanding of the world must take into account the ridiculous, laughable incongruities between man's silly pretentions and his real achievements, his attempts to play God and his human blunders. While the painful, tragic contrasts that exist between health and sickness, righteousness and sin, life and death, good and evil, may bring us to tears, the comic contrasts between life as we wish it and life as it is, found all around us, lead us to laughter, if we are wise.

Even God laughs. When the Psalmist said, "He that sitteth in the heavens shall laugh: the Lord shall have them in derision," (Psalm 2:4, King James Version) the writer had in mind God's humor upon beholding man's comic feelings of self-importance, when everything he is and has comes from Beyond himself. (If you seek evidence that God has a sense of humor, remember He made the camel, giraffe and pelican which look as if they were formed by a committee; look at some of those people Divine Providence allows to "run" for the presidency of the United States; see the odd sizes and shapes of humans on any bathing beach; and remember He made you and me!)

To be sure, there are kinds of laughter that are profane rather than sacramental; they debase rather than elevate us. Laughter at someone else's affliction or great discomfort is evil. Evasive laughter, as a means of covering up our lack of knowledge or of courage or of responsibility, is profane.

Indiscriminate laughter, laughter at just anything and everything, is unhealthy. As uncomfortable as the person may be who "cannot see a joke," far more distressing is the person who can see nothing but jokes wherever he looks. No matter the topic of conversation, it reminds him of a funny story or gag which he regards as hilarious, and anyone who will not join him in seeing every topic as funny he considers a wet blanket. By his superficial, half-witted attitude such a person discourages intelligent conversation, for who dares to bring up a matter of deep concern if some clown is certain to wise-crack it to death!

An old Hebrew proverb declares, "Too much laughter deadens the mind." It does, and especially it deadens a *real* sense of humor, for humor involves discrimination between life's comedy and its sobriety, a discrimination which the constant wisecracker soon loses, if he ever possessed it.

Thus, laughter, like every good thing on earth from eating to sex to religion, can be twisted into an ugly perversion. Nevertheless, its capacity for perversion may be evidence of the goodness of laughter, if only the good can be twisted.

Wholesome laughter is God's gift of emotional rest, relieving the strains of daily living. The more tired the soul, the more laughter is needed. When the outlook of the Civil War was most bleak, President Lincoln called a cabinet meeting and announced that the business to be discussed was most crucial. Members of the cabinet gathered in the company of the care-worn President. Lincoln looked into the anxious faces of his advisors, and then picked up a book written by Artemus Ward, his favorite humorist. The President read aloud from one of the most hilarious chapters, while his uneasy cabinet members shifted about in their chairs, indignantly wondering when Lincoln would get down to business.

At last Lincoln laid down the book, sighed as if some great burden had been slightly lifted from his soul, and said, "Gentlemen, why don't you laugh? With the fearful strain that is upon me night and day I should die if I did not laugh occasionally. You need this medicine as much as I."

Then the President lifted a document from his tall silk hat on a nearby table. He read from what Secretary Stanton called the "little white paper," the first draft of the Emancipation Proclamation, one of the most significant written records in all human history.

THE TINSEL AND THE HAY

Lincoln was one of the most dedicated, serious even moody, men ever to lead a nation, but the grace of laughter saved his sanity, giving him merciful, momentary relief from the terrible burdens of his office.

But laughter is more than emotional rest. It is a key to one's character. By what we find laughable we show what we are. In S. N. Behrman's drama, "No Time for Comedy," a character says, "It's all right to laugh under fire; that's character. But not sitting on the sidelines; that's callousness." It is reported that the beloved comic, Harold Lloyd, one time refused a million-dollar moving picture contract because he disapproved of the tainted "humor" in a certain scene. He explained, "If I cannot be funny and clean, then I'll just be clean." Healthy laughter is a sign of spiritual vitality. It bubbles up from the glad recognition of the goodness of God and His creation; it is gladness converted into music. It is joy made vocal when dawn colors the east with glory and awakens the mind to great expectations and an eagerness to get busy with significant work aimed at high purposes. It is the soul's rejoicing when a wild flower is found, when a bird sings, when a spotted fawn leaps from its bed at one's casual approach along a woodland trail, when a mother mallard appears swimming along the lakeshore with her downy ducklings paddling in her wake.

Laughter is the spirit's spontaneous response to the wide-eyed innocence of a kitten, a puppy, or human infant; the spirit's intoxication with a child's wonder and surprise upon seeing a newborn calf or colt or upon opening a birthday present or a Christmas gift. Laughter is the gay, uninhibited, appreciative reply we make to a friend's sharp witticism, or to a spouse's thoughtful surprise gifts that come on no special occasion. It is the sheer joy of being alive on a spring morning or a summer's night, or at autumn's dusk, or at any hour in the chill, bracing winter wind.

Laughter is glad employment of the comic side of human nature, because we are responsible for using all gifts coming from Him who is the Author of bubbling merriment as well as tears.

Laughter is the rainbow that shows God's sunshine is mixed with our tears and the joy of our security in God's love pervades even our troubles. Thus laughter is an affirmation of God's final triumph over the worst that can befall us.

When Pain Comes

O God, my Father,
Grant me faith enough
To trust
    that
Pain
  plays
    some
       vital
         part
In Thy plan
      for
        my
           soul's
             growth
               toward   Christlikeness.

Thus
May I accept pain
    without bitterness
        or
    rebellion,
With patience
        and
With grace.
May I use it well.
If
In Thy providence,
My pain does not
    become better,
May I become better
    because
        of
          my
            pain.
    In Christ's name. Amen.

Facing Life Courageously

Courage was one of the first character traits to gain the admiration of the human race. The welfare of the community, its food supply and clothing and its very survival, depended directly upon the willingness of tribesmen to risk facing great peril when hunting wild animals and engaging in tribal warfare. Nearly every able-bodied man in a primitive society was called upon to face physical hazards in the hunt and in war, and physical courage was therefore common and absolutely necessary.

In our time and civilization physical courage is less of a daily requirement for most people, because hunting is more of a recreation than a requisite for survival, and direct engagement in battle is reserved for a smaller percentage of the total population.

What happens, then, to courage when occasions for its use diminish? Does it wither and atrophy and finally disappear? The answer is this: the need for courage is as great as ever, but in our time it is *moral* courage that is constantly demanded, rather than physical heroism. Everyone who aims to live the good life must be willing to sacrifice comfort and undergo hardship for the sake of worthwhile goals and high causes. That willingness is what we call "courage."

Courage is not merely one of many virtues; rather courage is *every* virtue at the moment of testing. Courage is honesty when honesty is expensive and can cost you money, or "face," and embarrassment, or friends, and when a little deceitfulness would seem to pay huge dividends. Courage is standing by a conviction when no one else will stand with you or cheer you on, when all your friends believe you to be mistaken and beg you to alter your stand "for friendship sake."

Courage is chastity when the temptation is strong in the young to give into raw physical desire. Courage is charity, when one sees a desperate need for help, but when all that one owns seems barely enough to "get by on." Courage is mercy when revenge would be sweet and timely and it would "teach that fellow a lesson."

Courage is launching out into strange and dangerous territory when we crave a comfortable security. While cowardice creeps ever deeper into the cozy comfort of safety, courage is the willingness to break away, when necessary, from pleasant security and venture into the risky unknown. One young aspiring writer who was afraid to marry his fiance because his financial future was not assured, and he was reluctant to undertake a writing career because of fear of failure, confesses he was given courage by the sight of a squirrel. While sitting in a park worrying about his prospects in life, the young man looked up to see a squirrel leaping from tree to tree. Once the little fellow missed the limb he aimed for and fell, but caught himself on a lower limb. Then he leaped again and again until he arrived at his goal. An old man sitting beside the writer remarked that he had watched many squirrels swinging from one leafy trapeze to another, making their way from tree to tree. He had seen many miss a limb, but always they caught another hold, and no squirrel was ever hurt trying. Then the aged philosopher chuckled and said, "I reckon you've got to take some risks if you don't want to spend all your life in one tree." Two weeks later the lad married the girl and launched his writing career in earnest. And he always remembered the squirrel. Such risk-taking is courage.

Courage is persistence in spite of discouragement. Thomas Carlyle spent years researching and writing his history of the French Revolution. Before he took his finished work to the publisher, Carlyle loaned the manuscript to his friend and neighbor, John Stuart Mill. Several days elapsed and Mill did not return the manuscript. At last he came to Carlyle's door, pale and trembling, and confessed that Mill's housekeeper had stupidly used the book to start a fire. For many days the historian was alternately frenzied with anger and hopeless with despair. Years of hard labor were utterly wasted. He was convinced he could never bring himself to write another line of history. But one day while out walking Thomas Carlyle stopped to watch a mason building a brick wall. The man laid only one brick at a time, but still the wall was rising toward completion. Carlyle thought he did not have the heart to write another book on the French Revolution, but he would write one page at a time. And he did, and at last his magnificent work on the French Revolution was completed and published. The courageous are not free of despair; they struggle on toward their goals in spite of it.

Finally, courage is the conquest of fear, rather than the absence of it. It means looking fear in the face without flinching. Admiral Drake was standing on the quarterdeck of his ship before a violent naval engagement. An officer stationed near him saw the admiral shaking and heard him remark, "My flesh trembles at the many dangers into which my resolute heart will lead me." Courage implies knowing dangers, weighing them carefully, and then doing one's best, with God's help, to fulfill the mission in the world in spite of all peril.

Jesus challenged the traditions of His own people, attacked their race prejudices and fanatical nationalism, and dared to preach a gospel of love in a world insane with hate. He well knew, disliked and dreaded the suffering his actions would bring to him, but His chief aim in life was to do the Father's will, rather than to avoid hardship.

In a world with a slogan, "Safety first," the Christian follows One who taught "God's will first" and personal safety last. That is the highest courage of all.

In Praise of Prejudice

A backwoods wood-carver from America's deep South was well known for his "primitive" carvings of bears. Although he used almost any kind of wood and whittled with lightning speed, his small statues of bears bore a startling resemblance to the live animal. After watching him carve for some moments an astonished woman visitor exclaimed, "I don't see how you do it?"

"Well, Ma'm," the wood-carver replied, "it's like this: I look at a block of wood until I see the bear. Then I cut away the wood, and thar's the bear."

Such a tendency is an expression of one form of prejudice, a harmless kind. This wood-carver sees in a piece of wood what he wants to see—a bear. Another wood-sculptor, whose favorite animals were deer, would look at the block of wood until he saw such a creature and then carve a deer. Some woodsmen would see each block of wood as fuel for the cabin fireplace.

A forestry specialist might see it as an object of intensive study, and would look for signs of the tree's age and for indications of disease or insect damage.

Everyone is prejudiced. We seldom see things simply as they are. We see them through our interests. Especially is this so of human nature. We see other people not as they are *as a whole*, but fractionally—looking in them for what most interests us. But tragically, when we have found what concerns us, we attempt to cut away all the rest.

Too frequently our impulses and habits are the prisoners of our worst prejudices. Both impulse and habit have their good uses in taking care of some of life's routine details, like choosing a dish from a restaurant menu, or deciding which section of the newspaper to read first. But misused impulses and habits can get in the way of our appreciation of significant experiences with other people. They cause us to respond distantly in a critical or hostile way to people who attend a different place of worship than we do, or speak a different language or dialect, or salute a different flag, or sin in a different fashion, or inhabit skin of a different color.

Prejudice uses both impulse and habit. It causes us to react to a situation instantly, without thought, and it prompts us to react in the pattern of all of our past reactions, rather than acting in a new way in a new situation, with new people. Thus, a person who has anti-Jewish feelings reacts to all the known Jews he meets in the same way. The anti-Catholic, the anti-Protestant, the anti-Negro, the anti-white act toward the objects of their prejudice impulsively and habitually. No analysis is attempted. Behavior rests upon prejudgment, which is judgment formed before we think and formed on the basis of emotional considerations. Such prejudice is a time-saver. It enables us to express instant opinions of anybody without bothering to gather facts. But, of course, when we state our opinion, it is not about the essential person that we are speaking, but about our own surface judgments. We need to whittle away the layers of prejudice that form over the real person, hiding him from our sight so that his essential nature can clearly stand forth.

What would you think of a teacher who, on the day of a child's enrollment in school, inscribed the youngster's name in the class book, and opposite it wrote "failure" before the child had been in class five minutes, or had done an assignment, or had been called on for recitation? Unfair? Of course. Let us suppose that into every class the child entered on the first day of school each teacher wrote "failure" opposite the lad's name. How would you expect the boy to respond when he discovered he was prejudged by every teacher he met?

The natural response would be one of utter frustration, hostility and despair. Yet, every day people enter our lives and are labeled "failure" or "inferior" or "unwanted" in our record book before they have any chance to prove what is in them. There is something profoundly wrong with those of us who make and bestow these labels.

But prejudices can be good as well as evil. Jesus was one of the most prejudiced people the world has ever seen. He believed that every soul needed God, and before he met a person he was sure that such would be the case with that individual. Moreover, Jesus was convinced that God loved everyone, and therefore everyone that Jesus met should receive His love, too. This, too, was a prejudgment, a prejudice, the most magnificent prejudice the world has ever seen.

Thus Jesus unforgettably illustrated one meaning of the word "love." Dr. James Moffatt has translated the verse in the thirteenth chapter of First Corinthians that reads "Love believeth all things," to mean "love is . . . always eager to believe the best." This prejudice for "the best" does not imply a sentimental credulity, a foolish readiness to blind oneself to all evil in human nature or a weak-minded indifference to human perversity. Rather, such a bias is like that of the prospector for gold, who searches for riches amidst unsightly rocks. It means a determination to look upon all people searchingly, seeking for saving qualities even in the worst people. It implies a "mind-set," a prejudice toward goodness. No soul is so completely lost that every one of its qualities is as bleak as all the rest, nor are all of its tendencies equally evil. Very well then, love is eager to look for the best, to believe in it when it is found, to believe that a touch of goodness is a clue that God has been working in that life, to encourage the expression of good as much as possible, as patiently as possible, for as long as it is possible.

The world desperately needs more such gloriously prejudiced people.

Man's Search For Significance

The russet month of November witnesses the revival of hunting fever among American outdoorsmen. A zest for prowling after game ripens along with Indian corn and pumpkins. Now the autumn hunting season has opened throughout much of our country. In some states the bow and arrow season for deer began some weeks ago, and here and there we find an open season on bear. In some sections of America the season for gun shooting of small game is also open. Big game can now be taken by gun in some states of the Union and in some Canadian provinces.

Now the taxidermists will be busy mounting trophies brought to them from field and forest. Heads of deer, elk and moose, mountain sheep, antelopes and bears will be prepared to hand in conspicuous places as reminders of the hunter's prowess and shooting accuracy.

But although sportsmen will swat mosquitoes and kill blackflies and trap whitefooted mice that invade their hunting cabin cupboards, none of these will be taken home as trophies. Hunting wild game has an almost hypnotic effect upon some sportsmen, drawing them into extravagant expenditures of energy, even in the worst weather, because the problems encountered in the hunt challenge their energies, skill and knowledge. And hunting trophies give sportsmen a feeling of significant accomplishment. But no one ever mounts a mosquito, blackfly or mouse on the wall of his den. Why? Because they do not represent a sufficient conquest.

There is a nobility native to human nature that insists upon significance. Man is naturally hungry for meaning. He does not want his deeds to be trivial. As an old proverb puts it, "The eagle does not catch flies." A person may enjoy playfully tinkering with trifles now and then, but he does not want this whole life to be immersed in worthlessness. When he fails to find high purposes to which he can wholeheartedly give himself, he then lives in a welter of anxiety, fearing that his existence has no importance. He tends to display symbols of his real conquests over opponents that he considers worthy of his cunning, but he derives no joy from small victories over inconsequential foes. Deer heads are mounted in many a hunter's den, but mice never.

Here are some conquests worth making:

THE CONQUEST OF SPIRITUAL AND MENTAL NAR-
ROWNESS. Extend the areas of your awareness so that you
see and create more beauty and seek more truth about God
and man and God's world. Engage in reverence, wonder and
worship that stretch the soul, and enlist the imagination of
your compassion in seeking out human need and serving it.

Especially work for victory over selfishness, the worst form
of spiritual narrowness. As the Lord's Prayer suggests, we
must learn to say the unselfish "our" rather than the self-
centered "my." "After this manner therefore pray ye," said
Jesus, "Our Father," "Our daily bread," "our debts." Learn to
think of yourself as belonging to others, and of others as
belonging to you. Share the values of life, your goods, your

successes, your faith. Accept a share of the burdens of others, their disappointments, sorrows and woes. Instead of seeing what you can get from life, see how much of value you can add to the lives of others.

THE CONQUEST OF TIME. Learn how to invest time rather than "kill time," living one day at a time, not dragging along the burden of yesterday's failures and regrets or trying to live tomorrow before it arrives. Be victorious over your yesterdays by improving over what you were then. Life's great triumphs are not found in superiority over someone else. The big achievements in business, sports, art and character is to exceed the best you have ever done before. See if today you can add more than heretofore to the sum of good feeling and good deeds in God's world.

Thousands of workmen were employed in building the Hoover Dam (earlier called Boulder Dam) in Colorado. Eighty-nine of these laborers died while working there, some in tragic accidents. In memory of these martyrs to progress, who had laid down their lives to improve the lot of millions of people, a plaque was posted at the dam. It reads, "They died that the desert might bloom."

We gain significance when we live or die that the world might bloom with righteousness, justice, love, brotherhood, hope and peace.

Exciting Uncertainties

One of the most intriguing advantages of taking a walk through field or forest is that all of nature is stuffed with surprises and crammed with exciting uncertainties. The rambler never knows what lies just ahead. Something wholly unexpected is always leaping into one's awareness as if to cry a gladsome "Surprise!"

When I walk through our meadow, I never know what step may startle a whitetail buck from his daytime resting place in the shadow of a fallen tree. When I stroll through the gaunt autumn woods where October banks her fires with leaves against the cold of winter, any footfall may cause a snowshoe hare to burst from cover. Ruffed grouse unexpectedly thunder from underneath the apple trees in our wild orchard as I pass by. Where our small stream sparkles as it runs amber over its gravel-bed, brook trout take the watcher by surprise, none being expected at this time of day, in this season, in these particular shallows.

So it goes. Shore birds, not seen before on our pond's edge, suddenly appear and disappear. Indian pipe plants grow where none were ever found before. Bare maples and barren beech reveal nests where we've had near neighbors whose presence was unsuspected until autumn stripped away a thick veil of leaves. Nature is a realm of surprises, astonishments and uncertainties.

Life, like a walk through meadow or woods, is most exciting when it is abundant with the unknowns, the unproven and the uncertain. We all know for sure that two times two equals four, and no one is excited over the fact. Four plus four equals eight. That is certain, and annoyingly dull. But what will tomorrow bring, of success or failure, of joy or sorrow, of fulfillment or frustration? No one knows for sure. That makes tomorrow interesting.

We frequently complain about life's uncertainties, but how would we like to have all uncertainties removed from our existence? The plain fact is that we like a generous measure of uncertainty stirred into our days. If life is too tame, too secure for us, then we will add our own elements of doubt and mystery. We play mystery games to put some excitement into our days. Children play "Hide the thimble" or "Button, button, who's got the button?" or "Hide and seek." Older children, and grown-ups, too, play baseball, football and basketball. Who would play, and who would care to be a spectator, if everyone knew before the game began exactly how every move would be made and what the final score would be? The adventure in a game is in its uncertainties.

If excellence were guaranteed in every school examination, if success were promised when one undertook a profession, if exquisite happiness were automatic in every marriage, if a certificate of warranty of future perfection of character and personality were issued at the birth of every baby, if a "yes" answer were pledged to every prayer we uttered, how drab life would be!

Thank God for life's exciting uncertainties!

Death Is the Fulfillment of Life

(A LETTER TO A BEREAVED FAMILY)

Dear Friends:

Even though Ralph's illness had been long and critical, it was a shock to learn today that he has left us. Yet, if Ralph could have chosen his time of passing from this life to the life to come, it is likely he would have selected some moment such as this in the autumn season. This is because death for the man of faith is not a dismal end, but the glorious fulfillment of life, as autumn is the fulfillment of nature's year. Ralph, a man of taste, would think a radiant October day like this an appropriate time for his fulfillment.

Autumn is a parable of the meaning of death. Throughout most of the nation October is a harvest month, the epitome of earth's brimming fruitfulness and its generous grace. The liberal summer, now ended, has left memorials to earth's rich bounty and heaven's generosity. Corn is piled in corncribs, and mounds of golden pumpkins, squash and multicolored gourds are heaped high in storage buildings. Orchards have bestowed abundant blessings, and baskets and fruit-bins are filled with plump, shining gifts from the trees.

Autumn is fulfillment time when all that was bud has become flower, all that was but blossom has become fruit, and the green things of garden and field have ripened to readiness for harvest.

So on this autumn day, we who loved Ralph, we who already have begun to miss him, see his passing not as stark tragedy, but as his fulfillment. All that led up to his day of death was the ripening of his life, and I strongly believe that if our experience of bereavement would mellow, sweeten and ripen our own spirits, Ralph would like that and be gratified that our grief was not wasted.

Another comforting truth concerning Ralph's maturing toward fulfillment is this: all weathers and all hours made his soul grow, even storms and darkness.

There is a popular opinion that only the pleasant days turn pears golden yellow and apples a bright, shining red. And it is only on the radiant, warm days that trees push upward toward the sky. But lately scientists have told us that while trees need

95

light for photosynthesis and for manufacturing starch, it is during the darkness of the night that the day's store of energy is put to work and turned into growth. Day is for absorption of light, but nighttime is the greatest period of growth.

So, it is not only in the sunshine of good fortune that the soul stretches heavenward and grows. All troublesome, dark hours grow a soul if that soul belongs to God and knows it.

Those who did not know Ralph in the last several months of his life hardly knew the real Ralph at his best, for it was in his struggle with illness that the good which was always present in his life ripened, sweetened and matured, as if it was being prepared for harvest.

Those who watched his life during this last crisis saw the steady growth and enrichment of courage and patience and observed the quiet dignity with which he carried the burden of long illness. And they beheld a maturing of determination to live fully and faithfully as long as God would give him breath.

Ralph's love and concern for his wife and children, which had always been strong, and his immense delight in his grandchildren, became ever more pronounced. His glad acceptance of people as they were, his enjoyment of friendship and his love for the beauties of nature became even more intensified.

In recent months Ralph spent many an hour sending his roots deep into the meanings of faith. Suffering did not dim his awareness of God. Pain brightened it. He reviewed what he believed, and what was most worth believing, as very few of us have done when our days seemed bright, promising and pain-free.

So, as his disease worsened, his spirit strengthened and became more directed toward God.

Yes, it is true: as surely as trees grow in darkness, so does the soul that is sensitive grow toward God.

May this sorrow make us not bitter, but better. Because grief has touched us, may our spirits grow taller, our human ties and appreciations for each other grow stronger and our faith in God grow firmer.

And may heaven seem nearer, more attractive and familiar than ever now that one we have loved is there, at home.

Affectionately and prayerfully yours,
HAROLD